UNCLE SAM WANTS YOU

****

CHRISTOPHER CAPOZZOLA

UNCLE SAM WANTS YOU

✶✶

WORLD WAR I AND THE MAKING OF

THE MODERN AMERICAN CITIZEN

OXFORD
UNIVERSITY PRESS

OXFORD
UNIVERSITY PRESS

Oxford University Press, Inc., publishes works that further
Oxford University's objective of excellence
in research, scholarship, and education.

Oxford   New York
Auckland   Cape Town   Dar es Salaam   Hong Kong   Karachi
Kuala Lumpur   Madrid   Melbourne   Mexico City   Nairobi
New Delhi   Shanghai   Taipei   Toronto

With offices in
Argentina   Austria   Brazil   Chile   Czech Republic   France   Greece
Guatemala   Hungary   Italy   Japan   Poland   Portugal   Singapore
South Korea   Switzerland   Thailand   Turkey   Ukraine   Vietnam

Published by Oxford University Press, Inc.
198 Madison Avenue, New York, NY 10016

www.oup.com

First issued as an Oxford University Press paperback, 2010

Oxford is a registered trademark of Oxford University Press

Portions of chapter 1 originally appeared in "From Harlem to the Rhine:
New Perspectives on African-American Military Service in World War I,"
New York History 87 (Summer 2006): 365–77. Reprinted with permission.

Portions of chapter 4 originally appeared in "The Only Badge Needed Is Your
Patriotic Fervor: Vigilance, Coercion, and the Law in World War I America,"
Journal of American History 88 (March 2002): 1354–82.
Copyright © Organization of American Historians.
All rights reserved. Reprinted with permission.

Library of Congress Cataloging-in-Publication Data
Capozzola, Christopher.
Uncle Sam wants you : World War I and the making
of the modern American citizen / Christopher Capozzola.
p.   cm. Includes bibliographical references and index.
ISBN 978-0-19-973479-5 (pbk.)
1. World War, 1914–1918—Social aspects—United States.   2. Political culture—
United States—History—20th century.   3. United States—
Social conditions—1865–1918.   4. Consensus (Social sciences)—
United States—History—20th century.   5. Patriotism—United States—
History.   6. Citizenship—United States—History.   I. Title.   E780.C26 2008
305.48'896073009041—dc22   2007041191

1   3   5   7   9   8   6   4   2
Printed in the United States of America
on acid-free paper

This book is for my mother
and for Keith O'Brien.
And for my brother Jim,
who would have liked the Philadelphia parts the best.

Acknowledgments

⭑⭑⭑⭑⭑⭑⭑⭑⭑⭑⭑⭑⭑⭑⭑⭑⭑⭑⭑⭑⭑⭑⭑⭑

I can trace the roots of this book as far back as *The Look-It-Up Book of Presidents,* an illustrated volume that preoccupied much of my childhood. I have never truly overcome its charms, nor has my family ever really recovered from the many times I made them read it to me. Ever since, they have supported my historical interests in ways too numerous to list here, from food and phone calls to something called the "dissertation shed." My mother has believed in this from the beginning. My aunt and cousin, Theresa and Bill Gearty, made up a substantial portion of the audience for the first paper I ever gave, and I thank them for that. My brother Jim, who was perhaps my testiest critic and without doubt my biggest supporter, passed away last summer—far too soon. I am saving the first copy of this book for him.

Long after *The Look-It-Up Book of Presidents* had been lost in a move, I had the idea for this book on a spring afternoon in a coffee shop across the street from the National Archives in Washington. Alan Brinkley, Elizabeth Blackmar, and Ira Katznelson nurtured it in its initial stages and have continued to support it. So, too, have dozens of colleagues, friends, and audiences who have read it or heard me talk about it. For feedback, ideas, and overall inspiration, I would like to thank Barbara Ashbrook, Doug Barton, Katie Benton-Cohen, Anne Boylan, Richard Bushman, Vincent Cannato, David Ciarlo, Andrew Cohen, Aren Cohen, Michael Coventry, Lynn Dumenil, David Ekbladh, David Engerman, Paul Erickson, Ann Fabian, Eric Foner, Michael Fuquay, Beverly Gage, Robert Genter, Gary Gerstle, Aram Goudsouzian, David Greenberg, Ruth Helman, Meg Jacobs, Elizabeth Johnston, Martha S. Jones, Sue Leonard,

Alice Lipton, Pauline Maier, Gail Marcus, Timothy McCarthy, Heather Miller, Brett Millier, Sharon Musher, Christopher Nehls, Megan Kate Nelson, Cynthia Nieb, John Ochsendorf, Richard Polenberg, Daniel Rodgers, Caitlin Roper, Rosalind Rosenberg, Lucy Salyer, Andrew Sandoval-Strausz, Zachary Schrag, Bruce Schulman, David Sewell, Elliot Shapiro, Peter Shulman, Ryall Smith, Sarah Song, Ellen Stroud, John Summers, Jessica Wang, Christopher Wells, Chad Williams, Michael Willrich, Elizabeth Wood, Eric Yellin, and Julian Zelizer. Roy Rosenzweig was an enthusiastic supporter of this project from the beginning. He made the historical profession a more exciting place, and we all feel his absence.

Books don't get written without other books. *Uncle Sam Wants You* reflects the efforts of librarians and archivists too numerous to name, but special thanks go to Michelle Baildon at MIT, Renata Kalnins at the Harvard Divinity School, and Mitch Yockelson at the National Archives. Collected in my footnotes is a special obligation to generations of unpaid and underappreciated local historians without whose work this study would have been impossible. At MIT, I have benefited from research support provided by Lisa Bell, Laura Colón-Meléndez, Julia Dennett, Jessica Haurin, Yukyan Lam, Jenna Matheny, Mary Presley, Christopher Suarez, and Anya Zilberstein. Renee Brown, Mabel Chin, Margo Collett, Maria DiMauro, and Emily Megan Morrow Howe helped me navigate institutional bureaucracies.

Of all the libraries where I have worked, I would like to thank two in particular. I began this project at the Library of Congress, and I had the good fortune to return there in the summer of 2005 as a Jameson Fellow at the Kluge Center, where Mary Lou Reker helped me tap the library's untold riches. My thanks go as well to the Sophia Smith Collection and Smith College Archives. Several years ago, they took a chance on a sprawling and overly ambitious summer grant proposal, and their support made a crucial difference. I keep coming back, both to mine new sources and for the simple pleasure of working in the Alumnae Gymnasium, surrounded by people who love and believe in history.

I could not have written this book without the financial support and time to write that has come from so many generous individuals and institutions. The Columbia University History Department and Columbia's Institute for Social and Economic Research and Policy offered financial and logistical support. Participating in the workshops of the Social Science Research Council's Program on Philanthropy and the Nonprofit Sector connected me to a valuable community of like-minded scholars. Research grants from the American Historical Association's Littleton-Griswold Research Grant in American Legal

History, the Institute for Southern Studies at the University of South Carolina, and the Margaret Storrs Grierson Fellowship of the Sophia Smith Collection and Smith College Archives helped me collect the stories I tell. I finished this book with the generous support of the Carnegie Scholars Program of the Carnegie Corporation of New York, a Summer Stipend from the National Endowment for the Humanities, the J. Franklin Jameson Fellowship of the American Historical Association, and while in residence at the Visiting Scholars Program of the American Academy of Arts and Sciences, where James Carroll offered a model of passionate and thoughtful engagement with history's biggest questions.

From the outset, the deans of MIT's School of Humanities, Arts, and Social Sciences, Philip Khoury and Deborah Fitzgerald, have supported this project, and several others, particularly through a SHASS Research Grant and the Lister Brothers Career Development Associate Professorship. My chairs, Harriet Ritvo and Anne McCants, together with my colleagues in the History Faculty, have all made the institute an energizing place to work. David Kennedy introduced me to Susan Ferber at Oxford University Press. From the first day we met, Susan understood this project, and its author, and has patiently guided me through the publication process with advice and thoughtful editing. Christine Dahlin and Dawn Vogel took on the final production phase.

My final thanks go to Keith, for being next to me on the journey. We have adventures.

Contents

UNCLE SAM WANTS YOU

****

Introduction: Uncle Sam Wants You

★ ★

Sitting in his Manhattan studio on a summer day in 1916, James Montgomery Flagg took off his glasses, looked in the mirror, and saw there the image of America itself. One of the nation's most successful illustrators, the thirty-nine-year-old Flagg was working on a cover drawing for *Leslie's Illustrated Weekly Newspaper*. In the upcoming issue of the magazine, editors planned to urge Americans to expand the country's military force, in case world events dragged them into the ongoing tragedy that Americans at that point still referred to as the European War.[1]

Flagg was under a tight deadline and short on ideas; he didn't even have a model in his studio to work with. He had his own reflection—tall and lanky, with piercing blue eyes and wavy hair. In all likelihood, he also had a British military recruiting poster designed by Alfred Leete in 1914. That image featured Lord Kitchener, Britain's secretary of war and chief of its military recruitment, pointing at the viewer, with the words "Your Country Needs YOU." Flagg erased the caption, borrowed Kitchener's pose, and substituted his own face for the Brit's—then added wrinkles, whiskers, and gray hair, just for good measure. With that, Uncle Sam appeared, just in time for America's first world war.[2]

The picture ran on the cover of the July 16, 1916, issue of *Leslie's* under the heading "What Are You Doing for Preparedness?" Within a year, despite President Woodrow Wilson's stated intention to keep America out of the war, the nation began mobilizing young men into the ranks. In the spring of 1917, Flagg's image reappeared, this time on a U.S. Army recruiting poster, with its caption restored as "I Want YOU." By the Armistice, the War Department

Alfred Leete's 1914 military recruitment poster featuring Lord Kitchener, Britain's Secretary of State for War, likely served as a model for James Montgomery Flagg's famous image of Uncle Sam. (*Courtesy of the Library of Congress Prints and Photographs Division*)

had printed more than four million posters. Ever the patriot, Flagg served during World War I as New York State's official military artist; he volunteered for George Creel's Committee on Public Information, the federal government's official propaganda agency. He even offered a free portrait to anyone who bought a $1,000 Liberty Bond. Flagg composed forty-six posters as part of his wartime service. Of them all, the poster captioned "I Want YOU" has been the most enduring. Why has it become one of the most iconic images in American politics, even a visual metaphor for America itself?[3]

Perhaps Americans found that their Uncle Sam, like all good uncles, helped them out: by turning the vast machinery of war mobilization into a family relation, he gave political power a personal face and made sense of the government's presence in everyday life. On closer inspection, though, Flagg's Uncle Sam is a puzzling figure. He is at once watchful and protective, personable and authoritative, individual and institutional. And, like many uncles, he

James Montgomery Flagg's image of Uncle Sam, shown here in a 1917 U.S. Army recruiting poster, helped Americans make sense of the wartime state by putting a personal face on political power. By the war's end, the government had printed four million copies of Flagg's iconic image. (*Courtesy of the Library of Congress Prints and Photographs Division*)

is very badly dressed. His formal attire conveys the solemnity of war's occasion, and his furrowed brow and piercing stare show his seriousness, but his silly hat and ill-fitting suit suggest that Uncle Sam doesn't usually do this. He reassures viewers that war is not in America's lifeblood; the nation, like its uncle, would rather be doing something else.[4]

The poster helped Americans understand their relationship to the wartime government. When they sought a visual way to express that state, they chose—four million times—to depict Uncle Sam. What went through their minds in April 1917, when Uncle Sam pointed at them and said, "I Want YOU"? Or that fall, with a military draft in full force, as he told them to buy bonds, conserve food, and keep a vigilant eye on their German neighbors? That winter, as they faced a rising cost of living and shortages of coal and sugar, and as news of American deaths in Europe began reaching their communities, how did they feel when they saw that a poster had been vandalized? Did they share the anger of a group of New York women, who urged Congress to make the defacement of war posters a federal crime? Or were they the ones who had doodled on Uncle Sam in the first place? What did they think on November 11, 1918, when the same poster, faded and battered by the elements, was replaced with another announcing a victory parade?[5]

One thing we know is that the word *obligation* was very much on their minds. During World War I, when Americans discussed their relationship to the state, they used terms such as *duty*, *sacrifice*, and *obligation*. The language was everywhere: in congressional debates about entry into war, on the posters of military recruiters during the conflict, and even in the parades that marked the war's end. Political obligations energized, mobilized, and divided Americans during World War I.[6]

When philosophers talk about political obligation, they generally mean something quite specific: the question of what duties citizens owe to the state and under what terms they will obey its authority. At the beginning of the last century, Americans used the term with far less precision to encompass civic, social, and even psychological obligations. There were explicit political duties, such as jury duty and military service. A 1916 constitutional amendment had brought the new obligation of a federal income tax, although only the nation's wealthiest citizens paid it. Americans also had equally important—if less obviously political—obligations: to work, to be loyal to the nation, to conform to the norms of community. Women were told to obey their husbands, and immigrants' English-language classes taught sentences as straightforward as "I hear the whistle, I must hurry."[7]

Looking at the history of a liberal society like the United States, it might seem that Americans have never really had to think much about their political obligations, let alone act on them. In the later wars of the twentieth and twenty-first centuries, liberal individualism, an economy of consumption, a nationalized culture, legally protected civil liberties, and an expanded federal state all played more prominent roles in public life. But even so, throughout American history, a citizenship of obligation has always coexisted with one of rights, as a patchwork of political cultures supported a hybrid state as jumbled as Uncle Sam's ill-fitting suit.[8]

Americans' sense of obligation came from many places: political traditions of republicanism that valued the common good over individual liberty, utopian visions of community, Christian beliefs that made of duty a virtue, paternalist notions that legitimated social hierarchies and demanded obedience to them. In the early twentieth century, such language crossed party lines, from conservatives who sought to uphold the status quo to progressives who dreamed of a new era of shared sacrifice. It was a way of talking about politics that predated the war; the needs of war mobilization made its use pervasive.

Obligations were not just rhetorical flourishes on propaganda posters or phrases in philosophers' tomes; they were also social practices that made it possible for America to go to war. When Uncle Sam jabbed his finger at the American public, he pointed out their rights, and he also pointed out who was or wasn't an American. But mostly, amid the massive home-front mobilization for America's first world war, he pointed at people because he wanted them to do something.[9]

Uncle Sam got plenty of responses. More than 1.3 million men and more than twenty thousand women volunteered to serve in the armed services abroad. Those at home helped out as well. George Herbert Jones, a thirty-four-year-old self-described "very ordinary book-keeper" from Latta, South Carolina, wrote a congressman in August 1918 that "I feel that it is my duty as an American citizen to volunteer my services to our 'Wilson-American' government." Disqualified physically from military service, Jones still wanted "to do some kind of work for my Country. If there is anything in Government work that I can do," he begged, "please let me know." Mrs. Raynell Ryder wanted to serve the war effort on the factory line at the Winchester Repeating Arms Company in New Haven, Connecticut. Told that African-American women would not be hired for machine work, she asked her state's governor to intervene. "Why not give me a chance to help win the war?" she asked. "Although I am colored I am a true American and loves my country with my heart and want a chance to do my bit." A. E. Black, a baker in Fulton, New York, even offered Uncle Sam his hundred-pound bloodhounds. "They would be a good safeguard for supplys," he thought.[10]

Uncle Sam definitely needed the help, as new government agencies administered the draft, mobilized women's labor, and policed the home front. But the figure of Uncle Sam stood for more than Washington. In the years before the war, voluntary associations—clubs, schools, churches, parties, unions—organized much of American public life. Such groups provided social services, regulated the economy, policed crime, and managed community norms. Schooled in this world of civic voluntarism, Americans formed their social bonds—and their political obligations—first to each other and then to the state. Indeed, in the absence of formal federal institutions, these voluntary associations sometimes acted as the state. They organized public life and helped Americans feel a sense of collective identity, and they also carried out much of the practical work.

Americans of the early twentieth century thus owed allegiance to an overlapping array of authorities, of which Uncle Sam's federal government was only
one, and perhaps not even the most important.[11]

America's first world war marked an unprecedented mobilization of social
institutions, human labor, and popular will. Obligations to employers, families, schools, and churches had generally been considered outside the state, even
though the force of law often backed up personal responsibilities. Now, these
private obligations were suddenly fundamental to war mobilization in a moment
of crisis, prompting state intervention into American bedrooms, kitchens, and
congregations, places where the federal government hadn't always been before.

America's first world war was also deeply unpopular among large seg-
ments of the nation's population. Organized protest was rare after April 1917,
but bitter contests continued in fights over the terms of political obligation.
Time and again, Americans told Uncle Sam—whether he was a draft board,
a visiting nurse, a military tribunal, or an angry mob—what they believed
their political obligations were. As the state made ever stronger claims on its
citizens, wartime events prompted one of the twentieth century's broadest,
most vigorous, and most searching public discussions about the meanings of
American citizenship. In their language were rich theoretical expositions of
justice, fairness, and wartime democracy that make it possible to write a social
history of political theory and to understand what is at stake when citizens
debate their wartime obligations. The outcomes of those struggles mattered;
as Americans mobilized for war in these groups, they folded themselves into
government structures, transforming the state in whose name they spoke.[12]

Being a good citizen meant fulfilling your political obligations and doing
so through voluntary associations. Lending a hand to the war effort thus
became not just a good deed but a duty, and serious consequences ensued for
those who failed to join in. People were, therefore, obliged to volunteer in a
culture of coercive voluntarism. A paradoxical notion, to be sure, but one that
President Woodrow Wilson clearly articulated when he introduced America to
the Selective Service Act in a May 1917 proclamation. "It is a new manner of
accepting and vitalizing our duty to give ourselves with thoughtful devotion
to the common purpose of us all," he noted. "It is in no sense a conscription
of the unwilling; it is, rather, selection from a nation which has volunteered in
mass."[13]

A generation earlier, Wilson had already perceived the powers of coercion that can accrue to a democratic state when it left consent unexamined.
Long before he was president, Woodrow Wilson was a political scientist, and
in 1889, just before he returned to his alma mater, Princeton University, as

President Woodrow Wilson, shown here in 1916, conveyed the home front's political culture of coercive voluntarism when he announced that selective service was "in no sense a conscription of the unwilling; it is, rather, a selection from a nation which has volunteered in mass." (*Courtesy of the Library of Congress Prints and Photographs Division*)

a professor, Wilson published a massive treatise, *The State*. "Happily there are in our own day many governments...which seldom coerce their subjects, seeming in their tranquil, noiseless operations to run of themselves," he wrote. "In a sense," democracies "operate without the exercise of force." But "there is force behind them none the less because it never shows itself.... It is latent because it is understood to be omnipotent."[14]

The wartime state was not always latent and noiseless. In factories, food conservation programs, draft calls, and enemy alien registrations, Americans did not always do their utmost. Some of this was subtle resistance to an unpopular war. Given federal legislation such as the Espionage and Sedition Acts, which criminalized antiwar speech, many challenges to the politics of obligation took the form not of words, but of surreptitious actions—or inactions. Some 337,000 men successfully avoided the draft, antiwar neighborhoods consistently failed to meet their Liberty Loan purchase quotas, and at the battle of the Meuse–Argonne Valley in September and October 1918, more than one hundred thousand men fled the front lines and refused to fight.[15]

And so the calls of the home-front hectors grew more shrill. Even the normally placid *Ladies' Home Journal* intoned that "it is our nation that is now at stake: our manhood and our womanhood. . . . Not a single man or woman must be weighed in the balance and found wanting." Recalcitrant Americans were met by others whose sense of obligation went above and beyond Uncle Sam's call to duty. At times, voluntary associations were centers of resistance to militarism and the coercions of war mobilization; they sheltered draft dodgers, gave voice to workers' demands, and protected German Americans from the onslaughts of 100 percent Americanism. More often than not, though, as their members found a place for themselves in Uncle Sam's America, voluntary associations actively supported the war effort in a combination of coercion and voluntarism that proved explosive.[16]

The World War I home front witnessed some of American history's most brutal repressions of labor, of pacifism, and of ethnic difference. Convinced that the state had failed to act, Americans instigated notorious episodes of outright mob violence; more than seventy men and women were killed in public incidents on the home front during the war. In May 1918, in a thoroughly unexceptional episode that would be repeated hundreds of times across the country, a group of twenty shop clerks in Canton, Ohio, wrapped a coworker in an American flag, dragged her through the streets to the local bank, and forced her to purchase a $50 Liberty Bond. Other instances were less brutal but similarly coercive, as Americans reported their neighbors as draft dodgers, food hoarders, or subversive "pro-Germans." Such events filled newspaper pages nearly every day.[17]

The federal government had a hand in this violence, of course, but members of the nation's voluntary associations executed most of it. As it was happening—and even more so after the war was over—critics spoke out against what California senator Hiram Johnson identified as America's "peculiar sort of mental hysteria." Before the war was even a month old, federal Education Commissioner Philander Claxton warned Americans against "being carried away by a wave of hysteric patriotism." Norman Thomas, a socialist organizer who worked to defend conscientious objectors, spoke of "national madness"; the social critic Thorstein Veblen diagnosed "dementia praecox," or schizophrenia. Indeed, many of the events of the war years do seem irrational, almost crazy. But the violence was not a mere psychic aberration or a deviation from American political culture. Pervasive political violence, willingly undertaken, reflected politics as usual. Coercive voluntarism made America's first world war both its most democratically mobilized home front as well as its most violent.[18]

The arm-twisting was often gentle, a new version of the culture of collective participation that helped structure prewar citizenship and its obligations. A 1918 poster for the Liberty Loan depicted a crowded streetcar filled with patriotic loan subscribers and a single, menacingly mustached outsider. "You'll be uncomfortable," the poster noted, "without your honor button." Writing after the war in her semiautobiographical novel *Pale Horse, Pale Rider*, Katherine Anne Porter recalled a vague sense of dread whenever Liberty Loan salesmen, with their "stale air of borrowed importance," visited her office to ask her to buy a war bond. Fear could attend a visit from an agent of the Department of Justice; after one paid a call on a wartime critic in Storm Lake, Iowa, the offender "promised ... to keep his mouth shut henceforth."[19]

Before the war, Americans had certainly been accustomed to private citizens policing their ideas and behaviors, their labor and leisure. During the war, those ideas and behaviors and their labor and leisure had to be mobilized to defeat the enemy. Only then did these coercions come to be state projects, even when they continued to be conducted outside government auspices. As the needs of modern war blurred the lines between state and society, between mobilization and social control, the war made private coercions into public interests through the language of political obligation. When Uncle Sam said "I Want YOU," he invoked a culture of obligation at the same time that he threatened to enforce it.

Despite—or even because of—the collective gaze of Uncle Sam's agents and the passengers on streetcars, Americans carried on their conversation about the state. The previous decade's struggles over the regulation of industry and the provision of social welfare had convinced progressive reformers of the need for greater governmental power; political science textbooks proclaimed the further expansion of the state an inevitability. But plenty of Americans in 1917 remained unconvinced—whether they cherished their autonomy, feared centralized bureaucracy, or lacked any realistic alternatives. They chose state and local governments as political solutions and preferred voluntary associations as forums for public discussion and the execution of political agendas.[20]

Although the experience of war led to new political obligations and repressive state structures, the federal government did not hatch these ideas in smoke-filled Washington rooms and impose them on unwilling citizens. Some political leaders were ambitious state-builders, but most did not sit around wishing they could make the state larger; many, in fact, were quite reluctant to do so. In a war against the centralized bureaucratic state of Germany, accusations of "Prussianism" attended every expansion of federal power during the war. Rather, America's multiple political cultures created political obligations that were generally in close accord with, and sometimes even in excess of, federal war aims. Locally constituted political authorities then used a variety of forms—both old and new, local and federal—to see to it that those obligations were fulfilled, responding to the state's mobilization demands in one moment, calling on the state to expand its power the next. Atavistic violence coexisted with innovative repressions; a continuum of coercion ranged from gossip to flag wrapping to lynching, from the quiet discipline of bureaucratic record-keeping or postal censorship to the state-sanctioned torture of conscientious objectors.

The American home front was not a lawless frontier, a police state, or a great big meeting of the Elks Club. But it looked a little like all of these. It was an improvisational time, something Randolph Bourne clearly recognized. When the thirty-two-year-old radical thinker and progressive journalist died in New York in December 1918, one of the hundreds of thousands of victims of the influenza epidemic that devastated America at war's end, he left behind an unfinished manuscript on "The State." Bourne's sprawling essay has frequently been reduced to its memorable maxim that "war is the health of the state" and used to support the idea that war builds up the authority of bureaucratic institutions—which, often, it does. But Bourne meant something much more. In his essay, he distinguished "Government," which he called "a framework of the administration of laws, and the carrying out of the public force...in the hands of definite, concrete, fallible men," from the "State," which was both more pervasive and evasive than any existing institution. "That the State is a mystical conception is something that must never be forgotten," Bourne insisted. "Its glamor and its significance linger behind the framework of Government and direct its activities."[21]

Whether mystical or merely complex, the power of America's wartime state cannot be explained solely by the size or duration of its institutions. During the war, the lived experience of public and private, federal and local, rights and obligations was muddled—and up for grabs—in ways that American history's received wisdom about steadily expanding state power and steadily declining localism does not begin to capture. Uncertain of the duties of citizenship, embedded in long-standing traditions of private policing, wartime Americans engaged in lurching and ambivalent expansions and contractions of state capacities and bureaucratic authority.

Among the wartime thinkers who tried to sort out the meanings of violence and power in American political life was Randolph Bourne's teacher, John Dewey.

A fifty-seven-year-old philosophy professor at Columbia University, Dewey was perhaps the most respected intellectual in the United States in 1917. Dewey supported the war enthusiastically, but only after undergoing what he called an "immense moral wrench." By 1916, the war's barbarity had become apparent even to the Americans who still stood on its sidelines; that year, Dewey struggled to understand "the most stupendous manifestation of force in all history." "What is force," he asked, "and what are we going to do with it?" The philosopher sketched a distinction between "force," which was the "power of doing work, harnessed to accomplishment of ends," and "violence," which he thought of as "force running wild." With a valuable end in sight, "a hearty fisticuff may be the means of realizing it." It was a curious distinction, one that his former student Randolph Bourne would later seize on to discredit Dewey's passion for war. Where Dewey had stumbled, as any recipient of a fisticuff could have told him, was the matter of consent.[22]

Across the Atlantic, another political thinker spent the war years grappling with the relationship between politics and violence. The sociologist Max Weber, a towering figure on the German intellectual scene, took a wartime leave from the University of Heidelberg to run a nearby military hospital; "this war," he wrote, "is great and wonderful." By 1917, he no longer thought so, and he also began to rethink the relationship between violence and governance. In Weber's theory of the state, violence stood at the center: "force," he noted in a lecture on "Politics as a Vocation" delivered at the University of Munich in 1918, "is a means specific to the state." Indeed, Weber's definition of the state—"a human community that (successfully) claims the monopoly of the legitimate use of physical force within a given territory"—has since become scripture for generations of historians and sociologists.[23]

But as a description of the United States in the first world war, it is simply untrue. As self-appointed home guards wandered America's streets, terrorizing African-American sharecroppers in the Mississippi Delta, rounding up striking copper miners in Arizona, and boarding up Lutheran churches in small Midwestern towns, one thing was clear: the state did not hold a monopoly on the legitimate use of physical force. In a political culture of voluntarism locked in battle with an autocratic enemy, the state's legitimacy—its right to speak for the nation—depended not on the monopolization of legitimate violence but on its proliferation. And as every flag-wrapped shopgirl knew, the state was no less powerful for that fact. What the war did do, however, was prompt a struggle over that monopoly. It was a battle that would give new vitality to the language of rights, and would also give even more energy to the emergence of a powerful—if more latent and noiseless—state.

Of course, Americans didn't have only obligations; they also had rights. Woodrow Wilson sold the war as a battle for the "rights of small nations" and the "freedom of the seas." Suffragists fought for the right to vote, African Americans excluded from officer training camps demanded the right to serve, and there were as many invocations of the right of free speech as violations of it. But in a culture of obligation, ambivalence about rights abounded, and wartime discussion focused as often on their limits as on their defense. The population of wartime rights talkers included a range of Americans who claimed to be defending civil liberties even as they appeared to be limiting them. The American Association of University Professors spoke out for academic freedom but supported the dismissal of those scholars it deemed "pro-German"; the Federal Council of Churches, an association of mainstream Protestant denominations, claimed to defend the right of religious freedom in wartime but suppressed conscientious objection within its own denominations. Men and women who spoke of "responsible speech" sought to protect the rights of speech and press, but only for those citizens who had demonstrated that they could be trusted to exercise them responsibly. Such a conception of rights came straight out of the culture of obligation. It is a way of thinking about rights that seems unfamiliar today.

But if the rights talk of 1918 was the artifact of another era, contemporary Americans will recognize much in the wartime speech of progressive reformers like Jane Addams, radical thinkers such as Roger Baldwin, and African-American activists like Ida B. Wells. Wartime civil libertarians sometimes reworked or rejected the language of obligation, and they struggled to build institutional homes for their ideas. Pacifist and labor groups coalesced into the new American Civil Liberties Union; membership in the National Association for the Advancement of Colored People grew by leaps and bounds; agrarian populists and Jehovah's Witnesses filed lawsuits. These groups' members rearticulated Wilson's wartime rhetoric of making the world safe for democracy in the language of personal freedom and formed the basis of a rights-based vision of citizenship that would play a prominent role in twentieth-century America.

The outcome of the wartime debate over the state's incomplete monopoly on violence accelerated that shift. For generations, Americans assumed that self-government required the existence of vigilance societies that worked hand-in-glove with the state. These groups drew their legitimacy from that very cooperation, and they acted on the allegiance that Americans felt to the nation and to these groups, the nation's self-appointed local representatives. But as parades turned into riots, the wartime excesses of home defense guards and slacker raiders prompted a struggle over who could legitimately police the home front. Civil libertarian William Bayard Hale, an old friend of Woodrow Wilson who had even helped him draft his 1912 election manifesto, *The New Freedom*, wrote the White House in the spring of 1918 urging Wilson to create "a single special authority" to regulate "resident enemies and enemy sympathizers." Wouldn't that show, he asked, "that the Government at Washington is fully master of the situation, proposes to remain so, and needs no assistance from rioters?" It was not just that these groups employed physical violence but rather that their members' relationship to the institutions of law was so ambiguous. The authority to use force, which had been so diffuse, became increasingly tied to the state itself. As government actors authorized war, delegitimized vigilantism, and bargained with Americans for their wartime services, they repositioned the relationship between citizens and the government.[24]

"Lawlessness" became a crucial keyword during the war and the social upheaval that followed it. In the fight against mob violence, challengers asserted legal rights and called for due processes of justice, but they were not alone. Everyone, it seemed, was calling in the law—articulated by some as an angry demand for "law and order," voiced by others as a desperate plea for "the rule of law." It was even asserted from within the White House itself. These converging voices unwittingly accomplished a greater political and social transformation than could ever have been wrought by a weak, fragmented, and constantly harassed coalition of labor radicals, cultural feminists, and antilynching societies. Obedience to law challenged, and to some degree replaced, civic voluntarism as the central definition that Americans referred to when they talked about their political obligations.

The notion of legal obedience as political obligation was not new, of course. Political theorists of the early twentieth century had considered whether political obligation meant anything more than obedience to law. The influential British philosopher T. H. Green, whose *Lectures on the Principles of Political Obligation* was reprinted in 1917, had doubted law's significance, because "actual states at best fulfil but partially their ideal function," but many others highlighted the centrality of legal obligation to political obligation. In 1907, Supreme Court Justice David J. Brewer meditated on the "Obligation of Obedience," insisting that "the obedience of the American is not cowardly. ... It springs from a conviction that it is a duty." Moorfield Storey, a prominent Boston attorney and the president of the NAACP, reminded a graduating law school class in 1919 that the belief "that all men must obey the law is the doctrine on which free governments rest."[25]

After the Armistice, violence and voluntarism both continued. American Legionnaires broke up socialist meetings in 1919, and the white-hooded nightriders of the Ku Klux Klan menaced Americans in the early 1920s. But after the war—and in fact because of the war—law was more than ever a tool that ordinary Americans could use to challenge the political violence that had so characterized the American home front. Court cases and congressional hearings did much to destroy radical movements and ethnic associations, to be sure, but the same forums brought down an aggressive attorney general and the director of the Bureau of Investigation, unmasked violence against conscientious objectors and suffragists, and established the first substantive due process rights for African Americans in the rural South. They even reined in the Texas Rangers.

Movements against mob violence did much to erase the vigilantism and lawless violence that characterized nineteenth-century American political culture, but they also helped wipe away the era's vibrant political culture of associational life. They effaced the multiple authorities of prewar life—and thus diminished the multiple loyalties that operated there. Increasingly, Americans articulated their political obligations not to many things but to one: the state. When they imagined government rather than people as the source of rights, Americans unwittingly handed over to the state an array of coercive powers over matters previously governed by voluntary associations. Opponents of lawlessness thus helped to build the state that they were simultaneously being protected *from* and protected *by*. Government institutions had a hand in this as much as any social movement; the state helped make the rights revolution in part by acting so much like a state.[26]

That progressives—the people who brought America direct election of senators, direct taxation, initiative and referendum, and a philosophy of participatory democracy—should have turned away from "the people" is ironic but not surprising. As angry wartime crowds silenced pacifists, labor radicals, and small-town ministers, the idea of appealing directly to the people and locating democratic legitimacy in their associations lost some of its luster. The state—even the seemingly tyrannical state of the 1920 Palmer Raids that civil libertarians despised—appeared the better option in a devil's bargain. Progressives' faith in "the people" became, for many, a postwar fear of "the mob" and "the crowd."

This was not the world that Mary Parker Follett wanted, nor the one that she had worked for throughout the Progressive Era. When war came, Follett was forty-nine years old, living in Boston, and known in reform circles as both a social worker and a political writer. She worked for the Boston school district but was equally passionate about her work with the National Community Centers Association. Community, she thought, could rescue America, an idea she explored in *The New State*, published just after the Armistice in 1918. The book emphasized the need for institutions that could continually create what Follett called the "true group process." The basic unit of political theory, she argued, should not be the isolated individual but one in "continual relatings" with others. "My only rights," she argued, "are those which membership in a group gives me." Once her plans were fully realized, she hoped, Americans could "substitute for the fictitious democracy of equal rights and 'consent of the governed,' the living democracy of a united, responsible people." This was, she thought, "the task of the twentieth century." American civic voluntarism's most articulate prophet, though, could not confront its underbelly. About groups Follett wrote quite a good deal; about mobs, crowds, and herds, nothing at all.[27]

Walter Lippmann shared Mary Parker Follett's skepticism of the consenting, rights-bearing individual. A prominent journalist and a member of Woodrow Wilson's inner circle, the young Lippmann (not yet even thirty) was far more pessimistic than Follett. Amid the noise of wartime America, he heard silence. Out of fear, ambivalence, helplessness, or simple indifference, some Americans had remained silent—a stance that Lippmann knew could not be summarily categorized as either resistance or tacit consent. In a series of 1919 essays, Lippmann explored the sources of that silence, introducing into American political vocabulary the concept of "the manufacture of consent." Hopeful at first that objective journalistic methods could save the public from manipulation, by 1925, when he wrote *The Phantom Public*, Lippmann had wholly abandoned all faith that the people, in mass democracies, could govern themselves.[28]

An inauspicious beginning this was, indeed, for a century of civil liberties, as books were burned by librarians, suffragists were beaten by women, and conscientious objectors harassed by men of the cloth. Perhaps it was no surprise, then, that for much of the early twentieth century, rights talk was only that—talk. Civil liberties would never be sustained by the rich institutional networks of everyday life that undergirded the culture of obligation, and so the lived experience of rights proved far weaker than the culture of obligation that preceded it. Bereft of institutions at the local or national level to create and nourish a meaningful culture of rights, American political culture limped into the 1920s with a contested and fractured sense of the obligations of citizenship but with no real alternatives in place.

Uncle Sam Wants You begins with an examination of the Selective Service Act and the twenty-four million men who registered for military service under its terms beginning in June 1917. This was the nation's first experience with mass conscription; drafted men made up just 8 percent of soldiers in the Union army during the Civil War, but they constituted 72 percent of Uncle Sam's forces in World War I. The draft made the boundaries of state power a central question of wartime political culture; it was the most important, and the most controversial, of all the era's political obligations, all the more so because it claimed to be universal and selective at the same time. While legislators and political theorists discussed the fairness of conscription, drafted men and their families, who found the state an increasing presence in their everyday lives, argued with military officers and local draft boards. Selective service translated political culture into state institutions: without a massive state bureaucracy, and fearful of constructing one, Americans quickly realized that military mobilization required the nation's draft-age men to register on their own initiative. Ideals of voluntarism and obligation shaped the individual conscience; local institutions monitored its compliance. But not all Americans registered. The draft's supporters used coercive voluntarism to build structures of enforcement—particularly the slacker raids conducted by the volunteers of the American Protective League—that guaranteed Woodrow Wilson's nation would, in fact, volunteer in mass.

Conscientious objectors' political obligations stood in direct conflict with their religious ones; they knew better than anyone else what it meant for Americans to have multiple allegiances. But as chapter 2 shows, amid a war fought to defend Christian civilization, nothing less than 100 percent Americanism would do. Conditioned by the culture of obligation to see duty as an unavoidable aspect of citizenship, most Americans seethed at the objectors' refusals of military service. Nor did the objectors themselves entirely reject the idea that citizenship implied obligation; the vast majority demanded that they be allowed to perform an alternative national service that could reconcile their individual consciences with the power of the state. Many men became conscientious objectors because they rejected the state's authority, so it was ironic that of all Americans, objectors had the most direct relationship with the state, including the Board of Inquiry, a government tribunal whose members personally interrogated 2,300 objectors during the war. Faced with persuasion, ridicule, and court-martial, only a few thousand men claimed conscientious objector status, but their experiences revealed a new relationship between individual citizens and the state.

America's wartime culture of obligation lent itself to political coercion. Factory owners used violence to quell strikes; antisuffragists employed force to silence women's claims for the vote; whites hoped it could forestall black migration and political militancy. These coercive practices were sustained by, and exercised through, Americans' cherished voluntary associations. Chapters 3 and 4 demonstrate the close relationship between voluntarism and coercion in early twentieth-century American politics by examining the groups that mobilized women's labor and the vigilance societies that policed the home front.

Excluded for the most part from the ranks of the military, women were nonetheless obliged to volunteer, and millions of them did. Home-front volunteers found that fulfilling wartime obligations gave force to their political claims and offered their service enthusiastically, building dense connections between their organizations and the wartime state. More than 500,000 women collected pledges for the U.S. Food Administration; their coercive voluntarism included the indirect persuasions of house-to-house visits, gossip, and public shaming. Most women's organizations thought that fulfilling wartime obligations would help win the vote, but the radical suffragists of the National Woman's Party picketed the White House, insisting that suffrage was a right and not a reward.

If violence is as American as cherry pie, so, too, was the obligation of policing. Across America, citizens' leagues rounded up socialists, striking workers, and suspected prostitutes, and during the war vigilant citizens engaged in acts of political violence that they believed were part and parcel of the war effort. But home-front vigilantism had as many critics as participants. Wartime critics of mob violence began to undermine the authority of voluntarist coercion through their appeals to the rule of law, as they expressed new notions of rights and imagined a state that monopolized political violence.

Uncle Sam Wants You also traces the outlines of an alternative vision of citizenship that highlighted rights and individual liberties and rejected the culture of obligation. Stringent laws handed the power to police responsible speech to federal authorities—which, in practice, meant postmasters, juries, and librarians. As they faced off against small-town newspaper editors, dissenting ministers, and pacifist speakers, a new discourse on civil liberties emerged. Less a movement than a moment, the convergence of a fragmented and tentative collection of thinkers, activists, and ordinary Americans described in chapter 5 reshaped the forms that political opposition would take—as it challenged both the lawless doings of the mob and the lawful actions exerted by the wartime surveillance state. But in a culture of obligation, it was responsible speech that most Americans sought to defend, which required imagining new kinds of responsible citizens.

Following several high-profile espionage attempts by German agents, the U.S. government, and American people more generally, placed German Americans under official and unofficial surveillance, a story recounted in chapter 6. During the war, the U.S. government interned approximately six thousand persons. Most were soldiers or sailors in service of the German Empire; by war's end, though, many detainees were not even German citizens but European immigrants seized as "pro-Germans" and destined for deportation in the postwar Red Scare. Their experience, like that of German Americans nationwide, forced Americans to understand how cultural practices meshed with political obligations.

Wartime immigration officials turned the empty halls of Ellis Island into a mass detention center for enemy aliens; voluntary associations signed on, drafting plans for a possible mass internment of enemy aliens nationwide and assisting in the construction of powerful new government institutions regulating immigration and political subversion—institutions that would stand at the center of the twentieth-century American state. They passed English-only laws, assaulted Germans' voluntary associations, and even called for a federal Department of Education to remake America's immigrant mass into loyal citizens. German Americans won a few battles in court but lost the war; the devastation of their civic culture gave new meaning to the tacit consent of America's modern citizens.

It was a new state, and the obligations Uncle Sam demanded from his citizens were both more extreme in their possibilities and more limited in their connections to Americans' everyday lives. This was the transformation—both mystical and institutional—that Randolph Bourne confronted when he sat down to write "The State." Whether James Montgomery Flagg had seen some glimmer of it in the mirror as he sketched that summer day in 1916, we'll never know.

I

The Spirit of Selective Service: Conscription and Coercion

By 9:00 P.M. on September 12, 1918, the nation's work was done. Responding to President Woodrow Wilson's extension of the Selective Service Act to all males between the ages of eighteen and forty-five, more than thirteen million American men made themselves known to the state that day, reporting their birth dates, marital status, next of kin, and other vital statistics to local draft boards. A few days after the event, a *New York Times* reporter reflected on the day's events. He marveled that this unprecedented registration for military service looked almost like "part of America's second nature," with hardly any interruption of the nation's routine. "Without a military tradition...the manhood of this country...stepped before their draft boards and registered themselves for such service as the Government shall deem them fit; and having done so without any noise or fuss, they went back to their...peaceful pursuits as peacefully as ever until such times as the Government will need them for the serious tasks of war."[1]

The Selective Service Act of 1917 was the centerpiece of wartime citizenship and its defining obligation. America's first mass draft reflected the state's power at its most extreme—it demanded that its citizens die for it. The United States had always asserted the authority to coerce men into offering their lives for the nation-state. During the war, this basic premise—that political obligations implied military ones—went almost completely unchallenged, but Americans constantly tested its terms. Twenty-four million men and their families experienced a direct exercise of state power as they filled out their forms; they created new places for the federal government in their lives as they sought to enlist, to be exempted, to obtain their military paychecks, or to enforce the draft against recalcitrant neighbors. At the same time, conscription created new categories of citizens: conscientious objectors, draft dodgers, veterans. As drafted men and their families interacted with military administrators—whether far off in Washington or closer to home, in the person of local selective service boards or volunteer draft police—they reworked the meanings of political obligation and the institutions where it was practiced.

When Americans had these encounters with the federal government, who, precisely, were they talking to? The New York City newspaper correspondent wondered the same thing. Was the draft enforced by "heavily browed officers who overawed ranks of cowering registrants with their stares and sharp commands?" Hardly. The reporter saw that day that "the ruthless machinery of registration was wielded by no other hands than those of trim little school teachers...or mild-mannered citizens...taking a day off from business to help the Government." Most Americans, in fact, typically experienced federal power not through the physical coercion of "heavily browed officers" but through the efforts of "trim little school teachers" and "mild-mannered citizens" who staffed selective service draft boards. Every one of them was a volunteer.[2]

Selective service embodied the national culture of voluntarism: not only through individual effort but together with the institutions of everyday life—schools, churches, clubs, families, local newspapers. If military service was a new obligation of citizenship in 1917, it was linked from the outset to duties that weren't new at all. Americans had already formed social bonds, and war now transformed them into political obligations. America's vaunted culture of voluntarism intersected with and amplified state power, rather than acting as a check on it.

Voluntarism also shaped the "slacker raids," vast dragnet operations of interrogation conducted by the 250,000 volunteer members of the American Protective League. The APL was a private voluntary association with roots in local habits of vigilantism, but it was also an arm of an emergent surveillance state that employed modern methods of social control to uphold federal law. Like Flagg's poster of Uncle Sam, the American Protective League put a local face on a distant federal power, but that power was only possible in the first place because citizens voluntarily participated in the league. This was what bottom-up state-building was all about.

By the war's end, conscription would bring America courtroom battles, shoot-outs in the Ozark Mountains, and even a fistfight in the cloakroom of the U.S. Senate. There were torchlight parades and midnight raids; makeshift kaisers hung in effigy; a man hanged in a noose. And through it all, the registration forms poured into selective service headquarters. This was not lost on the *New York Times* reporter, who spent registration day in the rough-and-tumble neighborhood around Peck Slip on the East River waterfront in Manhattan. There, 3,528 men—many of them the longshoremen, dockworkers, and drifters who filled the neighborhood's lodging houses—registered, without complaint, at the makeshift offices of New York Local Board No. 92. "There was no use complaining," wrote the reporter. "To ask the average registrant what he thought of the whole affair would be to receive a shrug of the shoulder and the acknowledgment that he really saw no use in having any thought on the subject at all, further than that it was the law of the land, and that every loyal citizen owed it to himself and to his country to obey that law."[3]

"Accustomed to consider themselves more or less outside of the social organism of society," the reporter noted, neighborhood men "were suddenly compelled to locate themselves...ask themselves many questions that had not concerned them before—who they were—what they were—where they were." To the men, the forms were nuisances, beside the point of their political obligations. "The main fact" was "that they were ready to fight, if the Government would so have it." Submitting their names to Uncle Sam two months before the Armistice, few of these men would ever confront the main fact; nationwide, just 12 percent of men who registered were ever inducted. But the draft taught lessons to the rest of America. What the men of Peck Slip did not realize was that filling out the forms, "locating" themselves before the state, was the main fact—and their cards the symbols of the new terms of citizenship.[4]

★ *Soldiers and Slackers*

Conscription posed the toughest puzzle for Americans as they thought about their political obligations, and debates over military service dominated political discussion even before U.S. entry into war in April 1917. In battles over whether to adopt a policy of universal military training—which turned into a contest over conscription as Americans considered adopting the draft in May 1917—the nation grappled with the terms of political obligation. On one side stood organizations and individuals who had been pushing for a stronger, more professional military force during the years of American neutrality. The rank and file of the "preparedness" movement were mostly Republicans, men and women who hoped for a vigorous federal government, a standing national army, and a strenuous and militarized citizenship. A generation after the Rough Riders, Theodore Roosevelt was the movement's hero and, in fact, one of its leaders. In the buildup to war, the former president never passed up an opportunity to criticize the current occupant of the Oval Office. Nor did he have much patience for conscription's opponents, whom he derided as "professional pacifists, poltroons, and college sissies."[5]

Roosevelt, though, was mostly a figurehead and a blusterer, leaving the daily leadership of the movement in the hands of Major General Leonard Wood. A leading military statesman and a longtime proponent of universal male conscription, Wood argued that "manhood suffrage means manhood obligation for service in peace or war." A volunteer army, claimed preparedness advocates, would violate American principles of equality and fairness by allowing the faint of heart a free ride. "There is no reason," huffed Major General Hugh Scott, "why one woman's son should go out and defend... another woman and her son who refuses to take training or give service." The draft would also inculcate the virtues of political obligations even as it enforced them. "Our youth have been taught that government owes everything to them with no emphasis upon their debt to the government," complained former President William Howard Taft. "Military service will impress this counter obligation on the young man [and] teach him the value of respect for authority, of subordination to a lawful superior, and of the sacredness of his allegiance to his country." Draft supporters, influenced by republican notions of citizenship and wistful for the drama of Roosevelt's Rough Riders, gave their proposals a concrete form. They mobilized the membership rolls of turn-of-the-century patriotic societies and veterans' organizations; they collected funds for a voluntary officer training camp in Plattsburgh, New York; and they set up lobbying organizations such as the National Security League, with close connections to New York journalists and Washington policymakers.[6]

Preparedness advocates like T.R. pointed to the Revolutionary "Minutemen" to argue that universal conscription was no departure from national traditions. But the draft they envisioned, and the administrative bureaucracy they imagined would manage it, implied an army that would bear little resemblance to ragtag assemblies on colonial town greens. At the war's outset in 1914, Great Britain had relied on volunteer troops, diluting its military strength—not only by battlefield casualties but also through shortages of skilled labor at home, as industrial and technical workers left the factories of industrial England for the trenches of the Western Front. Heeding this cautionary tale, Leonard Wood therefore insisted that the United States build "a purely federal force," properly managed to guarantee the "detailed and careful organization of the resources of the country." Preparedness advocates placed obligations to the nation ahead of all others and favored the federal government as the institutional means of organization. A 1916 War Department memo disparaged voluntary recruitment as "undemocratic, unreliable, inefficient, and extravagant."[7]

Taking the other side were a host of progressive reformers and intellectuals, as well as a substantial proportion of the American public. Some opposed conscription because they opposed war. In July 1916, Randolph Bourne, an avid student of the philosopher William James, paid homage to James's famous essay "A Moral Equivalent of War" with his own effort in the pages of the *New Republic*. He attempted to extricate the valuable feeling of communal sacrifice found in military service from its connections to brutality and war. Bourne doubted T.R.'s dream of a military melting pot. "Military service is a sham universality," he wrote. Not only does it omit "the feminine half of the nation's youth" but it also "irons out all differences of talent and ability" and makes "a mere machine of uniform, obeying youths." Instead, Bourne proposed using the schools to solve the nation's social problems. "Our need is to learn how to live rather than die; to be teachers and creators, not engines of destruction."[8]

After war broke out in Europe in August 1914, Bourne and his fellow antiwar activists gathered in new peace societies like the American Union against Militarism and the Woman's Peace Party. As U.S. intervention loomed, they tried to assemble a coalition with other opponents of war. On Capitol Hill, they knocked on the doors of Southern and Western populists, most of them Democrats, politicians who consistently opposed centralized state power, particularly when it was concentrated in Washington corridors and East Coast banks. The alliance of populist politicos and New York intellectuals, though, proved fragile and uneasy at best.[9]

Woodrow Wilson's thoughts on the matter are difficult to discern. In March 1916, with war raging in Europe, he appointed as his secretary of war Newton D. Baker, a forty-five-year-old progressive reformer who not only had never served in the military but also was a proclaimed pacifist. As late as February 1917, Wilson himself was publicly on record against conscription. But at some point, he changed his mind. Ever the technocrat, Wilson found the military modernizers' efficiency arguments compelling; he was persuaded, too, by the voluntarist sheen that "selective service" cast over the draft's coercive methods. After looking over an early version of the draft law, Wilson asked Baker whether the proposed legislation would "authorize [us] . . . to call on the state officials, or is this just a friendly summons to cooperate?" suggesting that Wilson imagined a deeply voluntarist process based in the states rather than headquartered in Washington. But in April 1917, the president had a more immediate motivation: his bitter enemy Theodore Roosevelt was noisily agitating for the creation of a volunteer military regiment (which T.R., of course, planned to lead), and Wilson may have sought a means to forestall voluntarism in general so that he could block Roosevelt's voluntarism in particular. In any case, once he decided that conscription was "vital to the success of this grim undertaking," he was committed. By the spring of 1917, Wilson had become draft's most vigorous defender, and he even authorized Newton Baker to print and distribute thirty million draft registration forms before the Selective Service Act had even passed Congress.[10]

The debate about the military obligations of citizenship continued after the declaration of war, shifting focus to Wilson's proposed conscription bill. Pacifists and libertarians initially hoped for a way out; thousands gathered in Washington for a rally of the Emergency Peace Federation. Among them was Boston's Alexander Bannwart, who tried, with "a woman, a minister of the gospel, four other men," and his fists, to convince Massachusetts Senator Henry Cabot Lodge to see the light. (Lodge, with some helping hands, won the fight and voted for both war and conscription.) "This is wicked, wicked," moaned progressive reformer Lillian Wald.[11]

Conscription's opponents pointed to the nation's long history of military volunteers organized under local control. Petitioning Congress from Highland Park, Michigan, Stanley T. Rice felt that a draft was "not in accordance with the principals [sic] of American government and is undemocratic." Jessica Whitcomb of Topeka, Kansas, thought conscription was "imperialistic" and told her congressman it ran against the war's aims. "If war is pushed as one of Democracy against militaristic Autocracy, why should we... place ourselves under the rule of militarism?" What Rice and Whitcomb rejected, in a culture of voluntarism, was conscription's compulsory nature. So did Oklahoma senator Thomas Gore, who derided an "army of conscripted slackers" and asked, "Why should we brand the American boy as a conscript without affording him the opportunity to earn the glory of an American volunteer?" The draft smacked of coercion; as Speaker of the House Champ Clark memorably intoned during debate over the bill, "there is precious little difference between a conscript and a convict."[12]

The Selective Service Act, signed into law on May 18, 1917, was a compromise. The bill faced so much opposition from within Wilson's own party that he had to turn to a Republican, Representative Julius Kahn, to shepherd the legislation through Congress. The law required all male citizens of draft age (initially set at twenty-one to thirty years old), as well as aliens who had taken out first papers of citizenship, to register with local draft boards in anticipation of call-up by the army. Preparedness advocates got much of what they wanted: a universal obligation to register and a military controlled by Washington and committed to the melting pot ideal. "The Selective Draft Act," editorialized the *New York Times*, "gives a long and sorely needed means of disciplining a certain insolent foreign element in this nation."[13]

The law also protected federal authority to craft an efficient, modern military. Liability to registration was universal, but liability to service was "selective." In an era when just over 3 percent of Americans between the ages of eighteen and twenty-four were enrolled in college, there were no exemptions for students, although a tender regard for men of the cloth exempted clergy and divinity students. Rather, a man's health, his engagement in a "useful" war industry, or his obligations to dependent family members determined whether he would be called to serve. As Wilson put it, "The nation...needs each man, not in the field that will most pleasure him, but in the endeavor that will best serve the common good." Selective service was always intended not so much to create obligations as to manage them. But voluntarism was there as well. "The whole nation," said Wilson, "must be a team." Heading up Wilson's team in Washington was an unlikely assortment: on the civilian side, Secretary of War Newton Baker, described by an English visitor as a "nice, trim little man of the YMCA type," turned to his "little, short secretary," Frederick Keppel, a Columbia University dean "dynamic to his fingertips" and endowed with breathtaking bureaucratic ambitions. Baker's point man in the army was Provost Marshal General Enoch Crowder, a career lawyer-soldier and a snippy martinet who had little interest in taking orders from civilians.[14]

The voluntarists won the battle over the draft's day-to-day operation, for political more than bureaucratic reasons. The draft could never have been administered successfully from Selective Service System headquarters in Washington. The army lacked the funds or the manpower to embark even on registration, and the Department of Justice, with a Bureau of Investigation that was just nine years old, could offer little help with enforcement, especially in the face of the considerable opposition to conscription in many areas of the country. Hence the government's support of the concept of "selective service." By casting the registration process as a volunteer "service" by the individual to the state—which would do the "selecting" based on principles of efficiency it defined—the federal government gave the draft an aura of consent. Placing local draft registration offices at official polling places, rather than at police stations (as some had recommended), linked selective service with democratic political participation. As Wilson explained in the draft's initial proclamation, "It is in no sense a conscription of the unwilling; it is, rather, selection from a nation which has volunteered in mass." This notion of American men volunteering in mass to let the state make a coercive claim on their lives was crucial both for the draft's political legitimacy and for its operation on the ground.[15]

"We may trust to *American manhood* to come forward and *identify itself*," boasted a government brochure. Military mobilization required the twenty-four million men who came under the auspices of the Selective Service Act to register of their own volition for service. Although the draft boards had help in the task of identification from the U.S. Census Bureau, local post offices, private insurance companies, and ordinary telephone directories, voluntary registration was necessary because the state did not have the ability to locate or identify all those who lived under its authority. A generation later, draft officials could track a man down through his birth certificate, his driver's license, voter registration, passport, or Social Security card. In 1917, however, the average American man lacked most of these documents; some carried none of them at all.[16]

Selective service legislation tapped into Progressive Era traditions of associational activity to create a nationwide network of draft officials, legal advisers, medical examiners, ministers, and even dentists. Staff members who performed long hours of tedious clerical work occasionally drew a salary of $4 a day; most, however, were volunteers. Their work did more than just put a local face on the exercise of federal power. In some local communities, they *were* the federal government.[17]

By June 5, 1917, the nation's first registration day, the machinery of conscription was in place. "The man who stands back now is lost; lost to the ranks of citizenship," government officials announced that morning. Across the country, 9.6 million men between the ages of twenty-one and thirty appeared at four thousand registration sites for what Newton Baker correctly predicted would be a day of "festival and patriotic occasion." After processing the forms in just over a month, the army was soon ready for conscription itself. In a dramatic public ceremony in Washington on July 20, a blindfolded secretary of war plucked from a glass jar a gelatin capsule bearing the number 258. Within weeks, notices arrived ordering men with low draft numbers to report for medical exams; by the end of the summer, the first draftees headed off to hastily constructed military camps.[18]

Not everyone registered, of course. Attorney General Thomas Gregory divided the draft's opponents into two groups: "one class will consist of weaklings...and another of those under the influence of men and women...who are endeavoring to dissuade young men from serving." Some sought out antidraft organizations such as the American Union against Militarism, put together by peace progressives; others joined the socialists and anarchists who made up the more radical No-Conscription League. Even more significant were the methods by which draft-age men, acting as individuals before draft boards, rejected or challenged the obligations of the state.[19]

Conscription's opponents pursued their claims in court. Georgia's Tom Watson, a leading figure in the populist politics of the previous generation, emerged as a spokesman for draft resistance. Watson recruited two Atlanta

On July 20, 1917, just a few weeks after 9.6 million men had registered for the draft, a blindfolded Secretary of War Newton D. Baker drew number 258 out of a glass jar in the Selective Service System's draft lottery. (*U.S. Signal Corps Photo, Courtesy of the George C. Marshall Research Library, Lexington, Virginia*)

men, and $100,000, for a constitutional challenge in the summer of 1917. Later joining with civil libertarian and veteran New York litigator Harry Weinberger, Watson argued that selective service legislation violated the Thirteenth Amendment's prohibition against involuntary servitude and that the Constitution did not authorize the raising of armies by such methods. Weinberger added his own line of reasoning: by exempting clergymen and divinity students from the draft, the Selective Service Act had also violated the First Amendment's establishment clause separating church and state.[20]

Their arguments went nowhere. In January 1918, the U.S. Supreme Court unanimously upheld the constitutionality of conscription. Chief Justice Edward D. White, writing for the Court in *Arver v. United States*, dismissed the contention that the government had no power to exact enforced military duty. "The very conception of a just government and its duty to the citizen includes the reciprocal obligation of the citizen to render military service in case of need and the right to compel it." Any other notion, he wrote, "challenges the existence of all power, for Governmental power which has no sanction to it and which can only be exercised provided the citizen consents is in no substantial sense a power." Schooled in the language of obligation, White believed that citizens' responsibilities to the state came first, preceding their rights—including the right to an opinion about any particular policy. Consent followed from citizenship, not the other way around. *Arver*, while authoritative, announced nothing new. Every single court that heard a challenge to the draft denied it.[21]

As military call-ups began in the summer of 1917, open opposition to conscription emerged. On the Lower East Side of Manhattan and in Butte, Montana, throughout the rural South, and on Native American reservations in Nevada and Utah, Americans resisted the draft registration process; during the war, perhaps fifteen to twenty Americans died resisting the draft. Local traditions of rural radicalism prompted Oklahoma's Green Corn Rebellion in August 1917. The Working Class Union there included a mix of socialists and tenant farmers who agreed on little else besides their shared opposition to the draft. They proposed to march on Washington, feeding along the way on green corn picked from roadside farms. Spontaneous and diverse, bringing together white, black, and Native American farmers, the movement was rapidly crushed.[22]

Outright resistance, like that practiced by the Green Corn rebels, was less common than silent evasion. Some managed to avoid the draft with fraud and lies; Selective Service System records are replete with stories of dubious illnesses, missing toes, and feigned deafness. But given that Uncle Sam could not capture every draft-age man with his piercing gaze, and information about identity, birth date, and citizenship status was difficult to determine, dodging was relatively easy, particularly for the transient young working-class men who made up a substantial proportion of the draft-eligible population. Selective service officials reported 337,000 men who avoided service when called, but the army's own documents suggest that perhaps as many as three million evaded the draft by failing to sign up at all.[23]

These men quickly came to be known, in the slang of 1917 America, as "slackers." Their presence on the American home front—in numbers that alarmed both federal officials and local community leaders—prompted a widespread public movement for draft enforcement. The slacker was a problem of political obligation. The outrage directed at slackers, and the popular movements to capture and punish them, emerged from a political culture that defined citizenship through its obligations; whatever else a slacker was, he was first and foremost a man who would not do his duty to his country. Slackers were not conscientious objectors, who gave articulate voice to their criticisms of the state in formal documents. But through their actions no less than their words, slackers did just as much to redefine the terms of political obligation.[24]

Americans who hated slackers were pretty sure they knew who the slackers were. They knew, first of all, that slackers were not just bad citizens, but inadequate men. The antiwar radicals of the Industrial Workers of the World urged their listeners, "Don't Be a Soldier, Be a Man!" But this was the minority viewpoint, shouted down by militarist press editorials, popular films with titles such as *Shoulder Arms* and *The Slacker*, and the speeches of politicians—including, unsurprisingly, Theodore Roosevelt. Patriotic young women gathered outside the gates of the Hood Rubber Company in Watertown, Massachusetts. "We are going to get a fine bunch of white feathers," they announced, making reference to the traditional symbols of cowardice, "and present at least one to every man who is marked down on our list as a service dodger."[25]

The mental universe of the slacker-haters had some patience for clueless foreigners, who might be unschooled in the obligations of citizenship or maybe had been led astray by vicious radicals; as compensation, draft enforcers targeted ethnic immigrant communities. The legal obligations of aliens under Selective Service Act regulations only complicated the matter. All noncitizen males were required to register, but not all were required to serve, and those who were enemy aliens (citizens of Germany, Austria-Hungary, and the other Central Powers) were actually *forbidden* to serve, unless they renounced their enemy citizenship. A community with a large immigrant population, therefore, might also have a lot of young working-class men roaming its streets without uniforms. Native-born Americans quickly concluded that all such men were slackers. When police in Portland, Maine, noted more than a hundred draft-age strangers in the city's French-Canadian East End in August 1917, they worried that Portland was "becoming a Mecca for slackers."[26]

Like other recent immigrants, Jewish Americans struggled with the issue. For decades, Jewish immigrants had been associated with radical movements; in many of the nation's anticonscription organizations, Jews did play prominent roles. Many Americans concluded that all Jews were draft dodgers. Widespread assumptions of Jewish slacking found their way into a wartime manual for draft boards, which warned medical examiners that "the foreign born, especially the Jews, are more apt to malinger than the native born." In response, leading Jewish Americans went to great lengths to distance themselves from antiwar radicals. The American Jewish League supported the formation of a separate Jewish battalion in the hope that enthusiastic military service would cultivate mainstream acceptance, and the National Council of Jewish Women tried to combat suspicion with eager voluntarism. "We owe it to ourselves, to our people, and to our country," they claimed, "to disprove such insinuation by the practice as well as the preaching of real Americanism." Writing in the *North American Review*,

Lewis Brown pointed out that Jews were, in fact, overrepresented in the military population, making up 4 percent of the military even though they were at the time just 3 percent of the population. Brown's estimates are impossible to confirm independently, and the pervasiveness of such claims in wartime political discourse—asserted by every ethnic group, whether about military service, bond sales, or food production—suggests less about the precision of statistics than it does about the rhetorical power of voluntarism and the need, in the language of the day, to go "over the top."[27]

Asian immigrants faced a unique situation. In 1917, U.S. immigration laws barred them from naturalization, but wartime legislation that encouraged the rapid naturalization of any man who served in the U.S. military suggested (misleadingly, it would turn out) that the war might open the doors of citizenship to Asians. Thousands served in uniform; others volunteered as translators and censors. *Chung Sai Yat Po*, a Chinese-language San Francisco daily, urged its readers to buy Liberty Bonds and enthusiastically supported draft registration and enforcement. The newspaper published draft regulations and informed noncitizens about their duties under the law. "We overseas Chinese who reside in the United States are protected by the American flag (stars and stripes) and must abide by the order to register for enlisting and must not evade in any way." Military service by Chinese Americans was embedded in a debate about loyal citizenship: editors hoped that Chinese soldiers would serve with a distinction "no less than white soldiers" and "bring honor to the people of our race."[28]

In almost every case, there was far more division within ethnic groups than commentators noticed at the time or historians have recorded since. The ethnic elites who headed national organizations, represented immigrant communities in political bodies, or edited ethnic newspapers went to great lengths to assert that the draft-age men of their ethnicity were participating eagerly in selective service and turned the civic institutions of their community over to draft enforcement. Often they were successful in mobilizing their countrymen. But class divisions chafed raw the bonds of ethnic pride, and the spokesmen's protestations often masked considerable rates of evasion.[29]

Citizens also came up with their own definitions of draft evasion. In Worcester, Massachusetts, a French-Canadian machinist, whose skilled work in a war industry had exempted him from the draft, appeared before his local board eager to be reclassified as draftable: "Say, my girl says it's all bunk, this line of talk of me being more use here than in the army. If I don't go into the army, she won't marry me. She's right and you've gotta put me back in Class 1." When the board refused, the young man's girlfriend soon appeared, and she said, "I don't care how many classes you have or what the rules say.

Down my way, all single fellers between twenty-one and thirty-one are divided into just two classes, those who go, and those who don't go. That's my classification. Now if [he] don't go, I'm through with him. He simply has got to go." The board bowed to her request and reclassified the man; he soon found himself in uniform. In the end, the "draft dodger" was both a formal category created by the terms of American law and a figment of the nation's collective political imagination.[30]

★ *The Damnable Dilemma*

The universal obligation to register meant that selective service collected the names of millions of African-American citizens. A generation after Jim Crow had hardened from custom into a rigid legal structure, in the midst of a wartime atmosphere of political repression and intimidation, and building on traditions of voluntarism and obligation that they shared with other Americans, few black people openly questioned whether they owed military service to the state. The stakes were too high, as those who rebelled found out. In August 1917, a mob in York, South Carolina, lynched Reverend W. T. Sims for allegedly counseling draft resistance. The point was not if African Americans owed anything to the wartime state, but what. "If he fight, and fight he must, for what does he fight?" asked the author of a letter in the New York *Sun*. Selective service forms had a notation on their lower left-hand corners, telling draft board officials that "if person is of African descent, tear off this corner." By war's end, 2.3 million forms were missing a corner; 367,000 black men eventually served in uniform.[31]

The meanings of their participation remained elusive. Accounts of African-American military service often endow uniforms with alchemical powers, as if they were capable of transforming their wearers from pariahs to citizens. It's easy to understand why. When Noble Sissle, a sergeant with the Fifteenth New York Infantry during World War I, walked into a crowded hotel lobby in Spartanburg, South Carolina, in October 1917, he knew that the rules of white supremacy required him to doff his hat in the presence of a white man; he knew, too, that military regulations forbade him from ever removing Uncle Sam's cap. Walking out of the lobby, and away from this impossible dilemma, Sissle was challenged—with a sharp kick to the posterior—by a local white resident. But, for a change, his fellow soldiers, both white and black, protected Sissle and his stripes.

The power of Sissle's uniform that day contributed to the War Department's nervousness about the race question. Soon after the scuffle, they shipped the

Fifteenth New York off to France, lest race war consume Spartanburg; uniformed black men would be seen no more in the lobbies of South Carolina hotels. The next year, one Colonel E. D. Anderson of the U.S. Army General Staff decided it would be best for all concerned if conscripted African-American troops serving in labor battalions throughout the rural South were not issued uniforms at all. "Each southern state," he wrote, "has negroes in blue overalls working…with a pick and shovel." Drafted men dug for Uncle Sam within view of convict labor gangs and within earshot of blue-overalled sharecroppers, men and women who had been told in a wartime pamphlet *How the Colored Race Can Help in the Problems Issuing from the War* that they should "WORK! WORK! WORK!…The citizen who is unwilling to work is a citizen only by mistake.…We must save the cotton crop!" There were uniforms, and there were uniforms.[32]

Nor was a salute always a salute. Black men of the Fifteenth New York who had spent their working lives as redcaps and Pullman porters were accustomed not only to uniforms but also to saluting, and in the ranks, they practiced their own variation. After the regulation army version, "they would bow very low in the most approved style of a Saratoga Springs hotel head waiter," and with a snicker, murmur "Mawnin' Sus—mawnin'!" It was no laughing matter, though, when Private Sidney Wilson wrote his draft board to ask, "You low-down Mother Fuckers can put a gun in our hands, but who is able to take it out?" For his militancy, Uncle Sam gave Wilson ten years' hard labor, overalls and all. The wartime faith in uniforms sheds light on a catcall that came from the back rows of the Lafayette Theater in Manhattan one night in 1917, when the dashing, athletic, Harvard-educated Napoleon Bonaparte Marshall interrupted intermission there to urge men to join him in New York's all-black National Guard unit. One man shouted out, "What has that uniform ever got you?"[33]

W. E. B. Du Bois had an answer. His July 1918 "Close Ranks" editorial in the *Crisis*, the official paper of the National Association for the Advancement of Colored People, called for black Americans to "forget our special grievances and close our ranks shoulder to shoulder with our own white fellow citizens." African-American newspapers, churches, and clubs across the country added to Du Bois's words those of other black leaders who saw military service as a stepping-stone to equality. Others attacked him, in criticisms that poured in from across the country. Boston's noted publisher William Monroe Trotter denounced the accommodating rhetoric of his old ally; Du Bois "has at last finally weakened, compromised, deserted the fight, betrayed the cause of his race." "Crass moral cowardice," sneered the New York *News*.[34]

White people debated the meanings of African-American military service, too, particularly in the South, where the war's economic impact was disrupting the existing social order. Defenders of white supremacy dismissed outright the notion of the black citizen-soldier; Mississippi Senator James K. Vardaman called the idea "monstrous." In a vitriolic speech on the floor of the Senate, Vardaman claimed that African Americans "could not be relied upon in an emergency" and warned of "the final disaster, the . . . downfall and death of our civilization." Others were less fiery, among them the army's Enoch Crowder, who doubted African Americans' abilities and wrote in official reports of "a certain shiftlessness in ignoring civic obligations." Vardaman, Crowder, and others felt an urgent need to reconcile a paradox: the draft presupposed that men's political obligations were all alike, but white supremacy required the maintenance of distinctions and the inequality of citizens. In the rhetoric of many Southern Democrats who opposed the draft, fear of centralized power was hard to separate from fear of black empowerment.[35]

In the summer and fall of 1917, a white attorney from Blackstone, Virginia, exchanged with Virginia Congressman Carter Glass a series of letters that confronted this dilemma. On August 27th, Louis S. Epes expressed to the representative his concerns about inducting African Americans into the military. "If this is a white man's country then this war is a white man's burden and not the negroes'. . . . From a point of view of justice to the negro we have no right to demand his service in the firing line." Drafting black soldiers, he claimed, would alter the terms of their obligation. "The use of the negro" in war "is an admission . . . that this is no longer a white man's country but equally a black and white man's country; and I find that the negro is arriving at this same conclusion, the result of which I need not point out to you." The blame belonged to whites for trying to shift the burdens of citizenship to those who had not experienced its benefits. "For the protection of their own bodies they are willing to require of the negro a service which should only be required of an equal."[36]

In his reply, Glass assured Epes that "while I share in the fullest degree your racial prejudices," he saw things somewhat differently. "The negro, theoretically at least, is as much a citizen of the United States as you or I," he wrote. "The greater part of the country imagines that it would treat him without prejudice; hence the impossibility of enacting any legislation that would exclude him from the provisions of the Draft Act." He denied Epes's provocative claim that white Southerners were hiding behind a shield of black men and insisted that the obligations of citizenship must be distributed evenly, even if its privileges were not. "In my view, if the negroes are to be treated as equal citizens, even theoretically, . . . they should be made, in times of war, to defend the nation. . . . I would not free them from the obligation if I could," Glass wrote. "There is no reason why . . . my two boys should be sent to France to be killed in defense of their country, while strapping able bodied young negroes are permitted to pursue their peaceful avocations at their homes in Lynchburg." Glass and Epes struggled to come to terms with black men's military obligations; they had trouble, in part, because they could not agree on whether conscription was a process that demanded of the African-American citizen that he die for the state or deputized the citizen to kill in its name. Other than Louis Epes, few white Southerners had trouble with the former; it was the latter that they feared. And in reality, of course, conscription was both these things.[37]

In a nation less than two generations removed from slavery, where in southern states vagrancy and peonage laws had turned the duty to work into a formal political obligation, Uncle Sam's coercions were sometimes difficult to distinguish from those of other authority figures. Nor did they always have preference: an Arkansas draft board complained to Washington that the state's high rate of draft delinquency was due to "the withholding of mail by the landlord, often himself an aristocratic slacker, in order to retain" sharecroppers' labor. War amplified existing power with new "Work or Fight" laws adopted in numerous states and localities to deal with what an Ohio draft board called the "tramp nuisance." After May 1918, selective service regulations incorporated the policy as well. Georgia's law demanded that every able-bodied male citizen between sixteen and fifty-five be "regularly engaged in some…useful… employment" or find his way into the armed forces. Enforced disproportionately against African Americans (including African-American women), the laws also prompted vigorous protests. "This bill," wrote Reverend Henry Proctor of Atlanta, "has stirred up the colored people throughout the state."[38]

The culture of voluntarism shaped black wartime experiences in bitterly ironic ways. The navy and marines remained essentially closed to African-American volunteers throughout the entire war. When black nurses answered Uncle Sam's call, he turned them away. Such regulations affected the overall operation of the draft, which reduced local quotas according to how many men had already volunteered in a given community and therefore contributed to higher draft rates for black men. Racist draft boards played their parts too. In a political culture premised on voluntarism, African Americans often found themselves blamed for not fulfilling their obligations voluntarily when they were not even allowed to volunteer.[39]

★ *Before the Board*

In the meeting rooms of the nation's four thousand draft boards, draft-age men stood before the state and either accepted or challenged its authority.

Joined by their families and men and women from their local communities, they renegotiated the terms of obligation through their letters, editorials, and direct personal appeals. From the outset, selective service officials presented the draft boards to the American public as an embodiment of localism and voluntarism. But they were also government institutions on the advance frontier of an expanding state bureaucracy.

Selective service administrators were supposed to put a familiar face on federal policy, but outside the smallest of towns, they tended not to do so. Boards were appointed directly by President Wilson, who usually followed lists prepared by state governors. Lawyers and doctors, planters, bankers, undertakers, and heaps of county clerks filled the governors' lists. Selective service volunteers, who were predominantly native-born white men, shared the racial, ethnic, and class assumptions of their day and filled their reports to Washington with the stock characters of popular culture: in just a single write-up, one rural Iowa panel amused selective service officials with a drunken Irishman "full of fun and ready wit," inspired them with "a Mexican midget" who wanted to "help Uncle Sam drive back the unspeakable Hun," and told of several heartwarming grandmothers willing to sacrifice two generations of men, all for the nation's greater good.[40]

As the draft boards set out to administer the Selective Service Act's complex regulations, they did not always have an easy time. Their most difficult task involved managing the conflicts between family obligations and military ones. Local boards gave the first ruling on men's claims for dependency exemptions. Technically speaking, any man could claim exemption from the draft if he had a family member dependent on him for support. Many did not state the claim, though, having concluded that their obligations to the nation were more significant than those at home—or merely having concluded that army pay was higher than their current income or that military discipline and three square meals a day were preferable to the hardscrabble drudgery of turn-of-the-century working-class life. In response, women, children, and aging parents appeared before the boards seeking for their families the exemptions for which the men were legally eligible. From Forest Depot, Virginia, Mrs. R. K. Dooley wrote to her congressman in early December 1917 to ask his help with getting her son out of the army. "I am a widow and a very feeble one," she wrote. "My son's labor was my support and he was my only protection. Mr. Wilson himself could not be a good soldier if he knew his mother and sister was suffering from neglect, because they were not able to do for themselves and had no one to care for them."[41]

A man's dependency exemption could be rescinded if the board ruled that he was not properly married or not providing adequate support to his dependents. This regulation enabled some Americans to bring the state into their personal relationships in unprecedented ways. One woman wrote to an Iowa draft board urging that "if Uncle Sam can make any use of _____ then take him. He claims he is not able to work but his [*sic*] always able to fight and is constantly practicing on me.... Perhaps Uncle Sam could curb that a little for the benefit of all concerned." Emma Wolschendorf of East Bridgewater, Massachusetts, wrote to the draft board in May 1918 to ask them to draft her husband. "He is not a good father to his two little babies, and therefore I want our great 'Uncle Sam' to take care of him."[42]

Americans also enforced reciprocal obligations of the state toward its citizen-soldiers and the dependent family members they left behind. During the war, the War Department paid family members directly, building a complicated process of allotments and allowances justified in the language of obligation. "The call to arms does not annul the moral and legal obligations of every man to support his family and those who have a blood-tie claim upon his earnings," noted Columbia University's Samuel McCune Lindsay, a supporter of allotments and allowances. If Uncle Sam took men from their wives, he had an obligation to support them and their children. These payments, drawn from soldiers' pay before they ever received it, were not optional. No man could abandon his family obligations in order to become a soldier; state policy made men's economic obligations to their wives into political ones.[43]

Others simply asked the state to distribute political obligations more evenly. During the course of the war, thousands of letters arrived at selective service headquarters alleging slackerism or disloyalty on the part of neighbors, colleagues, and even family members. Edna Shaw of St. Louis, Missouri, wrote to draft officials to turn in her friend Otto Schaflitzel. "I wouldn't say anything about it," she wrote, "only he is so disloyal for only being 24 years of age and single. [He is] hurting my feelings, when he talks about the country, 'cause I have brothers in service and I will almost think . . . if I only had a gun I would kill him." To ordinary Americans like Edna Shaw, giving herself over to the spirit of selective service required confirmation that the government would do its part to make sure that draft-age men were honest about their situations.[44]

Draft boards had relatively little guidance, a great deal of latitude, and plenty of local pressures. Their policies varied widely. In Oklahoma, the Alfalfa County board required exempted men to purchase war bonds to demonstrate their loyalty, while in areas of the rural South where conscription remained unpopular, a handful of boards winkingly supported men's dubious claims for medical and dependency exemptions. Others refused to honor claims of conscientious objection or drafted aliens against both their will and the terms of the Selective Service Act. One Georgia board was deemed so racist in its procedures that it was dismissed by headquarters in Washington. In company towns, corporate management dominated the draft boards, and their policies reflected business-labor conflicts. In Kanawha and Raleigh Counties in southern West Virginia, the coal mine operators' version of a draft board was, literally, a board. On a slate outside the entrance to the mine, they posted the names of every miner and the amount of coal he had dug. "Slackers" in the mines lost their high-paying wartime jobs and, with them, their draft exemptions as useful war workers. The line between boss and government blurred—as did the definition of slacker.[45]

A man's interaction with a draft board typically included a conversation with a lawyer, particularly if he claimed exemption. Drafted men and their families quickly gained a legal education as they puzzled out complicated regulations regarding the payment of allotments and allowances to dependent family members. Immigrant women turned to organizations such as the New York Bureau of Legal Advice for help in making their cases before selective service appeal boards. This group, an important predecessor to the American Civil Liberties Union, did not tackle free speech issues until late in the war; its members were too busy counseling draft registrants. As a means of negotiating conflicting obligations and guaranteeing fairness, the law grew dramatically in popular importance and held a mediating position between the citizen and the state.[46]

Watching the draft in one American town reveals the intersection of selective service and coercive voluntarism. In 1917, Moosup, Connecticut, was a small mill town with just a few thousand residents. Moosup was not very diverse racially: when it conducted its draft registration in September 1918, the board counted 883 white registrants, 9 African Americans, and 1 Native American. But Moosup did include a substantial population of French-Canadian and Polish immigrants who worked in places like the Glen Falls and Central Worsted mills. Local institutions offered Moosup's residents plenty of opportunities to debate the war and express opposition to wartime measures. But more often than not, these institutions operated as mechanisms of enforcement by which, as President Wilson put it, "every man, whether he is himself to be registered or not [could] see to it that the name of every male person of the designated ages is written on these lists of honor."[47]

The means were often more implicit than explicit. Moosup's local newspaper had a hand in filling the ranks. In November 1917, the *Moosup Journal* noted that fifty men in the district had been called for their physical examinations; a month later, it listed their names and the results of their exams—as well as the names of six local men who had evaded the stethoscope. Names of men who claimed exemptions filled the paper's columns, along with the

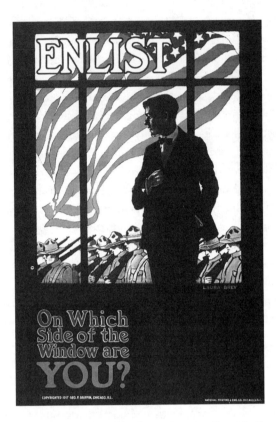

Military recruitment advertisements, like this 1917 poster by artist Laura Brey, used subtly coercive means to encourage wartime voluntarism. (*Courtesy of the Library of Congress Prints and Photographs Division*)

nature of their claims. Later, the *Journal* would regularly publish the results of questionnaires about deferment and dependency as they were returned to the draft boards. In fact, such policies may have protected draft-age men as much as they regulated them. Seemingly healthy young men who had been deferred because of family obligations or illnesses that were not readily apparent often found themselves subjected to extensive scrutiny and harassment in their communities, and a public acknowledgment of their deferment could protect them from trouble. Nor was a small town like Moosup unique; similar listings can also be found in newspapers nationwide, including larger cities such as Providence, Baltimore, and Denver.[48]

Call-ups required drafted men to report by train to the nearest camp, and the ceremony known as entrainment offered a visible public ritual of military obligation that honored, but also enforced, men's sacrifices. The *Moosup Journal's* most explicit, yet still indirect, enforcement of the draft came in an

April 1918 notice. "Edmund Paul, Louis Thaler and Raymond L. Block of this town have been called to appear before the bourd [*sic*] at Willimantic April 25, and they will entrain for the camp next day." As if Edmund, Louis, and Raymond didn't now have reason enough to show up in Willimantic on the twenty-fifth, the paper gave four men a special incentive to see to it that the draft law operated as planned. "As substitutes, to go to camp only in case of failure of the above men to appear, Alfred Beauregard, Joseph A. Jarvis, Arthur J. Jacques and Louis L. Rock have been named." That April, no substitutes were needed, but a few months later, when Emile J. Champagne, "said to be in Canada," failed to show up for entrainment, Louis N. Beaudry was sent to Camp Devens in his place, and the newspaper let everyone know.[49]

Churches did their part, too. In February 1918, the Knights of Columbus and the League of the Sacred Heart unfurled a service flag over the door of the All Hallow's Church in Moosup. The flag featured sixty-five stars, arranged in the shape of a cross, representing all the young men from the parish drafted into service. Across town, Methodists and Baptists flew their own service flags, joined by the Episcopal and Congregational churches in nearby Plainfield. The Roman Catholic St. John's Church in Plainfield even included three stars on its service flag for parishioners serving in the Canadian army. Needless to say, there were no stars for slackers.[50]

Over the course of 1918, the ties of social obligation became the binds of political obligation. A young man who was a member of a Moosup church or known to some of the town's newspaper readers would have found that those connections made it more difficult to avoid his political obligations. And yet it appears that the Franco-American community in Moosup may have sheltered Quebecois men from the Canadian draft, demonstrating that social networks could shield men from political duties when their institutions took a resistant stance. Even as conscription's defenders drew on existing patterns of social control, they often found them insufficient. In response, communities across America devised new mechanisms for enforcing the draft.

★ Slacker Raiding

At the outset of the war, the Justice Department's Bureau of Investigation had fewer than three hundred federal agents on staff, and letters pleading for the investigation of disloyal Americans were already swamping its offices. Among the first to arrive was an offer from a group of Chicago businessmen to create an "American Protective League," a new organization dedicated to guarding the home front. In March 1917, even before the declaration of war, the bureau's harried leader, A. Bruce Bielaski, accepted. By June, the American Protective League (APL) had one hundred thousand members in six hundred cities, and by the time the group dissolved in February 1919, as many as 250,000 men—and a handful of women, too, although official regulations denied them membership—may have served in this secret organization. The APL, a blend of local and federal power, and of old and new methods of social control, was the product of a political culture of coercive voluntarism. By the war's end, the APL would also contribute to that culture's undoing.[51]

American Protective League operatives were not alone in their zealous pursuit of 100 percent Americanism. Throughout the war, many Americans engaged in coercive violence against their fellow citizens. Even on the floor of the Senate, Mississippi's John Sharp Williams warned that "those who are not with us are against us...and if the law does not give them their medicine the people will." But the APL was not a lynch mob—it had a specifically state-sanctioned government status. Part and parcel of federal police power even as it operated largely outside it, the league came to the aid of the state at precisely the moment when the federal government was under pressure to expand its coercive mechanisms.[52]

The volunteers of the American Protective League were professional men, typically above draft age or otherwise exempt. They joined out of patriotism and a sense of duty, to feel important in their communities, or just for something to do. Surviving documents from the Kansas chapters of the APL record white men in their forties and fifties with ties to a wide range of professional and fraternal organizations. They included a doctor, a bank cashier, a barber, an undertaker, a minister, a wrestler, insurance and real estate salesmen, some sheriffs and farmers, a lot of lawyers, the business manager of the Atchison Railway, Light and Power Company, and a reporter for the *Emporia Daily Gazette*, personally recommended for service by its prominent editor, William Allen White.[53]

The American Protective League had an ambiguous legal status. Members wore identification badges mailed out from headquarters in Washington and noted in their literature that they were "authorized by and auxiliary to the Department of Justice." League men embarked on unwarranted searches and seizures, detained and arrested draft-age men without charges, intimidated allegedly disloyal Americans, and broke up strikes. Sometimes deputized en masse by local police, sometimes warned that they had no right to make arrests, operatives rarely paused over the difference. There was too much work to do, and too many enemies waiting: "Bolsheviki, socialists, incendiaries, I.W.W.'s,

Lutheran treason-talkers, Russellites, Bergerites, all the other-ites, religious and social fanatics, third-sex agitators, long haired visionaries and work-haters from every race in the world."[54]

Voluntarism mattered to the league. "What saves a country in need? Its loyal men," asserted the APL's authorized historian, Emerson Hough. "What reinforces an army called on for sudden enlargement? Its volunteers.... America always had Volunteers to fight for law and order against criminals. The law itself says you may arrest without warrant a man caught committing a felony. The line between formal written law and natural law is but thin at best," he asserted. Emboldened by what Hough called "a feeling based on the fair-play principle," the APL set out to enforce the nation's wartime obligations. Its members insisted that "the law was the law, and it played no favorites." "The fit man of proper age must show himself," wrote Hough, capturing the politics of coercive voluntarism in a single phrase.[55]

Initially, the American Protective League handled a wide range of cases: investigations of the character and loyalty of citizens and aliens, the circulation of seditious material or "enemy propaganda," claims for draft deferments. But by the spring of 1918—probably because of agitation by rank-and-file league men—draft dodging became most chapters' primary concern. Armed with earnest patriotism, their badges, and Section 57 of the Selective Service Act of 1917—which required men to carry their draft registration or classification cards at all times and show them to law enforcement personnel when requested—the 250,000 men of the American Protective League embarked on a series of large-scale interrogations that came to be known as slacker raids.[56]

The idea for slacker raiding developed from within the American Protective League itself. The Bureau of Investigation depended on the APL's detective work, and many operatives—even if they were not technically authorized to make arrests—did so. (They also eagerly claimed the $50 rewards that the U.S. Army offered for the delivery of alleged deserters to military camps.) Similarly, league men had been making individual interrogations and small-scale raids on their own initiative for some time. In the spring of 1918, authorities in the War Department, responding to the offers of the eager patriots of the APL, contemplated using their services to bring in slackers.[57]

On May 1, 1918, War Department lawyer Major Roscoe Conkling wrote to Colonel James Easby-Smith of the Provost Marshal General's office with a new idea. Conkling remarked that "every city throughout the United States has a paid or volunteer fire department" and asked, "Why should not the members of these departments in every community be appealed to to join with the police authorities or peace officers in running down delinquents?" As for legal authority, Conkling worried but little. "There is no need for attempting to confer any authority on these firemen, except to suggest to police officials, sheriffs and constables, if desirable, to deputize for this purpose certain members of the fire departments of their community." The folksy voluntarism of Conkling's plan appealed to Easby-Smith, and he eagerly assented. "I think we ought to go further," he added, "and organize a systematic plan for rounding up delinquents, of whom there appear to be over 250,000."[58]

But the APL had beaten Conkling and Easby-Smith to the punch. Its first citywide sweeps took place in Minneapolis and Pittsburgh on March 26, 1918, although it is difficult to distinguish the small-scale raids of 1917 from later, more ambitious counterparts. These were followed by the first multi-day, large-scale slacker raid, which took place in Chicago from July 11 to 14, 1918. There, more than 10,000 men from all branches of governmental authority participated, interrogating more than 150,000 men in the course of a few days.[59]

The Chicago incident typified slacker raids nationwide. For one thing, a wide variety of men claimed the authority to detain possible slackers. Chicago's APL operatives joined professional Department of Justice agents, city police, and soldiers and sailors on furlough in the city. Evidence from the Chicago raids and later ones in New York suggests that despite the presence of military personnel and local police, the Justice Department and the APL called the shots; the league handled about 75 percent of Chicago's cases. The Chicago slacker raid was a thoroughly modern phenomenon. It targeted places of mass entertainment and congregation: railroad stations, movie theaters, even a baseball game at Comiskey Park. It used automobiles to shuttle detainees across town, as well as telephones and telegrams to communicate with their draft boards. The scope and scale of the Chicago raid testify to the APL's ambition; this was no Sunday picnic.

Modern bureaucracy came in handy, too: what happened to a man during a slacker raid had little to do with his political views or, ironically enough, whether he was actually liable for military service. What mattered was his ability to demonstrate a state-sanctioned identity, age, and classification status to the satisfaction of the authorities by showing his card. As would be repeated nationwide, the number of draft evaders rooted out during Chicago's raids was trifling in comparison with the effort required to carry them out. Questioning in Chicago yielded some 20,000 detainees (mostly for failure to carry identity cards), of whom 1,200 alleged draft evaders were turned over to army authorities; nearly all were hastily released. These dismal results would be reproduced in cities across the country during the summer of 1918.[60]

The Chicago slacker raid met with general approval. The *Spy Glass,* the APL's official newsletter, noted that "there was little or no disturbance and few attempts to resist the authority of the League men who conducted the roundup. Most of the young fellows took their arrest as a disagreeable joke due to their own neglect and waited patiently until their identification could be completed." The public's praise for the APL's efficiency and spirit of wartime voluntarism would not survive the summer.[61]

Slacker raiding reached a fever pitch in the late summer of 1918, with raids at New York City's Coney Island on July 21 and in Trenton on August 2 (with a follow-up raid later that month). League men hit Atlantic City on August 15 and Galveston, Texas, on July 3 and August 28. On September 1, they rounded up San Francisco's slackers, moving on to Sacramento two days later. But of all the earlier drives, none matched the New York City slacker raids of September 3 to 5, 1918—in size or in controversy.[62]

It was quite a week to hold a raid. A faint whiff of national confidence filled the air as the wires brought uniformly positive news from the front in France; with the "World Series" (as Americans were starting to call it) between the Boston Red Sox and Chicago Cubs just about to begin, it was possible to think about Babe Ruth instead of the war. But other news was far more unsettling. A bomb exploded in Chicago's federal building soon after Bill Haywood, president of the radical Industrial Workers of the World, was convicted on sedition charges there. In Ohio, the trial of Eugene V. Debs, also charged with sedition, was about to get underway. And just days before, President Woodrow Wilson had called a third registration day under the Selective Service Act, this one scheduled for September 12th, just two weeks hence. For the patriot volunteers of the American Protective League, the time for action was now. And the place for action was New York City: "we find that the great states of each coast are practically foreign—New York most of all," bemoaned Emerson Hough.[63]

The War Department offered its own bit of foreshadowing for the raids, announcing in New York newspapers on September 1 that "a great organization, extending into every State...has been constructed to hunt down those attempting to evade the new selective service law." As Provost Marshal General Enoch Crowder noted in the same article, "The registrant's protection is to have with him at all times his registration cards....Failure to carry these credentials will render him liable to arrest at any time." The Justice Department would later point to this article as "fair warning" of events to come. Conveniently, the Justice Department also shut down the offices of the New York Civil Liberties Bureau and the New York Bureau of Legal Advice two days before the raids.[64]

Beginning at 6:30 A.M. on a hot, sticky day with on-again, off-again rain, the New York City slacker raids marked a unique marshaling of American political culture's powers of enforcement. The APL later estimated that somewhere between twenty thousand and twenty-five thousand men participated: city police, government agents from the Department of Justice, more than two thousand soldiers and one thousand sailors, and thousands of American Protective League operatives. For three days, they scoured the city's streets and public places, interrogating somewhere between 300,000 and 500,000 men. A man who lacked a draft registration or classification card found himself escorted by these self-appointed authorities to the nearest police station and from there to one of the city's armories or, in some cases, municipal jails. Although some men did complain afterward of rough handling, operatives had been cautioned to be "courteous but firm," and there is remarkably little evidence of physical violence; the *Nation* later marveled at "the long-suffering patience of the public."[65]

The raiders began their work that busy Tuesday morning by surrounding the exits and entrances of every train, ferry, subway, and elevated station; before rush hour was over, nearly 2,500 men had been seized from the stations alone. One couple, fresh from their wedding in upstate New York, stepped off the train in Grand Central Terminal and found themselves accosted by a sailor. "We were only married in Plattsburg [*sic*] yesterday, and you don't suppose I thought anything about draft board cards?" the husband asked. Unmoved by the couple's newfound marital bliss, the sailor whipped back, "Hard luck, but you'll have to come along."[66]

By noon, the raiders had shifted their attention to Manhattan's midtown and downtown business districts, often cordoning off whole blocks and interrogating the men on the street. Later, they raided theaters, saloons, billiard parlors, and boarding houses. Sailors wandered through the city's restaurants, moving from table to table inspecting the cards of diners. Frequently, they then moved from the dining room to the kitchen; one news report noted that "the chop suey restaurants yielded their usual percentage of men without cards." As the day's spectacle unfolded, rubberneckers gathered around the Sixty-Ninth Regiment Armory near Madison Square to watch the comings and goings. One of these was twenty-six-year-old Abraham Ituro, who had come to New York City from Russia fourteen years before. A slacker raider asked Ituro if he had registered for the draft, and he replied that he had not, "because he did not want to." Ituro soon found himself observing the armory's proceedings from the inside.[67]

Other men who were heartier supporters of the draft than Abraham Ituro nonetheless found themselves caught up in the APL's dragnet. By 1:00 P.M., authorities had gathered "a considerable crowd" at Lafayette Place and Fifth Street. A nearby truck driver volunteered to haul the men to the armory at Twenty-Sixth Street, but after performing his bit for the country, the driver was unable to produce his own draft card and had to leave his truck at the curb and go inside the armory. Operatives were soon told to cease interrogating drivers at the wheel because abandoned vehicles were interrupting the flow of traffic.[68]

One of the more dramatic raids took place at the Lexington Avenue Theatre, where soldier-actors from nearby Camp Upton performed the musical comedy *Yip, Yip, Yaphank* before a crowded house. Just before one of the intermissions, a slacker patrol—made up primarily of navy men, but under the direction of an APL inspector—entered the orchestra pit and, as the curtain fell on the act, demanded to see the registration cards of all the eligible men in the audience. Confusion ensued, and the investigation was put off until the end of the show, thanks to the intervention of a military officer: Sergeant Irving Berlin, the musical director of *Yip, Yip, Yaphank*, who was responsible for the men in the cast and furious that his performance had been interrupted.[69]

By the second day of the raid, New Yorkers had already learned to carry their draft cards; the intensity of the raids did not abate, but the number of arrests did. "Young men walking for two or three blocks in Times Square were usually held up six or seven times in that distance, but few complained," a reporter noted. "Nearly every one had his draft card handy and showed it with a smile." Many made hasty efforts to document their identities. So many men crowded the offices of the State Military Census Bureau looking for duplicate registration cards that the police had to be called in to disperse the crowd after the forms ran out.[70]

By the third day, the draft dodgers still did not appear, and some slacker raiders' initial enthusiasm began to wane. Others stepped up their methods, raiding a restaurant on the Lower East Side, where they captured a handful of men who had been wanted in association with socialist agitation (although their draft papers were apparently in order). Army privates and military police invaded the city's financial district, interrupting trading at the Wall Street curb market and closing off the Equitable Building, where they interrogated the building's seventeen thousand employees. They uncovered just twenty-two men without registration or classification cards; all of them were eventually released. In New Jersey, the league turned from the city's public places of amusement to its sites of employment, raiding every one of Passaic's fifty major factories.[71]

So what did the slacker raids turn up? Some caught in the dragnet were in fact delinquents, deserters, or enemies of the state, including Reinhold Wademan, hauled into Jersey City's Fourth Regiment Armory on the third night of the raids. Wademan, a German citizen, had never registered as an enemy alien and never intended to. "If you will give me my passport I will go quickly back and fight for Germany against the United States. I will never fight in your army." Another slacker was twenty-three-year-old George Miller, a night flagman on the New York City subway system, who heard about the raids just as he was about to come off the night shift on the morning of September 3. Rather than face the authorities without a draft card, he hid out in a flagman's shack in the subway tunnels deep under 145th Street, where he remained for three days before a fellow motorman turned him in.[72]

But authentic slackers and enemy aliens were few and far between. By the end of the three days, 60,187 men had been detained in New York City and its surrounding suburbs. But of these, only 199 were actual draft dodgers who would later end up in military uniform. And the number of "willful deserters"—men who had deliberately ignored Uncle Sam's call-up and were therefore eligible for court-martial—was even lower. New York City's draft director, Martin Conboy, could identify only eight men who were actually shipped off to Camp Upton as a result of the raids. So for every Reinhold Wademan or George Miller, there were approximately three hundred men who spent the night in a city jail solely because they could not document their identity, age, or draft registration status to their interrogators.[73]

If the slacker raids were a drama of political obligation, the league men were its star performers. Acting out of a sense of obligation, they organized themselves in voluntary associations and used tools of social control that bridged the gap between the face-to-face authority of the nineteenth century and the faceless bureaucracy of the modern administrative state. But of course they were also state actors, eager supporters of invasive and expansive federal policies who used the authority of government and cooperated with its most modern, centralized, bureaucratic institutions even if they were not really authorized to act in their name. The APL operatives tried to reconcile their modernizing impulses with older understandings of citizenship that were grounded in local institutions and private voluntarism. It was an improvisational response to the demands of volunteer draft enforcers. It would not outlast the war.

The coercions of the slacker raids did not go unchallenged. Little evidence remains to attest to resistance during the slacker raids themselves. On the contrary, newspaper accounts reveal that the military police's forced march of men detained at Coney Island was "much to the amusement of the onlookers," and the announcement of a raid at a theater in Trenton, New Jersey, met with cheers and applause—although there was probably some sullen or nervous silence as well. Women mounted much of the resistance to the New York City raids, protesting their personal inconvenience in the city's public places and the incarceration of men in their families. By the evening of the first day of the raid, women thronged the streets around the city's armories, armed with family Bibles, birth certificates, and other forms of identification for the men detained inside. Frustrated at the slow pace of the APL's investigations and resentful of the process as a whole, a crowd of women stormed the main gates of the Sixty-Ninth Regiment Armory and had to be dispersed by the police.[74]

A heated debate over the slacker raids took place on the floor of the U.S. Senate. Senator George Chamberlain of Oregon, chairman of the Military Affairs Committee, spoke out before the raids were even over. "Every red-blooded American citizen will protest against such proceedings conducted by some 'Meddlesome Mary' of the Department of Justice." In the senator's view, the crucial issue was not the goal, but the method. "There is not a man in the country who despises a man who undertakes to evade his military duty as much as I do," he noted, but "these men who are slackers ought to be reached by due process of law." For Chamberlain, due process meant a duly appointed and legitimate representative of the state, not an overeager volunteer. Those who challenged the league's authority to govern questioned an entire political culture of obligation that granted political authority to voluntary associations.[75]

Senator Chamberlain was similarly troubled by the fact that slacker raiding had interfered with industrial and military mobilization. He claimed that employees in Maryland's munitions factories had been taken off the assembly lines during slacker raids there and worried that valuable skilled men working under deferred draft classifications might leave their war work. The slacker raiders' disruptions also troubled Senator William Calder of New York. "Armed soldiers went into business offices and took men from behind their desks. They went into theatres and took men away from the ladies whom they were escorting."[76]

Some compared the slacker raids to the French Revolution or the methods of the German "Hun" himself. Senator Hiram Johnson of California called the slacker raids a product of "the Law of Suspects of the Reign of Terror." He warned those under the age of twenty-one or over thirty—who often could produce neither a registration card nor adequate proof of their birth dates and thus had the hardest time during slacker raids—to make their ages as clear as possible. "Oh... ye men well preserved, who may appear to be within the draft age, grow ye your gray whiskers... or an extrajudicial authority in the City of New York... will take you to the bull pen until you can demonstrate by a birth certificate a thousand miles away that liberty is yours!"[77]

Some senators defended the raids, among them Senator Miles Poindexter of Washington, who noted that "the showing is that these inquiries to separate the cowards and the slackers from those who had not violated the draft act was carried out as expeditiously and efficiently as possible." But the mood in the Senate was bitterly critical, and in a deeply divided Congress, it even crossed party lines: while Wilson's die-hard critics spoke out predictably, many of his loyalists denounced the raids too.[78]

Most senators seemed ready to rally around Utah Senator Reed Smoot's call for a national investigation. That spring, Senator Chamberlain had introduced legislation that would have made the entire United States an area of national defense and therefore subject to the rules of martial law; now he effectively renounced his earlier enthusiasm for disciplining the American populace. "The fact is, men are afraid, in this wartime, to assert their rights and stand up for their liberties. That's why so many innocent men were dragged off to jail. In other times men would have resented arrest, and would have killed those who tried to seize them without authority of law." Debate continued at a shrill tenor for two days, but legislative finesse effectively tabled Smoot's resolution and the investigation never got off the ground.[79]

The nation's newspaper editors, like its legislators, were not of one mind on the subject. Many leaped to the slacker raiders' defense. The *New York Herald* claimed that "every patriotic American welcomes an opportunity to contribute to the sending of such black sheep into the fold." Another paper thought that "much sympathy has been wasted upon those" caught in the APL's dragnet simply for having forgotten to carry a registration card. "It is not only a safeguard against the annoyance of arrest. It is a certificate of good citizenship." The New York *Evening World* came to the defense not of the slacker raiders, but of New York, which had been unfairly targeted as "a draft-dodging, unpatriotic town," a conclusion that editors chalked up to the "incessant aspersions [of] perfervid females and members of Amateur Patriots' Associations."[80]

More typical, however, were the newspaper editorials that, echoing Senator Chamberlain, criticized the raiders' methods even as they defended severe repression of slackers. On the same day that the *San Francisco Chronicle* commended employees of the Edgar Thompson Steel Works for dunking the head of their fellow worker Andy Tomko into a barrel of red paint after he refused to donate to the Red Cross war fund, editors denounced the methods of the New York City slacker raids as "a human rodeo" that "we had better do without." The *New York Times* felt the raids were being conducted "with more zeal than judgment," but its editors argued that "to raise a great tumult about it, makes the critic ridiculous; furthermore, this is no time for stirring up resentment against the draft by tearing passion to tatters…when agents of the Government blunder from excess of the sleuth spirit." The paper's only suggestion was more explicit prior publicity, which would ensure that future investigations would be "less spectacular and more practical."[81]

In the midst of all this controversy, President Wilson remained stonily silent. For several days, he followed the raids in the newspapers and read correspondence on the subject from state governors and ordinary citizens. His secretary, Joseph Tumulty, immediately suggested to Attorney General Thomas Gregory that he dispatch "a leading representative" of the Justice Department to investigate the affair, noting that "this is the only way to convince the people of New York that the Administration is interested." Wilson himself took no clear stand. He asked Gregory to look into the authority of the Department of Justice during the raids: "The arrests have aroused so much interest and are likely to give rise to so much misunderstanding that I would be very much obliged to you if you would let me know all the facts and circumstances." But Wilson never disavowed the raids, nor did he act on Gregory's eventual report. In fact, he appears to have been pleased with the outcome of the raids; Secretary of the Navy Josephus Daniels noted in his diary on September 10 that Wilson had commented to him that the raids "put the fear of God in others just before the new draft."[82]

The Justice Department and the APL vigorously defended their actions. Writing to Wilson, Attorney General Gregory cited the sections of the selective service law that authorized the arrest of delinquents and deserters and praised the American Protective League. He told the president that "some such dragnet process is necessary unless thousands upon thousands of delinquents and deserters are to remain at large" and insisted that the raids would continue "unless you give directions to the contrary." The raiders' most rabid defender was Charles DeWoody, superintendent of the New York office of the Bureau of Investigation, who "neither apologize[d] nor regret[ted] any act of his in connection with the roundup. He was sorry that members of the United States Senate had seen fit to criticize" his work. As the Bureau of Investigation faced public scrutiny in the aftermath of the slacker raids, DeWoody snapped at a reporter, "Nobody can make a 'goat' of me, and the Department of Justice is not a damned bit on the defensive."[83]

In the political aftermath of the slacker raids, the American Protective League quickly collapsed. Many factors were certainly involved: no more draft registrations followed after September 12, 1918; the influenza epidemic of September and October 1918 paralyzed military mobilization and kept APL operatives out of their offices; and, of course, the signing of the Armistice on

November 11, 1918, abruptly ended the draft. Even after these severe blows, slacker raiding did not disappear completely. In Detroit on September 8, APL operatives (under the close supervision of the city police) examined nearly three thousand men who had gathered at the Socialist State Convention there to hear Eugene Debs's last speech before his trial for violation of the Espionage Act. Other raids continued throughout the country, even sporadically after the Armistice.[84]

Over the course of the autumn of 1918, federal authorities systematically stripped the American Protective League of the quasi-legal authority it had once enjoyed. From the Bureau of Investigation headquarters in Washington, A. Bruce Bielaski emphatically told APL agents that they had never had the power to make arrests, and they definitely ought not test the matter now. New York chief E. H. Rushmore protested in response that "the New York Division has become an absolute necessity to the Local Boards both in this City and other sections of the country" but doubted that the APL could enforce the draft without permission to coerce. "It will be rather a hard matter," he reflected, "to persuade a deserter to accompany you entirely voluntarily, as Mr. Bielaski expresses it in his circular."[85]

The institutions on which the APL relied now shunned it. Just a week after the raids, the U.S. Post Office, which had provided addresses and access to private letters, officially closed its files to the APL. When other organizations followed suit, the league came apart at the seams. "The number of institutions who are refusing us information increases daily, claiming that we are a private organization. These same institutions formerly were always at our disposal," complained Rushmore. "The effect of these constant refusals upon the morale of our organization is bad.... We are very rapidly approaching the point where we will appear to have broken faith with our own membership."[86]

The last straw came when the APL operatives lost their badges, their precious symbols of state authority. In October 1918, APL national director Charles Frey instructed Rushmore to collect the badges of every one of his operatives. Apparently the Treasury Department, whose Secretary William McAdoo had long been an opponent of the league, had demanded the recall. The badges—which included the words "Secret Service"—might lead the APL to be confused with the officially sanctioned U.S. Secret Service, an agency of the Treasury Department. Frey assured Rushmore that new badges were on order. They were never issued.[87]

On February 1, 1919, the American Protective League formally disbanded. The organization's work in rounding up draft dodgers was abandoned; the only selective service prosecutions pursued after the war were military tribunals of conscientious objectors and courts-martial for a handful of high-profile draft dodgers whose actions had "been a red rag in the public's face." The War Department admitted that some 174,000 delinquents and deserters were still at large in 1920, but all that came of their painstakingly prepared card indexes—which stretched nearly the length of a football field in a former army barracks just outside Washington—was their publication in newspaper supplements well after the war's end.[88]

If the American Protective League was solely an arm of the state, then its demise seems not so significant: it was just one of many federal institutions dismantled in the immediate postwar period. Indeed, by the end of 1918, the director of the Bureau of Investigation, A. Bruce Bielaski, resigned his position, in part a reaction against his handling of the slacker raids. But the end of the league also signaled a move away from its extralegal practices and from the culture of civic voluntarism that had supported them. As critics disavowed the slacker raiders' methods of physical coercion, they affirmed the basic premises of the selective service legislation itself. The slacker raids didn't catch many draft dodgers, but they did reshape everyday politics and the meanings of American citizenship. The controversy questioned the legitimacy of governance by means of localized and quasi-legal voluntary organizations, it highlighted the primacy of political obligations to the federal government, and it placed law and legal process more firmly at the center of understandings of citizenship. League men had acted because they felt the state had failed to do so. Drawing on their sense of the obligations of citizenship, they claimed the right to enforce the law. Resistance to that authority brought about a more powerful state—just what the APL had demanded in the first place. By failing, they had succeeded more than they ever understood.[89]

★ *Sunday Drivers*

On September 8, 1918, after the dust had settled on the slacker raids, New York City joined a national experiment with voluntary restrictions on the use of automobiles on Sundays. Like the "meatless" and "wheatless" days that had preceded it, the "carless" days were designed to conserve precious resources for the war effort. But a ban on auto travel quickly ran up against the freedom of movement, and because automobile restriction was a presidential suggestion rather than an enforceable piece of legislation, the mechanisms for enforcement assiduously avoided any appearance of coercion. As New York's Mayor John Hylan noted in a proclamation conveying Woodrow Wilson's announcement,

"Those whom you have placed in high places during this time do not feel that they wish to command you in a matter of such vital importance."[90]

The mayor had clearly learned the lessons of the slacker raids. "Every citizen is urged to induce owners of cars not to use them," he announced. "By this is meant merely the employment of patriotic argument because insofar as the law goes at this time, there is nothing to prevent an owner from using his car if he persists." Hylan knew, however, that the mere "employment of patriotic argument" on the part of the citizen—despite effective use of the rhetoric of wartime voluntarism—would not always suffice. Accordingly, New York City's policemen were informed that "all traffic officers in the City are asked to take the license numbers of cars. . . . Names should also be asked." But, warned Hylan, "officers will understand that citizens have the right to use their cars if they wish to do so. . . . The conscience of each citizen must be the dictator."[91]

Conscience, indeed, would be the dictator, but of a changed body politic. The state—in its various personal and impersonal forms—had come and gone from the lives of wartime Americans. But it left its traces in the form of its bureaucratic record-keeping, memories of its power, and most important, in the transformed relationship between Americans and their political institutions. Writing after the war's end, the chief of the American Protective League branch in Hickory, North Carolina, reflected that "in my judgment, the psychological effect of an organization that could be felt but not seen helped wonderfully." A political culture premised on obligation and exercised through voluntary associations had attempted the task of enforcing an unpopular draft in a fair and equitable manner. In the absence of a strong federal government, this was the only alternative, but it was a political solution as well as a practical one, the product of a vision of civic voluntarism that would not survive the war intact.[92]

Nor, of course, did the draft. In a public relations move that also showed the Wilson administration's distaste for its wartime state-building, Secretary Baker ordered troop trains on the rails on the morning of November 11, 1918, to turn around when the Armistice bells rang at 11:00 A.M. Selective service call-ups ceased immediately. In 1920, the nation conducted another debate over peacetime conscription and universal military training. This time the draft failed, prompting the peace-loving William Jennings Bryan to dash a note to a fellow sympathizer, Louis F. Post: "I think we have militarism scotched." But the 1920 National Defense Act guaranteed the standing federal army that Roosevelt and Leonard Wood had fought for just four years before; America's military never returned to its prewar state. Nor, really, did its citizens.[93]

2

Between God and Country: Objecting to the Wartime State

★☆★☆★☆★☆★☆★☆★☆★☆★☆★☆★☆★☆

On November 2, 1918, Evan Thomas informed the commanding officer of the U.S. Disciplinary Penitentiary at Fort Leavenworth, Kansas, that he would not work anymore. Thomas, a conscientious objector, had refused to obey military prison officers as a protest against the treatment of six of his fellow prisoners. These men were Molokans, members of a small Russian Christian pacifist sect living in Arizona, whose religious teachings forbade not only any cooperation with war but also consumption of meat; impatient prison authorities had retaliated by cutting them off from all but bread and water. After his declaration of protest, Evan Thomas found himself in solitary confinement along with the Molokans. Writing two weeks later to his mother in Maryland, Thomas expressed both his hopes and his frustrations when he said of his fellow objectors: "This country is surely big enough for such people."[1]

It wasn't. As Evan Thomas penned his letter in the middle of November 1918, even the Armistice that marked the end of the war had not changed Americans' minds. Few agreed with Thomas's statement of tolerance; in fact, the attempt by conscientious objectors and their allies to convince the Wilson administration that America was surely big enough for them proved a failure. They had taken on a formidable opponent, and the state's wartime coercions proved more numerous, more fluid, and more insistent than conscientious objectors had ever imagined. As the war dragged on, their angry pamphlets revealed through their titles—*Uncle Sam: Jailer, Uncle Sam's Devil's Island*—the weight of their struggles. Nor did they convince the public at large. With few exceptions, Americans actively opposed draft exemptions for conscientious objectors. They employed scriptural argument in the pews of the nation's churches and applied physical torture in its military prisons. Not all opponents of objection menaced their charges with the sharpened edge of a bayonet, but behind the sword stood law, order, and the nation-state, as well as a population offended by the practice of conscientious objection.[2]

Objectors earnestly tried to reconcile the dictates of personal conscience with the needs of the state, and after extensive lobbying by peace groups and religious organizations, military and civilian policy makers ultimately crafted an official policy that recognized the category and found a place for them in the American state. That might suggest a modest victory, but the number of conscientious objectors who successfully claimed that status was remarkably small. Between May 1917 and November 1918, of the twenty-four million men who registered for the draft, 64,693 filed claims of conscientious objection. Local draft boards recognized 56,830 of these claims. Not all men who registered for the draft passed their physical examinations or were inducted; War Department records indicate that 20,873 objectors were called up for military service. Only 3,989 men pursued their objections after they had spent some time in army camps. About 2,600 of this small group accepted alternative forms of service on farms or with relief organizations working in France. A few hundred had just arrived in camp at the time of the Armistice; "absolutists," who refused any cooperation with the war effort, made up the remaining five hundred. Conscientious objectors played a role in the wartime politics of citizenship far out of proportion to their actual numbers. But why did they pose such a problem in the first place? Why did the military police officer at Leavenworth—and millions of Americans like him—come to believe that a Christian socialist and a half-dozen Arizona vegetarians posed such a threat to the state's war-making power or the nation's fundamental will?[3]

The answer has less to do with the individual objectors than with the history of the state to which the conscientious objected. Religious denominations were central components of the vibrant civil society that shaped turn-of-the-century American political culture; ordinary congregants, particularly in dissenting or pacifist churches, had to find a place for themselves in that culture and establish relationships with state power. Long accustomed to avoiding political entanglements, groups such as the Mennonites had discovered by the early twentieth century that protecting the distinctiveness of their own religious communities increasingly depended on assertive engagement with political and legal authority: obtaining U.S. citizenship, participating in electoral politics, petitioning officials, initiating court cases. It was that sense of the state—and how to navigate its waters—that objectors brought with them to military hearing rooms. The war amplified that consciousness. The substantial obstacles to CO status forced objectors to refine and rearticulate their challenge to the culture of obligation; by war's end, that sensibility had found new homes in politicized congregations and civil liberties organizations.[4]

The state changed along with its citizens, as seen most clearly in the work of the Board of Inquiry. Between June 1918 and the Armistice that November, a group of three War Department officials—including future U.S. Supreme Court Chief Justice Harlan Fiske Stone—traveled across the United States interrogating 2,294 conscientious objectors stationed at the nation's military camps. The Board of Inquiry's charge: to fix, with legal authority, the "sincerity" of each of the men they interviewed. Much depended on the board's decisions. Those it deemed sincere could be assigned to noncombat alternatives; the insincere faced the choice of donning a uniform and embarking for France or awaiting an Army court martial with the power to execute the guilty. Recent political and social history typically makes much of how ordinary people have "negotiated" state power. Negotiation was what the Board of Inquiry was all about.[5]

Conscientious objection confronted the conflicts between political obligations. Of course, the draft was never universal, nor did most wartime Americans think it should be; popular responses to conscription recognized the legitimacy of exemptions for married men and men in "useful" war industries, and Americans by and large accepted them, so long as they believed the draft was being administered fairly. Family duties could supersede political obligations as long as the state stood in the active role of neutral arbiter. But in this case, the conflict concerned religious and political duties. The soul was less amenable to investigation than marriage or employment, and Americans therefore demanded tangible measures to regulate the invisible consciences of their fellow citizens. The War Department embarked on a policy of scrutiny that officially evaluated the contents of American citizens' minds and souls. It was to this invasion that conscientious objectors had objected in the first place; wartime events, though, prompted the state to scrutinize more rather than less. As government officials got into the business rather than out of it, objectors pushed back, asserting their rights in a strident language of individualism. As they did so, they opened a window onto the process by which citizens make states, and states make citizens.

Although objection to military service has a long history connected to ancient practices, conscientious objection has specifically modern roots; it responds to the modern state and to modern war. The term typically appeared in quotation marks in the United States during World War I, suggesting just how new the phenomenon really was; even Secretary of War Newton D. Baker referred to "the so-called 'conscientious objectors.'" Conscientious objectors were men who explicitly refused to fulfill the military obligations of citizenship demanded by selective service and claimed religious or personal scruples for doing so. Conscientious objection's public nature distinguished it from slacking, draft dodging, and desertion—which, in practice, were also rejections of military obligation. Draft dodging and desertion were evasions of the state. Conscientious objection, by contrast, was a confrontation with it.[6]

The coming of war presented a crisis for the nation's pacifists. As Congress considered the Selective Service Act in May 1917, church leaders and political activists descended on Washington to advocate for provisions for those who rejected war on religious grounds. There they found an administration that was hostile, indifferent, or so distracted by the larger issues of war mobilization that it had little time to devote to the CO question. Leaders of the Hutterite Church lobbied Secretary Baker in person in what the *Washington Post* called "the most numerous collection of whiskers the War Department has seen in many a day." The Hutterites got most of what they wanted. According to the conscription law's final version, members of "any well-recognized religious sect or organization organized and existing May 18, 1917, and whose then existing creed or principles forbid its members to participate in war in any form" could claim exemption from combat service. The War Department counted 276,843 adult men in the congregations of the historic peace churches of the Quakers and the Mennonites, as well as newer, less familiar sects such as the Dukhobors, Seventh-Day Adventists, and Jehovah's Witnesses. Despite the provisions, though, lack of clarity abounded: the statute did not automatically exempt peace church members; it called for them to be inducted into the army and then assigned to a noncombatant service that the president would define at a later date.[7]

At the war's outset, simply to facilitate the processing of claims, the Selective Service Act provided exemptions only for duly recorded members of historic peace churches. In practice, this aided the congregants of well-established and widely known organizations such as the Mennonite Church and the Religious Society of Friends. Other churches, less familiar to draft boards or less meticulous in maintaining church rolls, faced greater difficulty. One military officer recalled the "astonishing number of different sects and denominations"; local draft boards frequently tired of the complications of Protestant schismatics in their communities, and they rejected CO claims by members of marginal religious groups they did not understand. Frustrated by the difficulties of accommodating all these sects, Newton Baker wrote jokingly to President Woodrow Wilson: "I am beginning to feel that nothing short of a comprehensive knowledge of Professor James's book on 'Varieties of Religious Experience' will ever qualify a man to be a helpful Secretary of War."[8]

The policy also reflected America's culture of voluntarism: if political obligations were exercised in groups, then religious ones should be worked out there, too, and not in the individual conscience; a church could speak for a congregant before the state. Reliance on official membership left a drafted man's political fortunes dependent on the institutional stance of his church. Objectors who were members of mainline Protestant churches or who were Catholic or Jewish found little support—and often outright hostility—in their own spiritual communities. Without backing from the church hierarchy, for example, only nine Catholics in the entire United States are known to have claimed conscientious objector status. The Federal Council of the Churches in Christ, a body of established Protestant denominations, pledged during the war "to protect the rights of conscience against every attempt to invade them" but made no efforts to protect conscientious objectors, actively discouraged them from filing claims, and pressured ministers to preach against them. Objector William Arthur Dunham recalled that "it was a common experience of conscientious objectors that their most bitter and intolerant enemies in the army were the chaplains and the YMCA men."[9]

★ *Power and Persuasion*

If we take the opponents of objection at their word, they were angry because conscientious objectors rejected their political obligations while other Americans went over the top. Writing after the war, Harlan Fiske Stone boasted that "the great mass of our citizens subordinated their individual conscience and their opinions to the good of the common cause," but "there was a residue whose peculiar beliefs…refused to yield to the opinions of others or to force." An editorial in the *Biblical World* accused conscientious objectors of hiding "dislikes" under "a pretense of conscience and religion." Like the draft dodgers they had done so much to control, Americans granted conscientious objectors little respect, no matter how firm the objectors' religious faith, and despite attempts by the COs' allies to cast them as heroes and martyrs. For many Americans, "conscientious objector" was just a fancy term for "slacker."[10]

The state, many argued, had a duty to test the objectors' beliefs and to dissuade them. Former President Theodore Roosevelt, declaring that "there is no room here for a 'fifty-fifty' citizenship," suggested in a January 1918 speech before four thousand enlisted men at New Jersey's Camp Merritt that conscientious objectors should be tested "by placing them on mine sweepers or by allowing them to dig frontline trenches." His statement was met with "wild cheering," an indication of heated wartime rhetoric, as well as a sense of political obligation that enlisted men shared with the former Rough Rider. Popular efforts to change the minds of conscientious objectors emerged from a political culture in which ordinary citizens claimed the right to police the home front; they thought their work was just as much a part of the wartime state as the interrogations of the Board of Inquiry. And, in practice, it was.[11]

Objectors exempted from military obligations, who supposedly retained all of the privileges of citizenship, had merely transferred their burdens onto the shoulders of those who bore arms. The *New York Times* felt that "a citizen's first duty" was to respond to military call-up; the man who shirked service made the load "heavier for his neighbors." Harlan Stone also gestured at the problem in his Board of Inquiry interrogations, where one of his favorite questions of absolutists was whether they had used postage stamps since the outbreak of war, convincing evidence (in Stone's mind, anyway) that these consciences could bear the benefits of the state but not its burdens. Theodore Roosevelt suggested that conscientious objectors should be deprived of the right to vote. That was no idle threat; Canada's War Time Elections Act of 1917 deprived conscientious objectors there of the franchise. The hatred directed at conscientious objectors reflected a bitterness at their supposedly cunning manipulation of the structures of political obligation.[12]

Antiobjectionists threw the book at conscientious objectors: persuasion, physical coercion, ridicule, and even psychiatric treatment. Straightforward verbal persuasion was the most common approach. Opponents tested the men's sincerity according to their own understandings of political obligation by subjecting them to interrogations about scriptural evidence, claims for the need to defend mothers and sisters from marauding Germans, and arguments linking the war effort to Christianity and presenting it as a spiritual crusade. "What would you do now if everybody would be just like you?" a military officer asked Mennonite Marvin King. "I wish they would," he replied. "Then there wouldn't be no war." Not all were as defiant as King. Considering that some 20,873 men arrived in camp bearing certificates from their draft boards testifying—with the authority of law—to their conscientious objector status, and yet only 3,989 held on to those claims to the war's end, many must have been dissuaded from their positions through cajoling, argument, and incentive.[13]

Direct physical coercion was the most extreme, but objectors of all types and in all parts of the country faced it. Military leaders even defended outright coercion as a wartime necessity. So did the British political theorist Sidney

Webb, who published an influential article on the subject in the *North American Review* in March 1917, as American policy makers began formulating CO policy. "If we are on a leaking ship," Webb hypothesized, "and the captain in authority declares that only by the most strenuous labors at the pumps...can the company be saved, I should not myself have any patience with a man who announced that he felt a stop in his mind about taking his turn at the pumps." Society's needs justified coercion of its members. "I could not logically refuse to apply all the violence and inflict all the pain necessary to coerce the will of that very inconvenient Conscientious Objector." Webb condoned force theoretically; Americans also practiced it widely, especially in the rural areas where pacifist communities clustered. The legal protections for peace church members that selective service administrators had drafted in Washington looked good on paper; they counted for little out on the prairies.[14]

Mennonite communities throughout the Midwest—particularly where members spoke German as their primary language—faced brutal harassment. About nine thousand adult Mennonites lived in Kansas at the war's beginning. They had, in fact, been invited to move there: in 1865, the state legislature had promised exemption from military service for anyone with religious scruples against war, a statute adopted specifically to entice Mennonite migrants, known for their agricultural prowess and their law-abiding ways. Migrate they did, starting in 1874, first from the eastern United States and then, by the late nineteenth century, from eastern Europe. Most spoke German at home, in their schools, and in worship services; although they eschewed participation in politics as worldly and sinful, they wanted to protect their children's bilingual education, so they had made sure to vote in school board elections. By 1917, therefore, most adult Mennonites had either been born or naturalized as American citizens. Mennonite communities were politically empowered, but in April 1917, their politics were in tumult: despite repeated assertions of national loyalty, Midwestern Mennonites, like many Americans of German descent, funneled donations to the German Red Cross rather than its American counterpart. Nor was pacifism always the sect's defining trait. H. W. Berky, from Pennsylvania, recalled that his community's prewar pacifism was "dormant....I mean, we had no discussions on pacifism that I recall, till the war came. And then all of a sudden, boy, everybody wanted to be a pacifist."[15]

By June 5, 1917, the first day of mass registration for selective service, neither the president nor the War Department had yet defined noncombatant service. But leaders of the Mennonite Church—which forbade any participation in war—had received so many assurances from Washington that few questioned the act of registration itself, and no ministers preached against it.

"To register requires the violation of no principle of nonresistance," wrote one Mennonite newspaper, and in Liberty, Illinois, Reverend G. O. Stutzman of the Church of the Brethren even signed on as a draft board official. Records in Kansas demonstrate no instances of refusal to register, no resistance to medical examinations, none even when notices arrived ordering men to entrain for camp. Of course, many with scruples about war found it difficult to give their objections an official bureaucratic character: the first thirty million draft registration forms, printed while Congress was still debating CO provisions in the selective service bill, nowhere asked if registrants were conscientious objectors; only those who knew they could do so claimed the status.[16]

Some did refuse to register. Members of the Molokan Church had fled Russia decades before and settled in isolated communities across the American Southwest. "We gave up everything to be free from military service," one later recalled. But in the early years of the war, church members in Glendale, Arizona, had been warned by a prophetess that a trial of faith was coming for believers; when registration day came, they recognized it as a test. Two of the church elders rushed off to Washington to meet with Secretary Baker, while in Arizona, draft-age Molokans took matters into their own hands. Thirty-seven men refused to register, and four days later, the entire community marched from their homes in Glendale to downtown Phoenix to support them. Outside the Maricopa County Courthouse, where the men faced charges of failing to register, the Holy Spirit moved many to sing and jump; inside the courtroom, it possessed twenty-nine-year-old Andrew Shubin during his testimony. Hastily convicted, the men faced the Selective Service Act's standard punishment for failure to register: immediate induction into the army.[17]

More dramatic events played out in the five counties of central Kansas where large numbers of Mennonites had settled. Mennonite men were more likely than many of their rural neighbors to be married and more likely to own their own farms, and thus they qualified in droves for dependency and agricultural exemptions. While other local boys donned uniforms, the wartime agricultural boom made Mennonites rich; observing similar events in northeastern Ohio, a Wayne County man grumbled at pacifist Amish farmers who "balked at everything... except taking the highest price offered for everything they could produce on their farms."[18]

Tempers quickly flared. "Due process of law," announced the head of Kansas's Harvey County Council of Defense, "will not be a feature in the punishment handed out," and frequently it wasn't. Crowd actions sometimes focused on members of Mennonite sects that believed it sinful to salute the flag. In McPherson County, two Mennonites were beaten and tarred and feathered. Two others were publicly shaved in Montezuma, Kansas. Across the border in Collinsville, Oklahoma, in April 1918, a crowd strung up Mennonite Henry Reimer and threatened to lynch him. The town police persuaded the mob to let him down only after promising that he would be tried by the Tulsa County Council of Defense the next day. The Night Riders, a wartime citizen vigilance society active in Barton and Pawnee Counties in Kansas, terrorized Mennonites and other German-speaking communities by leafleting and firing shots in the air.[19]

As Charles Gordon, a participant in mob violence in Burrton, Kansas, recalled decades later, "We was out to convert these slackers into patriots." Often, though, wartime violence against Mennonites targeted not the conscientious objectors but the older, established leaders of the community, as when a crowd of two hundred near Glendive, Montana, convened a "trial" for John Franz, a Mennonite town father there. "You are the man that is making all this trouble," Franz recalled being told. Lutheran and Catholic German Americans expressed little solidarity with the German-speaking Mennonites. This was not surprising, really; after all, they had had little connection with them before the war. Now, as German Americans labored to demonstrate their loyalty to skeptical Midwestern neighbors, they distanced themselves from pacifistic Mennonites.[20]

Members of the International Bible Students Association, a sect whose members were known at the time as Russellites and would later be called Jehovah's Witnesses, faced intimidation from every direction. The church's paper, *Kingdom News*, reported that "certain officers" raided church offices in Los Angeles; a Divinity School professor at the University of Chicago expressed "strong suspicion" that the church's money "emanates from German sources," a matter he thought "a profitable field for government investigation." In Chicago, a Polish immigrant woman ran to the American Protective League after her husband joined a Polish-language Russellite church; the league arrested the entire congregation in the middle of services. Five Witnesses were arrested in April 1918 in Walnut Ridge, Arkansas, for distributing copies of the *Kingdom News*. A mob battered down the jail door, took the four male prisoners from their cells, whipped them, and then tarred and feathered them. The *Memphis Press* reported the events with satisfaction: "After they had received the public indignity the men were told to get out of town, and they promptly obeyed." In the midst of this repression, the Witnesses also learned the power of worldly legal institutions: "We call upon all order-loving, law-abiding people to protest against this unholy persecution of innocent men and women," wrote *Kingdom News*.[21]

African Americans made up a very small portion of objectors. Walter Kellogg, one of the members of the Board of Inquiry, wrote in his memoir that he doubted the board had heard from "more than fifteen or twenty" black objectors. Repeated appeals from within the black community to perform military service in the hopes of gaining full citizenship set the tone, but the formal barriers imposed by selective service and the coercive practices of everyday life were the deciding factors. Although conscientious objection is often posited as the act of an individual against the state, in practice objectors have always depended on the support of institutions in civil society as well as their own ability to manipulate state power in order to make their claims successfully. During World War I, African-American pacifists were doubly disadvantaged. In later wars, black objectors found support in the Fellowship of Reconciliation or the Society of Friends, groups dominated by whites but actively multiracial as well as pacifist. In 1917, however, even though there were African-American Quakers, and some black pacifists had joined the Socialist Party, their numbers in these beleaguered institutions were quite small.[22]

Most black objectors were members of Christian sects that operated at a distance from mainstream African-American churches. In the South, about fifteen thousand Pentecostal Christians worshiped in the Church of God in Christ (COGIC) under the leadership of church founder Charles Mason. Although the church had no clear tradition of pacifism, Reverend Mason was moved by the war's horrors to preach against any participation. In September 1917, Mason drew attention from authorities in Lexington, Mississippi, for advising against registration. "I feel that it is wrong for me to kill my fellow-man," he announced. "I counselled them not to fly in the face of the government, but I told them if God showed them a way, to take it, and then the questionnaires came. They are claiming exemption." Lexington's local sheriff arrested Mason on June 18, 1918, charged the preacher with obstructing the draft, and hauled him off to Jackson—an intervention of law that probably saved the pastor from outright lynching by angry townspeople. The *Chicago Defender*, a black newspaper, reported that Mason had "distributed a large amount of disloyal literature of religious savor emanating from Los Angeles"; among the most galling were printed handbills that used visual examples to instruct illiterate congregants on how to claim CO status. The *New York Age*, another African-American paper, dismissed rumors that Mason was a German spy. "This is laying it on too thick," editors noted. Meanwhile, American Protective League operatives in California kept watch on a COGIC church in Los Angeles and tapped the minister's phone. Back in Mississippi, Mason faced $2,000 bail, and his draft-age congregants fared little better. In the wake of his arrest, "a large number of men in Holmes County," members of COGIC, were "rounded up by the Department of Justice and sent to Camp Pike."[23]

African-American objectors endured a constant barrage of cajolement, ridicule, and coercion from soldiers, both black and white. They also faced the racist hostility of fellow objectors. Bruno Grunzig repeated racist jokes in his letters to socialist friends in New York City, while conscientious objector Duane Swift complained to his father about sharing latrine facilities with African Americans, fretting that "many Negroes have syphilis." For an African-American CO, presenting his case required standing before an all-white draft board operating in his local community with the assistance of the sheriff—and then proceeding to appearances before military psychologists, the judges of the Board of Inquiry, and perhaps even the officers of a military court martial. Instead, black opponents of war and conscription generally chose to dodge the draft, in significant numbers.[24]

For all objectors, persuasion accompanied each stage of the formal exemption process, beginning on registration day, as local draft boards rejected approximately 12 percent of conscientious objection claims. Popular pressure had thus already worked the objectors over before they ever entered a military camp. And then it worsened. In the camps, exercises of terror and torture tried to break the firm wills of conscientious objectors. Some religious objectors who had personal scruples about diet, dress, or hygiene were forced into uniforms, required to drill at gun point, found their hair and beards cut, or were forcibly fed. A corporal at Kentucky's Camp Taylor paraded Adam Mumaw, a Mennonite objector from Ohio, before a group of three hundred soldiers, then told them that Mumaw had refused to wear a uniform. "I'll put you out under their influence and they can do with you what they want to." Soldiers stripped off his clothes and tossed him around the crowd until an angry lieutenant, disturbed more by Mumaw's nudity than the young man's humiliation, intervened. Noncommissioned officers held Sheldon Smith's face under a water faucet and forced him to kneel down and kiss the American flag. Camp officers then stripped, beat, and whipped Smith; finally they tied a rope around his neck, "all the while renewing their question about giving in." At Camp Funston in Kansas, after Ferdinand Schroeder refused to work on Sunday, "they beated us and I tell you pretty hard."[25]

Conscientious objectors were frequently attacked as unmanly or cowardly. It was an easy, albeit sloppy, bit of logic: if all men must serve, then those who refused were not truly men. Secretary Baker contrasted the "young men who had lived remote and apart from the stream of life" observing "curious customs" with more vital men who responded to the impulses that "quicken the pulse and strengthen the arm of the normal young American." And Theodore Roosevelt, who had made "the strenuous life" the signature of his muscular vision of citizenship, weighed in with predictable skepticism about the objectors' manhood: "Some are actuated by lazy desire to avoid any duty that interferes with their ease and employment,...some by sheer, simple, physical timidity." Objectors confirmed this gendered system when they asserted their masculinity. Bruno Grunzig, a secular objector, blamed soldiers' hostility on the unmanly religious objectors who surrounded him. "I am quite sure that this attitude has been caused mainly by the religious nutts [*sic*] and their effeminate ways, not to speak of their perpetual howling of puerile ditties," he harrumphed. "We must take our medicine like men," he claimed, "precisely because the natural reaction is *expected* to be the very reverse."[26]

Not every military camp was equally violent; many passed the war years without incident. Perhaps the worst was Camp Funston in Kansas, under the direction of Major General Leonard Wood. The father of the preparedness movement and the author of *The Military Obligation of Citizenship* had little patience for objectors; Wood thought them not just selfish but dangerous. "Not only are they refusing to play the part of loyal citizens," he wrote, "but they are also...spreading discontent among other men." Funston had its dissenting voices in the ranks; Lieutenant Colonel C. E. Kilbourne told a Mennonite minister that he was "so embarrassed in my inability so to govern events in this camp as to reconcile the claims of your people with my duty to the government." But Harlan Stone was right when he reflected that "the Army was not a bed of roses for the conscientious objector; and the normal man who was not supported in his stand by profound moral conviction might well have chosen active duty at the front as the easier lot."[27]

Violence, hushed up or overlooked, proliferated in the nation's military camps, helped along by the inaction of leaders in Washington. Selective service policy was a deliberate failure: regulations required COs to enter camp when called up, even though the government, all the way until early 1918, still had no idea what it would ask them to do. Administration officials saw nothing wrong. Baker assured President Wilson, for example, that the effect of sending the objectors to the camps "quite certainly would be that a substantial number of them would withdraw their objection and make fairly good soldiers." Wilson agreed. "I...believe with you that the matter will in part solve itself by the experiences of these men in camp." Navy Secretary Josephus Daniels noted in his diary that "the conscientious objectors are segregated, no harm done them, & one by one they come out and say they are ready to serve." The ability of camp life to persuade the conscientious objector pleased Secretary Baker. "To a very large number who presented themselves" as absolutists, he noted, "mere contact with their fellows was enough to enlarge their view and bring them into harmony with the thought of their generation." In theory, the process of persuasion that brought COs into harmony with the thought of their generation was democracy in action—just another part of the ongoing arguments of American political life. But in practice, persuasion and coercion were difficult to distinguish.[28]

Wartime policy makers grudgingly began to accept the objectors once they knew their numbers would remain small. After initial military investigations in the summer of 1917 demonstrated that conscientious objectors would be few, Baker breathed to Wilson a sign of relief that "it does not seem...as though our problem was going to be...so large that a very generous and considerate mode of treatment would be out of the question." The liberal state could tolerate conscientious objectors only if there were not very many of them. "I feel quite sure," wrote Baker that September, "that our policy of not announcing in advance the course to be taken has limited the number of these objectors to those who actually do entertain scruples of that kind."[29]

Officials were also confident they could persuade the objectors to abandon their positions. Harlan Stone believed that "before we can persuade the conscientious objector to accept our views of the duties of citizenship we must understand his views and know the forces at work in American life which produce them." Most conscientious objectors, in the words of Newton Baker, were merely ignorant of their duties to the state and of "the real meaning of our institutions." Corporal Alvin C. York's journey from conscientious objector to war hero shows how blurry the line between persuasion and coercion could be.[30]

Early in 1914, the tall, lanky twenty-six-year-old redhead joined the Church of Christ in Christian Union in Fentress County, Tennessee. York later recalled that after the war broke out, "I was worried clean through. I didn't want to go and kill. I believed in my bible....And yet old Uncle Sam wanted me. And he said he wanted me awful bad. And I jest didn't know what to do." York turned, repeatedly, to his minister, a man by the name of Rosier Pile, who in one of those curious circumstances of rural Southern bureaucracy was also his tax assessor, his postmaster, his distant uncle—and his Selective Service registrar. Pile persuaded York to claim conscientious objector status and entrain for camp. On registration day, the form asked "Do you claim exemption from draft (specify grounds)?" Alvin York wrote "Yes, Don't Want to Fight."[31]

It was not with Pastor Pile, but at Georgia's Camp Gordon where York had his true "conversion." There he encountered Major George Buxton, who stayed up with York late into the night, pacing the floor in front of him, barraging him with chapters and verses about the expulsion of moneychangers from the temple and the rendering unto Caesar that which is Caesar's. By dawn, Buxton had broken

When he registered for selective service, Alvin York claimed conscientious objector status but later chose to fight in France, where he won the Congressional Medal of Honor. The popularity of York's journey from pacifist to war hero reflected the nation's hostility to conscientious objectors. (*National Archives and Records Administration, Southeast Region*)

through. York donned his uniform, and in the fall of 1918 made headlines for single-handedly killing 25 German soldiers and taking another 132 prisoner during the Battle of the Argonne. Awarded the Distinguished Service Cross and the Congressional Medal of Honor, York was lionized in the popular press and received bundles of fan mail. A wartime icon to rival even Uncle Sam, York embodied for many Americans their hope that conscientious objectors were simply unaware of the obligations of citizenship, amenable to the persuasions of people like Pastor Pile and Major Buxton. If, that is, they were like York, who "loved and trusted old Uncle Sam and...always believed he did the right thing."[32]

Mennonites defended themselves strenuously. They had been prepared by their local religious leaders with biblical texts with which to refute their drill sergeants. They also had support—and pressure—from their hometown social networks. "Boy, you look out that you don't disgrace us," David Jantzen recalled his father telling him after he had been called up. Clergy wrote to, visited, and preached to Mennonite conscientious objectors at Camp Funston, despite the opposition of military authorities, who censored mail, seized religious literature, and tracked the visiting clergymen's movements within the camps. The ministers threatened the drafted men with excommunication if they took up arms. P. W. Pankratz actually wanted to join the army, and because he had never been formally baptized in the Lehigh Mennonite Church, he wasn't technically a conscientious objector, but back in Pennsylvania, Pankratz's father arranged a baptism for him in absentia. "They told my father if he didn't sign it, well, they'd throw him out of church."[33]

America's collective efforts at persuasion—and the objectors' acts of self-defense—yielded ambiguous results. The state did not get what it wanted: of 323 Mennonite men drafted in Kansas, for example, only 23 actually joined the army as combatants. Some went willingly, convinced that this war was a just crusade; others went cunningly, like Enos Stutzman, who found a place as an army bugler, even though his Old Order Amish teachings forbade musical instruments. "I couldn't see how the Lord would tell anyone how quick to read notes. It was one of the miracles again. . . . It was a direct deliverance." Of the remaining 300 Kansas Mennonites, 151 accepted noncombatant duty, and 149 refused cooperation or evaded the draft. But the Mennonite church leaders were disappointed, too; as objectors negotiated their conflicting obligations to church and to state, a clear majority chose some kind of wartime service, even though this was strictly forbidden by the tenets of the church.[34]

Conscientious objectors confronted an imposing army of dissuaders, only some of whom wore uniforms. Their opponents enforced a political culture that connected citizenship to the voluntary fulfillment of obligations. Those who refused might simply be ignorant of their duties and could be convinced. Those who still would not see the light might be mad or feebleminded and had to be interned, for their own good and the nation's. Those who persisted would have to be coerced—by collective actions in the objectors' hometowns, in army barracks, and in courts. The state, which created the category of the conscientious objector, was their only protector. But it offered little shelter.

★ *Scrutinizing the Soul*

"To discover and weigh and measure the secret motives which actuated the objector to resist authority," wrote Harlan Fiske Stone, "was no light undertaking." Draft officials hesitated to grant objectors generous protections lest the exemption of honest objectors encourage opportunistic claims on the part of more deceptive citizens. "To put it quite frankly," wrote Sidney Webb, "it is even more easy to pretend to a conscientious objection than it is to pretend to sciatica." Sincerity thus became a key concept in the debate surrounding conscription during World War I. Bureaucratic institutions demanded it, and selective service administrators tested it.[35]

To qualify as a conscientious objector during World War I, a man's religious scruples had to predate the outbreak of the war. Additionally, he had to reject all wars and not merely this particular conflict, its aims, or the political process that had led to the war's declaration. By insisting that the objector oppose war in the abstract, the law placed civic duty on a plane higher than mere politics; a citizen couldn't have a political *objection* to a political *obligation*. But what if the beliefs were sincere and universal but belonged only to the individual? John Nevin Sayre, a Pennsylvania-born pacifist active in the Fellowship of Reconciliation, was a member of the Episcopal Church of America, which supported U.S. involvement in the war. He had doubts about the war. He also had connections: his brother's father-in-law was the president of the United States. Sayre wrote Woodrow Wilson in April 1917, concerned that the proposed selective service regulations made no provision for objectors outside the historic peace churches: "To put the matter concretely, Quakers might be excused from going to the front, but individual Jews, socialists, or Episcopalians like myself...might be drafted into it....Conscience is always an individual and personal thing," he noted, "and...the creed or principles of a religious organization cannot be substituted for it." Sayre feared having to choose "between obedience to conscience or to our country's laws. I am sure you will realize," he told Wilson, "how deplorable this would be and how fundamentally un-American."[36]

Sayre thought concerns about dishonesty were too extreme. A law designed to safeguard the individual conscience had to gamble on sincerity, even if "slackers and cowards" might get through the law's loopholes. "Such persons, even if compelled to go to the front, would be of small use there.... If we must have a selective draft, would it not be far better to let some of these slackers escape rather than force the consciences of many good, true men?" Woodrow Wilson disagreed. The president recognized that reliance on church membership was a problematic proxy, but he thought it "impossible to make the exceptions apply to individuals because it would open the door to so much that was unconscientious on the part of persons who wished to escape service."[37]

Exceptional cases like Sayre's forced new ways of thinking. As War Department officials puzzled over what to do with the objectors, they groped toward a new understanding of citizenship: before the state, the citizen could stand as an individual, but his conscience must, therefore, be thoroughly regulated by state institutions. In a series of classified memos to the commanding officers of military camps, Secretary Baker quietly extended the CO protections of the Selective Service Act: first to individuals with "personal scruples" against war that might not match those of their churches, then to secular and socialist objectors. All the while, in public, he reiterated his disapproving stance.[38]

Alvin York's encounters with authority—whether the friendly advice of Rosier Pile or the all-night interrogation of Major Buxton—were individual, man-to-man confrontations. That might have seemed comforting to some COs, but for most the prospect was daunting. Resettlement into military camps severed objectors' ties with their supportive home environments, a tough task for young men taught to rely on their ministers as intellectual and spiritual guides. Despite the fact that selective service regulations imagined that men formed their religious obligations in groups, when it came time to confront the state directly, objectors increasingly did so alone. "The Government of the United States is not dealing in the matter, and cannot deal, with organized religious bodies, but must of necessity deal with individuals," wrote Newton Baker to Mennonite leader Silas Grubb in November 1917, in a direct reversal of earlier policies.[39]

Finally, on March 20, 1918, Woodrow Wilson issued an executive order announcing his plans for alternative service. Conscientious objectors could opt for noncombatant service "to the extent that such persons are able to accept...without violation of the religious or other conscientious scruples by them in good faith entertained." They could serve in the medical or quartermaster wings of the army or with its corps of engineers. Later provisions allowed the secretary of war to "furlough" objectors for volunteer work on farms, in wartime factories, or in service organizations such as the Red Cross. The new regulations also promised no "punitive hardships of any kind."[40]

The alternative service provisions were a victory for the army, for conscientious objectors, and for understandings of citizenship premised on obligation. Even before the war, Norman Thomas, a socialist and an organizer of the American Union against Militarism, a leading pacifist organization, had asked Senator George Chamberlain, chairman of the Senate Military Affairs Committee, to create "an alternative service of recognized value to the state." Entreaties continued after the draft became law. Church officials, pacifist groups, and the objectors themselves insisted that COs were willing to fulfill political obligations in non-combatant outlets. Secretary of the Navy Josephus Daniels recorded in his diary a conversation at an October 1917 cabinet meeting: "Heads of churches opposed to fighting are writing urging that these men be put to work and not remain idle."[41]

Quakers were particularly interested in alternative noncombatant service and urged the government to release drafted members so that they might join efforts in France led by the Friends Reconstruction Unit. Responding both to the war and the draft, a group of Philadelphia Quakers met in April 1917 and formed the American Friends Service Committee (AFSC), announcing that "we are united in expressing our love for our country and our desire to serve her loyally...in any constructive work in which we can conscientiously serve humanity." Secretary Baker initially rejected the Quakers' offer, telling Woodrow Wilson that relief work was too easy and would encourage "further 'conscientious' objecting." Continued lobbying convinced the War Department of the principle that "reconstruction of the desolated war-zones is...part of our national obligation"; Assistant Secretary of War Frederick Keppel was also convinced that it was easier and cheaper to send Quaker objectors to France than to lock them up at home. Approached by Keppel in April 1918 and asked to take informal jurisdiction over the matter, Quaker leaders agreed. Five hundred eventually served abroad in what they believed to be a fulfillment of their political obligations. "We did not consider our service *a way of escape* from military service," insisted the AFSC's Rufus Jones.[42]

The *New York Times* applauded Wilson's alternative service policies. "By clearly defining the sorts of toil which this country now can demand and insist on getting from 'conscientious objectors,'" President Wilson's executive order "will fairly well reconcile the ordinary American to the existence of these strange folk. Whether or not his decisions will be equally pleasing to the strange folk themselves remains to be seen," the paper quipped, "but their opinions on the subject are not of much importance." Ordinary Americans did not always take to the strange folk. Despite an urgent shortage of agricultural labor in the 1918 harvest season, farmers in Ohio and Iowa, for example, violently resisted the assignment of conscientious objectors to agricultural furlough positions in their communities. War Department officials reassigned the men and placed each "in a community which was not antagonistic to his religious beliefs" (although never his hometown). By harvest time, matters had reached an accommodation; farm owners cherished their steady labor supply, even though one Iowa farmer did express doubts about the objectors' pacifist principles after he heard them swearing at his mules.[43]

In practice, the Wilson administration's alternative service provisions frequently offered too little: local boards occasionally ignored the provisions, and

Harlan Fiske Stone, shown here after his appointment to the U.S. Supreme Court in 1925, spent World War I traveling the country interrogating conscientious objectors, whom he described as "a residue whose peculiar beliefs…refused to yield to the opinions of others or to force." (*Courtesy of the Library of Congress Prints and Photographs Division*)

some military officers refused to release COs for agricultural work. And often they arrived too late: although Wilson made his announcement in March 1918, Secretary Baker issued no supporting orders until June. Those orders included the War Department's official response to the problem of sincerity. A new policy established the Board of Inquiry, charged with the direct interrogation of objectors. Three legal heavyweights comprised the board: Major Walter Kellogg of the U.S. Army Judge Advocate Corps, progressive judge Julian Mack, and Harlan Fiske Stone, dean of the Columbia Law School and a future chief justice of the U.S. Supreme Court. The board traveled to every major military installation where COs had been encamped, and based on brief interrogations, usually no more than a few minutes, the board established the objectors' sincerity or insincerity.[44]

The board's mission betokened a new relationship between federal law and the souls of its citizens, as its members quickly learned. Harlan Fiske Stone noted that although the board was made up of attorneys, "the lawyer spends his life in dealing with the acts and conduct of men. Only in rare instances does the law try to fathom the human conscience." Secretary Baker hoped the Board of Inquiry would "provide the greatest generosity of treatment to the men whose sincerity is proved, while keeping the strictest check against giving an opportunity to the slacker or malingerer." But board policy was also designed to reduce objectors' numbers. Upon commencing work, the War Department proudly (if erroneously) noted that only six hundred objectors were at that time held in military camps, and that "this proportion...will be reduced still further when the Board...has reported." Baker had written to Wilson that he intended "to work out a plan which will be considerate of the embarrassment under which these people find themselves but will not encourage a simulation of conscientious objection on the part of others." Wilson heartily agreed.[45]

Those judged sincere could take a noncombatant furlough, while the officially insincere looked forward to immediate induction or a court martial. Take, for example, the operations of the Board of Inquiry at Camp Gordon near Atlanta. After the board interviewed 177 objectors there in June 1918, it persuaded 72 men to choose noncombatant service; 54 failed to convince the board of their sincerity and were forced to accept any service ordered by their commanding officer. Twelve men withdrew their objections "or it was found by the board that they had misunderstood the original questions" and weren't really conscientious objectors in the first place. At Camp Meade just outside Baltimore, the board ruled just twenty-three men sincere and recommended furloughs for them. In total, the Board of Inquiry heard 2,294 cases during its existence, and a majority of its subjects either relinquished their claims or were deemed insincere.[46]

The War Department also tried more scientific methods of scrutinizing American citizens. A March 1918 order by Secretary Newton Baker required psychological examinations of all conscientious objectors. Exam results had consequences, as Walter Kellogg, one of the judges on the Board of Inquiry, made clear: "Any inconsistencies in [an objector's] testimony were noted, and submitted to the Board upon its visitation." The belief that conscientious objection was a mental illness—that, in short, one would have to be crazy to be a CO—was never far from the surface. Secretary Baker thought that most religious objectors "really have no comprehension of the world outside their own rural and peculiar community. Only two of those with whom I talked seemed quite normal mentally." This vision of mental deficiency was no minor matter; some opponents of war—particularly those who had trouble articulating their concerns in the nice, neat language of liberal theory—found themselves labeled "feebleminded" or "insane" and interned for the duration of the war, or longer. But psychological inquiry was more than an attempt to label COs as deviant; it was an effort by modernizing state authorities to bring the most up-to-date methods to bear on the problem of political scrutiny.[47]

Edward Johnson was a farmer in Barronet, Wisconsin. With a wife and seven young children dependent on him for support, Johnson could easily have qualified for a draft exemption. But he didn't claim one. Arrested on May 14, 1918, for draft evasion, Johnson was sentenced to one year in federal prison at Fort Leavenworth for "teaching and preaching that it is unlawful to kill." Johnson's wife soon began a correspondence with William Morgan, the warden at Leavenworth. She told Morgan of her husband's physical and mental harassment in prison: "They put him in jail for 90 days and gave him bread and water for ten days. He was not allowed to talk to anyone or write. On the second day of bread and water they told him his wife was sick. This was not so, but it worried him and he could not find out." The warden wrote Mrs. Johnson to suggest that her husband's "soundness of mind" was in question, but Mrs. Johnson insisted that her husband had always been fine: "This was the first time I learned there was anything wrong with his mind. It all comes from worry. He always takes everything to heart. Some can take it light, but he never done that." On January 18, 1919, Edward Johnson was committed to St. Elizabeth's Hospital for the Insane in Washington, D.C. Records do not indicate whether he was ever reunited with his family.[48]

Psychological examination turned up unexpected results. After the war, Americans were consistently surprised to learn that the ranks of conscientious objectors were not made up of foreigners, pro-Germans, the feebleminded, or the insane. In January and February of 1919, the Surgeon General's Office of the War Department conducted a study of all inmates of the Disciplinary Barracks at Fort Leavenworth for a class in "Disciplinary Psychiatry." The study tested 2,416 prisoners and rated their intelligence from A ("very superior intelligence") to E ("very inferior intelligence"). Winthrop Lane, a progressive journalist and prison reformer, summarized the study in the *New Republic*, noting that "many people who were familiar with the kind of newspaper comment on conscientious objectors that was current during the war will probably be surprised to learn that fewer than eighteen per cent of political objectors and nineteen per cent of religious objectors fell below the 'average' in intelligence." Although the psychologists expected just 5 percent of men to fall in category A, 10 percent of the religious objectors scored at the highest level; some 39 percent of political objectors in general and 59 percent of absolutists were of "very superior" intelligence. Psychologists who expected to find rampant disrespect for law among

the objectors learned to their surprise that of the general prison inmate population at Leavenworth, more than 40 percent had had previous convictions, but
among the objectors, just 6.7 percent had any criminal record.[49]

Reliance on articulate verbal expressions as a measure of the soul's sincerity guaranteed that the privileges of citizenship were accorded primarily
to the privileged. In its dealings with illiterate Pentecostals from the moun-
tain South, with German-speaking Midwestern pacifists, and with immigrant
radicals who knew much Marx but little English, the Board of Inquiry placed
a premium on articulate speech. Walter Kellogg, for example, had little respect
for the Mennonite. "He shuffles awkwardly into the room—he seems only
half awake. His features are heavy, dull and almost bovine." Kellogg's views
on African-American objectors were hardly more charitable: "Their scruples
as respects war were frequently not well-reasoned," he complained, "but they
very probably believed honestly the things they claimed to believe." Secretary
Baker visited Camp Meade in September 1917. Of the eighteen thousand
men there, only twenty-six were objectors, and only one was a secular objector, whom Baker described to Woodrow Wilson as "a Russian-born Jew
who claimed to be an international socialist and who, I think, is simply lazy
and obstinate, without the least comprehension of international socialism."
Knowledge of the intricacies of socialism or biblical exegesis were crucial to
the men who faced the Board of Inquiry. Private Earl Robinson was interviewed at Camp Dix in New Jersey, ruled insincere because his understanding
of the Bible was "vague," and returned to the army, where he was later court-
martialed for disobedience and sentenced to twenty years' hard labor.[50]

Those who felt some comfort within the American polity possibly felt it
easier to make a claim on the state. John Nevin Sayre must have marked the
box for conscientious objection on his draft registration form with more confidence, knowing that a near relation had approved its design. Harlan Stone
recalled that "the Quakers produced a favorable impression by their high intelligence," and the Board of Inquiry deemed insincere only two Friends, both
of whom had joined as members after the declaration of war. (On the other
hand, Stone, a university dean, despised the "little group of college pacifists...
sublime egotists and glib talkers. Their self-confidence was monumental.")
The peace activists of the National Civil Liberties Bureau made much of the
ancestry of several prominent objectors. "I have had an essentially American
upbringing and background," announced Roger Baldwin at his sentencing
in October 1918. By the time the Surgeon General's Office administered its
intelligence tests to the conscientious objectors, the results were a foregone
conclusion.[51]

In practice, testing the sincerity of conscientious objectors helped thin their ranks. But there was more going on than the elimination of insincerity. Each of the tests was also, in its own way, an exercise of coercion practiced upon those with halting consciences. Expressing dissent, proving sincerity, and defending claims against the assaults of both state and civil society were so difficult that it does not seem surprising that out of the twenty-four million men who registered for the draft, a mere four thousand persisted in conscientious objector claims—not even two hundredths of 1 percent. In a sense, then, the tests worked. It is highly unlikely that among the 3,989 objectors who resisted all forms of military service there remained anyone who didn't mean what he said. No insincere men got through, but plenty of sincere men were left behind. The policy's success came at a cost—namely, that numerous citizens with sincere objections to organized killing found it impossible to claim a legal right that had been designed precisely for them.

★ The Trials of the Absolutists

Alternative service and the examinations of the Board of Inquiry did not end the debate over conscientious objection. Modern warfare, as a *New York Times* editorial pointed out, made alternative service theoretically problematic. How can a man "whose conscience will not permit him to assist in the actual destruction of his country's enemies...persuade that section of his 'psyche' to let him participate in activities that are just as essentially those of war as is that of going over the top or of firing a machine gun at an advancing German regiment?" asked the paper. "The fully explicable pacifist would go to jail—or the gallows—before he...would chop down spruce trees in an Oregon forest, if he knew that the resulting lumber was to be used in making war airplanes."[52]

Some in fact took that position. Absolutist objectors, whose numbers dwindled to just a few hundred by the war's end, refused the noncombatant option the Wilson administration offered them. Furthermore, most refused to obey the orders of military camp authorities, wear uniforms, or salute; a few even refused to follow military regulations concerning safety and hygiene. Some rejected noncombatant service because they believed their political obligations ought to be equally demanding as those of the men in the trenches. Absolutist objector Carl Haessler rejected the "bomb-proof" ease of hospital work: "If I am to render any war services, I shall not ask for special privileges." Absolutism and alternative service actually represented quite different understandings of the duties of citizenship: people willing to provide alternative service believed they owed obligations to the state but simply wanted to reconcile them with religious obligations. Absolutists, on the other hand, generally rejected the state altogether—which is why their ranks were made up almost exclusively of socialists, anarchists, or religious men who denied earthly authorities for spiritual ones.[53]

The absolutists were no one's favorite American citizens. Mennonite objector David Jantzen thought the absolutists he met "were sullen. They were just like a chip on the shoulder, you know?" Their claims that they had a right (or even a duty) to reject their obligations struck most American ears as preposterous. Even Norman Thomas admitted that "frankly . . . it is not always easy to deal with this class of men, and few officers have the patience and tact to carry out the liberal spirit of the War Department's orders." In late April 1918, the army decided to pursue court-martial proceedings for objectors "whose attitude in camp is sullen and defiant."[54]

Objectors who challenged the state's authority from within the gates of a military camp confronted Articles 64, 65, and 96 of the army's Articles of War, which required obedience to any order of an officer and punished all conduct of a "nature to bring discredit upon the military service." At a court martial, a single officer of the judge advocate general corps would sometimes serve as prosecutor, judge, and jury. Although COs were entitled to "counsel," that person didn't have to be a lawyer and rarely was. By war's end, more than five hundred objectors had been court-martialed, almost all on charges of disobedience under the Articles of War. Some were tried collectively: twenty-four men at Kentucky's Camp Taylor received ten-year sentences in May 1918 for refusing to work; authorities at Camp Travis in Texas handed down twenty-five-year sentences to forty-one absolutists there. One objector was convicted in just eighteen minutes. Of the 540 men, 17 were sentenced to death (although no executions were actually carried out), 142 received life terms, and 380 received shorter terms, averaging around 16.5 years, an average sentence higher than those meted out to draft-dodgers or war profiteers. Only one man was ever acquitted.[55]

Facing a court martial was a harrowing proposition. Erling Lunde, an efficiency engineer and volunteer scoutmaster from Chicago who called himself an "Independent Christian Thinker," was denied CO status because he "belonged to no established creed" and sentenced by a court martial to twenty-five years in prison. In a speech following his conviction, Lunde denounced "militarism and conscription, without which modern warfare is impossible." Carl Haessler, a Milwaukee socialist and self-described "patriotic political objector," told the court that sentenced him to twelve years in federal prison for refusing to wear a uniform that "I conceived it my part as a citizen to be opposition to the war." Raised in an Ohio Mennonite community, Ura Aschliman did not officially join the church until May 1918, thereby disqualifying him for CO status. After Aschliman refused to do kitchen duty at Camp Sheridan in Alabama, he, too, faced a court martial. An army officer asked the young man, "What does it mean to be a citizen of the United States, do you owe any duty towards your country…?" "For me," he replied, "it is to pray to Almighty God that He may rule through those whom [sic] are in authority." The officer was incredulous—"That is all his duty?"—and he soon lost patience. "What reward do you expect from all of this; are you a martyr, set yourself up as a martyr?" The court sentenced Aschliman to five years in prison.[56]

The three men—like most other convicted soldiers—were shipped off to the U.S. federal prison at Fort Leavenworth, Kansas, an outdated and over-crowded facility that had once been a model of American military justice, the creation of none other than Enoch Crowder, who had since been tapped to run the selective service system. They did not stay at Leavenworth for long. In the letdown after the Armistice, the nation's preoccupation with conscientious objectors quickly abated. Amnesty came faster and sooner than most Americans probably expected.[57]

Pressure on the War Department hurried the objectors' release. Religious institutions joined with socialist activists and civil liberties organizations such as the New York Bureau of Legal Advice and the National Civil Liberties Bureau. Activists campaigned to improve the prison conditions of the conscientious objectors and convince the Wilson administration to grant amnesty to court-martialed COs. Hundreds of Jehovah's Witnesses wrote letters to Congress. Ethel Thornburg of Reserve, Montana, begged for John Hardersen's release from the federal prison on Alcatraz Island in San Francisco Bay. "He is proving he is sincere…by what he is suffering," she insisted. "Such conditions," wrote Mr. and Mrs. S. S. Croy of Minco, Oklahoma, "ought not to exist in a land of so called freedom." Faced with a series of strikes at Fort Leavenworth in January and February 1919, War Department officials calculated the aggravation, and the cost, posed by the objectors' continued imprisonment. Most were sent home by the summer of 1919.[58]

Efforts to publicize the physical coercion of conscientious objectors connected religious activists and civil libertarians with contemporaneous movements against slacker raiding, mob violence, and lynching. At first, Secretary Baker denied all accounts of mistreatment, but news of the so-called "Funston Outrages," a series of assaults on objectors at Camp Funston, led to a few high-profile dismissals of army officers and a congressional investigation.

The scandal ended the military career of Major Frank White Jr., the judge advocate at the Kansas military camp and the son of a former senator from Alabama. White had little tolerance for the secularists, whom he termed "so-called conscientious objectors," dismissing them as men who "pretended to have conscientious objections based upon the view of the obligations which they owed to the country."[59]

After his dismissal, Major White, with the support of the American Legion, launched a noisy campaign against Secretary Baker and his supposed coddling of subversive pacifists. The Kansas legislature denounced Baker's actions as "an insult to the United States Army" that "has placed a premium on slackerism, cowardice, and mawkish sentimentality." The public apparently agreed: to forestall yet another congressional investigation (this one aimed at the secretary himself), Baker quietly changed the discharges of the military officers who perpetrated the Funston Outrages from dishonorable to honorable. But the attacks continued. When President Wilson granted amnesty to nearly all remaining COs in November 1920, Baker faced another round of attacks for releasing a "crowd of marplots and conspirators" on an "already outraged nation."[60]

★ *Modern Citizens*

The objectors themselves disappeared from the national stage, many of them sent home with so-called blue tickets. Neither an honorable nor a dishonorable discharge, these military papers told readers that "this is a conscientious objector who has done no military duty whatsoever, and who refused to wear a uniform." Most quietly returned home—often to rural German-speaking towns that emerged from the war much more subdued than they had been at the war's outset. Some felt a personal guilt over the difficult compromises they had made. "I wasn't proud of myself," recalled H. W. Berky. "I couldn't have been....I had sinned." Back in Montana, friends told John Franz to pursue a court case against the mob that had driven him out of town, but he refused, on religious grounds. "Vengeance is mine; I will repay, saith the Lord," he reminded his fellow Mennonites.[61]

Meanwhile, Alvin York had become a national hero. Thanks to the persuasive efforts of Major Buxton, men like Alvin York narrowly escaped what philosopher John Dewey asserted was the fate of all conscientious objectors: to become "victims of a moral innocency and an inexpertness which have been engendered by the moral training which they have undergone." Society,

Dewey claimed, had failed these men. The task of the government, therefore, was to help the objector see the light. "Enlightened by education," mused Harlan Stone, "they would have been loyal citizens, the first to offer their services to their country." Walter Kellogg wrote that "something must be done to uplift and to nationalize the backward people who need so sorely the broadening effects of education." But Kellogg thought the state could do only so much for such incorrigible citizens. "Something, as well, must be done to check the immigration of those aliens who bring to our shores their strange and un-American beliefs."[62]

In a culture organized around obligation, those who conscientiously refused it were no better than those who shirked it, and they found themselves, according to this definition, practically outside the terms of citizenship. In fact, many who had claimed conscientious objector status lost their formal U.S. citizenship or were denied when they petitioned for it. After the war, William Roeper asked a federal court in Delaware to naturalize him despite his refusal to swear that he would "support and defend the constitution of the United States against all enemies foreign and domestic." In June 1921, the court refused. "Citizenship is not merely a privilege, but an obligation as well," he was told, and absent Roeper's sincere and complete oath, naturalization could not proceed. "Ferdinand D—," a Hungarian immigrant, successfully claimed CO status in 1917, but six years later a federal court in Toledo, Ohio, found that fact sufficient evidence to bar him from naturalization. "Without any intention to reflect upon the quality of the profession of conscientious objector, we feel that it is enough that the country must endure the native-born of that persuasion whose citizenship is a birthright, without extending the number by the favor of naturalization laws." Mennonites John and David Goertzen fled to Canada to avoid the draft in 1918; when they returned to Henderson, Nebraska, two years later, they were arrested and court-martialed. Convicted as deserters, they were stripped of their citizenship. In case after case, courts refused to acknowledge that conscientious objectors could be citizens of the United States.[63]

The irony is that the objectors were some of twentieth-century America's first modern citizens. What made them distinctive was their assertion of individual rights against the modern state. As they seized a category of citizenship created by the federal government to mediate the conflicting obligations of minority groups, they forced the state to address not their group identities and their obligations, but their individual selves, and their rights. The legal regulation of conscientious objectors was not a response by the state to passionately individualistic sensibilities. In fact, government policy during World

War I did as much to create modern America's political individualism as to respond to it. Constant battle gave COs and their objectors valuable practice in how to confront the state and some sense of newfound power, even when they lost. "I feel myself part of a great revolt," Roger Baldwin announced before his sentencing. "It is a struggle against the political State itself."[64]

Only a few thousand men took advantage of the new category of citizenship that conscientious objection represented; their numbers grew in later wars, but always remained small. Numbers aside, America's struggle over conscientious objection did much to reposition the relationship between citizens and Uncle Sam. Years after the Armistice, Harlan Fiske Stone, then presiding over the Supreme Court, received a letter from a former CO who wanted to know if the chief justice, who had ruled against most wartime objectors' claims, had since had a change of heart. He hadn't. "I believe that inasmuch as I must live in and be a part of organized society, the majority must rule, and that consequently I must obey some laws of which I do not approve, and even participate in a war which I may think ill advised," he wrote, even as he crafted a more durable legacy of civil libertarianism during his tenure on the nation's highest court. During World War II, as America did battle with a totalitarian enemy, some Americans did change their minds, and the toleration of conscientious objectors was frequently lauded in self-congratulatory fashion as a sign of liberalism's durability. But it in its first world war, despite Evan Thomas's wish, America was surely not big enough for such people.[65]

3

The Obligation to Volunteer:
Women and Coercive Voluntarism

✮✮✮✮✮✮✮✮✮✮✮✮✮✮✮✮✮✮✮✮✮✮✮✮✮

Mrs. C. Douglass Smith of Pocatello, Idaho, summed up her wartime obligations quite simply: "Knit, knit, and then knit." When she did so, she joined an army of American knitters. Red Cross volunteers alone knitted 22 million items for hospitals, 1.5 million refugee garments, 15 million military garments, and 253 million surgical dressings. The women of New York City's Cosmopolitan Club beat their drums with knitting needles as they marched down Fifth Avenue in a victory parade reviewed by President Woodrow Wilson. But the figure of American women knitting for Uncle Sam, like the image of Uncle Sam himself, is deceptively simple.[1]

America's knitting army included elite women, for whom the task was a pleasant and diversionary hobby; rural women who depended on their own labor to produce clothing; and working-class immigrant women who labored in textile factories, sweatshops, and their own tenement kitchens. Knitting was publicly lauded as an inclusive form of voluntarism that all women could undertake, and the knitting woman provided a powerful image of a female citizen fulfilling her wartime obligations, but the items that the U.S. military needed required labor skills that recreational knitters often did not have. Many women who had promised Uncle Sam that they would knit spent the war years simply learning how to do so. Despite its warm and homey image, women's knitting was sometimes bitterly contested, just like wartime obligations more generally. On a cold Friday afternoon in January 1918, seventy-year-old Emma Furman went to downtown Macon, Georgia, with her daughter Bess to knit for the Red Cross. Ordinarily, "it was quite an inspiration to see so

AMERICAN RED CROSS

OUR BOYS NEED SOX KNIT YOUR BIT

Millions of American women volunteered to knit socks for soldiers, but when George Freerks of Minnesota claimed that "no soldier ever sees these socks," he was prosecuted under the state's sedition law. (*Courtesy of the Library of Congress Prints and Photographs Division*)

many women at work," but finding "no one to direct the work" that day, the women left. "Bess [was] much disgusted," Furman confided to her diary. Others avoided the work altogether. In Pocatello, the Navy League Knitting Club noted in April 1918 that some two hundred women had obtained supplies from the club without completing any products; by the spring of 1918 Smith College students had made only about half the surgical dressings that in the beginning of the school year they had sworn an obligation to knit.[2]

Some openly questioned the value of knitting, circulating rumors that military authorities were tossing out shipments of knitted materials after they reached the military camps. In Atlanta, the Rev. Billy Sunday urged the wrath of God on whatever "German spy" destroyed nineteen sweaters at Red Cross headquarters there; Mrs. Spencer R. Atkinson surely relieved Atlantans when she noted that "Germans had nothing to do with it. Mice did it." *Red Cross*

Magazine battled rumors in an article that chronicled "The Saga of the Socks." Chicago's Mrs. Richard Folsom denounced knitting rumors as "German propaganda," and a court in Big Stone County, Minnesota, agreed. A grand jury there indicted George W. Freerks for obstructing the war effort after he complained in January 1918 that "the war is managed just the same as they are doing with these old hens. They get them to knit socks and sweaters to try to make them believe we are at war. No soldier ever sees these socks. What good are all these damned sweaters? It is all bunk." Minnesota's Supreme Court later upheld Freerks's sedition conviction.[3]

But when another Idaho woman wrote to the *Pocatello Tribune*, wondering in print why knitting "must be done personally rather than be contracted out to large firms," she was on to something. Why, as the United States mobilized the home front for mass participation in war, did such work have to be done "personally"? Even if some soldiers did see those socks, the uniforms they wore had typically been sewn on machines in factories. Indeed, by the summer of 1918, contracts for the production of soldiers' sweaters had also been parceled out to factories, and when government planners at the War Industries Board began to exert control over the nation's yarn supply, *Red Cross Magazine* switched its tune. "Don't Make Sweaters!" it urged readers of the September 1918 issue. So much for the obligation to knit.[4]

Voluntarism had many definitions. It denoted an expression of consent. It referred to organized activity outside state auspices. It was also an act of unpaid labor. Viewed from that angle, the picture changes. Winning the war meant capturing the hearts and minds of the home front, as well as extracting significant amounts of unpaid labor in an economy in which women had long worked without monetary reward. Voluntary service, boasted clubwoman Mrs. Coffin Van Rensselaer, "is the means of saving millions of dollars."[5]

Even as the war's pamphlets and posters theorized voluntarism as an obligation, it remained a privilege to provide unpaid labor to the nation in 1917. Few working-class women could have telegraphed the U.S. Food Administration, "No salary," as one woman did in reply to an inquiry about the payment she required for wartime service. They found it hard to spare time on behalf of a war effort that many of them didn't much care for in the first place; few working women in Philadelphia could have visited the clubrooms of the Philomusian Club, which knit bandages on Mondays and Thursdays from 9:00 A.M. to 5:00 P.M. Nor would they have cared to stop by the "Volunteer Factory" that the city's Red Cross chapter established to make garments for European refugees with "the factory method." And women who worked in the garment industry were already sewing all day in any case, some of them on military uniforms. George Hall of New York's Child Labor Committee observed pushcarts filled with uniforms and middlemen behind them, calling, "Who wants coats or pants to finish?" But when working-class women and their labor advocates tried to convince Uncle Sam that "it is not fitting that the soldiers of freedom should go to the firing line clad in garments which are the product" of tenement housework, they were denounced as traitors. Other women's efforts were simply ignored; no African-American knitters marched before Woodrow Wilson in that Fifth Avenue parade.[6]

In a political culture organized around voluntarism, including women's voluntarism, Americans struggled to understand the difference between voluntary sacrifice and unpaid, or even forced, labor. Coercion also operated differently in women's organizations than in the male vigilante societies that dominated headlines. Although women did not by and large experience or participate in physical violence, coercion still abounded. When women were subject to political violence, as happened to the radical suffragists of the National Woman's Party who protested in front of the White House in 1918, the war's dynamic of violence and disavowal played out predictably, and the nation's struggle over "the pickets" dovetailed into other wartime debates over mob violence. Less visible, but no less significant, were the steps that women took within their own organizations or households, or as they traveled from house to house on behalf of Uncle Sam. And shaping all these events was the wartime struggle for suffrage, which remade women's relationships to each other, to the state, and to the obligations of citizenship.

As the war mobilization machine geared up, military uniforms rolled off the assembly lines, unmasking the knitting woman as a political, rather than an economic, necessity. She symbolized the home-front volunteer, a civilian female version of the male recruit to whom Uncle Sam pointed in James Montgomery Flagg's "I Want YOU!" poster. Her image persists, a vision of citizenship that binds up voluntarism and obligation in the person of a white-capped, needle-clicking, civic angel. The image drew on long traditions of women's civic voluntarism at the same time that women challenged and reformulated it.

★   *The Obligation to Volunteer*

President Wilson aimed his perplexing call for the service of "a nation which has volunteered in mass" as much at civilians as at drafted men. Winning the war required the mobilization of manpower for military service overseas, but war demanded the women and men of the home front as well: their material resources, their industrial labor, and their political consent. Americans worked out the terms of consent in the institutions of everyday life where they actually experienced their obligations to one another: schools, churches, the workplace, the family. Especially important were the nation's voluntary associations, where women and men gathered regularly for socializing and civic engagement. Countless wartime speechmakers told Americans they had to volunteer; it was in their clubs that they expected to do it.[7]

Women and men of the Progressive Era had a penchant for clubs, reflecting the social life of a time before mass entertainment and the political impulses of an era when many Americans remained skeptical of the state. Two generations removed from Civil War, region and location still mattered; local government solutions appeared more flexible and more democratic than federal ones. Elites disdained corrupt urban machines, preferring organizations of like-minded individuals, informed by experts. The various social movements that gathered under the label of progressivism practically built a shrine to their own voluntarism. The legal foundations of public life, too, lent a hand—and clear incentives—to associational formation. Law and political culture made room in the political arena for vigorous action by voluntary associations—all the more so for American women, who still encountered obstacles in the public sphere and barriers before the voting booth.[8]

What happened, then, when a rhetoric of voluntarism meant to mobilize men for military service encountered an existing politics of voluntarism organized in large part by women? Plenty of women responded to Uncle Sam when he asked for their services—most notably, the eleven thousand women who joined the U.S. Navy and some twelve thousand who served as nurses in the U.S. Army. At home, women marched in parades, wore ribbons, and flew flags. They offered up labor in the production of clothing and the conservation of food, and they secured capital for the war effort by selling and purchasing war bonds. They demanded abstention from alcohol and commitments to moral purity—not only their own but also that of the women who socialized in the environs of military camps. They sacrificed sons and husbands to the war effort and adjusted to the challenges of household maintenance posed by absent wage earners in their families.[9]

They carried out much of this work in women's clubs. During the period between 1890 and 1920, women's organizations stood at the intersection of local organization and national power. Clubs and their local networks fostered intimate social relationships and female autonomy, while at the same time organizing a collective national voice in an era when nearly all government institutions excluded women from full participation.[10]

Organized women's groups had been meeting in America for decades, beginning with a burst of religious and benevolent societies in the 1830s, women's relief efforts during the Civil War, and ultimately leading to the formation of the General Federation of Women's Clubs in 1890. The GFWC was actually a loose collection of thousands of local clubs. Some were literary or artistic clubs, others addressed themselves to "municipal housekeeping" and social service, and the federation included both suffrage and antisuffrage locals. By 1917, the GFWC counted some three million members, and with its motivated leadership, broad communication networks, and deep local roots, the General Federation was unquestionably one of the most effective political organizations in the country. Clubwomen's activities in the Progressive Era brought them in close contact with party politics, even as they continued to be excluded from electoral politics at the national level and most state levels. But clubwomen also made a virtue of their distance from the rough-and-tumble world of partisan electoral politics as they promised to raise the standards of society and political life through their public interventions.[11]

Most GFWC local clubs remained unapologetically restricted to white women, even as African-American women developed their own vigorous club movement. By the World War I era, the National Association of Colored Women (NACW) counted fifty thousand members in more than a thousand local clubs. Black women joined for companionship, for status, and for reform, but in African-American communities, clubwomen's voluntary activities carried an added significance that white women's club work often did not: black women's initial national organizing efforts in the 1890s developed at a historical moment when black men were being systematically forced out of participation in political life, particularly in the South. The organization of municipal services or the provision of loans, insurance, and poor relief by black voluntary associations responded directly to the political concerns of communities that were inadequately served by government institutions, private banks, and insurance companies—if they were served at all.[12]

Before the United States even entered World War I, women's clubs had already concerned themselves with the war, especially by throwing themselves into fund-raising for European refugees. Some, like the elite women of the American Fund for French Wounded, even went to France in ambulance and motor corps. "I believe it's worth a good deal more than a year out of anybody's life to be over here," wrote Theodora Dunham, a college student active with the American Fund, to her parents. The National League for Woman's Service, a pro-interventionist organization that drew heavily from female patriotic societies, established a motor corps by January 1917 and began training women

Among America's home-front volunteers was twenty-year-old Amelia Earhart (third from right), who volunteered to take an automotive repair class in Northampton, Massachusetts, in the spring of 1918. (*Courtesy Smith College Archives*)

as wireless operators just a few weeks later. By early April 1917, the National League had fifty thousand members "demanding to be organized and prepared" and was training women in thirty-two states. For these women, as for others in groups such as the Women's Navy League and the Daughters of the American Revolution, U.S. entry into the war was a welcome event. "I am glad," wrote Dunham in a 1917 letter, "that America has at last taken a stand."[13]

That the General Federation of Women's Clubs would also enthusiastically support the national war effort was not a foreordained occurrence. Just a few years before, in the heyday of the Progressive Era peace movement, nearly every state federation included a peace committee; as female pacifists busied themselves with essay contests, pageants, Fourth of July peace rallies, and weekly newspaper columns, they folded their activities into the GFWC's national agenda. Later, as war loomed, these women would break away to form their own peace organizations, most notably the Woman's Peace Party, founded in 1915. The General Federation, meanwhile, slowly drifted toward war. In 1916, the New York City Federation's Peace Committee renamed itself the Peace through the Army and Navy Committee and agitated for increased military spending and national conscription. On February 20, 1917, clubwomen telegraphed President Wilson that "the General Federation of Women's Clubs stands loyally behind the Government." Mrs. Herbert A. Cable offered the president the services of the California Federation of Women's Clubs, "enlisted for the period of the war, to work as soldiers work, under centralized authority and obedient to command." Clubs soon suppressed pacifism in their own ranks. Moderate women's clubs such as the National Council of Jewish Women suspended their collaboration with peace organizations; when the antiwar British poet Siegfried Sassoon addressed New York City's Cosmopolitan Club, which included elite literary women such as novelists Ellen Glasgow and Willa Cather, "guests swept from the room in indignation, and pacifism and patriotism boiled over together."[14]

Clubwomen professed their readiness to serve, but it remained unclear what precisely they proposed to do, especially in social clubs that had good intentions but little political experience. In central Massachusetts, the Worcester College Club voted to give up refreshments and raised a modest sum to donate for the care of wounded soldiers. They performed war-related dramas and sang patriotic songs. But although they voted on three different occasions to undertake "some form of war work," they never actually did so, and lifted their ban on refreshments during the club's annual whist parties.[15]

The nation's actual voluntarism, clearly, did not match its voluntarist rhetoric. Diatribes against the "woman slacker" soon filled the popular press and the minutes of women's clubs. A wartime editorial in *Ladies' Home Journal* described the woman slacker as "a woman who cannot take anything seriously,...who cannot put aside her little dolls and playthings: who must consume in social frivolity the time and strength that other women are putting into salvatory work." Selfishness perplexed the politically engaged women who were daily giving all to the nation. Like the draft dodger and the conscientious objector, the woman slacker had cast off the burdens of citizenship with a shrug of her shoulders, leaving others to carry the load.[16]

Government officials and leaders of major organizations also worried that uncoordinated voluntarism would be inefficient. Among draft-age men, unmediated voluntarism was thought to be prompted by boyish excitement, a gung ho goodwill that Selective Service System administrators sought to channel and put to good use. Reckless female voluntarism was different, frequently dismissed as a frivolous search for entertainment that needed to be controlled rigorously lest it detract from the serious business of war. Student Anna Davenport Sparks told her Smith College classmates that their service, "if it is to be efficient, must not be in an orgy of enthusiasm, but rather in sane, well-planned, quietly-executed activities." The *Ladies' Home Journal* urged readers to serve but serve smartly: "Let every woman ... be sure of her talent, and not hinder or complicate by offering herself for work for which she is not fitted." These concerns reflected the political culture of the era. No one could quite decipher what women's wartime voluntarism was; since it wasn't work, they feared it might merely be leisure.[17]

And so the nation's clubwomen attempted the same solution the War Department did: selective service under a broad regime of voluntary registration. During the early months of the war, women's organizations canvassed their members, dutifully filling note cards with lists of skills that might be useful to the war effort: nursing, sewing, driving, shooting. Philadelphia women gathered ninety-five thousand cards "during the hot summer months" of 1917. Rhode Island and New York included women in the counts of each state's "Military Census"; the General Federation urged a full government-administered census of women to replace piecemeal registration work within clubs. The Massachusetts Federation aptly scheduled its census for June 5, 1917, the same day young men registered for selective service. "The hearts of the women of the Federation, many of whom were mothers, were full to over-flowing as they, too, registered for service," noted a club history. The equation of women's registration with selective service could at times be explicit. The *Smith College Monthly* editorialized in June 1917 that "though there be, tech-nically speaking, no Selective Conscription for college women, it might be well for us voluntarily to conscript ourselves to one specialized form of work rather than to spread our energies over many fields." In southern Illinois, Mrs. Henry Schmidt was even more direct: "We are needed—we are drafted—we cannot refuse!"[18]

For some, it was a short step from registration to military dress. A mem-ber of the Illinois Federation of Women's Clubs claimed that "since our men are required to wear service uniforms, our women are requested to dress in harmony with our great national thought," and when thousands of women on the home front donned makeshift uniforms, they equated their own work with soldiers' service, insisting that women's citizenship could be harmonized with great national thoughts. But the ambiguity of women's wartime voluntarism rested in the easy shift in the Illinois speaker's words. Soldiers were "required," and women were "requested." It was a distinction, but was it a difference?[19]

Clubwomen had debated the relationship of their organizations to the war effort and defined the obligations of their members; they had begun to position the volunteer work of their clubs within a politics of obligation that reserved the highest honors of citizenship for male soldiers. Soon, as they

sifted through the pledges rendered—or not—during women's voluntary registration drives, they would find a place for their clubs within the state itself.
They would also face the failures of many women to meet the obligations of
wartime loyalty and service that they had prescribed.

★ *Volunteers within the State*

When Uncle Sam pointed to the home front and asked for wartime service,
he tapped a thriving network of voluntary associations organized by men and
women alike. The war brought voluntary groups under the umbrella of state
power in ways that strengthened their political legitimacy. Americans who felt
localized obligations to institutions in their hometowns witnessed and participated in the transformation of these groups into appendages of the nation-state.
Leaders of these organizations ambitiously attached themselves to the government
in its moment of expansion as the advance guard of a wartime legion of bottom-
up state-builders. Voluntarist women were the foot soldiers of this army.

Like the editors of *Ladies' Home Journal*, policy makers, too, feared duplica-
tion of effort and dissipation of energy. And so the federal government—out of
necessity as well as a desire for control—harmonized home-front voluntarism by
establishing close working relationships with existing national voluntary associations. Seven major national organizations that did work with the U.S. military
came together in the National War Work Campaign: the American Library
Association, American Red Cross, the Jewish Welfare Board, the Knights of
Columbus, the Salvation Army, the Young Men's Christian Association
(YMCA), and the Young Women's Christian Association (YWCA). Some
worked independently, funded and staffed largely through their own efforts,
and remained free to set their own agendas. Others collaborated closely with
the federal government: the American Red Cross drew funds from both the
government and private contributions, and it responded obediently to demands
by War Department officials. Gathering more than eight million Americans
into 3,870 chapters and 31,000 branches and auxiliaries, the Red Cross worked
closely with the military during the war. Similarly integrated into the state, the
YMCA and YWCA provided social and spiritual services to soldiers abroad,
their families at home, and communities located near military installations. In
other cases, the government did not tap national associations but was co-opted
by them, as groups effectively turned their own prewar organizational agendas
into national wartime aims. Such was the case with the General Federation of
Women's Clubs, which colonized the Woman's Committee of the Council of

National Defense, and the American Library Association, which exerted similar control over the War Library Service, an official governmental agency.[20]

These organizations coordinated the local efforts of millions of volunteers, but they did not include all Americans. Jewish and Catholic organizations had to fight their way into the National War Work Campaign—YMCA leaders told War Department official Raymond Fosdick that their exclusion of Catholics was "a necessity"—and found a place only after the Y refused to set aside its explicitly Protestant proselytizing mission. Women fit uneasily into the male-dominated national organizations that mostly made up the National War Work Council. The National Council of Catholic Women coordinated the volunteer efforts of women in 4,470 church societies nationwide, but its appointed leadership was entirely male, and it always held a subordinate place in the National Catholic War Council. The Red Cross and the American Library Association excluded women from leadership roles, even though their rank-and-file memberships were over-whelmingly female. "The great trouble," one volunteer remarked, "is that now, as always, men want women to do the work while they do the overseeing."[21]

Nearly all of these groups segregated or excluded African-American volunteers. The wartime Committee for the Advancement of Colored Catholics, for example, was part of the National Catholic War Conference, but African Americans never served in any other branch of this group. Philadelphia's Protective Association for Colored Women was dominated by white women. In May 1918, anticipating the noted "Close Ranks" editorial that W. E. B. Du Bois would publish in the *Crisis* two months later, YWCA member Florida Ruffin Ridley wrote that "colored women are ready, willing and able to stand shoulder to shoulder with white women in rendering service." But while African-American women in the YWCA signed up for such projects as the New York State Military Census, tensions over decision making in the Y continued throughout the war.[22]

Black women turned to their own institutions as outlets for voluntarism. Relief activities organized for African-American soldiers drew heavily from the expertise of black clubwomen; Josephine Ruffin, the principal organizer of the National Association of Colored Women, helped found the Soldiers' Comfort Unit in 1918; the unit's president, Mary Louise Baldwin, had been active in Boston's settlement houses. In their meeting rooms, African-American clubwomen found a space to work out their relationship to the wartime voluntarist state and to criticize President Wilson's rhetoric of citizenship. "He has used up all the adverbs and adjectives trying to make clear what he means by democracy," argued Nannie Burroughs in a report to the Woman's Convention of the National Baptist Convention. Ada Thoms insisted that whether Wilson "meant to includes us or not makes no difference. We are included."[23]

Clubwomen's organizing experience proved vital as they moved in small numbers into official government positions during the war. In April 1917, President Woodrow Wilson established the Woman's Committee of the Council of National Defense to coordinate the mobilization of women's voluntarism across the country. He drew on women's clubs' demonstrated mobilizing abilities and their leaders' known political commitments. Wilson appointed twelve women to the Executive Committee of the WCCND; all twelve were clubwomen, and three were current or former presidents of the General Federation of Women's Clubs. Similar patterns appeared at the state and local level; at a meeting of the Woman's Committee of the Nebraska Council of Defense, Mrs. Addison E. Sheldon asked all clubwomen in the audience to identify themselves, "and scarcely a woman failed to rise."[24]

Clubwomen installed themselves as leaders of wartime organizations and worked closely with Uncle Sam. When a man registered for selective service, he usually handed his form to a woman, and women also aided in the draft's enforcement: through their work with state Councils of Defense, women helped round up deserters and draft dodgers in twenty-six states. In some communities, the government supported the recruitment of women as public speakers and propagandists, and despite the objections of many men that the sale of war bonds was not "women's work," clubwomen took part in the Liberty Loan.[25]

Women also went to Washington. Before the war, Edith Guerrier was a librarian at the North End Branch Library in Boston, active in the settlement house movement, and a member of the Women's City Club. Her life followed an ordinary routine that included, as she later recalled, "library work, the clubs, and pottery" until she signed up at the City Club for wartime clerical service. Within a few weeks, "new duties and responsibilities engaged my attention." Guerrier moved to Washington, took up residence with other women volunteers in a group house, and began work as a librarian for the U.S. Food Administration. After the war, Guerrier returned to her routine in Boston, but not all women did: Emily Newell Blair, who joined the Council of National Defense in Washington during the war, grew increasingly active in Democratic politics and served as one of the first women on the Democratic National Committee from 1921 to 1928.[26]

The war brought women such as Blair into the state in new ways, but war could also stifle women's participation when the government took over an issue that had been on clubwomen's agendas. Such was the case with national prohibition. Ever since its founding in 1874, the Woman's Christian Temperance Union had been among the most prominent organizations in the national movement to suppress alcohol. In 1917, the WCTU counted more than 400,000 members, a track record of seventeen state victories, and some well-placed friends in

Washington: Secretary of War Newton D. Baker and Navy Secretary Josephus Daniels both were committed to keeping the armed forces dry. Anna Gordon, the WCTU's president, denounced "the Un-American liquor traffic...of alien and autocratic origin," and individual members of the WCTU labored under the group's wartime motto: "Every White Ribboner a Prohibition Patriot."[27]

In December 1917, Congress passed national prohibition as a wartime measure; the states ratified the Eighteenth Amendment by January 1919, events that ironically left the WCTU largely shut out of the wartime ruling coalition. As a women's organization that sought to exercise power over the behavior of men in military camps, the WCTU faced an uphill battle against the prerogatives of gender and the state; military police would enforce the military prohibition's policies. Nor did the WCTU's full-throated Protestantism easily square with wartime rhetoric of the military melting pot. And despite their claims to be a nonpartisan organization, the WCTU had frequently opposed Democratic candidates; party leaders in the Wilson administration had little affection for the women of the WCTU.[28]

There was plenty at stake in women's efforts. Anna Howard Shaw, serving on the Woman's Committee of the Council of National Defense, wanted women to be full partners in the war effort. Shaw, nearly seventy years old, was president of the National American Woman Suffrage Association and one of the nation's leading feminists. "Neither the Government nor society can longer afford to regard women's efforts as merely supplementary to men," Shaw felt, implying for her that "women should become integral parts of all bodies organized for war work." Often, though, it didn't work out that way. Relegation to secondary roles in the nation's war machine frustrated ambitious women. From her position as head of Connecticut women's wartime activities, Caroline Ruutz-Rees fumed that women "are still to a great extent 'helping' in the old volunteer manner...regarded meanwhile by the governmental power...with a tolerance half respectful, half amused." And, in fact, women exerted little control over formal policy making in the federal government. But in other areas, women wielded great power, especially over other women. When they did so with the authority of the state behind them, clubwomen did much to remake the relationship between citizens and the federal government.[29]

★ Kitchen Soldiers

Three years of total war had devastated the farmlands of Europe, and the production of foodstuffs in the United States supported not just American doughboys but Allied soldiers and European civilians as well. Anna Howard Shaw saw food's global significance: "Modern warfare demands…the armed force in the field and the arming-and-supporting force at home: and it is impossible to predict which is more important in securing ultimate victory." Old World countries facing desperate food shortages adopted strict rationing policies; to Americans not yet feeling the pinch of wartime hunger, such measures smacked of coercion, and they rejected them in public debates. Increased production and decreased consumption, prompted by the goodwill and self-sacrifice of the civilian population, would be the American plan.[30]

Herbert Hoover wouldn't have had it any other way. During the war, both men and women helped turn the forty-two-year-old California business executive into the prophet of wartime voluntarism and an unlikely war hero. Hoover, who coordinated international relief efforts in Belgium in the initial months of the war and then returned to the United States to head up the U.S. Food Administration, hoped that war mobilization could capitalize on the nation's traditions of voluntary association. "People fear beaurocrocy [*sic*] [and] would wish dictatorship ended when the war closes," he wrote in a letter to Navy Secretary Josephus Daniels.[31]

Politicians presented the U.S. Food Administration as a model of voluntarism, "intended," as Woodrow Wilson announced, "only to meet a manifest emergency and to continue only while the war lasts." Hundreds of thousands of news articles, lectures, and posters—emblazoned with such slogans as "God Bless the Household That Boils Potatoes with the Skins On"—urged American households to stock up on local foods that would otherwise spoil, to forgo wheat (which was easy to ship overseas), and to substitute fish for meat. Except for modest controls on the distribution of sugar and regulations on wholesalers and restaurants, rationing never appeared. Hoover opposed it because it would require a "hundred thousand bureaucratic snoopers." He even made a virtue of necessity: "I hold that Democracy can yield to discipline."[32]

For centuries, women had been preparing food in their own households without getting paid for it, thus making food a logical site for the political mobilization of women's voluntarism during the war. "There is no service in this war…in which the women can so well enlist themselves as in this," Herbert Hoover intoned. But while a few of the politicians who peddled food conservation probably hoped it would divert nosy women from the male world of wartime politics, many leading women wanted to use their voluntarism as an entering wedge to pry open the doors of politics. Jane Addams had been pursuing this strategy for a generation. The founder of Chicago's Hull-House, Addams had already done much to turn women's household concerns into a distinctive political agenda. In a 1918 speech on "The World's Food Supply and Woman's Obligation" given before the General Federation, Addams drew attention to woman's "old obligation to feed the world." But at the same time that she summoned prevailing notions about women's work, Addams urged federation members to connect their duty to feed their families with political obligations toward the nation and the world. She told listeners that despite women's leisure, at which "European visitors never cease to marvel,... the American woman is not, however, relieved of her responsibilities." She would do well, Addams argued, "if... in response to a great crisis she is able to... enlarge her conception of duty in such wise that the consciousness of the world's needs becomes the actual impulse of her daily activities." Clubwomen acted on Addams's insistence that women citizens had obligations to fulfill.[33]

Their first task was to establish a unified home-front fighting food force. And so, on April 12, 1917, just days after the declaration of war, the General Federation asked every member to pledge to conserve food: "I will use only those amounts of food required for adequate nourishment. I will endeavor to control the waste in all kinds of materials in the household and to live simply. I will begin now." The rank and file responded wholeheartedly. The New York State Federation of Women's Clubs supported food conservation in a November 1917 resolution; Dallas women joined in, too. Thirteen thousand Minnesota clubwomen signed the GFWC pledge.[34]

Women's clubs expanded their pledge drives nationwide under the auspices of the U.S. Food Administration, and as they blended state action and civic voluntarism, they also began to blur the line between mobilization and social control. The Hoover Pledge Drives—so called because they were administered by U.S. Food Administration and its director, although in fact Herbert Hoover had very little to do with them—sought the signature of every woman who ran a household. By the time that blank Hoover Pledge Cards began circulating across America, thousands of clubwomen had long since pledged their loyalty, and these volunteers—almost 500,000 of them—now turned their attention to women outside their own organizations, explicitly taking on the task of regulating the political obligations of other women. Responding to a series of three drives in June and October 1917 and June 1918, as many as fourteen million households signed the pledge.[35]

Clubwomen formed the vast majority of pledge collectors, acting both through their prewar organizational networks and in new, state-based institutions. In Alabama, Governor Charles Henderson assigned the task of collecting pledges to the Alabama Federation of Women's Clubs, and some 180 of the state's 228 federated clubs took part, including the As You Like It Club of Odenville and the Young Matron's Study Club of Ozark. Mrs. Francis E. Whitley directed the Hoover Pledge Drives in Iowa just months after she had administered them among the Iowa State Federation of Women's Clubs; unlike in Alabama, the "patriotic women canvassers" who spread out across the state included the members of the Iowa State Federation of Colored Women's Clubs.[36]

Edith Guerrier recalled seeing the cards as she traveled across twenty-four states for her Food Administration work: "wherever there were homes, I had seen the food-saving emblems." But Guerrier's recollections tell only part of the story. Not every window had a sticker. In southern West Virginia, some towns reported 100 percent compliance from local women; in others, clubwomen worried that residents were "not aroused to the situation yet." Across the country, women resisted signing the pledge. Lou Hoover, Herbert Hoover's wife and a leading clubwoman, assured listeners in Rockville, Maryland, that Uncle Sam "doesn't care to know what any woman has in her pantry," but women who feared that pledging meant signing over their entire food stocks to the state held out as long as possible. One woman saw the matter in political terms: "As a being with no political rights in Massachusetts, I fail to see why my signature on one of your cards would have the slightest weight." Others resented the invasion of their personal liberty. In the small town of Savannah, Missouri, Mrs. Wirt Ball refused to sign on the grounds that she didn't "think this is a free country any more." Another Missouri woman released her dogs when the pledge volunteers came by, and one went so far as to tell them that "if we would give [a card] to her, she would wipe her butt with it, [she] wasn't going to feed rich people."[37]

"No one is to be forced to do anything in this matter," Iowa's food administrator J. F. Deems assured the state's women on the eve of the pledge campaign there. "It is a subject for the conscience of the individual." Voluntarism was the language of the day. Women who signed the Hoover Pledge Cards were said to have "joined" the U.S. Food Administration—as if it were a voluntary association and not an official government agency. But despite the cozy rhetoric, the Hoover Pledge Drives mirrored selective service more than a kitchen canning club. The USFA administered its pledge drives with cooperation from the media, schools, libraries, and workplaces. Even churches mobilized: clubwomen encouraged ministers to form committees to survey entire congregations and compose lists of those who had not yet taken the pledge. Herbert Hoover wrote directly to clergymen, urging them to preach on the subject of food conservation. The subtle coercions of the house-to-house canvass marked the pledge drives, along with the indirect surveillance that accompanied the food pledge posters that women displayed (or didn't) in their kitchen win-

Wartime voluntarism reached the youngest Americans, including this group of schoolchildren in Syracuse, New York, who did their bit for the Red Cross. Children were not only urged to save pennies and recycle tin cans but also were encouraged to report wasteful classmates or disloyal teachers. (*Courtesy Zachary M. Schrag*)

dows. Philadelphia clubwomen boasted that "more than four thousand people of alien birth were visited." Oklahoma pledge collectors turned over the names of the unwilling to the State Council of Defense. Such a campaign went a long way toward guaranteeing that, in Deems's words, "there are no slackers."[38]

Women's adherence to their pledges was also enforced. "Anyone neglecting or refusing to comply with our government's food regulations will be marked as a traitor in the community," announced South Dakota's Food Administration head in 1918. P. M. Harding, who ran the USFA in Vicksburg, Mississippi, announced public hearings, "so that persons failing to co-operate in the nation's hour of emergency may be known to their fellow citizens." In Macon, Georgia, in July 1918, Emma Furman's daughter Bess returned from the Red Cross knitting circle with news that a neighbor, who had been permitted to purchase twenty-five pounds of sugar after pledging that she would use it for canning, had been caught baking "sweets galore" for her daughter. "She was visited by authority and ordered to show the preserves or the sugar," Furman noted in her diary. "Not being able to do either [she] was put under a $300 bond." Furman didn't pause to identify the "authority" in question, perhaps because authority at that moment was so diffuse. Compulsion could even be internalized within the household itself. Mary Aldis found half a slice of bread in her kitchen garbage can during the war. She recounted to readers of the *Journal of Home Economics* how she "call[ed] my household staff together" and "asked who was the guilty one." Hanging in Aldis's kitchen? Not only the Hoover Pledge poster, but also a sign, "in red letters": "To waste a crust of bread is an act of treachery to the nation."[39]

Wartime food conservation continued an ongoing politics of food production and consumption. In the 1910s, America was still on the road toward a more urban, consumption-oriented economy, and the preparation of food included older customs of local knowledge along with new methods and mechanical gadgets. Progressive Era experts in the fields of home economics and domestic science disdained many traditional cooking methods as woefully outdated. Before the war, rural and farm women had battled with county demonstration agents and other self-appointed experts over proper methods of farming, canning, and cooking. When the Hoover ladies came around in 1917 to talk about food, they knocked on doors of houses they had visited before.[40]

The political terrain on which this debate took place shifted after April 1917, as efficient food preparation became a political obligation. For the domestic scientists, women who used traditional food preparation methods were no longer just backward but treasonous; canning was not simply a modernist option but a patriotic duty. And they could back up their arguments as never before, with help from clubwomen, national and local media, and the authority that accrued to their "recommendations" now that they delivered them with Uncle Sam's stamp of approval.[41]

Hoover work also brought the state into political contests over food consumption in southern households where white women employed black women as domestic servants. The practice of "pan-toting" supplemented the wages of domestic workers with leftover food brought home from their employers' kitchens. Domestics generally disliked pan-toting, which perpetuated an unequal power relationship and kept their wages down, but they were even more dismayed when their employers forbade it. During wartime efficiency and conservation crusades, white women cracked down on pan-toting as wasteful, a move that domestics bitterly resented and surreptitiously fought. Tensions of labor between employers and workers now took on an added layer of politics: a white southern householder was doing war work as she kept an eye on her maid. The unwritten labor contracts that black women domestics had forged in the tense politics of the southern kitchen, meanwhile, were newly recast as seditious.[42]

The intersection of labor and obligation also appeared in conflicts among women during strikes in wartime canning factories. Hundreds of Italian immigrant women in San Francisco who had formed the Toilers of the World used Hoover's rhetoric to justify their strike against Bay Area canning companies in July 1917. The middle-class clubwomen of the Oakland Defense Unit, however, saw matters another way. Convinced that the production of food was a political obligation, they gathered a group of student volunteers from the University of California, set aside their half-finished peach preserves, and stepped out of their kitchens into the factories to can peaches—believing themselves not strikebreakers, but wartime volunteers. So many women were leaving Baltimore's canning factories for higher-paying jobs in munitions that elite clubwomen organized a Food Reserve Corps in the city to fill the assembly line's empty seats with volunteers. In September 1917, John Gibbs, of Baltimore's Gibbs Preserving Company, applauded the effort, which "helped to impress all the more forcibly upon the public, in which the working classes are included, the dire necessity of working in canning factories."[43]

Most historians agree that the promptings of voluntary societies and government organizations added little to the nation's harvests. For every clubwoman's family that munched through a bland and meatless dinner, there was surely another in which a steady paycheck from a factory job made possible a fuller dinner table than ever before. Wartime meat consumption, by most estimates, actually increased. Minor changes in the patterns of food consumption aided the Allied war effort rather little; in the midst of rapidly escalating prices for needed agricultural products, farmers had all the incentive they needed to produce more wheat and less corn and quickly brought an additional twenty-eight million acres of land under agricultural production.[44]

The political obligations that clubwomen enforced had little, actually, to do with food. Like knitting, food conservation was part of a symbolic politics of female voluntarism marked by coercions that went largely unexamined. In the postwar period, as Americans battled over the political legacies of wartime violence, they denounced slacker raiders, CO torturers, and lynch mobs; the Hoover Pledge collectors did not come up for discussion. But efforts to turn American housewives into an army of "kitchen soldiers" were no less significant manifestations of coercive voluntarism. They were merely less visible, because of how most women moved through their daily lives: a woman's consent was enforced by signing a pledge card in the private space of her kitchen, rather than in the baseball stadiums, saloons, streetcars, and billiard parlors that the slacker raiders targeted. And the fact that physical force was rarely applied should not obscure the exertions that were so frequently exercised.

At times, women's efforts brought them foursquare into the dynamics of home-front policing. They monitored other women's loyalty closely. Fear rocked clubrooms in Philadelphia after Red Cross officer Albert Staub told women there of the discovery of surgical dressings soaked in poisonous chemicals, which Staub attributed to sabotage. "You women of Philadelphia must clean house. Go over the list of your members and make sure of the loyalty of every one. . . . You do not realize the desperate extremes to which those who are against us will go." Settlement house workers at New York City's Greenwich House collaborated with army and navy intelligence bureaus. The New Jersey Federation of Women's Clubs established an espionage committee, "asked to be 'eyes and ears' for the government, to report suspicious actions, seditious remarks, interference with government meetings and the circulation of false reports concerning war organizations." Members boasted that "reports sent through this committee to the Department of Justice at Washington were of material assistance to the government."[45]

The National League for Woman's Service combined surveillance work with weekly target practice and military drill. In New York City, the Women's Motor Corps, loosely affiliated with the National League, cooperated with the New York City Police Reserve, adding to their assigned duties of transporting and entertaining wounded soldiers the additional burden of examining the citizenship papers of women who entered and left the Port of New York, as well as other unnamed domestic surveillance projects on behalf of the American Protective League.[46]

Surveillance efforts regulated the behavior of women within clubs as well. Controversy rocked the women of the New York City Federation when they convened at the Hotel Astor in October 1918. At the podium was the president of the American Relief Legion, Mrs. Oliver Cromwell Field, clad in the uniform of the Women's Police Reserve. "Mme. President, there are five tons of German-made toys which have landed in this country. Are we to stand for their being sold here?" The room buzzed, and Mary M. Lilly, a candidate for the State Assembly in the Seventh District, jumped at the chance to speak: "They shall never be sold here. Let us do as my ancestors did so long ago with the tea in Boston Harbor. Let us throw them into the sea." The clubwomen formed a committee for further study, and "every woman went home vowing that not a child or grandchild of hers should have a German-made toy for Christmas."[47]

During the middle of the war, E. Marguerite Lindley, a member of the National Society of New England Women, sketched a timeless ideal of women's wartime obligation. "This conflict means patriotism, and especially women's patriotism—sacrifice, deprivation, probably frugality such as characterized the ancestors of whom we are so proud." She hoped that her fellow clubwomen would help defend America against the "savagery of the German horde" and "prove our heritage by living up to the letter of requirements set forth by the Federal Food Administration." So too, women should "arous[e] all unpatriotic Americans to a realization of their privileges in helping end this brutality." The Food Administration, of course, had set forth recommendations, not, as Lindley called them, "requirements." But the difference was often effectively blurred during the war.[48]

C. E. Clark, a bank cashier in Poole, Nebraska, wrote the White House to tell the story of "one old lady Mrs. Mary McDonald," whom he had observed on September 12, 1917, when women in the small prairie town registered for national service. A sixty-six-year-old widow with rheumatism and two sons in service, McDonald "came in and insisted upon registering. . . . For one who has no money or home of her own to be willing to do this, we would call this patriotism." Illinois clubwoman Mrs. Clarence Rainwater called her efforts patriotism, too. She believed that women's fulfillment of political obligations had demonstrated their readiness to assume the tasks of full citizenship. Before the convention of the state federation, she asked, "Who then can deny woman her place in this co-partnership, even to suffrage?"[49]

★ *The Loyal Votes of Women*

Voting fit uneasily into wartime theories of political obligation, because voting and citizenship did not clearly overlap. In an era marked by the wholesale disfranchisement of African-American men and of women of all races, it was clear that voting could not be called a universal obligation of citizenship. Especially because you didn't have to be a citizen to vote—immigrants who had taken out their first naturalization papers had access to the ballot box in a few states and localities. And of course, you didn't have to vote at all. If suffrage was not an obligation, it was obviously a right—but in a culture of obligation, rights were sacred trusts, whose conferral on women could be allowed only after they had proved their trustworthiness. Many argued that women's wartime service had proved that trust.

Women's voluntarism was indispensable to suffrage victory, which came with the ratification of the Nineteenth Amendment in August 1920. But clubwomen's wartime service took place in the changed political climate of war, with its rhetoric of democracy, new engines of federal power—and suffragists chained to the White House gates. Successful arguments about woman suffrage resonated with the prevailing culture of obligation, not because women used their service as a bargaining chip but because they showed through the fulfillment of obligations that they could be entrusted with rights.[50]

Of course, not everyone saw it this way; there were almost as many arguments for suffrage as there were suffragists. For Jane Addams, along with many of the middle-class women who avidly read her books, voting was an end and a means, a necessary tool that would improve society by bringing a uniquely female perspective to a political arena that corruption and partisan politics had sullied. The votes of women would extend their efforts at "municipal housekeeping." Arguments like this echoed the rhetoric of obligation, made all the more convincing by women's home-front voluntarism. Such claims, they argued, were not self-interested; suffragists in Washington displayed on their banners Susan B. Anthony's words during the Civil War: "We press our demand for the ballot at this time in no narrow, captious or selfish spirit, but from purest patriotism for the highest good of every citizen." Women of this mind-set typically felt most at home in the National American Woman Suffrage Association (NAWSA), under the leadership of Carrie Chapman Catt and Anna Howard Shaw. With more than a million members, NAWSA was America's biggest suffrage organization, but hardly the boldest: its members pursued an slow and steady approach that by the eve of the war had all but ground to a halt.[51]

The obligations of citizenship also led women to oppose women's suffrage. For the "Antis," Progressive Era club work demonstrated that women were already wielding significant power without the ballot; they feared, too, that extending suffrage to immigrant or African-American women—whom they believed unable to bear the full burdens of political obligation—would only further degrade the political process. Responsible citizenship dominated the rhetoric of these women, who emphasized that despite eager wartime service by some, too many women were not ready to assume the full duties of citizenship and that the "silent majority" they spoke for did not want the ballot.[52]

In every wartime club room, suffrage lurked in the corner—when, that is, it did not sit center stage. Several groups attempted to suppress the issue. The League for the Civic Education of Women, an elite society in New York City that included several leading antisuffragists, tabled all further discussion of suffrage to focus on its mission of teaching women "how to participate efficiently, accurately and intelligently in civic affairs." In September 1917, as a wartime measure, members of the Lanham Study Club in Maryland voted to postpone all discussion of suffrage for the duration, and the women of Sorosis in New York City nearly came to blows when the group's leaders attempted in October 1917 to prevent any discussion of suffrage.[53]

Most clubs, though, debated suffrage openly. After years of stalling by southern clubwomen, the GFWC approved a federal suffrage amendment plank at its 1914 convention. The National Council of Jewish Women voted down a suffrage resolution when they met in 1917; a year later, members changed their minds. The Meridian, an elite club in New York City, was dominated by Helen Kendrick Johnson, one of the nation's most prominent female antisuffragists, who had testified in Albany and Washington against the franchise. But by 1917, the rank and file of the Meridian supported votes for women, noting that "suffrage could hardly be denied to those who had done such valiant war service, and were still doing it." Johnson conceded defeat, grumbling that she hoped women would "accept citizenship seriously."[54]

Women in suffrage organizations found themselves contemplating their response to the war. Some suffragists saw both a duty and an opportunity to display women's good citizenship in action. Florence Ellinwood Allen was an active clubwoman in Cleveland who lost two brothers in World War I; she spoke on behalf of the Liberty Loan and lectured on citizenship for the Cleveland Federation of Women's Clubs while playing a leading role in the Ohio suffrage movement. African-American women in Texas did not set aside their work for the Negro Women Voter Leagues while they cared for black soldiers in that state. NAWSA activist Ida Husted Harper responded angrily to criticisms that suffragists had put their own aims ahead of the nation's. Their loyalty is "above all question," Harper wrote in response to a negative editorial in a Dallas paper. Suffragist women were not putting rights ahead of obligations; they "made their own cause entirely secondary to military service. Their 'war work' has not been equalled." New York suffragist Mary Garrett Hay echoed Harper's claims. "We have always put our country first, and we shall continue to do so," she insisted.[55]

Some of the nation's leading suffragists were also pacifists, and under their pressure, some suffrage groups made no public commitments in support of the war, in hopes of preserving the single-issue focus they had worked so hard to craft. Other groups actively suppressed pacifist women, either out of a strategic concern that peace talk would brush the suffrage movement with the tar of sedition or, for some, because of their own support of American intervention in the global crisis. "I felt that we should have entered the world war even earlier than we did," radical suffragist Harriot Stanton Blatch later reflected.[56]

Many women found themselves in the middle, among them Carrie Chapman Catt. As president of NAWSA, the fifty-nine-year-old Catt was single-minded in her focus on the vote. But she hated war, too, had vigorously opposed it, and together with Jane Addams had organized the Woman's Peace Party in

1915 to fight it. But by early 1917, she saw matters in a new light. Catt framed the dilemma in a letter to NAWSA leaders. "Our suffrage work would unquestionably come to a temporary stand-still," she wrote, closing off members' fight between war and suffrage. Rather, she focused on the consequences of voluntarism. "The big question presents itself, shall suffragists do the 'war work' which they will undoubtedly want to do with other groups newly formed, thus running the risk of disintegrating our organizations, or shall we use our headquarters and our machinery for really helpful constructive aid to our nation?" Knowing that NAWSA women would volunteer for wartime service, Catt sought to protect the group's massive membership base and its institutional networks.[57]

Under Catt's reluctant guidance, NAWSA women poured themselves into war work. NAWSA officially supported the war before it was even declared. "We stand ready to serve our country with the zeal...which should ever characterize those who cherish high ideals of the duty and obligation of citizenship," members resolved in February 1917. The pacifist Catt even joined former NAWSA president Anna Howard Shaw on the Women's Council of the Committee of National Defense, even though Catt herself did little to aid the council and sheltered peace activists within NAWSA. At its 1917 convention, the group voted to give up lobbying Congress on the suffrage question for the duration. They canceled their 1918 convention as a war measure and devoted substantial resources to operating a hospital behind the front lines in France.[58]

"Bullets, not ballots," urged the *Woman Patriot*, as antisuffragist women tried to upstage their rivals in demonstrations of loyalty and patriotism. "Let us all quit being suffragists and anti-suffragists, and just be women backing up the men in every phase of fighting the war," echoed prominent antisuffragist Alice Hill Chittenden. In the war's early months, that sometimes happened; during an April 1917 military recruiting drive in New York City, suffragist women traveled the streets in cars lent or driven by antisuffragist women. But by October 1917, with women's suffrage on the upcoming ballot in New York State, suffragists and antisuffragists locked horns, and calls for unity became little more than attempts to stifle debate. Both sides urgently claimed the mantle of good citizenship. Mrs. A. J. George of Massachusetts argued that suffragists' claim on the vote as a reward for wartime loyalty revealed such women as "contingent patriots," and antisuffragists cast such frequent aspersions on the loyalty of suffragist women that Catt publicly complained that her opponents were trying to "impugn my loyalty as an American."[59]

Election Day in 1917 brought victory to the suffrage forces in New York, but the state's antisuffragists refused to admit defeat. They made first use of their new political power by petitioning the state legislature to repeal their right to vote, and they continued to wield their war service as a weapon against the suffragists. New York antisuffragists blamed radicals for the passage of women's suffrage and formed a "society of women who will conduct a militant campaign against socialism, against pacifism, and against all forms of pro-Germanism in New York City and State." Membership was open to all women, "provided only that they are unqualifiedly pro-American." The *New York Times* applauded the group's formation, noting that the women showed "sound judgment as well as sound patriotism," particularly in their campaigns to teach immigrant women the dangers of pacifism and socialism. "Suffrage being forced upon them, they are going to make, and help others make, the best use of it....They will be a force of intelligence, conservatism, and Americanism directed against the bedevilment and Bolshevikation of representative free government."[60]

Antisuffrage women often opposed the extension of the franchise because they feared the political influence of unassimilated immigrants and ethnic minorities; suffragists sometimes supported the vote for precisely the same reasons. Radical suffragists, frustrated that the Jones Act of 1917 had granted citizenship (and manhood suffrage) to residents of Puerto Rico, flew a banner asking "Mr. President... [Is] This the Porto Rican's Hour?" NAWSA President Carrie Chapman Catt had long made clear her dismay that black men and immigrant men could vote while responsible white women were excluded from the ballot. As she surveyed the home-front scene of wartime America, she grew even angrier. "Every slacker has a vote. Every newly made citizen will have a vote. Every pro-German who can not be trusted with any kind of military or war service will have a vote. Every peace-at-any-price man, every conscientious objector, and even the alien enemy will have a vote," she moaned. "It is a...danger to a country like ours to send 1,000,000 men out of the country who are loyal and not replace those men by the loyal votes of the women they have left at home." As she knocked on senators' doors, Catt claimed that suffrage women were loyal—and claimed suffrage for loyal women—at a moment when loyalty and citizenship were both under intense scrutiny.[61]

Women like Mary Church Terrell also came to Capitol Hill. Raised among the African-American elite of the new South that W. E. B. Du Bois called the "talented tenth," Terrell had been active in Washington politics for decades. A founder and former president of the National Association of Colored Women, the fifty-three-year-old Terrell actively supported the war effort by traveling the country to give speeches on "Uncle Sam and the Sons of Ham" and "How the War Will Solve the Race Problem." In June 1917, in a graduation speech at a black high school in Baltimore, Terrell reflected hopefully on the war's impact on African Americans. "A better time was coming for us," she told the students, firm in her belief that "for the first time in history the major portion of the civilized world was fighting for democracy and universal freedom." Despite recent racist violence, Terrell believed that "patriotic, justice-loving citizens in this country would do everything in their power to renew their allegiance to the principles for which this Republic has always stood." This, she thought, "would mean greater freedom and increased opportunities for my heavily handicapped race." For this mild rhetoric, Terrell was viciously attacked. The comptroller of the city of Baltimore, a white man who spoke after her at the commencement exercises, could barely control his rage. "You people need not expect to get any more liberty after the war than you are getting at the present time," he shouted, to the hisses of the audience. The *Baltimore American* denounced her speech as "seathing [*sic*] and bitter remarks at the white race." Fulfilling wartime obligations did not always expand Americans' rights.[62]

In the White House, suffragists confronted a president who ignored them, dismissed them, or evaded them. As late as 1913, Woodrow Wilson openly opposed women's suffrage, and a journalist close to the president recalled that Wilson thought "the only women interested in woman's suffrage were aggressive and masculine with harsh voices." But ever the consummate politician, Wilson tried to appease suffragists with words while insisting, as he told a 1914 delegation, that, limited by his party's platform, "I am not a free man." He told a 1916 suffrage convention in Atlantic City, New Jersey, that the vote was something "for which you can afford a little while to wait." At a meeting with suffragists on January 9, 1917, Wilson again insisted he was powerless to help them. Frustrated at Wilson's inaction, the fiery young suffragist Alice Paul walked out of the White House determined to do something.[63]

Raised by Quaker parents near Philadelphia, the thirty-two-year-old suffrage activist Alice Paul was absolutely uncompromising. And she was ambitious—so much so that she earned a law degree at night so that she could take on the nation's flawed suffrage laws. A decade before, fresh out of the University of Pennsylvania and living in London, Paul studied the tactics of militant British suffragists. Soon after returning to the United States, she led eight thousand women in a tumultuous protest at Woodrow Wilson's 1913 inauguration; political fallout from the Inauguration Day riot led to a congressional investigation and the sacking of the District of Columbia's police chief. Alice Paul quickly tired of the clubroom decorum of NAWSA, which she dismissed as "an immense debating society." After failing to convince the group to adopt more aggressive tactics, Paul bolted NAWSA and established

Alice Paul and other members of the National Woman's Party argued that suffrage for American women could not wait until the war's end. The opposition faced by the "pickets" in Washington linked suffragists to other victims of wartime violence. (*Courtesy of the Library of Congress Prints and Photographs Division*)

the National Woman's Party (NWP), which soon set up its headquarters across the street from the White House.[64]

The radical suffragists who joined Paul in the NWP chafed at the culture of obligation, and their arguments represented a direct feminist challenge to political obligation itself. For the radicals, suffrage was a fundamental right of citizenship, and no citizen could be complete without it. They also rejected any suggestion of a wartime social contract. "We will not bargain with our country for our services," said one NWP leader. "We will not say to our government: 'give us the vote and we will nurse your soldiers,' but we will insist on suffrage now." Paul's suffrage comrade Doris Stevens recalled that, during the war, "we did not regard Mr. Wilson as our President. We felt that he had neither political nor moral claim to our allegiance. War had been made without our consent." Woman's Party members objected to terms of citizenship made without their input, and unlike NAWSA, they explicitly voted to continue their suffrage work in wartime.[65]

The *Masses*, a radical paper that counted NWP members among its sub-scribers and authors, cheered them on. "The spectacle of women anxious to assist a military bureaucracy...in order to gain a political privilege, has been viewed with intense chagrin by those who regard the political emancipation of women as part and parcel of human emancipation." But to most Americans, the radical suffragists' message sounded like evidence of the same irresponsibil-ity practiced by conscientious objectors and civil libertarians. Indeed, one U.S. senator dismissed the suffrage protestors as "selfish and silly," almost exactly the words that the *Ladies' Home Journal* had used to describe the woman slacker. Alice Paul remained defiant: "if the lack of democracy at home weak-ens the...fight for democracy 3000 miles away," she said, then "the responsi-bility...is with the government and not the women of America." In a time of war, statements like Paul's could seem treasonous or even deranged. Charles L. Dana, a prominent neurologist, diagnosed a mental illness: suffragists were "neurotic women who want what they want right away and are impatient because the State does not...respond at once to their demand." It was hardly a mental leap, then, when Washington police attempted to commit Alice Paul to St. Elizabeth's Hospital for the Insane; she was temporarily detained there at about the same time as Edward Johnson, the conscientious objector from Wisconsin. The frenzy of reaction against the radical suffragists shows how hard these women pushed against reigning definitions of political obligation, and the ensuing tumult once again forced a contemplation of the place of violence in American public life.[66]

On January 11, 1917, Alice Paul did something that no one in American history had done before: she protested in front of the White House. In the past, groups had protested in Washington's public spaces or even rioted in the city, and some had politely petitioned at the gates of 1600 Pennsylvania Avenue. Although labor organizations had been fighting for decades for the right to assemble on picket lines, Alice Paul and the National Woman's Party "pickets" began something new—so new, in fact, that the term repeatedly appeared in quotation marks during the war, just like "conscientious objec-tor" and "slacker." Alice Paul, who had little connection with the labor move-ment, originally referred to her protest as a "perpetual delegation" rather than a picket. "Then they called it picketing. We didn't know enough to know what picketing was," she recalled, somewhat disingenuously, in a 1972 interview.

Beginning with a group of only twelve women, who gathered with a banner reading "How long must women wait for liberty?" Alice Paul and her fellow suffragists would continue to picket the White House, every day except Sunday, for over a year.[67]

Initial responses were favorable. Although Ohio Congressman Henry Emerson demanded that "the suffrage guard be withdrawn, as it is an insult to the President," the president himself seemed initially unfazed. He waved at the suffragists from his limousine and sent his guards out with hot coffee on winter days. The women knitted socks, sang songs, and courted publicity. But the tide began to turn just a few weeks later. In March 1917, NWP members hoped to meet with President Wilson on his second Inauguration Day. They found the White House gates locked; the time of their meeting came and went; and when Wilson's limousine sped out of the driveway onto Pennsylvania Avenue, he looked straight ahead. The Inauguration Day's events reveal a political culture in transition: the suffragists drew from older notions of entreaty and petition, recalling the days when presidents really did meet with "delegations" of strangers who walked up to the White House door. Wilson's refusal, his guards, and his presidential limousine all symbolized a powerful new state in action. "It looks like President Wilson's move," muttered one suffragist.[68]

On June 20, 1917, the women of the NWP crossed the line. In response to President Wilson's decision to send a diplomatic mission to Moscow, members of the National Woman's Party unfurled a banner comparing Americans' freedom to that in Russia, then in the first stage of what appeared to many Americans to be a democratic revolution. Their banner featured a particularly incendiary claim: "This Nation Is Not Free." The suffragists had deliberately aimed to provoke. "We did not expect public sympathy at this point," Stevens recalled. Nor did they get it. A crowd of several hundred women and men gathered angrily around the picketers. "Why don't you take that banner to Berlin?" shouted one woman. Walter Timmis of New York City was angry, too. "It's a shame that we have to give our sons to the service of the country and be confronted by such outrageous statements at the very White House gates."[69]

The question, though, was what to do about it. "Won't the police pull that thing down?" one man shouted to Secret Service guards standing nearby. But the guard had not yet finished transcribing the banner's text, which he hoped to use in criminal proceedings. "Can't you wait until I finish copying this?" he asked. Timmis then asserted his authority. "Come on, boys, let's tear that thing down," and they promptly did so. Others threw eggs and tomatoes; a sailor threw a punch, aimed directly at the jaw of suffragist Georgina Sturgis.

When she asked, "Why did you do that?" he paused. "I don't know," he said, then ran off. Women responded to Timmis's call, too, among them Mrs. Dee Richardson, who knocked a suffragist down, straddled her, and shouted "you dirty yellow traitor" while tearing the banner to shreds. Meanwhile, "the policeman industriously collected the bits for possible use as evidence."[70]

Wilson and the Washington police decided not to protect the picketing women but to regulate them more strenuously, substituting the power of the state for the collective voice of the people. They dusted off the statutes of the District of Columbia, and two days later, on June 22, as soon as the women commenced their protests, the police "started making arrests wholesale," charging forty-eight women with disorderly conduct, parading without a permit, "obstructing traffic," and "loud and boisterous talking." As women appeared in court to defend themselves, NWP activists connected with an emerging civil liberties movement. Suffragist Helen Hill Weed hardly knew her way around a courtroom; she stumbled as she attempted to defend herself at her trial in July 1917. "I am not a lawyer and am not certain as to what I may properly ask," she said, although that did not stop her from arguing her own defense—or articulating her own vision of political rights. Alice Paul, a practicing attorney, knew her way around a courtroom, and she recruited important allies, among them Dudley Field Malone, an eccentric crusading lawyer who would later work as Clarence Darrow's right-hand man during the Scopes trial in 1925.[71]

Malone, a faithful Democrat who had been appointed collector of the Port of New York, used his White House connections to set up a meeting with Woodrow Wilson on July 18, 1917, in which he confronted the president with evidence that his own cabinet members, together with the District of Columbia police, had provoked the crowds. Malone carefully avoided implicating the president; Wilson denied any knowledge of the plan but pardoned the women the next day. Released on July 20, the women immediately returned to the picket line. Every day the suffragists unfurled their banners; on August 14, 1917, they debuted a new sign referring to "Kaiser Wilson." And every day crowds attacked them. The crowds' methods "became physically more brutal and politically more stupid," recalled suffragist Doris Stevens. "Their conduct became lawless in the extreme."[72]

As crowds repeatedly attacked the suffrage signs—and the suffragists themselves—events played into the ongoing wartime debate about who held the authority to regulate responsible citizenship: the crowd or the police. In the private all-male confines of Washington's Chevy Chase Club, Attorney General Thomas Gregory expressed his views to fellow members—among them the NWP's lawyer, Dudley Field Malone. "Whenever women raised a disturbance as these women had done," Malone recalled him saying, "the thing to do was to ridicule them." Gregory reportedly said he "would like to sprinkle them with a hose." In October 1917, Alice Paul herself was arrested and sentenced to seven months in prison. The next month, police charged thirty-eight more women under the city's traffic regulations. Within weeks, dozens of radical suffragists filled the jails of the nation's capital; the most stubborn found themselves in "the hole" of Virginia's Occoquan Workhouse, where women experienced solitary confinement, psychiatric treatment, and forced feeding.[73]

Malone resigned his position in the Wilson administration on September 7 in protest over its repressive policies toward the suffragists and what he saw as a violation of the social contract—although he expressed his views in terms rather different from the radical suffragists: "How can the Government ask millions of American women . . . to give up by conscription their men and happiness . . . while these women citizens are denied the right to vote?" The NWP continued its charge for the suffragists in Occoquan. "The people . . . should publicly know what kind of a prison they have in their midst," thundered Malone. The assaults—and the hunger strikes—drew the attention of the national media, much to the embarrassment of the White House. The Wilson administration urged newspapers to bury their coverage of the NWP inside their papers in "a bare colorless chronicle," but the papers continued to splash the pickets across their front pages.[74]

Mainstream suffrage leaders repeatedly disavowed radical tactics. Members of the more moderate New York City Woman Suffrage Party reaffirmed their "belief in the quiet educational methods of propaganda" that they claimed had won suffrage for women in that state. They protested the "militant policy" of the National Woman's Party and "emphatically condemn[ed] its tactics as lamentably lacking in dignity, utility, common sense, and in the respect due the President of the United States as the head of a great nation." The radical suffragists didn't mind such attacks. "People who had never before thought of suffrage for women had to think of it," recalled Doris Stevens, "if only to the extent of objecting to the way in which we asked for it."[75]

Other women, who did not picket the White House but closely followed the fortunes of the imprisoned suffragists, developed interests in prison conditions and called for congressional investigations. As the suffrage radicals struggled to assert their vision of citizenship, they foregrounded a different vision of political obligation than the clubwomen: they imagined a solitary individual doing battle with the repressive power of the state. Many balked at the notion that the right to police the home front extended to the exercise of physical force against women.

"Unity is not to be obtained by dragging women to filthy jails for the crime of bearing banners upon which are inscribed the words from the President's lips," insisted one small-town Democratic politician in a letter to Woodrow Wilson. Draft dodgers and "pro-Germans" were one thing, but the flower of American womanhood was another. Colorado's Representative Edward Keating said he did "not like to see an exhibition of the mob spirit." If the pickets "were violating a law they should have been stopped in an orderly manner....A mob should never take charge of things in this country." The *New York Times*, echoing wartime arguments about pacifists and conscientious objectors, claimed the women of the NWP should be punished by neither mobs nor courts. "The place for them is the clinic of the pathologist or the psychiatrist....Witchcraft, tarantism, suffrage obsession, and its violent phenomena, are proper subjects, as this humaner age knows, for psychotherapy."[76]

Late one night in November 1917, David Lawrence walked into Alice Paul's cell at Occoquan. Friendly to the Wilson administration, Lawrence was a journalist, and no one knows how he gained access to her cell when no other reporter ever did. According to several accounts, Lawrence acted as an emissary from the White House, there to offer Alice Paul a bargain. If she would call off her picketing, Wilson would support the Nineteenth Amendment. No record of Paul's response remains, but soon after their meeting, her sentence was commuted, the picketing stopped, and within a year the president stood before the Senate of the United States. On September 30, 1918, as autumn broke the heat of Washington's summer and the war's tide had turned toward victory, Woodrow Wilson urged Congress to send the Nineteenth Amendment to the states for ratification. "We have made partners of the women in this war," he proudly noted. "Shall we admit them only to a partnership of suffering and sacrifice and toil and not to a partnership of privilege and right?" "We will not bargain with our country for our services," Paul's fellow suffragist had once insisted with passionate commitment and with disdain for the wartime bargains of the moderate suffragists knitting socks in clubrooms. What Alice Paul did not realize was that the state could make her bargain with her principles.[77]

★ *A Final Luncheon*

By the time the members of the New York City Federation of Women's Clubs sat down on Friday, February 1, 1918, for the luncheon concluding their annual convention, the women were restless and tired. Much had been accomplished, and the women had resolved to undertake even more to aid the nation during this time of crisis. The presence at lunch of Governor and Mrs. Charles Whitman showed the clubwomen's vital significance to the ongoing war effort. After the Whitmans left, Mrs. Thomas Massey rose to address the club.

And then the bombshell hit. Mrs. Massey announced that the New York City Federation of Women's Clubs was infested with disloyal clubwomen. The day before, Massey had overheard "strong pro-German sentiments," including those of one member who called the American flag a "dirty rag." Massey did not sit idly by in the face of such disloyalty. "I did not know who those women were, but I soon found out, and gave their names to the police. One of those women, I have seen in this room today." As the volume in the Astor Hotel ballroom rose noticeably, Massey pressed her point. We must act quickly, she said. "We must put all traitors out of our clubs. The Government should receive loyalty and co-operation from us and we can only give it by putting out every pro-German, or pacifist, or anyone who stands for a slacker."[78]

Massey proposed a resolution, which began by affirming that the club-women of the New York City Federation were "true patriots, whose loyalty could not be questioned," and resolved that any member who "favors pacifism or express [sic] sentiments of a disloyal or treasonable character, shall be reported to the Executive Board." As she stepped back from the podium, the room exploded. The response in the ballroom was immediate and heated; several women rose to speak in favor of the resolution. Violating the federation's strict rules of order, one woman shouted out from the floor that "the names of any women who are traitors should be made public." Federation President Mrs. John Francis Yawger replied that the police had urged Massey not to reveal the names, but another clubwoman remained indignant. "Do you mean that these traitors among us should not receive a public trial?" she called. Massey's resolution passed in a nearly unanimous rising vote; only two women remained seated, among them one said to be a dedicated suffragist and a supporter of Alice Paul's radical protest tactics.[79]

But the work of the clubwomen was not yet done. At the end of their luncheon, Mrs. J. Hungerford Milbank rose to propose that the federation form a regiment of volunteers and place itself at the service of the country. Milbank had been actively recruiting a female detachment even before the United States entered the war and since that time had taken to wearing a self-designed khaki uniform. She believed that the Germans would certainly reach America, and soon. "You will need to know how to handle a gun, either to kill an enemy or yourself," she warned her listeners. For Milbank, war and suffrage had fundamentally transformed the political obligations of the women in her audience that day. "With your enfranchisement, you have been given liberty with one hand and obligation to serve with the other. Will you do it?"

"Yes, yes," shouted the women.[80]

With that simple articulation of the tension between liberty and obligation, Milbank captured the wartime dilemma of many of America's women. The hearty replies she received in the ballroom of the Astor Hotel suggested how far they would go to resolve it.

4

Policing the Home Front:
From Vigilance to Vigilantism

✮ ✮

In the early morning hours of April 5, 1918, a mob lynched Robert Prager, a German-American coal miner, near Collinsville, Illinois. On April 3, a group of miners, who believed Prager was a German spy, had forcibly marched him through a nearby town and delivered him to "protective custody" in Collinsville. The next night, a bigger crowd came for Prager. They stripped him of his shirt, pants, and shoes, wrapped him in the American flag, and marched him through the streets. The mayor looked on passively; when the crowd passed the town line, Collinsville's police turned back. A few hours later, the mob strung Prager up on the branch of a lone hackberry tree on the outskirts of town and then dropped his body three times, in the words of one participant, "one for the red, one for the white, and one for the blue."[1]

Violence has been a persistent feature of American political life, a point that was not lost on Robert Prager, who told the mob to "go ahead and kill me, but wrap me in the flag when you bury me." The era of World War I marked the high point of one kind of political violence in American history, as the actions of repressive state institutions, private organizations, and spontaneous crowds left more than seventy Americans dead and thousands terrorized by tar, flame, or the noose. Yet the same years also witnessed the invigoration of political arguments that questioned extralegal authority and laid the groundwork for the legal and political dismantling of vigilantism in the twentieth century.[2]

One such effort came from the White House on July 26, 1918, when President Woodrow Wilson condemned mob rule in America. Wilson was angered that the enemy German press had used Prager's killing in its wartime propaganda, and he felt increasing pressure from civil libertarians at home. In a public proclamation, Wilson insisted on the rule of law, particularly in wartime. He claimed that "no man who loves America, no man who really cares for her fame and honor and character,...can justify mob action while the courts of justice are open and the governments of the States and the Nation are ready and able to do their duty." The mob spirit, Wilson averred, was irreconcilable with American democracy. "Every American who takes part in the action of a mob or gives it any sort of countenance is no true son of this great Democracy, but its betrayer, and does more to discredit her...than the words of her statesmen or the sacrifices of her heroic boys in the trenches can do to make suffering peoples believe her to be their savior."[3]

Widely reprinted, Wilson's address found an eager audience in the press and among private citizens. Writing from Washington, Reverend J. Milton Waldron called Wilson's words "strong, manly, righteous" and his stand "one of the finest things you have ever done for oppressed humanity." The *New York Times* called the speech "a pondered admonition with whose purpose and expression" no American "can disagree." Opponents of wartime lawlessness consistently called vigilantism "un-American"; several even went so far as to suggest it was the work of German spies. If violence is so integral to American history, then why was Wilson's denunciation so stirring? The explanation turns on the distinction between vigilance and vigilantism. On the home front, Americans proudly called themselves vigilant citizens and believed that they were doing work much needed—and explicitly requested—by the national government. In that assumption, they were not wrong. Leading public figures, drawing on long-standing traditions equating citizenship with obligation, did call on Americans to stand vigilant during the war. Appealing to habits of voluntary association, they supported the organization of vigilance movements nationwide: committees of safety, women's vigilance leagues, home guards. The government depended on the voluntary work of such groups for the success of the nation's war mobilization effort. "This country," boasted Justice Department official John Lord O'Brian just two weeks after Prager's killing, "is being policed more thoroughly and successfully than ever before in its history."[4]

Yet some of those same figures also spoke out against vigilantism, few more eloquently than Woodrow Wilson in his July 1918 statement. When they did so, they did not have the vigilance societies in mind. What Wilson and those who shared his outlook meant was something more specific and rarer: the mob, conceived as a violent, spontaneous, and extralegal public group. As national leaders denounced the mob in ever more frequent calls for "law and order," they attempted to separate vigilance and vigilantism. They cast the former as a valuable work of service and voluntarism that embodied American democracy, and they attacked the latter as incompatible with what Wilson had called the nation's "standards of law and of right."

The distinction took on great significance. Americans who engaged in extralegal actions to support the war effort insisted that they were exemplars of vigilant citizenship. Their victims denounced them as lawless vigilantes unworthy of the nation's honor. In their sudden preoccupation with the distinction between legitimate and illegitimate political coercion, Americans partially revised the place of law in the system of political obligation. The attack on mobs and vigilantism gave new energies to civil libertarians; wartime events that made political violence possible and visible also undermined the legitimacy of that violence. Government officials who denounced lawless vigilantism focused on physical violence, which they said was politically illegitimate because it subverted the spirit of a nation of laws. The wartime and postwar concern with mob violence led many to ignore legal and nonviolent forms of state and private coercion that arose alongside, and outlasted, crowd actions. The distinction obscured the ways that Americans wove coercion into the fabric of their political culture during this period.

★ The Obligation of Vigilance

As long as Americans have claimed the right to rule themselves, they have also insisted on the authority to police each other. In the early republic, they tied vigilance to concepts of popular sovereignty, but vigilance was also a political practice whereby collective policing by private citizens contributed to community defense. By the time of the U.S. entry into war in April 1917, Americans were long accustomed to the idea that citizens had a positive obligation to police one another. Such policing, many believed, could involve coercion.[5]

Vigilantism, too, has played a recurrent role in American history. Vigilantism is often equated with mob violence and thought to consist of political terror and violent coercion, and use of the term conjures up images of night riders and frontier justice. Violence is clearly an element—the years between 1767 and 1951 witnessed more than 5,400 killings by organized and unorganized groups. But although vigilantism could and did often become deadly, neither killing nor physical violence is a necessary component. Rather, vigilantism is fundamentally about law, and political arguments about it articulate relationships between citizens and the system of law in which they operate. The citizens who undertake vigilante actions are not public officers, even if they sometimes cooperate with officials or claim to act in the name of the state. To be a vigilante is to operate outside the strictures of law as articulated by the legitimate regime, even if the aim is to establish social order on its behalf.[6]

Anglo-American common law traditions demanded that citizens—particularly male citizens—participate in defending the community. Self-defense included community policing: individuals could initiate a citizen's arrest or be deputized by local authorities; those who heard the "hue and cry" of distressed persons were obliged to come to their aid; militias gathered most able-bodied adult men for service; the common-law rule of *posse comitatus* gave sheriffs the power to summon the same men to preserve the public peace. In the years immediately preceding World War I, those practices appeared to be on the decline. Policing had been partly professionalized, particularly in urban areas, and the newly reorganized National Guard had begun to replace state and local militias. But while the reach of law enforcement had displaced the posse and the hue and cry in most of the United States by 1917, this process was hardly complete and universal, as extralegal actions in the Jim Crow South demonstrated. Nor were myths and memories of colonial days and the western frontier far from the minds of either the general public or the national elite. Wilson's Attorney General Thomas Gregory had commented favorably on the Reconstruction-era Ku Klux Klan in a 1906 speech. In 1915, former President Theodore Roosevelt, discussing the work of vigilantes in the western territories in the nineteenth century, claimed that their work was "in the main wholesome."[7]

In 1917, private and community methods of maintaining order dominated labor relations. Corporations regularly employed private police such as the Pinkertons to break up strikes and infiltrate unions. To supplement such mercenary forces, business leaders recruited citizen volunteers. State and federal officials who saw little active role for the state in economic life generally supported antilabor vigilance groups. From time to time, politicians disputed the groups' methods, and labor organizations consistently challenged their legal status. But in the pre–World War I era, when the courts were no more sympathetic to labor than were other arms of the American government, workers often saw little to gain by appealing to the rule of law.[8]

The obligation of vigilance made Americans the guardians of the moral welfare of their fellow citizens as well, as in the national prohibition campaigns that gathered force before World War I. Similarly, efforts to curtail prostitution coalesced in the 1910s into a movement to abolish it. Supporters of the prohibition and purity movements pursued legislative campaigns and established vigilance societies. For more than thirty years, Anthony Comstock's

Society for the Suppression of Vice sought to cleanse New York City's nightlife. Beginning in 1910, the Progressive reformer Maude Miner recruited working-class young women into the New York Girls' Protective League. "Girls do not go out as detectives," Miner wrote in 1916, "but when they come face to face with it . . . they recognize their obligation to help in remedying it." This volunteer police force sought to discipline young women both by force of law and through what reformers called "personal work"—informal practices of public lectures, household visits, and even accusatory letters. Antivice activists viewed the legal system with ambivalence. Often, frustrated by corrupt police and judges, they chose to work outside the system. At other times they cooperated with courts, either when using the law to crack down on prostitutes, madams, and pimps, or when they sought to help women by establishing special courtroom procedures or reforming women's prisons.[9]

A similar tradition of collective policing, predominantly but not exclusively in the South, suppressed African-American militancy and controlled African-American labor. Vigilance groups enforced white racial supremacy with force and terror. The number of lynchings had somewhat declined since the 1890s, but the war years saw an increase in violence and the formation of new white supremacist citizen groups, none more notorious than the Ku Klux Klan, reestablished in 1915. Such groups enjoyed the support of formal state institutions at every level of American government, which consistently declined to intervene in matters deemed local or wholly private. Leading black reformers strenuously challenged the methods and even the legitimacy of such groups, and genteel New South reformers politely petitioned for order. In the tumult of wartime politics, their calls for action would grow more strident, but by 1917, they had made little headway.[10]

In many areas of everyday life, therefore, Americans participated in or endured citizen vigilance, and by 1917, some were already debating how to rein in extralegal coercion. With war's declaration, vigilance movements expanded, and their relationship to the state changed: vigilance organizations gained force and authority as they spoke in the name of the wartime state, but their new position also exposed them to criticism by those who denied their legitimacy. The wartime debate about political violence, although not entirely new, was conducted on an altered terrain.

Government officials and other leading public figures called on American citizens, male and female, to stand vigilant for the duration. A poster from New York's Conference Committee on National Preparedness urged defense against spies and traitors: "Men of America, be of clear vision! . . . Promptly deliver up these advance agents to public scorn and to the law, so that when you go to your home at night you can look into the innocent eyes of your children and be unafraid." A similar poster printed by the New Hampshire Committee on Public Safety urged "promptness in recognizing and reporting suspicious or disloyal actions to your local authorities or to us. . . . [Help] your local Committee on Public Safety in every way." In a 1917 Flag Day speech, President Wilson warned that "vicious spies and conspirators" had "spread sedition amongst us" and "sought by violence to destroy our industries and arrest our commerce," and throughout the war he consistently encouraged private citizen vigilance. "Woe be to the man or group of men that seeks to stand in our way," Wilson ominously concluded.[11]

Americans who wanted to do their part for the war found explicit instruction in an editorial in New York State's *Albany Journal* akin to those published in thousands of wartime newspapers:

> If you ever, on the street or in a trolley car, should hear some soft-shell pacifist or hard-boiled but poorly camouflaged pro-German, make seditious or unpatriotic remarks about your Uncle Sam you have the right and privilege of taking that person by the collar, hand him over to the nearest policeman or else take him yourself before the magistrate.
>
> You do not require any official authority to do this and the only badge needed is your patriotic fervor. The same thing applies to women. Every American, under provisions of the code of civil procedure, has the authority to arrest any person making a remark or utterance which "outrages public decency."[12]

Hundreds of thousands of men and women responded to calls for national defense on the home front by forming voluntary vigilance associations. They varied widely in their aims, structures, and membership. Elite societies such as the National Security League and American Defense Society engaged in more lobbying than policing. The American Protective League enrolled more than 250,000 men, and some women, in the largest vigilance society, but there were many others. Philadelphia Mayor Thomas Smith called for twenty-one thousand men, "physically normal, of good character," to defend the city; in Berkeley, California, the Nathan Hale Volunteers signed up "to cooperate with the United States Army, Western Department." More menacing organizations included the Sedition Slammers and Terrible Threateners, and even the Boy Spies of America.[13]

The work of these vigilant citizens uncovered not a single German spy, and much of what they did was ineffectual or even absurd. Volunteers in New Haven, Connecticut, kept a round-the-clock watch at an antiaircraft device they had installed to protect the city against a highly unlikely aerial invasion from Germany. The earnest patriots of a vigilance group in Portland, Maine, seized a suitcase abandoned in downtown Longfellow Square. They "gingerly" brought the bag to police headquarters, where it was "carefully examined and was found to contain a quantity of men's soiled underwear."[14]

Other stories, however, offer little comic relief. During the war, vigilance societies targeted pacifists, suffragists, ethnic minorities, religious fundamentalists, trade unionists, and socialists. Incidents of violent, spontaneous pro-war crowd actions abounded, but organized groups conducted most of the political coercion, often in close collaboration with the institutions of government and civil society already in place in local communities. Those organizations glossed over or ignored issues of legal process and wasted little energy in precisely establishing their authority to make arrests. They were not thoughtless mobs who believed the Constitution was a meaningless scrap of paper, even as they appeared to treat it as such. They were organized men and women deeply concerned about the survival of American democracy as they understood it.

Wartime calls for citizen vigilance raised the demand for volunteer policing; wartime rhetoric and fears of subversion heightened its significance. The war also altered the relationship between private political coercion and the state, turning social control into a political obligation. Americans were accustomed to private citizens policing their neighbors before World War I. Yet it was only during the war—as their neighbors had to be mobilized, regulated, and governed—that the practices of citizen policing came to be state projects, even when they were not conducted under state auspices. The needs of modern war tied private coercions to state interests.

★ *Defending the Connecticut Home Front*

If you didn't go to France, you could guard the home front. Men in the Citizens' Protective League of Covington, Kentucky, stockpiled arms, and other townspeople volunteered as public speakers. Their female patriotic counterparts in New Jersey formed an espionage committee and a gun club as they knitted socks and scarves. Whether federal or state governments had legally authorized the groups was not always on their minds. Good citizenship for the wartime civilian required voluntary service for the war effort and vigilance in all matters. Events in the industrial state of Connecticut demonstrate the role of volunteer policing in war mobilization.[15]

On March 9, 1917, facing the prospect that the existing state militia would be federalized and shipped off to France, the Connecticut legislature authorized the formation of the Connecticut Home Guard, "a body of armed troops for constabulary duty within the state." By the time of the Armistice, 19,336 citizens had worn its makeshift secondhand cotton uniforms. All were men, mostly above draft age or otherwise exempt. Their leaders were bankers, lawyers, and doctors, but its rank and file included small businessmen, farmers, traveling salesmen, and clerks. Most were experienced members of fraternal organizations; only a few were military veterans. Nearly all were native-born white Protestants in a state deeply divided by ethnic and religious tensions.[16]

The Connecticut Home Guard was dedicated to the defense of the state and its industries, especially munitions. Charles Burpee, a local historian and himself a colonel in the Home Guard, later wrote that "though the mass of the so-called 'foreign' population was devoted to Connecticut principles, Germans included, a very contrary socialistic element . . . had organized, and the Deutschland genius for working mischief behind the lines had been evidenced." The Home Guard's authorizing legislation limited its powers. It had little legal authority; its members, for example, were specifically forbidden to make arrests. Guardsmen, however, regularly disregarded such formalities.[17]

The Home Guard quickly started work, collaborating with other voluntary associations, industrial corporations, and the federal government. Their first task was to coordinate the state's military census of May 1917, which aimed to record vital data on every adult man in the state in preparation for military conscription. They later stood watch during selective service registration calls and showed their strength in Home Guard parades in towns across the state just before registration day. As the Home Guard noted in its official report, the parades "gave to certain inhabitants of the State a salutary object lesson and warning which they needed" at a time when some of Connecticut's young men were surely considering draft evasion. The Home Guard also vigilantly protected the state's railroad bridges and power installations from all enemies foreign and domestic. In January 1918, acting on a spurious tip that the radical unionists of the Industrial Workers of the World (IWW) planned to set fire to industrial facilities and bomb the bridges of the New York, New Haven and Hartford Railroad, four thousand guardsmen stood watch through the cold winter night.[18]

The Connecticut Home Guard also collaborated with other wartime organizations, particularly the American Protective League. In April 1918, just days after Robert Prager's killing, members of the two groups were so angered to learn that the U.S. Attorney's office had refused to indict Hartford's socialists for sedition that they invaded the radicals' weekly meeting. Seizing the stage, Charles Burpee demanded that the socialists pledge allegiance to the flag and warned them of the dangers of their disloyalty. "This city must be purified," he announced. "The law will act according to the law's own course. In this city we have plenty of citizens ready to back up the law and show the law its course....All law depends on public opinion. Public opinion makes law. No law can be supported without public opinion. When the people enter a great war like this, they are the law." Burpee offered the vigilant citizen's understanding of political obligation: not bald-faced disrespect for the law (although it must have seemed that way to the Hartford socialists) but a theory of citizenship that located sovereignty in the people and would not separate the power of the state from that of the citizens who constituted it and had been authorized to act in its name.[19]

The men of the Connecticut Home Guard described themselves as the descendants of the Minutemen who had defended the New England countryside more than a century before, and in retrospect, the work they did seems unexceptional in the state's long history of industrial strife and ethnic tension. Fearing revolution or subversion, the men of the Home Guard viewed the law as a tool they could manipulate, rather than a set of institutional constraints to obey. Nor, it appears, did they deem violent coercion illegitimate, as their raid on the socialist meeting demonstrates. As Burpee later noted, the guardsmen "were comfort and satisfaction especially to the munitions plants and the managers of the railroads." If corporate bosses cheered them, so, too, did the thankful crowds that filled Hartford's streets on Armistice Day, and Governor Marcus Holcomb decorated them in front of the state capitol. Their coercions were not unknown in prewar industrial centers such as urban Connecticut, but the war effort folded them into the national war project in ways that highlighted their ambiguous legal status. In Connecticut, there was little public opposition to that ambiguity. Elsewhere the actions of vigilance organizations led some critics to try to disentangle the interwoven threads of public and private that these groups represented.[20]

★ Keeping Vigil over the Copper Mines

Bisbee, Arizona, a small copper-mining city near the U.S.-Mexican border, witnessed a crisis of coercion, authority, and political legitimacy in July 1917. The rule of law did not have a firm hold in Arizona that summer. Mining companies wielded enormous power at their own mines, with private police forces and citizens' groups on hand. Government backed them up, too; state and local officials regularly sided with the corporations against the workers and left the day-to-day governance of much of the state almost entirely in the hands of the mine bosses.

War mobilization changed both the copper industry and the significance of labor unrest, which reached new highs nationwide during the war. "These labor troubles in the West disturb the President," wrote Secretary of Labor William B. Wilson. "The need of copper is tremendous." Indeed it was: military demand for copper sent the mineral's price skyrocketing, along with corporate profits, even as the wartime inflationary spiral left workers feeling pinched. Labor shortages, caused in part by draft call-ups, made workers at the Phelps-Dodge mines in Bisbee more confident about unionizing in response. Some opted for the more moderate International Union of Mine, Mill and Smelter Workers, a branch of the American Federation of Labor, but most workers in Bisbee chose the radical unionism of the Metal Mine Workers Industrial Union No. 800, affiliated with the IWW.[21]

On June 27, 1917, more than half the 4,700 workers at the Copper Queen mine in Bisbee walked off the job. Their bitter strike dragged on for weeks; copper production reached a near-standstill. Mine owners, town leaders, and the national press interpreted the strikers' actions as disloyal and outrageous. No one was more disturbed than Harry E. Wheeler, a forty-one-year-old former Arizona Ranger captain who served as Cochise County sheriff. Wheeler's hard-won reputation for being evenhanded in his dealings with labor and capital may have led to his selection to the county draft board. But in the summer of 1917, Wheeler was troubled by labor unrest, and in the shadow of the Zimmermann Telegram's hint of a German-Mexican conspiracy, he worried about immigrants as well. "The majority of strikers seem foreign," he announced, and telegraphed Governor Thomas Campbell in distress: "The whole thing appears to be pro-German and anti-American." Bisbee residents could not call on the Arizona militia, which had already been called into federal service. So they formed two organizations to oppose the strike: the Citizens' Protective League gathered business leaders and middle-class locals, and the Workmen's Loyalty League organized nonstriking mine workers. Wheeler would later testify that after the leader of the IWW strike committee "said he could no longer control his men, I made up my mind that something had to be done.... To protect the law-abiding citizens of the community, I decided that I would strike first," he claimed. "I was left here alone. Everybody deserted me."[22]

Before dawn on July 12, 1917, Sheriff Wheeler deputized more than two thousand members of the two leagues, as well as hundreds of privately hired

On July 12, 1917, more than two thousand members of local vigilance groups volunteered to expel striking workers from the copper-mining town of Bisbee, Arizona. (*Courtesy of the Arizona Historical Society/Tucson, AHS 42669*)

detectives and the president of the Phelps-Dodge Corporation, who "happened to be in Bisbee on the day of the deportation." Wheeler told the men that the federal government had authorized the leagues to deport the strikers (although they had not been so authorized), gave his new deputies white armbands, and set them to work rounding up "on the charges of vagrancy, treason, and of being disturbers of the peace of Cochise County all those strange men who have congregated here." The deportation itself was a political circus that indiscriminately detained men, women, and children, regardless of their opinions on the war or their actions during the strike. Two men—one a striker and the other a member of the Citizens' Protective League—were killed during the raid. By midday, Bisbee's workers huddled under armed guard in a baseball park in a neighboring town. After each man "was asked if he wanted to go to work or if he could give the name of a reliable citizen who would vouch for him," the league men marched almost 1,200 of them at gunpoint onto trains provided by the El Paso and Southwestern Railroad and "deported" them to New Mexico, where they were unceremoniously dumped in the desert town of Hermanas.[23]

For the next four months, the Citizens' Protective League, along with the more patrician Chamber of Commerce in nearby Douglas, effectively ruled Bisbee from a temporary headquarters in a building owned by the copper companies. The league issued "passports" to town residents after oral examinations that mingled questions about the war with questions about the strike. No one could enter or leave Bisbee without a pass; no one found work—or got a draft exemption—without one, either. Men and women who failed the league's loyalty tests were excluded from the city, deported, or imprisoned and sent to work at the copper mines in convict labor gangs. The rule of the Citizens' Protective League continued until late November 1917 and was suspended only after pressure from President Wilson and orders from Arizona's attorney general.[24]

The Citizens' Protective League claimed that its work was vital to the war. Its spokesmen argued that they had taken the law into their own hands to defend law, not to violate it. Wheeler intended his deportation not as a seizure of power from the federal government but as an invitation to the state to act. When asked why he ordered the train cars to take the striking workers to New Mexico, Wheeler replied, "I wanted the troops to have them." In a telegram to the president, Governor Campbell noted that "citizens in the many mining communities affected, feeling that peace officers cannot afford adequate protection, are acting,...meantime praying for federal intervention." Campbell, Wheeler, and the corporations insisted that it was the IWW strikers who were lawless. Asked under what law he was operating, the sheriff admitted he didn't know. "I have no statute that I had in mind. Perhaps everything I did wasn't legal.... It became a question of 'Are you an American, or are you not?'" As Wheeler told the state attorney general, "If we are guilty of taking the law into our own hands, I can only cite to you the Universal Law that necessity makes.... I would repeat the operation any time I find my own people endangered by a mob composed of eighty per cent aliens and enemies of my Government." Across the country, many Americans cheered the raiders' work, distinguishing their vigilance from lawless vigilantism. The *Los Angeles Times* congratulated the posse, noting that "the citizens of Cochise County, Arizona, have written a lesson that the whole of America would do well to copy." Former president Theodore Roosevelt insisted that "no human being in his senses doubts that the men deported from Bisbee were bent on destruction and murder."[25]

The deportation's critics placed the leagues on the other side of the divide between vigilance and vigilantism and insisted on the need for legal process. From Florence, Arizona, J. Sheik claimed that the copper companies "had taken, as it were, the government from out of [the Governor's] hands and were running it to suit their needs." Samuel Gompers, the president of the American Federation of Labor, also blamed the leagues. "Some of the men deported are said to be law-abiding men engaged in an earnest effort at improvement of their condition.... There is no law of which I am aware that gives authority to private citizens to undertake to deport from the state any man. If there be lawlessness, it is surely such conduct."[26]

"I made up my mind that something had to be done," insisted Cochise County Sheriff Harry Wheeler, who led the Bisbee deportation. (*Harry Wheeler Papers, Courtesy of the Bisbee Mining & Historical Museum*)

Robert Bruère, a labor journalist, investigated events in Bisbee after the deportation. Amid World War I even Bruère could not countenance subversion of the war effort by striking workers, and he echoed the copper corporations in his criticisms of IWW radicalism. But Bruère insisted that the wartime need for order still did not outweigh the value of legal process. The citizens' leagues, he suggested, were the dangerous and lawless elements in southern Arizona. "When...we look more closely at the things which the copper companies did, we are startled to find their policy inspired by the same distrust of the State, of the constituted authorities of Arizona and the Federal Government, for which they themselves condemned the I.W.W. as an 'outlaw' organization." The *New York Times* solemnly intoned that "Bisbee had the right to defend itself against violence, not to do violence," although editors suggested that the proper solution would have been to arrest all 1,200 strikers on vagrancy charges.[27]

The Bisbee raids prompted conflicting responses from officials in Washington. Immediately after the workers walked out in June, Labor Secretary William Wilson expressed his relief that the secretary of war had decided not to dispense "troops or secret service men" to deal with the situation in Bisbee. Hours after the raid, President Wilson assured Governor Campbell that federal troops were on their way to quiet the town, but added, "Meantime may I not respectfully urge the great danger of citizens taking the law in their own hands as you report their having done. I look upon such action with grave apprehension. A very serious responsibility is assumed when such precedents are set."[28]

The federal government had encouraged citizen vigilance through its support for the Arizona Home Guards and its toleration of private policing in a mining industry necessary for war production. Writing from Camp Sevier in Greenville, South Carolina, the Arizona native Clifford Faires noted that in Globe, another Arizona mining town, the Loyalty League was busily "preserving law and order and . . . fostering patriotism in a community where it was sadly lacking." Boasting that recently "notice was received from Washington that this effort at safeguarding the peace is to be rewarded by Federal recognition and supervision," Faires perceptively identified the complicated and contradictory response of a government that depended on citizen vigilance yet actively tried to rein in vigilantism.[29]

As details of the Bisbee deportation reached the White House in July, key figures in the administration came to regret their slow response to the crisis. Wilson ordered an investigation and appointed the President's Mediation Commission (PMC), a board of lawyers and labor bureaucrats generally liberal and sympathetic to labor. The PMC, under the direction of Labor Secretary William Wilson and his trusty assistant, Felix Frankfurter, worked in southern Arizona throughout the fall of 1917 and the next year issued a report highly critical of the deportations. The report also condemned the postdeportation reign of law and order by the Citizens' Protective League and the Chamber of Commerce; as a cure for industrial strife, it urged greater cooperation between labor and management, to be facilitated by the federal government. But one of the PMC's greatest concerns was that the leagues had undermined the effectiveness of other wartime loyalty organizations: "Such agencies of the 'public' as the so-called 'loyalty leagues' only serve to intensify bitterness, and, more unfortunately, to the minds of workers in the West serve to associate all loyalty movements with partisan and anti-union aims."[30]

The report was not without its critics. Governor Campbell insisted that the IWW posed the true threat to law: they had "brought about a reign of lawlessness, invading the constitutional rights of the whole body politic." Theodore Roosevelt called the report "as thoroughly misleading a document as could be written on the subject," angry not only at the PMC's coddling of strikers but of its criticisms of one of the leaders of the roundup, Jack Greenway, who had been a Rough Rider with T.R. twenty years before.[31]

The wartime mobilization of American industry had changed the context of the tense relations between labor and management. Accustomed to maintaining order through citizens' groups and private police forces, the copper companies and the town leaders who supported them drew on traditions of antilabor vigilance in Bisbee in the summer of 1917. In part, the war was only a pretext that gave extra force to the bosses' existing authority. But it was more than that. Raiders tied their work—and the actions of the strikers—to the fortunes of the war effort and claimed to speak with the authority of the state in their ongoing contests over power. Sheriff Wheeler justified the July 12 raid by saying of the strike, "This is no labor trouble. We are sure of that; but it is a direct attempt to embarrass the government of the United States." The wartime need for industrial mobilization made the government dependent on such organizations even as some of its officials questioned their legitimacy. Most of the leagues' actions were supported, even in the U.S. Supreme Court, which heard a challenge to the deportation on the grounds that it had infringed freedom of movement. The Court dismissed the claim as a state issue in which the federal government had no interest.[32]

By making a labor dispute into a high-stakes matter of war mobilization, the leagues also opened the door for workers to use that formulation as a weapon and to call on state institutions in their own defense. The press debated the leagues' coercion, and the Wilson administration condemned it. The fundamental idea that citizens had a duty of vigilance—which had prompted the formation of such organizations as the Citizens' Protective League—was never fully discredited. But the court challenges and federal investigations laid the groundwork for new approaches that would come to the fore in later decades.

★ *Protecting Women from Themselves*

As soldiers gathered in the nation's hastily constructed military camps, their presence transformed the surrounding communities. Many residents welcomed the young men and organized recreational and social service opportunities; others worried that the camps betokened imminent moral collapse. Secretary of War Newton D. Baker felt the army had an "inescapable responsibility" to uphold its half of the social contract. "We can not allow these young men, most whom will have been drafted into service, to be surrounded by a vicious and demoralizing environment," he said, and in May 1917 he warned state governors that he would move military facilities if "clean conditions cannot be secured." "These camps," he announced, "shall not be places of temptation and peril."[33]

Military police operating with the authority of law undertook much of the antivice work of the World War I era; Sections 12 and 13 of the Selective Service Act made it a federal offense to sell alcohol or operate a house of ill repute within five miles of a camp. But the enforcement of that legislation folded into—and dramatically transformed—the obligation of moral vigilance and citizen policing of personal behavior and female sexuality. Some of the young women brought under suspicion as "charity girls" were in fact commercial prostitutes, but most were guilty only of offending middle-class understandings of proper female behavior. Many Americans lumped them all together as a subversive assault on the effectiveness of U.S. troops. As D. J. Poynter of Albion, Nebraska, wrote to Secretary Baker: "Shoot the lewd women as you would the worst German spy; they do more damage than all the spys [*sic*]."[34]

The suppression of vice brought federal policy together with voluntary associations, particularly the American Social Hygiene Association, an antiprostitution group bankrolled in the prewar years by John D. Rockefeller Jr. Soon after the passage of the Selective Service Act, the War Department established, in conjunction with its Commission on Training Camp Activities, its Law Enforcement Division and installed at its head Bascom Johnson, the attorney for the American Social Hygiene Association and a veteran of decades of antivice work in San Francisco. It was a vision of cooperation between state and civil society that warmed many voluntarists' hearts. It even went by the name of the "American Plan."[35]

One arm of the Law Enforcement Division was the Committee on Protective Work for Girls (CPWG). The committee was charged with patrolling areas around military establishments to protect soldiers from the dangers of prostitution and, as Jane Addams bluntly put it in a December 1917 public discussion on the topic, to "care for foolish girls who do not know how to take care of themselves." Suppressing vice was a federal policy, and women and men in official positions dominated the bureaucracy that oversaw it, but the military authorized and coordinated the volunteers who conducted the nightly work of surveillance, investigation, and internment. The CPWG established a Protective Bureau in every city that had a military training camp. Conceived as official police forces, the bureaus were in practice staffed largely by volunteers, mostly because of the CPWG's insistence that the enforcers be female. In the words of one War Department official, "it is a woman's job to work with women."[36]

The official endeavors of the CPWG intersected with the private initiatives of middle-class women's clubs in military communities. It also gave them new power: in Portland, Oregon, policewoman Lola Baldwin had been struggling for a decade for the authority to clamp down on vice; suddenly, armed with specific instructions from the War Department to "obtain by special ordinance any regulations or facilities germane" to her work, Baldwin forged ahead. The convergence of governmental and private policing brought the structures of coercion down hard on allegedly loose women. Henrietta Additon, the CPWG's assistant director, noted that "all the resources of occupation, education, health, recreation and religion in the community are brought into play." "Such is the power of patriotism wedded to the ideal of a great cause," boasted Lieutenant George Anderson.[37]

Maude Miner transferred her energies from volunteer work to wartime government service. In a lecture to the War Work Council of the YWCA National Board, Miner urged the women of the Y to practice vigilance, and she tolerated no slackers: "Every one who has been around can help. At times you are too busy at work and too tired to do anything. Combine a little trolley car ride with some scouting work. You will find you cannot help but follow some of these youngsters home and help them." When asked after the lecture how women could get authority for the patrols, she told her listeners, "Just by asking for it. . . . All of us have a certain amount of power. We can stop a little girl and find out about her and learn of the danger and start the work, and then go to the Chief of Police and to the different officials of the city." Miner gave voice to her understanding of women's obligations, but she also claimed a space for vigilant women in the coercive work of the war effort.[38]

Volunteer antiprostitution squads already existed in some cities; in others, war prompted their formation, even without an army camp nearby. "Communities that were not included in military zones [also] started cleaning house," recalled Raymond Fosdick, the wartime head of the Commission on Training Camp Activities. Women's patriotic leagues policed the streets of cities across the country. In Massachusetts, social worker Helen Pigeon and her colleagues hid in the bushes of the Boston Common at night to spy on and detain women who were consorting with soldiers. In Chillicothe, Ohio, just outside Camp Sherman, one army captain found the patrols quite effective: "The worst kind of women do not parade the streets as the Girls' Protective League operates under the 'arrest on suspicion' rule, and strangers are not in town long before being picked up."[39]

Women suspected of prostitution were detained, interned, and frequently forced to submit to medical examination, often without any legal charges filed against them. At best, women were quickly released; others, particularly those infected with venereal disease, languished indefinitely in hospitals and prisons, makeshift detention centers, "no-privilege cottages," or workhouses—some behind barbed wire—where they performed manual labor under the watchful eye of armed guards. The vigilance societies' definition of prostitution was frequently vague. Juanita Wright, a young woman originally from Spartanburg, South Carolina, was committed indefinitely to the Sherborn Reformatory for Women in Massachusetts after word reached the protective bureau there that she was living with a soldier without benefit of marriage. In a public protest in Oakland, California, Katherine Bushnell insisted that authorities used the laws to target socialist women.[40]

Bushnell's July 1918 meeting was one of the rare instances of opposition to the army's policy. Montana representative Jeannette Rankin spoke out in the halls of the Capitol, and after the war, Roger Baldwin and the American Civil Liberties Union took an interest in the cases of accused prostitutes. But most challenges went nowhere. War Department officials who met in 1919 with Bushnell, a missionary with the Women's Christian Temperance Union, dismissed her as "altogether like a fanatic, or insane person."[41]

Moral vigilance and state power intersected with the emerging discipline of psychology, as suspected prostitutes were subjected to psychological examinations. Women found to be "feebleminded" were regularly turned over to institutions without their consent and with no public hearing. Marine Major John O. Cobb told a Chicago audience that "two thirds of the immoral women of the country are of the moron type." Further complicating matters, between 1910 and 1917, sixteen states passed laws authorizing the sterilization of the feebleminded, and some of the presumptive prostitutes were sterilized. It is unclear how many women faced the strong arms of the law, of medicine, and of the nation's moral vigilance groups during the war. Official documents from the period report as few as fifteen thousand women arrested as prostitutes, but the number may be closer to thirty thousand in federal facilities alone, excluding an even greater number who encountered local laws and organizations but were not formally arrested. It was, as Lieutenant Anderson boasted, "a united and coherent front... for the drastic suppression of the offence."[42]

Both the War Department and leading clubwomen considered the policing of women's sexuality a specifically female obligation. But patriotic women on the home front could choose from options that ranged well beyond moral vigilance societies. Women formed gun clubs for armed self-defense. Within days of the declaration of war, the American Defense Rifle Club, under the leadership of June Haughton, "an expert rifle shot," established a rifle range on the roof of the Hotel Majestic in New York City. The women of the Albany

Colony of the National Society of New England Women learned how to use rifles in self-defense under the direction of a staff member from the nearby armory. In Bayonne, New Jersey, nineteen women formed the Women's Revolver League and, using borrowed weapons and an instructor on loan from the local police station, trained at the police practice ranges at the Bayswater Yacht Club. Like other vigilant Americans, these women employed a rhetoric of self-defense to prompt state action. In this case, women claimed that both the state and male citizens had taken inadequate steps to protect them from the sexual violence of an impending invasion; veiled references to wartime atrocities in Belgium filled the women's writings.[43]

Women formed patriotic leagues, surveillance societies, and women's auxiliaries to all-male militias and guards. Connecticut women, for example, could not enroll in the Home Guard, but the Minute Women of New Haven and Bridgeport formed a quasi-military uniformed alternative that drilled and paraded just as men did. Some women even joined men's vigilance organizations. Charles Diener, attacked repeatedly in Spring Valley, Kansas, in April 1918, recalled that on one occasion mobbers brought their wives to view the violent spectacle. But women did more than watch: even though Sheriff Wheeler did not issue white armbands to Bisbee women, they were among the perpetrators of the Bisbee deportations, despite the fact that the town's morning paper on July 12, 1917, urged "All Women and Children Keep Off Streets Today." The obligations of citizenship were gendered, but the barriers between the sexes were permeable. Lines of race and class sometimes were not. In Utica, New York, the elite members of the National Society of New England Women helped guard the Utica Gas and Electric Company, the Savage Arms Corporation, and nearby bridges against sabotage by German spies and striking workers. But the radical socialist Ella Reeve Bloor also spent much of the war in Utica, where she organized women workers at Savage Arms, who struck in an effort to obtain equal pay for equal work.[44]

Nothing that occurred, from the formation of vice squads to forced sterilization, was entirely new. But moral vigilance took new forms during the war; mobilization efforts incorporated ongoing campaigns for citizen vigilance. Antivice work also had new meanings for the citizens who undertook it, as women folded private policing efforts into state institutions, enthusiastically embracing law and the state, when once they had dismissed such institutions as corrupt. Questions about coercion were answered differently in this instance than in others. Radicals in Connecticut and elsewhere had vigorously protested the Home Guard's breakup of socialist meetings in Hartford. In the wake of the Bisbee deportations, national labor unions and liberal intellectuals defended labor against the leagues. But few organizations or individuals spoke out on behalf of the working-class women who were interned as feebleminded prostitutes; nor did many challenge the coercions of either the state or voluntary associations. With governments, laws, voluntary associations, psychologists, and reformers arrayed against them, and the relative political powerlessness of their gender and class and sometimes race as well, these Americans bore a heavy burden of political coercion on the World War I home front.

★ *Keeping Vigil in the Delta*

Many African-American veterans, concurring in W. E. B. Du Bois's strident claim "we return from fighting, we return fighting," agitated for political rights both in the South and in the urban North, where African Americans migrated in large numbers during the war. War brought to the rural South economic changes that opened up job opportunities, a new federal presence that sometimes upset existing power relations, social connections to political organizations in Chicago and elsewhere, and—thanks to Uncle Sam's paychecks—an infusion of cash to pay for it all. But white vigilance organizations, fearing subversion and "pro-Germanism," rededicated their efforts to enforcing African-American participation in the draft and suppressing black people's organizing around issues of labor, migration, and violence. An Arkansas factory owner, who blamed wartime social unrest on the Wilson administration, thought it time for Southerners to "take down their rifles from over the mantelpiece [and] put down the internal rebellion." Such sentiment was not limited to Dixie, as race riots rocked Northern cities during the war; Mayor Thomas Smith called out every volunteer of the Philadelphia Home Defense Reserve during a race riot there in August 1918.[45]

Matters worsened in the summer of 1919, with at least twenty-five episodes of racial violence in cities nationwide, from Washington and Knoxville to Birmingham and Longview, Texas. In Chicago, at least thirty-eight people died in two days of rioting that began on July 27, 1919. In Omaha in late September 1919, a crowd of six thousand attempted to lynch the city's mayor when he defended Will Brown, an African-American packinghouse worker who was the mob's initial target; federal and state troops and American Legion volunteers intervened to end the episode. In the year following the Armistice, at least seventy-six African Americans were lynched, ten of them veterans, some still in their military uniforms. African Americans found that they could affirm their loyalty and lawfulness and plead for the rule of law, or they could form their own vigilance societies for self-defense. They attempted both approaches.[46]

Some tried to stop the lynchings and race riots of 1919 by convincing white Americans that their fellow citizens needed legal protection from the rule of mob violence. This was an ongoing tactic of the antilynching movement, but African Americans made the message clearer and more urgent by pointing to their wartime loyalty. The National Association for the Advancement of Colored People (NAACP), in its annual report for 1919, called for law and order and affirmed the rights of black Americans by insisting that the fact that "lawabiding colored people are denied the commonest citizenship rights, must be brought home to all Americans who love fair play." Writing in the *Independent*, W. S. Scarborough, president of Wilberforce University, a historically black college in Xenia, Ohio, appealed to the rule of law and concluded by asking, "Will not the American white people come halfway—put aside their prejudices and play fair with this people that has done so much to help win this war?" Such positions continued decades of activism against mob violence, much of it drawing on the extensive networks of voluntary association among African-American clubwomen. Hopes for a vigorous response from the government foundered in the White House, where President Wilson dismissed a petition bearing thirty thousand signatures that protested the violence against African Americans in the Washington riots in July 1919. Wilson insisted that the fight for the League of Nations treaty required all of his attention.[47]

In the Mississippi River Delta, however, where white listeners ignored patient appeals to law and fairness, another version of fair play arose. In the spring of 1919, citizens of Phillips County, Arkansas, formed an organization to keep watch over their fellow citizens and maintain peace and order in their community. They met in secret, swore oaths of allegiance to "defend this Government and her Constitution at all times," and perhaps even stockpiled arms for self-defense. These were not the night riders of the Klan. These vigilant Americans were the black sharecroppers of the Progressive Farmers and Household Union of America. Their story demonstrates the multiple uses of citizen vigilance in early twentieth-century America and the contest over its significance.[48]

On September 30, 1919, black sharecroppers filled the pews of a small church in Hoop Spur, Arkansas, near the town of Elaine, to hear about the work of the Progressive Farmers. Although accounts of the earliest incidents conflict, the sharecroppers ended up in a gun battle with a group of white men outside the church, triggering three days of violence across Phillips County. Crowds of local whites roamed the countryside, and African Americans

The defendants accused of starting a race riot in Elaine, Arkansas, in 1919, shown here, brought questions of legal authority and mob violence before the nation's highest court in their appeal, *Moore v. Dempsey*. (*Courtesy of the Butler Center for Arkansas Studies, Central Arkansas Library System*)

returned fire; more than a thousand were arrested, and as many as two hundred people may have died. Federal troops from nearby Camp Pike restored order, but they turned over control of the county to the Committee of Seven, a privately organized white vigilance organization composed of local business and political elites. The Committee of Seven quickly established its own rule of law in Elaine, launched an investigation of the riots, and arrested seventy-nine African-American men. In the wake of the Committee of Seven's investigations, the trial that followed can hardly be dignified with the name: deprived of counsel and forbidden to call witnesses on their own behalf, every one of the black defendants was convicted by the all-white jury, some after just seven minutes of deliberation. Twelve men were sentenced to death and sixty-seven others to lengthy prison terms in what NAACP Chairman of the Board Mary White Ovington called a "lynching by law." The Progressive Farmers and Household Union was seen no more in Phillips County.[49]

Coming at the end of a months-long wave of racial violence in the "red summer" of 1919, the riots in Elaine contributed to a movement by African-American activists to stop lynching and mob violence. The NAACP convened the Conference on Lynching and Mob Violence in May 1919 at which leading white and black politicians spoke, and its leaders continued to document ongoing incidents; the NAACP's Walter White traveled through Phillips County just weeks after the riot. Ida B. Wells-Barnett worked to publicize the violence in Phillips County through a fund-raising campaign, articles in the *Chicago Defender*, and a pamphlet that she circulated in Arkansas. Public criticism of mob violence supplemented courtroom challenges. Speaking in Columbia, South Carolina, in the summer of 1919, Moorfield Storey, a distinguished former president of the American Bar Association and the NAACP's president, told his audience that after the war "there never was a time in the history of the world when it was more important to teach the knowledge of and respect for the law." Like other critics of mob violence, Storey insisted, "that all men must obey the law is the doctrine on which free governments rest"; he argued that "there is no more dangerous tyranny" than "mobocracy." Within months, Storey was part of a legal team that challenged the Arkansas convictions and brought questions of legal process and mob violence before the nation's highest court.[50]

In his brief to the U.S. Supreme Court, Storey argued that the formal mechanisms of law offered insufficient protection when coercion pervaded the entire atmosphere of public life. "If any juror had had the courage to investigate said charge, with any spirit of fairness, and vote for acquittal he himself would have been the victim of the mob." Even when the law operated according to its own rules, claimed Storey, it might be an insufficient safeguard against the mob. In a dramatic departure from earlier reasoning, the Court agreed with the NAACP, ruling in 1923 to overturn the verdicts. As Justice Oliver Wendell Holmes Jr. wrote in the majority opinion in *Moore v. Dempsey*:

> If the case is that the whole proceeding [of a trial] is a mask—that counsel, jury, and judge were swept to the fatal end by an irresistible wave of public passion...neither perfection in the machinery for correction nor the possibility that the trial court and counsel saw no other way of avoiding an immediate outbreak of the mob can prevent this Court from securing to the petitioners their constitutional rights.[51]

The law, in other words, could itself be a form of mob violence. In such a situation, said Holmes, appellate courts could intervene to guarantee a fair trial.[52]

In *Moore v. Dempsey*, postwar concerns about mob violence and legitimate authority found one resolution in the judicial process. The ruling also held out the possibility, eagerly hoped for by civil libertarians and African-American activists, that the law might act as the arbiter of the boundaries of political coercion. In the meantime, Arkansas's black residents responded to vigilantism in more direct ways: they moved. Phillips County's African-American population dropped by 20 percent in the decade after the riot, and a local white-owned newspaper sympathetically recounted the plight of "one planter who had 300 acres of fine cotton and not a negro on his plantation."[53]

★ Law and Order

Even as their members marched in Armistice Day parades in November 1918, few of the nation's vigilance societies felt their work was done. The Connecticut Home Guard, for example, petitioned Governor Marcus Holcomb not to disband the organization. Its officers noted that "the State should have at its command during the time of reconstruction and readjustment ... a well-disciplined and reliable military force of sufficient strength to protect life and property within its borders in any emergency." The governor granted their request, and guardsmen helped quell a town-gown battle in New Haven on May 28, 1919, when three hundred soldiers and five thousand townspeople, outraged by student catcalls at a military band concert, stormed the Yale University campus and beat students until authorities forcibly intervened.[54]

But critics grew increasingly more vocal after the Armistice. A few had spoken up during the war. E. D. Verink, head of the Red Cross in heavily Mennonite McPherson County, Kansas, announced in June 1918 that he would refuse any donations that had been "secured by these night riders." In Oklahoma City, where an aggressive State Council of Defense and groups such as the Knights of Liberty acted with the support of the state government, *Harlow's Weekly* denounced the fact that "the Councils rapidly assumed judiciary and almost legislative rights ... armed with the great authority of public opinion." Or, as the *Omaha World-Herald* argued in October 1919 in the wake of the riot there, "We have learned how frail is the barrier which divides civilization from the primal jungle, and we have been given to see clearly what that barrier is. It is the law. It is the might of the law wisely and fearlessly administered. It is the respect for and obedience to the law on the part of the members of society. When these fail us, all things fail. When these are lost, all will be lost."[55] Such a vision—that legal process, not violence, divided legitimate from illegitimate political coercion—rested on a view of the place of law in political life different from that held by members of vigilance societies.[56]

On Capitol Hill and in the halls of the nation's state houses, talk of reform filled the air. Responding to the postwar wave of violence, activists pressed Congress to consider a bill making lynching a federal crime. In 1921, Missouri Representative Leonidas Dyer introduced legislation "to assure persons within the jurisdiction of every state the equal protection of the laws." The House passed the bill, but in the Senate, Southern Democrats filibustered, and the measure went down to defeat. Although such initiatives opened debate at a national level, battles would have to be fought more locally. There were some surprising victories. In Texas, José Tomás Canales, a Tejano member of the Texas House of Representatives from Brownsville, demanded that the state legislature investigate wartime violence by the Texas Rangers against Mexicans and Americans of Mexican descent. Canales supervised the inquiry as it called dozens of witnesses and gathered two thousand pages of evidence. Within a year, the Rangers had been drastically reorganized and brought under closer control by the state government.[57]

Most Americans, though, articulated their calls for law as a demand for "law and order," a strengthening of constituted legal authorities' control of political coercion. After the slacker raids of 1918 revealed that the volunteers of the American Protective League wore pins saying "Secret Service," the Treasury Department quickly shut them down, but the Justice Department was simultaneously hiring a dozen new federal agents a week. Postwar legislation similarly took away from women's volunteer vigilance societies the power to regulate prostitution while it dramatically expanded the reach of state power by authorizing the intervention of boards of health and local police. *Harlow's Weekly*, which had spoken out passionately for the rule of law, hoped that its exercise would rein in lawless German Americans "because they failed to use the caution so necessary in this time of stress." In the wake of the Washington riots, some sought to use law to control not white rioters but African-American citizens. "Already a bill before the Senate seeks to separate the races on street cars," noted the *Independent*. The nationwide May Day violence of 1919 led one senator to state that he would introduce legislation outlawing strikes or advocating "the 'overthrowing of the Government of the United States, or any other Government.' In California the wholesale arresting of 'undesirable aliens' is already under way."[58]

In the immediate aftermath of the war, the political situation was presented as a choice between law and order and social chaos. Among the growing community of civil libertarians, a stark picture of American politics also prevailed, but they viewed it from a different angle. The activists of the National Civil Liberties Bureau—like their opponents, the law-and-order conservatives who clamored for stricter loyalty laws—wanted more laws, and they wanted them more consistently enforced.[59]

Another area in which civil libertarians and conservatives concurred was in their denunciation of "mob violence." Where one side saw jingoistic superpatriots, another feared subversive anarchist strikers, but both groups understood the mob to be made up of the same social types, and both thought mob rule posed similar dangers to American democracy. One commentator denounced the mobs that had broken "the long record of good order in the National capital" during the July 1919 riot in Washington, as a crowd "made up almost wholly of boys between eighteen and twenty-five years of age. In part these were composed of young roughs of the city. The rest were soldiers and sailors, either discharged or from near-by camps, and from their appearance doubtless of the hoodlum element of their home towns." Statements attributing public violence to spontaneous, disorganized gatherings of lower-class men were common throughout 1919, despite the fact that they were simply untrue.[60]

Some leading postwar intellectuals contributed to this vision of the mob as they reformulated their thoughts on crowd psychology and mass politics. European sociologists at the turn of the century considered the significance of mob psychology in an extended debate that voiced their underlying concerns about mass democracy. Prewar American thinkers often challenged the antidemocratic assumptions of this literature. Writing in 1916, historian Allan Nevins chastised a European theorist of crowd psychology for ignoring "the immense hopefulness in the gradual rationalization of the crowd which is going on all around us" and suggested a progressive interpretation: "Not even in the backward parts of the world is the crowd, in any sense of the term, so excitable and blind as it once was." This view would not prevail in the postwar years. By then, intellectuals had come to fear the mob instinct. Walter Lippmann, a progressive intellectual who had spent the war years working in the inner corridors of the White House, reflected on postwar America and worried that "at the present time a nation too easily acts like a crowd."[61]

In their sociological and intellectual assumptions, the critics of mob violence—who had witnessed the violence of the American home front firsthand—were not entirely wrong. But such a viewpoint acted to make the workings of American political coercion invisible, in two ways. It obscured the central role played by organized groups and local elites in the narrow category of events called "mob violence." And by focusing on violent passion and ignoring the ways that vigilance groups had exercised their powers with the consent of the government, this literature helped sweep the more systematic, organized, and passionless coercions under the rug of political legitimacy.[62]

In the fall of 1917, Bisbee witnessed what the city's *Daily Review* called "a splendid gathering of high-class, patriotic business men and workers and professional men of the district." Sheriff Harry Wheeler, who had led the deportations that July and who would be viciously rebuked in the President's Mediation Commission report, was the guest of honor. Accepting the accolades of his fellow community leaders, Wheeler said, "My friends, you pay me too much honor.... There were scores of men in that drive the morning of July 12 who...did more than I that day for the district and our home fires. I merely did my duty. I couldn't shirk."[63]

On the World War I home front, there were many men and women who, like Sheriff Wheeler, felt they could not shirk the duty of vigilance in service of the war effort. And so they responded, drawing on social practices they knew and creating others as they went along. During the war, Americans policed their fellow citizens as part of a culture of obligation that pervaded nearly every facet of national life. At the factory and at school, in churches and in dance halls, on the streets and on the telephone, ordinary Americans were watched and governed by their fellow citizens. The apparatus of surveillance would not have been constructed if Americans had not viewed vigilance as basic to good citizenship and had not officials at all levels of government tolerated and even encouraged that vision of political obligation.

In May 1919, the *Public*, a progressive reform magazine, editorialized on the role of law in American life: "This is a country of law. If it is not that it is nothing at all. And being a country of law those who assume to set up private judgment are undermining its foundation.... If this system is not self-sustaining then democracy itself is at fault." Events on the home front demonstrate that the system was not self-sustaining, as the editorialist had suggested. Those who called for the rule of law while they oversaw a system of coercion that continued to operate outside the law were neither devious, duplicitous, nor hypocritical. They were obedient citizens trapped in a paradox of their own making, dedicated to a nation of laws that asked them to ignore laws. In the postwar push for law and order, the worst manifestation of citizen vigilance—mob violence—had been denounced, and even as it persisted into the postwar years, the intellectual, legal, and institutional weapons wielded against it would grow more powerful. But new ways of enforcing the obligations of American citizens would gradually take its place. The mob, narrowly defined, had been tamed. But the coercion had not.[64]

5

Responsible Speech: Rights in a Culture of Obligation

★ ★

In a time of national crisis, the people of Philadelphia could always count on the Liberty Bell. Despite having cracked severely in 1835, the Liberty Bell had appeared throughout the intervening years at international exhibitions and local patriotic celebrations, and Independence Hall—where it was then housed—was the most visited museum in the country. During the war, Americans who came to see the Liberty Bell saw their ancient patriotic relic displayed next to a new one: the glass jar from which Secretary of War Newton Baker had drawn the Selective Service System's first draft lottery numbers. Liberty Loan salesmen paraded the Liberty Bell through the city on a float in October 1917, accompanied by a military color guard and Uncle Sam himself. But soon after the war, the *Literary Digest* announced that "Miss Liberty Bell is sick." American scientists debated whether the bell's distinctive fracture could be repaired using new technologies of metallurgy and soldering. But the scientists said that the Liberty Bell could not be fixed, and Americans decided that, in any case, they liked it better cracked.[1]

During the war, Henry Glintenkamp, a cartoonist for the radical magazine the *Masses*, used the Liberty Bell's cracks to suggest the fragility of wartime civil liberties. For publishing that image, the magazine's editors would end up in court. But out of their struggles, they built something new. During America's first world war, a broad but tentative and fragmented coalition developed around the concept of civil liberties, using rights as a weapon of defense. They resisted obligation's coercive aspects and gave voice to a politics that imagined the citizen first and foremost as an individual and as a bearer of rights, and then they formed social networks, voluntary associations, and political institutions dedicated to realizing this vision. Out of this wartime crucible emerged the American Civil Liberties Union, modern First Amendment jurisprudence (articulated, at the beginning, only in dissent), and understandings of individual rights in popular political culture that would transform American politics in the twentieth century.[2]

Or at least they thought they did. Early civil libertarians would never have been able to cultivate the seed of rights had there not been fertile soil in which to sow it. They found such ground—perhaps without even knowing they were looking for it—through their interactions with an older understanding of citizenship, centered on obligations. Speech was an ancient right, as its defenders repeatedly insisted when they appealed to courts for its protection. Before the war, such thinking exasperated many progressives, who had seen "personal liberty" used to strike down the aggressive state interventions they put forward. Many dismissed such notions as relics of the horse-and-buggy age Americans were rapidly moving out of, and fought for the rights of individuals to speak publicly or publish on controversial topics. Labor organizers formed the fundamental element of the constituency for free speech, as they sought the right to assemble and to "picket" unfair employers. "Free speech fights" prompted by radical speakers from the Industrial Workers of the World (IWW) shook the nation's cities, particularly in the upper Midwest and the far West. Cultural radicals supported the freedom of artists and playwrights; atheist professors demanded academic freedom at denominational colleges; feminists took on obscenity laws and other strictures of moral purity that blocked public access to birth control. African Americans had fought for the right to assemble and to speak long before Ida B. Wells published the first issues of her Memphis newspaper, *Free Speech*. Similar concern for the liberty of citizens galvanized some immigrant communities to resist prohibition or fight restrictions on private schooling. Legal theorists and philosophers had addressed questions of civil liberty well before World War I, and lower courts had heard cases on speech and censorship, even if the Supreme Court yet had not.[3]

All these groups wanted "free speech," and most Americans, mindful of the First Amendment even if they could not quote it, agreed on its importance. But there were few institutional networks to connect them to each other. Theodore Schroeder founded the Free Speech League in New York City in 1902 to fight for his belief that there should be no limits on expression whatsoever, but his group had few members and was hardly a presence in public life. Some free speech activists really were little more than rebels and cranks. Political efforts were uncoordinated; many pursued single-issue agendas without linking them up into a coherent vision of citizenship premised on "civil liberties." Antivaccination, drama production, and labor relations rarely came together in the public sphere, let alone the public's political imagination—until war came, that is, and the state began to lump them all together as threats to the nation.[4]

Wartime proponents of "responsible speech" believed that rights were limited entities that were balanced by political obligations—a balance that had been readjusted by the war. An October 1917 editorial in the *Outlook* succinctly defined the notion: "A man has no more right to use his tongue to the injury of his neighbor or his country than he has to use his fist to their injury. The right of free speech does not mean irresponsible speech." This vision of citizenship imagined a self-restrained citizen operating within community norms; desires for free expression were self-indulgent. Such a position drew on ideas for the limitation of free speech that were as old as the First Amendment itself. The antebellum period had seen the Alien and Sedition Acts and gag rules against antislavery speakers. Interference with the press was common in both the North and the South during the Civil War, and for every "free speecher" who defended Margaret Sanger, there were far larger political constituencies that not only supported her suppression but also regarded it as a political necessity.[5]

Proponents of responsible speech, schooled as well in the politics of voluntarism, believed that civil liberties were as much about groups as about individuals. A member of a supposedly disloyal group—such as the Woman's Peace Party or the IWW—was presumed incapable of responsible speech. People who spoke for groups—legislators, preachers, journalists, professors, librarians—were thought to be under a special burden to balance freedom against the obligations they owed to the institutions and collectivities they spoke for. And they agreed that speech would be regulated by groups. Armed with expanded coercive powers, Americans could and did enforce responsible speech in new ways. They demanded responsible speech of wartime critics and had violent face-offs with pacifists, socialists, and even barroom drunks. But during the war, Americans questioned the popular enforcement of norms of speech and increasingly turned to the state for its regulation.

World War I changed American civil liberties by altering the role of the state in debates over legitimate speech. On one level, free speech justified the state—a war against German militarism heightened support for the idea of the free press, even as it massively expanded formal and informal controls on publications. Civil liberties activists also used the state as a tool for their own defense. The southern populist speaker Tom Watson, New York radical editor Max Eastman, and the men and women of the Nonpartisan League all challenged the state's intrusions on civil liberties. But the war did more than try the souls of its progressive citizens. It taught Americans new lessons in how to regulate and control themselves. Increasingly they did so, not so much in relation to each other but in relation to a newly powerful state.

✷ The Trial of Jane Addams

Wartime pacifist speakers were particularly vexing. In Portland, Maine, local business leader Halbert Gardner told an audience at City Hall in the spring of 1917 that "it must be evident to any thinking person that the time has come, when no man can…talk any more peace piffle about the meek inheriting the earth." Before the Kansas State Historical Society, George Morehouse denounced the "bloodless, spineless, cringing drivel of 'turning the other cheek' sentimentalism."[6]

At times, vigilant citizens took it upon themselves to silence pacifist voices. In Baltimore, a crowd of four thousand people, led in part by faculty members from Johns Hopkins University, surrounded Baltimore's Academy of Music in April 1917 to protest the "unpatriotic" David Starr Jordan and a group of "Jew radicals" who joined him at an antiwar rally there. Kenneth Guthrie of New York wrote to the *New York Times* after he had received in the mail a publicity letter from the pacifists of the American Union against Militarism (AUAM). He thought such people were "either aiding the foes of democracy or sufficiently mentally deficient to see that against a mad dog none but arguments that appeal to him are possible." In the former case, he thought, "the Government should suppress them; in the second they should be put into schools for the defective." Like the government agents who interviewed conscientious objectors and the clubwomen who rounded up working-class charity girls, Guthrie asserted that those who disagreed with his vision of citizenship had simply failed to comprehend it.[7]

In the summer of 1914, when war broke out in Europe, Jane Addams was a national hero. Her memoir, *Twenty Years at Hull-House*, was a best-seller and an inspiration to progressive reform. Addams was a confirmed pacifist who had dedicated herself to peace as a labor and women's issue for decades. She faced public criticism long before the United States entered the war in April 1917 but persisted; even the death of her nephew in France did not dissuade her. Her wartime speeches, though, would not find as receptive an audience as her reform writings. Her popularity made her a target—and a problem. Because Addams was so prominent, she could not easily be suppressed; rather, her stance forced proponents of responsible speech to articulate their objections to her continued speaking.[8]

Jane Addams, once the nation's hero for her writings and social service work, found herself denounced during World War I as unpatriotic. After the war, the Daughters of the American Revolution voted to rescind her membership. (*Courtesy of the Library of Congress Prints and Photographs Division*)

On April 17, 1917, Jane Addams told the Women's Club of Chicago that she could "see no reason why one should not say what one believes in time of war as in time of peace." The Women's Club disagreed with her direct challenge to responsible speech; that June, they notified Addams that her peace organizations could no longer meet in its clubrooms. Addams reaffirmed her beliefs in a speech on "Patriotism and Pacifists" delivered before the Congregational Church of Evanston, Illinois, in June 1917. "Opposition to the war," she insisted, "is not necessarily cowardice." She also suggested a place for the dissenting pacifist in the culture of obligation. "The pacifist must serve his country by forcing definitions if possible.... Since war was declared, some of us have had a feeling that we are shirking moral service." Rising from the audience, Addams's former colleague and fellow reformer Orrin N. Carter, now the chief justice of the Illinois Supreme Court, politely challenged her. "I think that anything that may tend to cast doubt on the justice of our cause in the present war is very unfortunate," he said as he stood before the congregation. "In my opinion no pacifist measures should be taken until the war is over." Justice Carter became an overnight hero in the press.[9]

The criticisms continued. The *Birmingham Age-Herald* worried that "if Miss Addams's plea prevailed thousands of men who never had a conviction about any moral issue would get busy and have a conviction against fighting, and thus shirk a true man's duty." A women's club newspaper correspondent complained of Addams's unwavering political commitment: "Jane Addams is losing her grip. She is becoming a bore. Sometimes she represents a worthy cause, but she doesn't help it." Mary Simkhovitch, a fellow settlement house worker, denounced her, noting that "it has been very painful to many of us . . . to find that we cannot think or act in unison with her." Addams was not without her supporters, including Secretary of War Newton Baker and U.S. Food Administrator Herbert Hoover, but she remained outside the fold for the duration of the war. Not long after the war, the Daughters of the American Revolution even voted to purge Addams from their membership rolls. She had failed to police herself—to exercise the obligation of responsible speech.[10]

The suppression of pacifist speech energized civil liberties organizations, and they responded in a manner altogether fitting for the political culture of the Progressive Era: they formed a club. The American Union against Militarism, the nation's leading voice against war before April 1917, took up the cause of pacifist speakers with the president. In an open letter published just weeks after the war's declaration, Lillian Wald urged Wilson to remind Americans "of the peculiar obligation devolving upon all Americans in this war to uphold in every way our constitutional rights and liberties." Six months later, a splinter group—the National Civil Liberties Bureau—left the AUAM's overworked Bureau of Conscientious Objectors to focus more directly on issues of speech and assembly. Pacifists' wartime isolation increasingly forced them to rethink the relationship between the individual and the group in their political theories, which brought home to many—especially modernist progressives who had dismissed individual liberty along with the horses and buggies—the need for legal protections for individuals.[11]

★ *Regulating Speech: The Espionage Act*

How would troublemaking speakers be regulated? Sometimes Americans policed speech outside the color of law. Wartime vigilance organizations dedicated much of their energies to monitoring the boundaries of responsible speech. In Birmingham,

Alabama, just after the war, a citizens' group organized to limit the right of assembly among railroad workers who were organizing a union. They broke up meetings by force and posted the following message on the meeting hall door:

> We, the Patriotical Committee, understand that you have allowed the
> I. W. W. or German agitators to hold meetings in your hall.... We the
> Committee feel that you did not know some things that we did and...if
> you allow these meetings to continue you may loose [sic] your hall some
> how or something may happen. We can't tell you except be loyal to your
> country & State.[12]

The Knights of Liberty, a vigilance society in central Oklahoma, had formed as a labor surveillance group in 1917, but a year later, they turned their attention to the *Oklahoma Vorwärts*, a weekly German-language paper published in the small town of Bessie. On September 20, 1918, they ordered editor Julius Hüssy to cease publication. He refused. On October 17, a group of approximately fifty men took it upon themselves to shut down his operation. As with most other vigilance societies active on the home front, this was no spontaneous mob mad with war hysteria but a systematically organized group acting under the control of local elites. Hüssy noted later that "well-known men were among them, men whom we never would have expected to be party to mob-justice, men who have been or still are active in positions of public service."[13]

As pacifists tried to find a place for themselves within the polity, most Americans excluded them from it with the same combination of legal sanction and popular pressure that characterized other aspects of home-front policing. Local authorities had a great deal of latitude to regulate speech and assembly under existing laws. States and localities used vagrancy statutes, disorderly conduct charges, and nuisance laws to control irresponsible speakers, just as the Washington police had applied them to Alice Paul and the suffragist pickets. During the war, nearly half the municipalities of Oklahoma adopted laws forbidding "seditious remarks" or the circulation of disloyal literature. Speakers who had addressed audiences of West Virginia coal miners were imprisoned on vagrancy charges, despite miners' protests. In New York City, a history professor was sent off to Bellevue Hospital "for observation as to his sanity" after he engaged in "a conversation on internationalism near a recruiting station." President Woodrow Wilson dismissed pacifists in a wartime speech before the American Federation of Labor, noting that "what I am opposed to is not the feeling of the pacifists, but their stupidity. My heart is with them, but my mind has a contempt for them." In the summer of 1917, the federal government turned its contempt into legislation: the Espionage Act.[14]

For most Americans who lived under its regulations, the Espionage Act had little to do with espionage. It was an omnibus bill that collected a series of legal innovations that wartime Justice Department officials had been clamoring for but had been unable to pass until the war emergency changed the tenor of Congress. On the home front, its most significant provisions were those that aimed to suppress speech. The Espionage Act punished with fines up to $10,000 and prison sentences of up to twenty years anyone who "shall willfully make or convey false reports or false statements with intent to interfere with the operation or success of the military or naval forces of the United States or to promote the success of its enemies." The act also gave the U.S. Postmaster General power to withhold from the mails any matter "advocating or urging treason, insurrection, or forcible resistance to any law of the United States."[15]

The bill did not become law without opposition; many of the same congressional voices that had spoken out against the war and the draft opposed the Espionage Act as well. But it was initially thought mild, in part because newspaper editors had successfully eliminated a provision that would have given broad power to the president to define when the press had published information useful to the enemy. Publishers insisted that they could be trusted to regulate themselves. The Espionage Act's proponents touted it as a protective measure. Post Office Solicitor General William Lamar told readers of the *Forum* that the law shielded soldiers and workers from dangerous propaganda and protected "thoroughly loyal" Americans "who don't want disloyalty dinned into their unwilling ears."[16]

To state that the wartime Espionage Act authorized the federal government to regulate speech is to say that it handed over those powers to employees of the Post Office Department. At its head was Albert S. Burleson, a fifty-four-year-old Texan who served as Woodrow Wilson's postmaster general. Burleson was a Democratic Party loyalist—a requirement for any postmaster general in an era when the job involved handing out thousands of lucrative patronage positions, but particularly so in the case of Burleson, who enjoyed friendly relations with two of the men closest to Wilson, his Attorney General Thomas Gregory and his personal adviser Edward House.[17]

Attorney General Gregory urged that the Espionage Act should not be "permitted to become a medium for personal feuds or persecution," but often it was. In their local communities, postmasters were politically well connected—precisely how they had earned their federal appointments in the first place. During the war, they took on a special role in regulating speech, prompting Oswald Garrison Villard, the patrician editor of the *Nation*, to complain about the delegation of power to "some third assistant or $1,200 clerk who has passed upon the details of the thing." Across the country, local elites and postmasters colluded to suppress small socialist, labor, and foreign-language papers. In Minnesota, agrarian populist radicals were so wary of post-masters that they left the motors running in their cars when they drove up to the post office to drop off their mail. German Americans in central Oklahoma who subscribed to the *Oklahoma Vorwärts* complained to the editor that their papers were not being delivered, and Lillian Wald informed President Wilson that even first-class mail was being inexplicably delayed. Such reports were echoed across the country as postmasters often went above and beyond the already strenuous demands of Albert Burleson.[18]

After the war, Burleson boasted of the power of the Post Office, "the one department of the Government that had a nation-wide organization thoroughly effective that could do things." There was much to be done and no reason the postmasters—a ready army of the wartime state—shouldn't do the work. Burleson's right-hand man William Lamar insisted that "for us to permit an exaggerated sentimentalism, a misapplied reverence for legal axioms which our courts have held have no true application to the questions involved to restrain us, would be criminal."[19]

★ *A Tale of Two Papers*

The Espionage Act passed on June 15, 1917, and Albert Burleson went to work the next day, sending out to postmasters across the country a secret memo urging them to keep "close watch on...matter which is calculated to interfere with the success of...the government in conducting the war." The policing of responsible speech required cooperation between government officials and local volunteer efforts. The *Saturday Evening Post* ran advertisements asking Americans to turn one another in; Attorney General Gregory noted that "complaints of even the most informal or confidential nature are always welcome." The Justice Department was soon receiving a thousand letters a day.[20]

On August 15, 1917, Albert Burleson approved the decisions of local postmasters in New York City and Savannah, Georgia, who had declared two very different publications to be in violation of the Espionage Act. The *Masses*, a monthly magazine edited by Max Eastman, circulated primarily among labor and cultural radicals in New York's bohemian scene, which included many who opposed the war. The *Jeffersonian*, ruled unmailable the same day, was the mouthpiece of southern populist Tom Watson, engaged at that moment in a strident anticonscription campaign. The struggles of the two editors revealed the strange alliance that wartime civil liberties cases sometimes created.[21]

In rural Georgia, Tom Watson found himself the target of popular and federal repression. Always a crusader, Watson denounced the declaration of war, conscription, the mobilization effort, and more or less everything else he encountered, including Catholics, Jews, African Americans, and Freemasons. He was also immensely popular. Thousands of agrarian populists came to hear him speak, and his newspapers circulated across the rural South, offering an intellectual and cultural community of antiwar resistance in the region. After war's declaration, though, many believed he had gone too far; angry Southerners would have been pleased by a June 1917 sermon at Atlanta's First Baptist Church, where Reverend Charles Daniel preached that "an immediate stop should be put to this obnoxious propaganda he is spreading by means of his paper."[22]

That same month, Marion Lucas, the local postmaster in Savannah, Georgia, withheld Watson's weekly newspaper, the *Jeffersonian*, from the federal mail; later, in a separate incident, Tampa's postmaster did the same. Watson immediately went on the offensive, asking whether Americans must "begin our war upon European autocracy by creating one, here at home." In a moment of particular spirit, he demanded: "Don't abuse me—ANSWER ME!" He continued to lead his popular movement against conscription and defend his own right to speak, noting in an interview: "Freedom of speech, within your limitations, as I have said—I have had a good deal of it. Sometimes I have not had quite as much as I would like to have had. It takes a good deal of freedom of speech and press for me, I assure you."[23]

For legal aid, Watson turned to an unlikely ally—Harry Weinberger, a thirty-one-year-old New York attorney who was a "confirmed pacifist," an aspiring theater director, and Jewish. If their backgrounds had little in common, the two men shared a hatred for conscription and similar views on individual liberty. "I believed the people were not made for the State; the State was made for the people," Weinberger would later write in his memoir. The two began a correspondence in the summer of 1917, with Weinberger offering informal advice on how to navigate the Espionage Act's complicated provisions; eventually the two collaborated on Watson's unsuccessful court challenge to the Selective Service Act.[24]

When the Cabinet discussed Tom Watson's case in August 1917, Woodrow Wilson was exasperated at "Damned Fools" like Watson. "We cannot go over all the DFs," wrote Navy Secretary Josephus Daniels in his diary. "They know Tom Watson is a fool. We have better things to do." But the postmasters, the bottom-up state-builders of the Espionage Act, had already started the ball rolling. On August 15, 1917, Burleson affirmed the Savannah postmaster's ruling. Watson pled in federal court for an injunction. Three days later, Watson and Post Office Solicitor William Lamar met at a federal hearing hastily assembled at the summer residence of federal judge Emory Speer. Speer was unconvinced by Watson's claims. "Had the Postmaster General longer permitted the use of the great postal system which he controls for the dissemination of such poison, it would have been to forego the opportunity to serve his country afforded by his lofty station." William Fitts, the Assistant U.S. Attorney who prosecuted the case, was blunter. Watson "should go in a hole and pull it in after him . . . the further he goes and the longer he stays the better it will suit the Government."[25]

Tom Watson kept trying. In Thomson, Georgia, where Watson published the *Jeffersonian*, the local postmaster was an old supporter; he helped Watson continue distributing the paper until authorities learned of their collusion and threatened further prosecution. Then, to evade restrictions, Watson bought up a defunct paper in Thomson and started publishing it under another title, but it, too, was soon suppressed. Admitting defeat, Watson abandoned publication in late September 1917.[26]

The *Masses* faced suppression at precisely the same time, and its supporters also fought back. On July 3, 1917, just weeks after the passage of the Espionage Act, the magazine's editors presented the August issue to postal authorities. Postmaster of New York Thomas Patten spent the Fourth of July perusing the issue, and the next day he informed the journal's editor, Max Eastman, that it was unmailable. Patten mentioned some articles and a couple of cartoons—one of a broken Liberty Bell, another of Uncle Sam dragging a ball and chain—but he also alluded, more indistinctly, to the magazine's "general tenor."[27]

Eastman was infuriated and responded in the press and the courts. Allies at the AUAM's Civil Liberties Bureau organized the Free Press Conference in New York on July 13. Speaking before the crowd assembled there, which included the likes of John Dewey and Dudley Field Malone, Eastman was obviously dejected. "The worst thing I can say for this situation is that it actually surprises me," he told the audience. "I never succeeded in thinking up anything half so bad as this." Four friends of the *Masses*, including attorney Clarence Darrow, traveled to Washington a few days later to meet with President Wilson in person. They had to settle instead for an audience with an unsympathetic Albert Burleson, who, one of the delegation thought, "seemed to look at the whole problem with a degree of aloof extremism."[28]

The *Masses* won an initial victory in the district court in New York. On July 24, Judge Learned Hand ruled that Postmaster Patten had applied the Espionage Act too vaguely, had confused advocacy of radical ideas for incitement to lawbreaking, and, more capaciously, had endangered "the tradition of English-speaking freedom." But this initial win only prompted further repression; the magazine's editors were later prosecuted not for violating the Espionage Act but for obstructing the draft. The beleaguered editors found support for free speech in the jury box; tried on two different occasions, both proceedings ended with hung juries. But the damage had long since been done: denied access to the mails again in September 1917, the *Masses* quickly folded.[29]

Both publications had their defenders. Isaï Kahn of Chicago wrote to Postmaster General Burleson "to record my protest against the depriving the American Socialist and the Masses from the Mails with out due process of law." Kahn defensively noted that "in the first place I want to say I am french and not german as my name might indicate." He insisted that he was "apposed to the stand both papers take in regard to the war but I am more apposed to the squelching of free speach in this free country." Writing from Monroe, Georgia, after the war's end, J. H. Maddox defended the *Jeffersonian* in a rambling and angry missive that blamed Catholics and Jews for the suppression of Watson's paper. The "move was against Watson for opposing the sending soldiers from here to fight over seas. Now Mr. Burleson Watson may have been the only Editor to say that he was not the only man by thousand that thought so.... For the good of the country... I beg for Watson's relief."[30]

The government's campaigns temporarily derailed Tom Watson, but they gave new life to his sputtering political career. He ran for the U.S. Congress in 1918, and even though his opponent denounced him as a "miserable creature whose every word is against his country," Watson nearly won (and, in fact, may have, if his charges of corruption are to be believed). Immediately after the Armistice, he started publishing another newspaper, in which he demanded a repeal of federal censorship legislation. He went on to run for president, standing in Georgia's Democratic primary in 1920. Later that year, he was elected to the U.S. Senate on a platform that called for the restoration of civil liberties.[31]

The events of the war years had convinced Watson and thousands of his supporters of something most of them already believed—that the basic building blocks of democratic participation required protection, not from the mob, but from the federal government. The suppression of Watson's papers shaped a popular constituency for free speech that drew on an older language of states' rights and opposition to centralized authority rather than the language of modern individualism that circulated among Greenwich Village bohemians. Watson's was a populist interpretation of civil liberty: "We buck privates and non-coms are with you, Uncle Tom," read a banner at a 1920 election stop. Watson's vision of free speech was not the same as that of the New York City radicals, even if they used the same words and fought in federal courtrooms against the same laws. In a 1917 letter to Harry Weinberger, Watson complained that the "Bureau of Civil Freedom [sic] has not had one word of aid or comfort for us," and only "recognize[d] us...when we can be useful in contributing a fee." Indeed, after the war, the *Nation* did not greet Watson's 1920 election victory as a triumph for civil liberties, but as "essentially the victory of a Fifth Estate, of the sinister forces of intolerance, superstition, prejudice, religious jingoism, and mobbism." Of all the groups active during this civil liberties moment, these two never found common ground, even though Albert Burleson thought they posed comparable threats. Instead, the suppression of the two publications demonstrates the fissures and tensions within the twentieth century's emerging culture of rights.[32]

★ *Provocative Speech: The Sedition Act*

For every prominent national figure like Jane Addams or Tom Watson, there were hundreds of local figures—preachers, teachers, and loudmouths—who tested the line between responsible and irresponsible speech. Small-town free speech battles during World War I often centered around ministers. It was their job to speak publicly, and popular deference to religious authority required community members to listen. But because clergymen had extraordinary power, they also had unique obligations and were carefully monitored during the war. The vast majority of the nation's clergy sided with the war effort, and some of them were among the home front's heartiest watchdogs of dissent, radicalism, and pacifism. Dissenting clergymen paid a heavy price for their statements, including two ministers in Audubon, Iowa, who were nearly lynched on New Year's Eve in 1917 for their "pro-German" sermons, or Reverend Jesse Payne, "pastor of the colored holly [sic] roller church" in Blytheville, Arkansas, who in April 1918 was tarred and feathered to the tune of a John Philip Sousa march. More commonly, troublesome preachers were forced to resign, usually under pressure from their own congregations. Such removals took place in almost every denomination.[33]

Clarence Waldron served as minister of the First Baptist Church in the small town of Windsor, Vermont. The war affected Waldron profoundly, and he increasingly found himself drawn to Pentecostal teachings that put him at odds with most of his Baptist congregation. Waldron's reputation as an outsider was confirmed by the fact that the thirty-one-year-old minister had moved to town just two years earlier with his wife and her German-born mother. Watching world events unfold, Waldron not only came to believe that war was contrary to the teachings of Jesus Christ but also feared that the Apocalypse was imminent, and he expressed his faith in increasingly dramatic ways; townspeople dismissed him as a "Holy Roller."[34]

On "Liberty Loan Sunday," October 21, 1917, Waldron refused to preach on the war, as Treasury Secretary William McAdoo had urged every American clergyman to do. An angry crowd of several hundred people gathered that night; in self-defense, Waldron wrapped himself in the American flag and sang "The Star-Spangled Banner." By Christmas, he was under arrest, charged with violating the Espionage Act by circulating *The Word of the Cross*, a pamphlet that claimed that "a Christian ought not and should not fight." Waldron turned down help from the National Civil Liberties Bureau, concerned it would be "a trap which would get him into more trouble." Free speech had some supporters in Windsor, though; Waldron's case was initially dismissed after a hung jury. After a retrial that brought most of the town's ministers out to testify against him, Waldron earned a fifteen-year sentence applauded by Attorney General Gregory. The *Christian Register*, a Unitarian newspaper, agreed, noting that "the penalty took into account the important influence of a minister; and we might add, of a preacher in a church whose members are blindly devoted to queer religious ideas. They make susceptible subjects in a time of stress." Released a year later, Waldron never returned to Vermont.[35]

Members of the International Bible Students Association, or Jehovah's Witnesses, faced intimidation in almost every community where they were active during the war. A jury convicted a group of church leaders in Brooklyn of violating the Selective Service Act in June 1918, and the *New York Times* applauded. Their conviction taught "a lesson long needed by the too numerous people who have utterly wrong ideas as to the extent to which 'the free exercise of religion' is permitted by our Constitution," the paper editorialized. "They take the phrase literally, regard it as a right to do anything they please." The *New York Times* thought there were limits to both free speech and religious freedom: "We may all believe what we choose, but if our beliefs lead us to do things repugnant to the settled and general sentiment of our fellow-countrymen as expressed in their laws, then it will be vain for us to raise the plea of religious liberty." As members of the clergy balanced political and religious obligations, duties to God, the state, and their congregations, they were warned that "above all individual rights stands that of the Government to defend and perpetuate itself."[36]

Across the country, many Americans found themselves in trouble for things they said in haste, in frustration, or under the influence of alcohol. In the early weeks of the war, New Yorker Stephen Kerr's reference to "you skunks of Americans" earned him a citation for disorderly conduct; a year later, in McLean County, Illinois, Amanda Murphy was arrested under the Espionage Act for her attack on a Red Cross volunteer. "God damn this war and God damn President Wilson too and God damn the Red Cross nurses.... Don't another one of you come on this place; not a cent do we give to the Red Cross." Patriotic citizens in Earle, Arkansas, offered a flag button to Earl Beal to wear with pride; Beal went to jail after "he threw the emblem down and cursed the government." Joseph Balough, who told the patrons of a saloon in Granite City, Illinois, that Germany was "all right" was sentenced to two years at Fort Leavenworth. Elsewhere, three men found themselves sentenced to six months in a workhouse for singing "The Watch on the Rhine" on their way home from a bar.[37]

After the war, Justice Department official John Lord O'Brian would mock such cases, noting that prosecutions for fighting words "gave the dignity of treason to what were often neighborhood quarrels or barroom brawls." But "loose talk" was no laughing matter at the time, particularly for the war's most important loose talker: Ves Hall, a rancher in Rosebud County, Montana, who in January 1918, in "badinage with the landlady in a hotel kitchen" and in "hot and furious saloon argument," had called Woodrow Wilson a "tool, a servant of Wall Street millionaires, and the richest and crookedest ____ ever President." After George Bourquin, a federal judge with an unorthodox streak, overturned Hall's Espionage Act conviction, the Montana legislature passed a stringent state sedition law that would soon serve as a model for new legislation in Washington.[38]

By the spring of 1918, it was clear that the Espionage Act wasn't working. It was under attack by pacifists and civil libertarians, who were devoting more of their organizational resources to free speech issues. The NCLB was at the forefront of civil liberties litigation during the war, petitioning politicians and engaging in lawsuits and publicity campaigns on behalf of civil liberties. Socialist organizations undertook similar work, and the legal branch of the NAACP launched several cases focusing on First Amendment issues. In the middle of the war, civil libertarians opposed federal power but called for federal action nonetheless; Roger Baldwin urged "that the President indicate clearly...the line which in his mind can properly be drawn between those matters which can be fully discussed without prejudice to the country's interest, and those which cannot."[39]

Supporters of law and order didn't care for the Espionage Act, either, not because it was too stringent, but too weak. "The demand is that some positive action be taken or vigilance committees will be organized and the citizens take it into their own hands," wrote a Montana businessman to his senator. In the wake of the highly publicized lynching of Robert Prager in Illinois in April 1918, many insisted that the federal government expand its regulatory powers in order to rein in local actions. Even the attorney general blamed "most of the disorder throughout the country" on "lack of laws relating to disloyal utterances." Popular regulation of speech would not suffice. "It becomes doubly important... that the line be drawn by the administration itself," editorialized the *New Republic*.[40]

Woodrow Wilson was a student of history and politics; no surprise, then, that he believed himself to be a staunch defender of the ancient traditions of liberty to which many appealed during the war. In April 1917, he told a newspaper publisher that "I can imagine no greater disservice to the country than to establish a system of censorship that would deny to the people... their indisputable right to criticize their own public officials." But Wilson clearly believed in responsible speech, telling the pacifist John Nevin Sayre, his son-in-law's brother, that "there is such a thing as the indecent exposure of private opinion in public."[41]

Early in the war, Wilson responded to Lillian Wald's letter that "you may be sure I have the matter in mind," but in practice, he was indifferent to the Espionage Act's day-to-day administration, which he happily turned over to Albert Burleson. He even returned one of Burleson's memos unread, assuring the postmaster general that "I am willing to trust your judgment." Burleson's extremes, however, eventually chafed at Wilson and the rest of the Cabinet. On repeated occasions, the Justice Department declined to prosecute the editors whose papers Burleson had declared unmailable. After Burleson targeted *Pearson's Magazine* and the *Nation*, whose editors were friends of the president, Wilson intervened, urging "the utmost caution and liberality in all our censorship." Burleson, always a stubborn man, grew defensive and petulant; Wilson, never to be outmatched in a contest of stubbornness, increasingly ignored his longtime ally.[42]

In the meantime, however, Congress had responded to popular demands for an increased assertion of federal authority over the regulation of speech. On April 10, 1918, just days after Robert Prager's death, the Senate passed a series of amendments to the Espionage Act that would be known as the Sedition Act; President Wilson signed them into law on May 16. The new regulations drastically expanded the punishments for "disloyal, profane, scurrilous, or abusive language" and gave postmasters even more authority—in this case to block the delivery of mail that violated the act's provisions. The accusations continued to pour in from across the country as popular efforts to regulate speech intersected with new federal powers. By October, the Justice Department, overwhelmed in its caseload, ordered local U.S. attorneys to hold off any further indictments.[43]

★ *Defending the Nonpartisan League*

Even with the Sedition Act in place—and in part because of it—Americans defended their own definitions of free speech, often at great danger. Supporters of civil liberties mobilized on a mass scale in response to attacks on the Nonpartisan League. Founded in North Dakota in 1915 as a voice of agrarian dissent, the NPL was active primarily in the upper Midwest, where its leaders called for cooperative ownership of the agricultural economy. During World War I, despite the fact that the NPL officially supported U.S. entry into war, the NPL's radicalism put it on the wrong side of the fence. In Twin Falls, Idaho, denunciations of the Nonpartisan League so overwhelmed the County Council of Defense that council officials asked townspeople to take a temporary break.[44]

But the league also had a supportive constituency, and NPL politicians held political power in several areas, particularly in North Dakota, where they controlled the legislature and had seated one of their own, Lynn Frazier, in the governor's chair. NPL organizers traveled across the Midwest raising new supporters and defending civil liberties in the language of Midwestern agrarian populism. When they traveled, they carried Liberty Bonds and copies of Woodrow Wilson's *The New Freedom* with them to show as evidence of their loyalty, just in case they encountered hostile audiences.[45]

The NPL's political strategy included the publication of partisan newspapers in every county where it operated. Once war came, such a strategy smelled of treason. Nebraska Governor Keith Neville, no friend of the NPL, worried that it promoted "circulation of seditious literature, calculated to arouse anti-American sentiment, class hatred, and in general interfere with the successful prosecution of the war." But threats of suppression also mobilized NPL members to defend their newspapers. On the stump in public meetings, in the pages of the rural penny press, and in the region's courtrooms, members of the Nonpartisan League waged a campaign for civil liberties. When NPL organizer Beryl Felver was almost lynched in Merrick County, Nebraska, in May 1918, he sued the city, invoking an existing anti–mob violence statute. Sometimes the NPL found allies. A sympathetic sheriff in Fargo, North Dakota, protected the free speech rights of Nonpartisan League speaker Walter Thomas Mills when an angry crowd threatened him; in an attempt to keep order, the sheriff deputized all of the NPL organizers instead of the mob. In Nebraska, the league and its opponents eventually reached a compromise over speech rights. In return for permission to hold public meetings, the NPL agreed not to circulate materials that the State Council of Defense objected to, a list that included not only the NPL's *War Aims* pamphlet but also—in a telling irony—Woodrow Wilson's *The New Freedom*.[46]

They contested ideas of citizenship and civil liberties in the courts as well. The Nonpartisan League maintained a legal bureau dedicated to protecting its members from legal assault. Its wartime record was mixed. In North Dakota, where the NPL held power at the state and local level, the league had considerable success, but in Minnesota, where the league was a weaker association targeted for almost constant harassment, the NPL Legal Bureau offered little shelter. Friendly juries occasionally acquitted NPL leaders accused under Minnesota's state sedition statute, but at other times, judges who smelled a rat handed down directed verdicts. The league's appeals won few victories. The U.S. Supreme Court upheld the conviction of NPL organizer Joseph Gilbert under the Minnesota Sedition Act; Justice Joseph McKenna was incensed at Gilbert's First Amendment claims. "It would be a travesty on the constitutional privilege he invokes to assign him its protection." And the Supreme Court gave its blessing to repressive state and local sedition laws when it ruled that "the state is not inhibited from making the national purposes its own purposes."[47]

The Nonpartisan League was not alone. But if the civil liberties coalition was newly tied together by the war, its members were joined by weak and fraying strings. For Roger Baldwin, director of the National Civil Liberties Bureau, free speech was a privilege of American citizenship. Baldwin never tired of telling his listeners that he was descended from two passengers of the *Mayflower*, and he noted his favored class upbringing even when he resisted it. "If I was conscious of the 'better people' it was only to know I was one of them," he recalled. Such assumptions influenced his civil liberties work. He noted that "I liked society so much that I was certain democracy would perfect it, and that good people, like us, could hasten this triumph." Civil libertarian and Harvard Law School professor Zechariah Chafee Jr. likewise defended the rights of free speech with vigor but drew boundaries of responsibility and respectability around them. "The man who insists on waving the red flag" of socialism "has just as little common sense" as those who would punish him. "I do not believe that man should be arrested for carrying a solitary red flag in the street any more than for wearing a sweater at a dance, but ordinary polite-ness ought to keep him from doing either."[48]

Roger Baldwin had an ambivalent relationship with the democratic pub-lic that invigorated so many progressives before the war. Baldwin first encoun-tered direct democracy as a social reformer in St. Louis in 1910, when he enthusiastically supported legislation authorizing citizen initiatives on the bal-lot. The citizens of St. Louis frustrated him, though, when they immediately used this new mechanism of democracy to pass a law supporting racially seg-regated housing. "My too-simple theory of democracy had to be changed," recalled Baldwin of this moment. Only a short time after these events, he found himself involved in his first free speech fight to defend birth-control advocate Margaret Sanger, and it was during this same period that he stud-ied anarchist literature and listened with eagerness to the speeches of Emma Goldman.[49]

Baldwin would return to individualism when he was prosecuted in October 1918 for violating the Selective Service Act after deliberately refusing to appear for a physical examination. In a statement before the court, Baldwin made the remarkable claim that he was not a member of any radical organiza-tions, portraying himself instead as a free-floating individual drawing from various groups and their thinking, while owing allegiance to none. "I presume that myself, and not the National Civil Liberties Bureau, is on trial before this court this morning." This radical individualism was on the one hand a sharp challenge to a political culture that embedded individuals within groups. But it was also a betrayal by Baldwin of the groups that had done so much to nurture him and were under attack by federal agents. Baldwin's defense rested on a claim to full citizenship that derived from his individuality and his con-nections to his 100 percent American forebears. He would agitate, within organizations, for the rights of others, but on the stand that day, he tried to leave them behind.[50]

Radical individualism made little headway in the courts. For most believ-ers in responsible speech, individual liberties were moderated and bound by people's commitments to the groups of which they were members: the church, the university, the nation-state. Attorney General Thomas Gregory insisted that "no person should be prosecuted or interned solely by reason of his membership in any...organizations, that guilt is always personal, and that under no circum-stances should any organization or body of men be prosecuted as such," but in practice, legislatures and courts disregarded Gregory's wishes in favor of a vision of citizenship that located the citizen as a member of social groups. Criminal syn-dicalism laws passed by the federal government and the states primarily targeted radical groups. The courts confirmed this vision of citizenship and speech in cases such as *State v. Lowery*, decided by the Washington Supreme Court in 1918. Frank Lowery was convicted of criminal anarchy in Washington state on the evidence of his membership in the Industrial Workers of the World. The justices refused to consider Lowery's claim that his beliefs differed from those of an inflammatory IWW pamphlet that was submitted as evidence against him. Rejecting Lowery's demand to speak as an individual, the court insisted that his membership in a group spoke for him. "The defendant made these doctrines his own by accepting membership in the organization by which they were promulgated, and an exposition of whose principles they represent."[51]

Civil libertarians at times also shared the belief of their opponents that the declaration of war had shifted, at least temporarily, the boundaries of legitimate and illegitimate speech. Lillian Wald was a founding member of the American Union against Militarism, but when the United States entered the war and the AUAM showed no signs of letting up its oppositional stance, she resigned in protest, insistent that the group should work with, not against, the government. She distanced herself from more radical pacifists—even though she remained a leading member of the Woman's Peace Party—but to no avail, as she shared the common fate of denigration and dismissal that attached to all pacifists during the war.[52]

Reverend Herbert Bigelow, a radical antiwar preacher active in the Cincinnati area, shared Wald's view. In October 1917, a vigilance society whipped and almost hanged Bigelow "in the name of the poor women and children of Belgium" after a speech in Newport, Kentucky, and his case became a rallying cry for the nascent civil liberties movement. Three months later, the NCLB invited him to address the topic of "American Liberties in Wartime" in front of an eager crowd at New York City's Liberty Theatre. Still bearing the scars of his attack, Bigelow tempered free speech with obligation. "I disagreed with the country's going to war....But when we were once in the fight I have considered it my duty, and I have so informed my friends, that we should stand by our country right or wrong."[53]

For all the episodes of repression, it would be inaccurate to paint a picture of the American landscape peopled with armies of loyalty leagues and postmasters imposing a regime of terror against fellow citizens. Americans consistently needed less outright repression than the wartime alarmists claimed. Nor did the repressions of distant and unresponsive elites mobilize a robust populist constituency for free speech. Complicated intellectual and political motives and understandings were at work even among the most committed civil libertarians. For some progressives and populists, the war years felt like a state and corporate usurpation of power and a move against democratic control. But others feared the mob and looked for ways to control its actions. Some merged populism and progressivism with civil liberties on a democratic scale; others sought protection from the winds of mass politics under the umbrella of radical individualism. These were dangerous bedfellows, and their collusions and compromises would have durable legacies.

★ *Men Must Be Held Accountable*

It was only a matter of time before responsible speech reached the U.S. Supreme Court. Between 1917 and 1925, the justices heard a series of cases on freedom of expression, and in their rulings, they engaged with, and transformed, the law of responsible speech. The Constitution's First Amendment forbade Congress to make any law impinging on the freedom of speech or the press, but that had been little tested in the years before 1917, mostly because it applied only to the federal government and not the states. Issues of expression had come before lower courts, and questions of press and speech had been litigated in the context of labor law and libel law, but until the passage of the Espionage Act, the Court had not ruled directly on these matters.[54]

The war's cases piled up on the docket, and the Court began hearing them in January 1919. The first concerned Charles Schenck, general secretary of the Socialist Party in Philadelphia, charged with violating the Espionage Act when he and his colleague, Elizabeth Baer, circulated fifteen thousand copies of an anticonscription pamphlet. "Do not submit to intimidation," it warned, and offered numerous quotes from the war's opponents—among them Representative Champ Clark's comment during the debate over the Selective Service Act that "a conscript is little better than a convict." Schenck urged readers to "assert your rights." Schenck's pamphlet went even further, radically insisting that citizens had an obligation to dissent: "If you do not assert and support your rights, you are helping to deny or disparage rights which it is the solemn duty of all citizens and residents of the United States to retain.... You must do your share to maintain, support and uphold the rights of the people of this country." In briefs submitted to the Court, government attorneys dismissed Schenck's First Amendment claims as "frivolous and unsubstantial."[55]

The justices agreed. Speaking for the Court in a March 1919 ruling, Justice Oliver Wendell Holmes Jr. encoded the principles of responsible speech into his decision, articulating a vision of civil liberties in the context of a broader political culture organized around duty and obligation. Holmes began by defending free speech and admitted that much of what the socialists wrote had earlier been said by "well-known public men," including the Speaker of the House of Representatives. But like so many others, Holmes agreed that the war had changed the terms of political obligation. "We admit that in many places and in ordinary times the defendants...would have been within their constitutional rights. But the character of every act depends on the circumstances in which it is done." Holmes then gave voice to American history's most memorable articulation of responsible speech: "The most stringent protection of free speech would not protect a man in falsely shouting fire in a theatre and causing a panic." Holmes believed that claims for the protection of freedom of speech must be considered, but carefully. "When a nation is at war many things that might be said in time of peace are such a hindrance to its effort that their utterance will not be endured so long as men fight and that no Court could regard them as protected by any constitutional right." This was responsible speech at its most limited, in which the burden rested on individuals to regulate themselves and to navigate the boundary between responsible and irresponsible speech.[56]

The remainder of 1919 brought a wave of courtroom defeats for radical speakers. Jacob Frohwerk's conviction for calling it a "monumental and inexcusable mistake to send our soldiers to France" was upheld, as was that of the editors of the *Philadelphia Tageblatt*, prosecuted not for the words they wrote, but for their translations and deletions of other articles, which federal authorities found seditious. Before the year was out, justices could also read an array of criticism of their work in magazines and law reviews as legal scholars challenged Holmes's definition of responsible speech.[57]

The Court that had been unanimous in *Schenck* divided several months later when it took up the case of Jacob Abrams and his colleagues, who had been sentenced to twenty years in prison for circulating two pamphlets in New York City in August 1918. In the pamphlets, the radicals attacked the Allied intervention in Siberia against the Bolshevik Revolution and proclaimed the imminent demise of the capitalist system. They also presented a challenge to prevailing understandings of national loyalty when they pledged outright resistance: "We, the toilers of America, who believe in real liberty, shall pledge ourselves...to create so great a disturbance that the autocrats of America shall be compelled to keep their armies at home, and not be able to spare any for Russia."[58]

As in *Schenck*, the appellants called on the First Amendment, with attorney Harry Weinberger at their side. And like Charles Schenck, they lost. The Supreme Court upheld their convictions. For proponents of responsible speech, *Abrams* was an open-and-shut case. Writing for the majority in November 1919, Justice John Clarke thought that the precedent of *Schenck* disposed of the claims of Jacob Abrams, and he wasted little time in saying so. For Clarke, the matter came down once again to responsibility. "Men must be held to have intended, and to be accountable for, the effects which their acts were likely to produce." And in this case the intent was clear. "The manifest purpose of such a publication was to create an attempt to defeat the war plans of the government of the United States." Its circulation was doubly unacceptable, given New York's position as the nation's leading port, as a transfer point for military embarkation, and as a center for wartime production. Such behavior, reasoned Clarke, clearly failed the clear and present danger test that Holmes had earlier set out; as irresponsible speech, it merited no protection.[59]

Nevertheless, *Abrams* prompted a vigorous dissent by Justices Holmes and Louis Brandeis, both of whom had sided with the majority in *Schenck*. Holmes's dissent is often read as an epochal shift to the defense of free speech, but if so, it was articulated in the language of responsible citizenship. Holmes reiterated his certainty that the state could regulate speech more strictly in time of war, and he understood why wartime efforts to do so had reached such proportions: "If you have no doubt of your premises or your power and want a certain result with all your heart," he wrote, "you naturally express your wishes in law and sweep away all opposition." But Holmes insisted that "the ultimate good desired is better reached by free trade in ideas, that the best test of truth is the power of the thought to get itself accepted in the competition of the market, and that truth is the only ground upon which their wishes safely can be carried out."[60]

The marketplace of ideas sounded like a broadly inclusive vision, but its participants were limited to America's responsible citizens. It was they whom Holmes sought to protect, more so than the irresponsible anarchists and socialists whose fates were in his hands that day. In his dissent, Holmes indicated that he would have accepted punishments for the *Abrams* defendants, although "the most nominal punishment seems to me all that possibly could be inflicted." For these were not responsible citizens, in Holmes's view, but "poor and puny anonymities" whose pamphlets could not but fail to dissuade good citizens from their obligations. "Now nobody can suppose that the surreptitious publishing of a silly pamphlet by an unknown man, without more, would present any immediate danger," Holmes wrote dismissively.[61]

Both the majority and dissenting opinions in *Abrams* emerged from a culture of citizenship that imagined rights could be responsibly exercised by responsible citizens. Only slowly did civil libertarians lay the ground for the obligation to protect dissent that Charles Schenck had defended in his socialist pamphlet; when Eugene Debs told his listeners that they were "under infinite obligations" to "the minorities who have made the history of the world" and that "the only way we can discharge that obligation is by doing the best we can for those who are to come after us," he was promptly arrested. But the idea had gained a judicial foothold in Holmes's belief in the value of legal process in his *Abrams* dissent—that people would come to value the free trade in ideas "even more than they believe the very foundations of their own conduct."[62]

Responsible speech still ruled, but it regulated new citizens. The socialists and anarchists who stood before the Court in *Schenck* and *Abrams* had moved through a process most remarkable for the palpable presence of the federal government. Draft laws, Espionage Acts, and immigration and deportation laws caught the defendants in a web spun from Washington. They were punished by the state; only to the state could they turn. But not all regulations of speech featured the federal government so prominently. Sometimes, as in the case of the nation's libraries, the state was hardly visible at all.

★ *Responsible Readers*

Americans boasted that they fought a war with soldiers who read: men who understood the terms of citizenship and could therefore consent to them. Libraries, like newspapers, created such citizens. As the *Denver Times* editorialized, "The Hohenzollern thinks he is fighting an American army and navy but this is a serious error; he's fighting the American home spirit, which is invincible.... Books for soldiers!" Of course, if libraries were good for the war effort, the war could also be good for librarians, who in 1917 wanted eagerly to demonstrate both their national patriotism and their professional efficiency. During the war, the American Library Association, a relatively small professional society, found itself mobilized as a supporting war agency along with such massive organizations as the Red Cross and the YMCA.[63]

Librarians gathered books and magazines to send to soldiers overseas, worked in war libraries at military camps across the country, and helped inform the civilian reading public about the war. They also stood at the forefront of wartime movements for censorship. Most Americans, though not all, took censorship for granted as something that responsible citizens did, and many volunteered in moral vigilance societies that guarded the nation's culture against dangerous or immoral ideas. Women's clubs frequently supported the censorship of films and books, voluntary societies patrolled theaters in New York and other cities, and grassroots African-American organizations campaigned for the censorship of offensive works such as the inflammatory film *Birth of a Nation*. A 1918 report of the NAACP boasted that "the branches keep up a steady censorship of the press."[64]

Wartime posters boasted of the democratic nature of an army filled with soldiers who read. At home, librarians quietly censored or purged suspicious books from library shelves. (*Courtesy of the Library of Congress Prints and Photographs Division*)

During the war, librarians collaborated closely with state agencies and voluntary associations that undertook campaigns to monitor the nation's reading. A newspaper in Lincoln, Nebraska, pushed a successful campaign to remove a thousand German-language books from the State Library Commission collection; the commission ruled the books essentially "harmless" but removed them from circulation nevertheless. In Ohio, the Columbus public library sold its German collection for scrap paper. Public libraries in Chicago, Cincinnati, Cleveland, St. Louis, Minneapolis, and Los Angeles all removed German books from their shelves.[65]

There were occasional instances of criticism, as when a War Department list of books deemed unacceptable for military libraries found its way into national newspapers in February 1918. The *Detroit News* denounced "the deadly censorship fever" and took the exceptional position that access to books ought to be greater among soldiers than among civilians. Comparing library censorship to the antivice work of Anthony Comstock, the paper complained that "in peace days our national literature was puritanized and mollycoddled practically out of existence by the Comstockery of the post office department and the public libraries. Now the camp libraries are threatened by the same malady." The paper insisted that "a man fighting for democracy has a right to choose his own reading matter" just as "the people—not the superior people, but all the people—have the right to rule themselves."[66]

On December 4, 1917, Mary Couthouy Smith, an author and member of the pro-war writers' collective the Vigilantes, asked John Cotton Dana, director of the Newark Public Library in New Jersey, to remove eight books that she thought tended "to misrepresent history and deceive the young and innocent." With the support of the Newark trustees, Dana refused. "I came to the conclusion...many years ago," he told Smith, "that liberty of thought is a very desirable thing for the world and that liberty of thought can only be maintained by those who have free access to opinion." Dana was denounced in the popular press; one newspaper called his decision "reprehensible folly." The library profession agreed; as one journal noted, "common sense application of [censorship] should be the solution of the present problem."[67]

Dana himself was no opponent of the war—he organized an exhibition of war posters that traveled to libraries nationwide. Nor was he a free speech radical, even as he suddenly found himself the newest member of wartime America's impromptu civil liberties coalition. In a postwar article on "Public Libraries as Censors," Dana called censorship a "benign necessity," emphasized the librarian's obligations to the community, and noted that a librarian "should check his efforts by a skillful anticipation of what his community will quietly accept." He phrased an opposition to censorship in the language of responsible speech: "One of the aids to the growth in a democracy of wisdom and of the habit of self-control and of the feeling of individual responsibility...is the lack of autocratic censorship." Internalized self-censorship would make the kinds of citizens who could be entrusted with rights.[68]

Libraries in Connecticut had to confront "seditious" literature on their shelves. In Hartford, as elsewhere in the country, policy makers and local patriots worried about the circulation of enemy propaganda; in July 1918, the Connecticut State Council of Defense decided to act. In a memorandum to each of the state's libraries, council member W. E. Gifford noted that "from time to time we have been advised by various State Councils that certain books of supposed pro-German tendency are in circulation in the various public libraries," and he offered the states a list of books that had been investigated by the American Library Association.[69]

Some of the lists came back to the Council of Defense with nothing but check marks of removed books—silent notations that might have been either eager compliance or sullen obedience. But other librarians noted that the work suggested by the Connecticut Council had long since been completed. Dotha Stone Pinneo, the librarian at Norwalk, cheerfully informed the state council that "we had, the moment relations were severed between the United States and Germany, removed everything which seemed to us harmful, but I am glad to have the full list," while Grace A. Child, librarian of the Gilbert School in Winsted, tartly informed the state council that "we do not circulate any books containing German propaganda or those otherwise harmful or disloyal as connected with Germany."[70]

Alice Coffin of the public library in Windsor Locks assured the state council that "there is no demand for any of these books here"; A. M. Clark of Groton wrote that "there being no call for any, it doesn't make much difference about there being on the shelves, but as I am not always at the desk have done as you ask." Margery Abell of East Hampton remarked that "we have had very few calls for books on Germany of late." In the thirty-eight letters that remain, only the librarian of Yale University sounded a mild note of dissent, arguing that his library had a special mission to keep such books for scholars to use—not now, but in the future.[71]

Did the effort by the Council of Defense eliminate the views expressed in the books that librarians had tucked away for the duration? Perhaps. After all, fewer books were available after Gifford's letter circulated than before. Many books, however, were gone from the shelves before the state authorities sent out their letters, as popular movements regulated speech at the local level. Formal censorship was just one of many mechanisms that guaranteed loyalty to the nation. The most curious fact of this correspondence is the repeated insistence by the librarians that whether the books were on the shelves or not, no one was checking them out anyway. War had already changed both librarians and readers as citizens.

Finally, what criticisms there were of censorship policies—whether those policies came from state actors in the Council of National Defense, industrious librarians, or groups like the Vigilantes—took on new meanings as well. Librarians were not indifferent to intellectual freedom and knew the need for the circulation of ideas and the freedom to write and publish one's views. But they saw these rights in tension with the obligations of citizenship and the special obligations placed upon them in their position as custodians of culture. They didn't think they were violating anyone's civil liberties. They protected the rights of responsible citizens capable of self-regulation, men and women who understood that there could also be obligations to keep silent, and obligations not to read. Those citizens who could not so regulate themselves could not be defended and would ultimately be suppressed. This was nothing so simple as war hysteria, even when librarians were among those who gathered books in the town square and set fire to them. This was the culmination of a culture of obligation in a moment of political crisis.

★ *Honest Injun*

As the culture of obligation, grounded in voluntary associations and the politics of everyday life, faded over the course of the twentieth century, so, too, would the assumptions of responsible speech that accompanied it. But civil liberties after World War I were never sustained by the same institutional networks of everyday life that undergirded the prewar civic culture, and the lived experience of the culture of rights proved far weaker, and open to a far smaller segment of society, than the culture of obligation. Just as scientists abandoned the proposals to mend the Liberty Bell as mere alchemical wishes, the wide array of Americans who labored on behalf of civil liberties found that the practical science of politics could not always mend the Constitution they believed the war had broken.

The mending began soon after the war was over. On November 27, 1918, President Wilson ordered Burleson to stop the wartime censorship, later telling his postmaster general that "I cannot believe that it would be wise to do any more suppressing. We must meet these poisons some other way." A few months later, Wilson pardoned hundreds of Espionage Act prisoners; Justice Department officials openly acknowledged that many were "victims of wartime passion or prejudice." Their shared victimhood was a political experience. "The conduct of the Postmaster General," noted the *New Republic*, "is driving...all citizens who believe in the freedom of the press, to make common cause." For others, the mending came too late. Radicals like Max Eastman had lost faith in free speech altogether. "Words are not going to make any difference. Words are nothing." The Espionage Act remained in force until July 7, 1921, when the United States quietly signed a separate peace treaty with Germany. The law remained on the books, however, and the Supreme Court upheld it in a case involving the *Milwaukee Leader*, a paper that had met the passage of the Sedition Act with a disheartened editorial advising readers that "your best course is not to talk about the war at all." The Court seemed almost tired of the whole question, dismissing technicalities of the Post Office Department's administration of the Espionage Act as "settled law."[72]

Albert Burleson knew that he had done right by the country. In an April 1919 speech in Washington, he defended his actions against critics. "Considering these conditions, are you surprised that criticism should be directed against the Postal Establishment?" During the war, proponents of responsible speech had turned to the state and urged it to act; civil libertarians sought protection through state action as well. What both groups overlooked was that regulation was handed down not only by courts and postmasters; it also came from librarians and emerged inside individual consciences. The pacifist writer Lowes Dickinson, reflecting on the impact of war in 1920, thought that in postwar society, people "seem to be terrorized by the fear each individual has of what all the other individuals taken together are supposed to be feeling and thinking, till it sometimes appears as if public opinion were the opinion which nobody holds, but which everybody supposes other people to hold." During the war, George Creel had reasoned that "the less said about any sort of censorship the better.... It is desirable that no one should know just where the censorship is working."[73]

"Honest Injun," said Burleson, "I have no complaint whatsoever."[74]

6

Enemy Aliens: Loyalty and the Birth of the Surveillance State

News reports and soldiers' writings reveal that as American soldiers departed New York Harbor bound for France, some cheered when they saw the Statue of Liberty. But how did these same soldiers react as their ships steamed past the nearby immigration processing center at Ellis Island? They certainly knew what it was: many of the soldiers themselves had passed through the facility in the years since its opening in 1892. And many knew that with the coming of war, the island now served a different purpose. The outbreak of World War I had effectively halted America's steady prewar stream of immigrants. Instead, the federal government turned the empty halls of Ellis Island into a detention center for enemy aliens—citizens of America's wartime foes, particularly Germany. Ironically, despite its place in contemporary American collective memory as a place of welcoming, Ellis Island was always a site of regulation—never more so than in 1917, as Uncle Sam's troopships floated by.[1]

The ironies abound. Not a single person held at Ellis Island was a soldier captured on the battlefields of Europe, even though the press referred to inmates as "German prisoners of war." About half were German sailors and merchant seamen captured immediately after the United States declared war, and others were German citizens caught in the net of wartime legislation. But many—and indeed, by war's end, most—were not German at all, but immigrant radicals from many nations, all deemed dangerous to national security. From the outset, then, America's German enemy alien program had as much to do with contests over domestic politics as it did with international affairs.[2]

German Americans' wartime persecution was a surprise and an aberration. Coming to terms with its effects is difficult; surely theirs was an ethnic community already in the midst of declining distinctiveness. Instead, as the politics of obligation meshed with the politics of identity, ideas about national belonging helped formalize new categories of citizenship: the "enemy alien," the "pro-German," and finally—the "un-American." Political obligations, too, were transformed. Voluntary associations carried out much of the day-to-day work of regulating enemy aliens on the home front, as members drew on traditions of voluntarism and responded to the realities of a small federal bureaucracy. Loyalty was debated and enforced by Lutheran chaplains, progressive reformers, and even angry mobs—and then ultimately by the state. By war's end, new procedures—internment, denaturalization, deportation—joined new state structures such as passport agencies, immigration offices, and the Justice Department's Bureau of Investigation as features of a twentieth-century American state that owed much to wartime concerns about German immigrants and their beer halls, but neither began nor ended there.[3]

The obligation of loyalty stood at the center of this debate. Men, money, and materials could be mobilized under Uncle Sam's watchful eyes, but how could something as immaterial as national loyalty be measured, and how could it be assured in the divided political climate of the home front? In the study of his sprawling house just steps from Harvard University's campus, the sixty-year-old philosopher Josiah Royce spent the summer of 1916 pondering the duties of Americans in the global crisis that surrounded them. Born and raised in Gold Rush California, Royce's upbringing gave him a unique perspective on the Progressive Era's broader obsession with social solidarity. Sociologists parsed the distinctions between the lost world of a homey *Gemeinschaft*, or community, and the cold, impersonal *Gesellschaft*, or society, that had dawned in the twentieth century; radical agrarian populists and Christian socialists sought to reclaim an evaporating republican past; historical nostalgists, devotees of flag cults, and Daughters of the American Revolution gathered in patriotic societies nationwide; Progressive reformers labored in search of the Great Community.[4]

Community meant everything to Royce, and loyalty, in his view, was its foundation. In an influential 1908 book, *The Philosophy of Loyalty*, Royce proposed loyalty as a way of life. He defined the term as "the willing and practical and thoroughgoing devotion of a person to a cause." But which cause? Mindful that people of goodwill might differ, and fearful that people might dedicate themselves to wrong or even evil causes, Royce concluded that the only solution was to have "loyalty to loyalty" in the broadest sense, in order to foster the "great community" for which he hoped so eagerly. Without loyalty, the "detached individual" could be enticed by dangerous causes. Royce's vision resonated with American political culture. Most Progressive Era theorizations of loyalty—but especially Royce's—emphasized group attachments and looked skeptically at individualism. His way of thinking lent itself to obligations. "I fully agree with those who believe that men can reasonably define their rights only in terms of their duties," Royce wrote in 1916. "I have a right to get some chance to do my duty. This is, in fact, my sole inalienable right."[5]

The world war broke Royce's heart. Already in the fall of 1914, Royce had set aside his philosophical work to devote himself to war relief; tentatively neutral at first, he vigorously denounced Germany after one of its submarines sank the British passenger liner *Lusitania* in May 1915. In June 1916, he shared with the graduating class of Clark College in Worcester, Massachusetts, his hope that war could bring "a very far-reaching and earnest revival of interest in the idea of duty." But he remained throughout an unwilling patriot. In his essay "The Hope of the Great Community," Royce depicted the war as "a conflict between the community of mankind and the particular interests of individual nations." The war, he felt, would ultimately decide the fate of the community he had worked so hard to build.[6]

In the everyday politics of the home front, loyalty proved even more difficult to define than in Royce's philosophical system. Loyalty raised complicated questions of consent, coercion, and—most fundamentally—evidence. Naturalized immigrants had deliberately chosen to live under the American regime and sworn allegiance to it. Those Americans who were citizens by birth had rarely (if ever) been asked for explicit consent to the social contract that they had implicitly entered, yet the state nonetheless took their consent for granted. During World War I, evidence of disloyalty gathered. The obligations of some Americans to multiple states or to multiple languages frustrated the defenders of national loyalty. Draft resistance and evasion, demands for suffrage and higher wages, conscientious objection, pacifism, and Bolshevism: were these not selfish evasions of duty in the midst of trying times? Surely, some Americans concluded, the bonds of national loyalty were dissolving.

But what to do about it? The loyalty of enemy aliens was as difficult to decipher as the sincerity of the conscientious objectors. Whether they read Royce's works or not, Americans knew that he was right: people had multiple, overlapping, and even sometimes irreconcilable loyalties. Cultural pluralism had its defenders, thinkers such as Randolph Bourne and Horace Kallen, as well as Louis Brandeis, who echoed Josiah Royce: "Multiple loyalties are objectionable only if they are inconsistent," Brandeis wrote. "A man is a better citizen of the United States for being loyal to his family, and to his profession or trade; for being loyal to his college or lodge." But during the war, many Americans rejected Royce's solution of a "loyalty to loyalty" that could hold all of humanity's interests at heart. Some loyalties, they decided, mattered more than others. Those who could not prove they had put their loyalty to the nation-state first—despite all the wartime speechifying, pamphleteering, and propagandizing that surrounded them—would now have to answer to the law. For German Americans, the days ahead would be trying indeed.[7]

It was far easier to police manifestations of alternative loyalties than American loyalty itself. Under wartime pressure, therefore, public symbols of conflicting loyalties—flags, languages, voluntary associations, schools—withered. If the obligation of loyalty could not be coerced, the obligation of silence could—and during the war, it was, with new tools of state power that changed the relationship of the citizen to the government. Time and again, German Americans chose silence—at times out of a stubborn resistance, sometimes out of nervous fear, sometimes without realizing they had done so. Whatever its motivations, silence helped German Americans walk the line between loyalty and disloyalty in a hostile America. But silence had consequences for Germans' cultural institutions and their relation to national citizenship. This silence, somewhere between voluntarism and coercion, showed that tacit consent was the easy way out of the paradoxes of American political obligation.

Tony Smollok understood that paradox. At some point in the winter of 1920, the Polish immigrant met in a federal prison with Reverend Constantine Panunzio, himself a naturalized citizen of Italian birth who had spent the war years working with the YMCA on the Italian front. Although convicted of no crime, Smollok had been arrested, either for advocacy of radical ideas or membership in a proscribed organization; that winter, his deportation was imminent. "When I came to this country, and saw the Statue of Liberty, I tipped my hat to it and I was happy," he told Panunzio. "The final result is that...I am arrested by the government which I tried to understand and obey."[8]

★ *Creating the Enemy Alien*

On April 6, 1917, the five hundred congregants of St. Matthew's German Lutheran Church in Hoboken, New Jersey, shuffled into their pews for Good Friday services. The war surely weighed heavily on their minds. Four days earlier, President Woodrow Wilson had asked Congress for a declaration of war; that morning, he had signed it. Many in the congregation entered church that day with a new state-sanctioned identity: enemy aliens.

Ever since August 1914, the war had pulled German Americans between their mother country and their newly adopted homeland. This was particularly true for the residents of the German immigrant community of Hoboken, a city that counted several German churches besides St. Matthew's and was proud to be the port of call for the North German Lloyd and Hamburg-American steamship lines. The ethnic assertions of Hoboken's Germans—which extended to the sale of German war bonds at the Steneck Trust Bank on River Street—had raised eyebrows even before war's declaration and before episodes of espionage and sabotage set the nation on edge. On July 30, 1916, just a few miles from Hoboken, the munitions factory at Black Tom, New Jersey, exploded in a blast said to be heard as far away as Philadelphia. Bridges had been blown up across the country, submarines had sunk ships just off the Outer Banks of North Carolina, and spies had been captured red-handed even before the publication of the Zimmermann Telegram, which promised Mexico the return of the southwestern states in the event of a German victory. German disloyalty was not entirely a figment of the American mind, although that imagination did sometimes get carried away. Some of these episodes were the handiwork of the German Empire, whose cloak-and-dagger diplomats and spies had been apprehended sporadically since 1914. Other incidents were almost certainly the doings of domestic radicals. As war neared, few Americans saw any need to make such fine distinctions.[9]

Whatever preaching the Germans expected from their minister, the real sermon on their minds was Woodrow Wilson's Proclamation of War. Promulgated that morning, the text was oddly short on rousing patriotic sentiment; instead, it dealt almost exclusively with the regulation of enemy aliens. Invoking the somewhat dusty clauses of the Alien Enemies Act of 1798, Wilson defined all male German citizens in the United States age fourteen and older as "enemy aliens." Members of this new category faced a series of specific regulations: "liable to be apprehended, restrained, secured, and removed," they would have to surrender "any firearms, weapons, or implements of war," including the newly popular wireless radios. Aliens could not live or even travel within a half-mile of any "military installation," which included munitions factories and seaports—a provision that meant that those congregants of St. Matthew's who lived near the Hudson River would technically now need permits to enter their own homes. Aliens could not print any attack on the government of the United States. Their property could be seized. They could be deported.[10]

Hoboken Lutherans heard in Wilson's words a call for tolerance but not very much of it; German citizens, he stated, should be treated "with all such friendliness as may be compatible with loyalty and allegiance to the United States."

Across the river, New York City Mayor John P. Mitchel, noting the city's ethnic diversity, urged "kindly consideration, self-control, and respect"—while in the same speech noting the legal definition of treason and its punishment (namely, execution). The city printed Mitchel's announcement "in all the principal languages" and displayed it in public places and store windows. Attorney General Thomas Gregory was blunter: "No German alien enemy in this country, who has not been implicated in plots...need have any fear of action...so long as he observes the following warning: 'Obey the law. Keep your mouth shut.'"[11]

The pastor, by now, was noticeably late. As his congregants sat in the pews, they might have reflected that Wilson's proclamation came as neither a shock nor a surprise. Legislation regulating aliens was not new, as evidenced by the fact that Wilson invoked a 120-year-old law in his initial proclamation. During the Progressive Era, guarding the borders of the state had become key to regulating the shape of the nation itself. New initiatives to monitor aliens in the United States had emerged, through shifting statutes regarding immigration and naturalization, the passage of alien land laws in western states that forbade Asian aliens from owning land, and a 1907 act regulating the citizenship of married women. New powers of deportation and denaturalization issued from Congress. Nor was the United States alone in its wartime efforts. The Hague Conventions of 1907 had specifically laid out most of the policies Wilson now enforced; other belligerent nations regulated aliens with methods that made American policies seem almost mild by comparison.[12]

But perhaps the enormity of the situation did not fully sink in until the congregation learned that there would be no Good Friday service at St. Matthew's German Lutheran Church. Herman Hexamer, St. Matthew's lay leader, entered the church and told everyone simply to go home. In the next day's paper, they read why. Their pastor, Reverend Herman Brückner, had been under surveillance for his connections with the German Seamen's House in Hoboken, a charity that brought him into steady contact with German naval personnel; agents, who had been tracking suspicious aliens since 1914, also noticed his work as a neutral intermediary on behalf of German sailors interned by the British in Jamaica. That morning, Brückner had been taken from his home and carted off to Ellis Island.[13]

★ *The Duty of Hatred*

Many of the men and women who settled in to services at St. Matthew's had an ambiguous citizenship status, suggesting that, after decades of mass migration and rapidly changing citizenship laws, the concept of American national loyalty was even more complicated in 1917 than philosophers such as Josiah Royce had let on. On the day war was declared, the United States included a substantial minority of people who were not fully, or not only—or not at all—American citizens. A series of 1913 amendments to Germany's citizenship law insisted that its citizens retained full citizenship rights even when they were also citizens by birth of another country, as most children of German immigrants were. American law and customs added another layer of complexity: in seven states, German immigrants (among others) could vote after a brief term of residence without having becoming naturalized U.S. citizens. Now, as Good Friday brought a declaration of war, commentators denounced Germany's law as the sign of a vast German conspiracy; one critic believed that "such a man readily perverted his acquired citizenship, together with the rights it afforded, to the purposes of his old allegiance." Within months, angry legislators repealed alien voting laws in nearly every state where they were still on the books.[14]

Statutes insisted that enemy status was a formal category that attached to national citizenship alone. In practice, during the war it remained an open question whether belief, action, or cultural identity—rather than territorial location or legal paperwork—might make someone into an enemy. The loyalties of German Americans, went this argument, could not be deciphered simply from a glance at the covers of their passports. Some proposed language instead, among them Gustavus Ohlinger, a tireless anti-German propagandist from Toledo, Ohio, who was himself of German birth. "A nation's life is embodied in its speech," and loyalty to the United States implied an obligation to use English. "No man of German descent," he insisted, "can become thoroughly American while retaining allegiance to the German language." Wartime movements to regulate or suppress German culture were always about more than what appeared on the surface. They revealed Progressive Era anxieties about immigration, surely on Ohlinger's mind as the president of the Chamber of Commerce in a diverse city where Germans were just one of forty-three different ethnic groups. They were surely fostered—if not caused—by the hateful propaganda that poured forth from state agencies and the mass media. And they reflected debates about political obligation. Language and culture—visible markers of multiple loyalties—emerged as flashpoints as Americans puzzled out the ethnic and linguistic obligations of American citizenship.[15]

The 1910 U.S. Census reported a total national population of just under 92 million people. More than 13 million were foreign-born (whether naturalized or not), and Germany stood first in the list of home nations, with 2.5 million. With plenty of native-born Americans of German descent added in, the census counted 8.6 million people of either German birth or parentage. Fully 9.2 million respondents identified German as their first language. Germans concentrated more heavily in some areas than in others. In 1900, fifteen cities had German-born populations of more than fifteen thousand, but these made up 36 percent of the total German-born population in the United States. Germans and German Americans made up 14.7 percent of Nebraska's population; in Wisconsin, nearly 29 percent.[16]

Through strength of numbers, German Americans supported national ethnic associations such as the National German-American Alliance, with more than three million members, as well as small-town churches, community groups, sport and shooting clubs, and singing societies. Organization in groups like the Turner societies gave Germans a collective political voice, and they dominated political party machines in such cities as Cincinnati, St. Louis, and Milwaukee, which also had vibrant German socialist communities. Literature and theater thrived in a transatlantic print culture; even the small German population of Oklahoma could choose among seven weekly papers printed in the mother tongue. Twenty-four percent of American high school students studied German, and many schools, particularly parochial elementary schools in the Midwest, employed German as their primary language of instruction. Despite these figures, however, the institutional supports of a distinctively German culture were already on the wane: immigration rates from Germany had been falling off since the 1880s, and the younger generation was decidedly more American in its focus and interests.[17]

Between 1914, when war broke out, and April 1917, when the United States entered it, it was still safe to be an outspoken supporter of Germany. The war prompted a burst of German nationalism among *Deutschtum* abroad. A Philadelphia speaker called for "the final, decisive victory of the Teutonic race," and a July 1915 editorial in the *New Haven Anzeiger* urged readers to "Speak German; write German; think German; walk German; behave German!" More muted support could be found in newspapers that defended Germany against Allied propaganda and pled for a stricter enforcement of American neutrality. George Sylvester Viereck, editor of the *Vaterland*, and Charles Hexamer, president of the National German-American Alliance, were the boldest spokesmen; most German Americans cared more about bilingual and religious education or the cultural threats embedded in campaigns for prohibition than they did about the international diplomacy of a Kaiser whom many of them despised. Indeed, even the National German-American Alliance devoted most of its energies to the fight against prohibition; its secret stash of funds—denounced during the war as funding from the German imperial government—in fact came from the German-dominated brewing industry. Such efforts at self-defense had little to do with allegiance to a foreign power. The culture that these groups protected was a specifically German-American one that blended two national traditions ("Germany my mother; America my bride," went the saying) and fiercely defended local political control against intrusions by the state.[18]

But before 1917, German-American civic life did reveal significant loyalties to Germany, and not only strident nationalists lent Germany a hand. The German-Bohemian communities of New Ulm, Minnesota, famed for their wooden shoes, shipped more than ten thousand pairs to the German Army. The pacifist Mennonites of Kansas, who despised all war, still chose to raise money for the German Red Cross and not its American counterpart. In a political culture that interpreted the actions of civic voluntarism as manifestations of political obligations, it is no wonder that it was charitable work that brought Hoboken's Reverend Brückner under government scrutiny and into federal custody. During the tense period of neutrality, charity had become a continuation of politics by other means.[19]

Even as Woodrow Wilson declared German citizens to be enemy aliens, some Americans marked them as political outsiders. Chilling anti-German statements steadily replaced prewar admiration for German efficiency and progressivism. In 1915, prominent journalist Stanhope Sprigg painted a picture of German conspiracies in Milwaukee, Cincinnati, and St. Louis in consort with fearsome German-Jewish bankers, whom he blamed both for the war's outbreak and for President Wilson's timid neutrality. Noted evangelist Billy Sunday preached that "no nation so infamous, vile, greedy, sensuous, bloodthirsty ever disgraced the pages of history." In a pamphlet that urged Americans to *Throw Out the German Language and All Disloyal Teachers*, the patriots of the American Defense Society claimed that "any language which produces a people of ruthless conquestadors [*sic*] such as now exists in Germany, is not a fit language to teach clean and pure American boys and girls" and encouraged the public burning of German-language books. All too soon, they would get their wish.[20]

Where did wartime anti-Germanism come from? Some of it had deep roots. Stereotypical Germans filled the pages of nineteenth-century periodicals, temperance movements targeted Germans' political power, and diplomatic tensions accompanied German militarization in the 1900s and 1910s. Most antipathy toward Germany, though, developed only after 1914. Some Americans became anti-German after hearing about German atrocities in Belgium, others out of fear of German espionage and subversion at home. At a deeper level, though,

While wartime propaganda was rarely as lurid as this 1918 poster by Frederick Strothmann, the war's events fostered anti-German sentiments that reshaped the meanings of citizenship not only for German Americans but also for all recent immigrants. (*Courtesy of the Library of Congress Prints and Photographs Division*)

anti-Germanism had little to do with anything specifically German. Native-born Americans projected general anxieties about immigration and ethnic difference onto unlucky Germans placed by the forces of history in the wrong place at exactly the wrong time. That's why wartime Americans often seemed so confused about whether the culprit was the enemy German state, a barbaric German culture, or the German people themselves. Whatever the source of the concern, though, their feelings intensified suddenly and dramatically after 1917.[21]

Some voiced the view that opposition to—or even hatred of—Germany was an obligation of American citizenship. Josiah Royce insisted that "our duty is to be and to remain the outspoken moral opponents of the present German policy," but he distinguished that from German culture more generally. The chancellor of Syracuse University thought it "religious to hate the Kaiser," and Horace

Bridges of the Chicago Ethical Society expounded on "The Duty of Hatred" in the *Atlantic Monthly*. "Hatred, within the limits of the purpose of ending this war and all war…is not merely tolerable," he wrote. "It is our bounden duty."[22]

The assault on German Americans ranged from small, personal incidents—what writer Hermann Hagedorn called "hand-shakes less friendly than they used to be"—to mob violence and legal strictures. It grew out of the political culture of voluntarism; vigilance against German espionage in fact framed the entire project of policing of the home front. But the assault was also, from the very first day of the war, a federal undertaking. Tensions over how the obligation of loyalty would be enforced—of how the very borders of citizenship would be defended—prompted a remaking of the political culture of obligation and laid the foundation for the state that emerged from the war.[23]

Three years of hard fighting over whether the United States would enter the European war had thoroughly politicized civil society, all but guaranteeing that the home front would witness a battle between voluntary associations. State councils of defense joined with citizen vigilance groups to wage war on the institutions of German-American civic life, where immigrants practiced their multiple loyalties so visibly. Congressional investigators hounded the National German-American Alliance (NGAA), once the cornerstone of German-American national organization. Membership declined steadily throughout 1917, until finally, in April 1918, the group voted to disband voluntarily and turn its remaining funds over to the Red Cross. American superpatriots applauded the vote, but a deeper level, the NGAA's decision had already been made for it. Across the country, smaller organizations dedicated to German-American life also closed up shop. The ethnic press was hit hard. German publications declined from 554 in 1910 to 234 in 1920; daily German newspaper circulation plummeted to a fourth of its 1910 numbers.[24]

German music had captured the ears of prewar America with the compositions of Beethoven and Wagner and the popular concerts of singing societies. During the war, few other elements of German culture were so savagely attacked. The American Defense Society, an elite patriotic society, fumed that German music was "one of the most dangerous forms of German propaganda, because it appeals to the emotions and has power to sway an audience." The group found receptive audiences across the country. The mayor of Lincoln, Nebraska, ordered all German composers eliminated from the program of the visiting Minneapolis Symphony Orchestra. In Tampa, the Florida Federation of Women's Clubs led a similar charge. Teachers in Columbus, Ohio, pasted over the pages of music textbooks containing German songs; in California, they cut them out with scissors. Crowd actions targeted German singing societies for intimidation, arson, and destruction.[25]

Some audiences and musicians mounted a spirited resistance, including Karl Muck, conductor of the Boston Symphony Orchestra (BSO). Already under suspicion for his love of German composers and his German birth (his formal citizenship status was unclear), the fifty-eight-year-old Muck crossed the line in Providence, Rhode Island, on October 30, 1917, when he refused a request to conduct "The Star-Spangled Banner." "Art is a thing by itself, and not related to any particular nation or group," he insisted. The Rhode Island Council of Defense's resolution against his "deliberately insulting attitude," issued the next day, was only the beginning. The *Providence Journal* demanded his internment as an enemy alien. Across the country, his appearances prompted violent protests: BSO concerts were canceled in Pittsburgh, Baltimore, Detroit, and Chicago. Despite a vigorous defense from the symphony's patron, the aging Brahmin and Civil War veteran Henry Lee Higginson, and even despite his performance of the anthem on a symphony hall stage that was ostentatiously draped with a massive American flag, Muck's days were numbered. At 11:00 P.M. on March 25, 1918, having just completed rehearsals for the next day's performance of Bach's *St. Matthew Passion*, Muck returned to his home in Boston's elegant Fenway neighborhood. With enemy alien regulations in hand (but not an arrest warrant), federal agents and Boston police seized the conductor, dismissing Muck's assertions of Swiss, not German, citizenship. Stripped of his post (and its whopping $28,000 annual salary), Muck sat out the war on Ellis Island.[26]

But for all the resistance of Karl Muck, for all the blustering of the American Defense Society and the *Providence Journal*, a careful ear turned to the American home front hears less discordant noise than compliant silence. German music had often been discontinued long before laws banning it were propagated: New York and Chicago opera companies chose to stop performing in German rather than face legislation or hostility. Often German-American organizations made the decisions themselves, as when members of the Northeastern *Sängerbund* voted in October 1917 to postpone their annual *Sängerfest*. The obligations of loyalty required the elimination of visible signs of multiple allegiances. Wartime Americans told the German immigrants who dismantled their musical cultures that the political violence they did to themselves was a sign of their patriotic affirmation; they were honored for displaying only one political obligation.[27]

Assaults on German music soon turned to German books. Book-burning rallies took place all across Nebraska; the faculty of the University of Colorado laboratory school organized Boulder's event. Other public celebrations included a "stein-breaking fest" in Omaha sponsored by the Red Cross and the slaughter of German dog breeds in Columbus, Ohio. Public flag rituals reached German Americans in episodes like one in Huron, Ohio, in April 1918, when a crowd forced the local German pastor to salute the American flag in a public ceremony. In Papillion, Nebraska, a mob beat the town's German Lutheran pastor. Another mob in Detroit dragged a German-American man through the city, shaved him, and threatened to drown him in the Detroit River. In California, a San Jose man was tarred and feathered and chained to a cannon in a public park. When the townspeople of Collinsville, Illinois, lynched Robert Prager on the night of April 4, 1918, they carried wartime violence to its most extreme.[28]

Local councils of defense gave the duty of hatred a legal force, combining the culture of voluntarism with the authority of wartime state power. In the minutes of their December 29, 1917, meeting, members of the Oklahoma State Council of Defense noted that "a few men convicted in Federal courts, a few fined, a few held up to the ridicule of their neighbors, and perhaps a few shot, would mean the stamping out of pro-Germanism in Oklahoma." Law could sometimes provide modest cover: Muskogee, Oklahoma, averted a lynching when the city's judge stepped in and arrested two German men on the dubious charge of hoarding flour so that he could protect them from mob violence. But as often as not, the law only amplified the repression that Germans experienced. In Texas, the Nueces County Council of Defense supervised the whipping of a Lutheran pastor accused of preaching in German after the council had warned against it.[29]

Addressing government officials and investigators in Washington, letter writers urged a more powerful response—and thereby imagined a more powerful state. Harry Walker of New York City sent a telegram to Woodrow Wilson's secretary Joseph Tumulty in July 1917, worried that the "greatest traitor I know is employed in Harvy Restaurant. I know he is Prussian." D. H. Rittenhouse wrote from Trenton to turn in two nurses at the New Jersey Hospital there. "Insane Hospitals are good places for German spies to work," wrote Rittenhouse, who proudly noted that he was "70 years of age and 100 per cent American and if I can aid in doing anything to thwart the aims of German rulers I shall be glad." Velma Brundage of Centralia, Washington, wrote to turn in her neighbor, Mike Urban, as "a German spy." When Justice Department agent Tom Howick visited the small Washington city, he found that "Miss Brundage proved to be a member of the seventh grade of the primary schools and but thirteen years of age." From ages thirteen to seventy, Americans exercised the duty of hatred both inside and outside of state institutions.[30]

★ *Interning Enemy Aliens*

Even before the war, the Bureau of Investigation kept careful watch over Germans in America; by March 1917 it had compiled a list of 98 whom it wanted interned on the very first day of the war and another 1,300 it planned to keep under surveillance. But before too long, the federal government had a problem on its hands. In the nation's custody were 1,356 German naval personnel, 2,300 German merchant crewmen from both domestic American ports and in the U.S. territories in the Philippines and the Panama Canal Zone, and eventually a total of 2,300 civilian enemy aliens deemed dangerous to the United States—among them Hoboken's Reverend Brückner. What was it going to do with them?[31]

As the Wilson administration pondered its options, leading figures in the War Department had at their fingertips a report by the National Committee on Prisons and Prison Labor. At some point in early 1917, the progressive prison reform group established a Committee of Internment of Alien Enemies with such distinguished members as former U.S. Attorney General George Wickersham and Raymond Fosdick, a reformer whom Wilson would later name director of the army's Commission on Training Camp Activities. The committee drew up elaborate plans for the mass internment of the nation's entire population of German enemy aliens. True to their progressive sensibilities, the reformers insisted that internment would be for the aliens' own good, "to safeguard the public from their depredations [and] the aliens from unfriendly acts of citizens."[32]

In the light of the internment of Japanese-American citizens and aliens that would follow a generation later—an internment that was both more massive (more than 120,000 were seized) and more sweeping (plans in World War I never contemplated the internment of U.S. citizens, as would happen in World War II)—it is difficult to gain perspective on the prison reformers' proposal. The plans were elaborate and detailed, going so far as to count out the total requisition of silverware an internment policy would require and to prescribe a bedtime for potential internees. This was far too practical to belong in the same category as the empty blustering of xenophobic newspaper editors. And in fact, officials at the highest levels of the U.S. government contemplated mass internment. They discussed the subject in the halls of the War Department and at Cabinet meetings, where Secretary of State Robert Lansing and Treasury Secretary William McAdoo both supported the policy. Internment's opponents argued not from principle, but from utility. The War Department was never enthusiastic about the plan and strenuously claimed that scarce resources would

German enemy aliens whiled away the time playing board games at an internment camp at Fort Douglas, Utah. More than six thousand Germans were interned during the course of the war. (*Used by permission, Utah State Historical Society, all rights reserved*)

be better spent in prosecuting the war itself. Wilson demurred, too, knowing that the government could hardly handle the task. The federal government did not unleash wartime anti-Germanism by ceding its monopoly on the legitimate use of violence against German Americans. It had explicitly decided not to seek it in the first place.[33]

But there was still the matter of the prisoners. Government policy ultimately assigned the Germans to one of four locations. Fort Douglas in Salt Lake City, Utah, received several German naval crews and all enemy aliens west of the Mississippi. Those east of the big river ended up at Fort Oglethorpe in Georgia. A smaller group of prisoners, all German sailors from the Atlantic, was held at Fort McPherson in Georgia, and merchant crewmen went to Hot Springs, North Carolina. Germans captured by Americans as prisoners of war on the European battlefields were never transferred to the United States, in part because of custody battles with French and British authorities and also because hostilities ended before a transfer system could be implemented.[34]

Camp facilities earned a thumbs-up from a visiting Swiss legation in the fall of 1917; certainly, by comparison with prisoner-of-war camps near the front lines in Europe, conditions were excellent. Internment, though, was no vacation; the camps resembled something between a military barracks and a domestic U.S.

prison. Some of the Germans at Fort McPherson were attached to the Atlanta Federal Penitentiary's road gangs, and internees elsewhere performed agricultural labor at the standard prison labor wage of fifty cents a day.[35]

By design, the internees had very little contact with the outside world. Those held in temporary detention at Ellis Island received visits from spouses, friends, legal counsel, and the YMCA. The camps, however, were another matter; it appears that the only civilians allowed to visit the German internees were their spouses and a select group of ministers, sent by the National Lutheran Commission for Soldiers' and Sailors' Welfare. But even the ministrations of the Lutheran pastors were not without complication. One, Reverend Walter Schmitt, also acted during the war as an informant for the Military Intelligence Division of the U.S. Army, reporting back to headquarters what he had learned during his pastoral visits. German Americans reinforced their distance from the German internees. Fearful of appearing too sympathetic, they took up few public collections, although they did offer hospitality to internees' wives, some of whom took up residence in the nearby communities of Salt Lake City, Chattanooga, and Atlanta.[36]

As the war unfolded, incidents of popular scrutiny intersected with the construction of an apparatus of surveillance within the federal government. On November 6, 1917, Wilson ordered all male German aliens age fourteen and older to register. On April 19, 1918, he extended those regulations to women. At their local post offices and police stations, some 482,000 German citizens in the United States filled out forms, submitted photographs and fingerprints, and swore an oath of loyalty to the United States. About four thousand more were detained and then released on parole, a policy that Attorney General Thomas Gregory found thoroughly satisfactory. Detentions "for a limited period to produce a disciplinary effect," he noted, were "a powerful deterrent against alien-enemy activity." But the government never entirely abandoned its internment plans: American Protective League operatives across the country were asked to prepare "a place of confinement accommodating from 200 to 500 persons...available upon an hour's notice."[37]

In April 1917, the federal government ruled that enemy aliens could not work in or live within one-half mile of a military installation or a munitions manufacturer. In New Haven, the Connecticut Home Guard forcibly evacuated some residents from homes near the Winchester Repeating Arms plant, but factory bosses who depended on German-born trained machinists worked out a compromise to keep the assembly lines moving. For the remainder of the war, about three hundred Germans moved about New Haven carrying passes that established their identities, marked out local neighborhoods approved for visit, and even noted their officially sanctioned paths to work. "Geschäft ist Geschäft," muttered one employee of Winchester Arms. "Business is business."[38]

Hoboken's Germans faced similar strictures. Days after the war began, President Wilson seized the German-owned port facilities and turned them over to the army as a launch site for troop transports. Beginning on June 14, 1917, and ending only with the Armistice, nearly 1.8 million American soldiers left for France from the former German piers, a fact they recorded in their battle-field rallying cry, "Hell, Heaven, or Hoboken by Christmas!" Military officers were fearful of sabotage or espionage but hard put to find a way to enforce the half-mile travel and residence restrictions in a small city that was only one square mile in area. Authorities forcibly shut down the city's 237 saloons and carefully monitored the aliens' identity papers, but no residents were moved. The army and the Hoboken Germans managed a tense and watchful truce for the rest of the war.[39]

German-owned property also came under legal, as well as popular, sur-veillance. Wartime battles over alien property often reflected concerns about Americans' multiple loyalties. But they also revealed selfish attempts to seize property from individuals made powerless by their problematic wartime citi-zenship. In territorial Hawaii, the islands' tense politics boiled over in 1917, following the arrest and indictment of Georg Roenitz, a former German con-sul in Honolulu and a vice president of the German-owned sugar company H. Hackfeld & Co. Within weeks, the entire company was in the hands of the Justice Department's Office of Alien Property. By the summer of 1918, Alien Property Custodian A. Mitchell Palmer, an ambitious Pennsylvania politician who would be the next attorney general, had parceled out Hackfeld's assets to its old competitors, organized under the new flag-waving name of American Factors, Ltd. By the war's end, even Attorney General Thomas Gregory felt compelled to restrain Hawaii's virulent anti-Germanism.[40]

As incidents of anti-Germanism reached a peak in the spring of 1918, Americans had all but forgotten the words of Josiah Royce: "Our people must learn that loyalty does not mean hostility to another man's loyalty." There were a few who sought to rein in the excesses of coercion. Writing in the *Northwestern Christian Advocate*, a Methodist bishop worried that the duty of hatred ran the risk of debasing the American war effort. "The gospel of hate is not a necessary spur to make Americans fight....It can be done without resorting to the debasing tactics of Germany herself."[41]

They often did so by appealing, as had so many other critics of mob violence, to law. After Robert Prager's death, newspaper editors called for the adoption of a stronger federal sedition law, then under debate in Congress.

"Already the news comes over the wire that patriotic citizens are taking the law into their own hands," warned Senator William E. Borah of Idaho. "If we do not do our duty, the impulses of loyal men and women will seek justice in rougher ways." Attorney General Gregory, no friend of German Americans, nonetheless insisted on the rule of law. "One of the grave dangers confronting the nation is that our own people will not be sufficiently liberal in their treatment of aliens." Gregory made clear that those "who are antagonizing our national interests and sowing dissension among our own people" would find no haven on his watch. But the federal government's approach was the best one. "Any improper or unreasonable attack" on enemy aliens "could only produce trouble." Surprising words from a man who, just one year before, had been ranting about obeying the law and keeping your mouth shut.[42]

It was not that Gregory had undergone some kind of conversion into a civil libertarian—far from it. He believed that law could both punish the disloyal and protect loyal German Americans. But Gregory left so much vagueness in phrases such as "antagonizing our national interests" or "sowing dissension" that German Americans had no way of knowing where they stood in the eyes of the local communities that actually enforced these laws. The means of demonstrating loyalty were so uncertain, and the penalties for disloyalty were so crystal clear, that German Americans ultimately found little refuge in the nation's legal structures. Nevertheless, some of them turned to the courts as they battled to protect the teaching of the German language.

★ Robert Meyer's Case

"In the future we must become a one-idealed, one-languaged, one-loyaltied people," editorialized the *Century* magazine on the eve of the war; educator Miles Gordy, writing at the war's end, agreed. "Our manner of speech is an index of our moral selves." But when the beloved English-speaking community failed to materialize, energies soon focused on the suppression of German instead. This was the logical outcome of the book burning and dog killing—and it brought the concept of multiple loyalties before the nation's highest court.[43]

Legislative regulations of language had an extensive prewar history, particularly in education, where concerns about citizenship and cultural identity were hardly new. Most language laws passed before 1917 actually protected the teaching of foreign languages; despite repeated introduction of bills, only fourteen states required education in English in 1903. They were bitter contests, and most of them involved German immigrants. Passage of Wisconsin's

Bennett School Law of 1889, which required that children must learn all basic subjects in English, galvanized a popular movement among German Americans that successfully achieved its repeal. Nebraska's 1913 Mockett Law required the teaching of German in any school district that gathered the signatures of fifty parents on a petition; politically organized German Americans had pushed it through to preempt legislation that would have required all children to attend public schools at least three months a year.[44]

During World War I, the balance of power in these battles shifted, and the race to pass language legislation was on. Once again, local and state councils of defense took the lead. In South Dakota, the State Council of Defense ordered a ban on German-language instruction in public schools in February 1918, even though it had no legal authority to do so. On June 1, 1918, it extended the prohibition to cover the use of German at all public gatherings, including church meetings, and extended the school law to include private as well as public schools.[45]

Local councils showed even more variation: in Texas, the Panola County Council of Defense declared the German language "extinct." In May 1918, the council in Hall County, Nebraska, decreed an end to all German teaching, the removal of German books from the schools, and the closing of the German-language paper in Grand Island. In a final flourish, it ruled that two local German associations, the Liederkranz and Plattdeutscher Verein, must switch their meetings and their constitutions to English. Cordell, Oklahoma, forbade the use of German within city limits; when a farmer was heard speaking the forbidden tongue to a friend in public, a local deputy beat him over the head. In the same state, in October 1918, the Grant County Council of Defense required telephone operators to refuse calls in German for the duration of the war.[46]

Widespread legislative assaults on the German language narrowed in 1919 and 1920 to the matter of education. Some states put a stop to German-medium instruction; others restricted the study of foreign languages. Some explicitly named German as the foreign language in question; most did not. (Louisiana's law referred only to the "enemy language.") The most extreme laws extended these strictures to outright bans on private schools and religious instruction. By 1923, a total of thirty-five states had adopted laws requiring English-medium instruction, and twenty-two forbade schools to teach foreign languages at the elementary level.[47]

Support for these laws came from all corners. The Indiana State Teachers' Association called for the elimination of all foreign languages from the elementary schools; teachers in Oklahoma enthusiastically supported English-medium laws. Many states acted in anticipation of pending federal legislation they thought sure to pass. The Smith-Towner Bill, introduced in October 1918, would create a Department of Education in Washington and distribute federal funds, but only to states that "shall have enacted and enforced laws requiring that the basic language of instruction in the common-school branches in all schools, public and private, shall be the English language only." Wartime nationalists thought federal control was the only way to ensure 100 percent Americanism; immigrant communities and some factions within the Catholic Church mobilized against what they perceived as an assault on their institutions.[48]

But by the time that states began enacting laws after the war's end, much had already changed. In the fall of 1917, the U.S. Bureau of Education surveyed 163 cities of 25,000 people or more and found that only 19 of them continued to offer German-language instruction in the first eight grades. In 1916–17, there were 231 students enrolled in German classes at the University of Oklahoma; the following year, just 76. The overall numbers are the most striking. In 1915, 24 percent of high school students nationwide took German; by 1922, only 1 percent did. Most decisions to withdraw German teaching came about before any legislation was passed. At the University of Colorado, wartime regents actually voted to keep German in the school's curriculum, not in a defense of academic freedom, but confident because student enrollments had already precipitously declined.[49]

How did German Americans respond to these events? Some resisted, either by affirming their loyalty or by launching courtroom challenges. Embattled small-town editors and ethnic community leaders spoke out for a more pluralistic and tolerant vision of American citizenship. The *Lutheran Witness*, a national church paper published in St. Louis, pointed out that "the change from German to English is progressing rapidly. It need not be accelerated through the policeman's billy." Julius Hüssy, the Swiss-born editor of a small-town German newspaper in central Oklahoma, demanded the right of free speech for German Americans in editorials as early as March 1917 and continued undaunted until the State Council of Defense shut his paper down in October 1918. Sometimes German Americans circled the wagons and made outsiders unwelcome; some North Dakota officials were "afraid to visit the German counties…on public business, such as Liberty Bond or Red Cross drives."[50]

The church turned out to be both a haven and a place to fight from. Lutheran churches, for decades models of political quiescence, began to mobilize. The newly formed American Lutheran Publicity Bureau in New York and the Lutheran Publicity Organization in St. Louis took a lesson from their opponents as they waged a battle of ideas and images with George Creel's

Committee on Public Information. Midwesterners formed the National Lutheran Education Association, and the American Luther League defended parochial schools. As the American Luther League in Fort Wayne, Indiana, wrote in its 1919 pamphlet *Lutherans, Awake!* "Never...have we Lutherans found ourselves in so great danger as at the present minute, and it is our duty by all just means to protect and defend ourselves against this real, earnest, and threatening danger." When several Midwestern councils passed legislation forbidding religious services in German, they were overwhelmed with so many requests for exemption that the policies had to be, as the South Dakota Council delicately put it, "modified." So many Germans in Nebraska voted with their feet in the wake of a similar decree there that the Nebraska State Council, faced with the silent resistance of empty pews, briefly considered a further ruling "that the Germans be forced to go to church whether they want to or not."[51]

German Americans also resisted in the voting booth. They rewarded Chicago mayor William "Big Bill" Thompson for standing up against anti-German efforts in that city, and they punished Ohio's wartime governor, James M. Cox. When Cox ran for president in 1920 on the Democratic ticket, he boasted that his state had "preserved good order...within its borders by cultivation of such a spirit as made open or covert disloyalty dangerous to the disloyal." In a bald-faced lie about one of the most violently anti-German states, Cox stated that "there was no untoward incident affecting peaceful alien enemies." The Cox campaign made his wartime anti-Germanism a centerpiece of his appeal, even going so far as to ask "traitors" to vote for his opponent, Ohio's Republican Senator Warren G. Harding. German Americans responded to Cox's prompting; heavily German counties went for Harding in 1920.[52]

Finally, some turned to the courts and insisted, as did the *Lutheran Witness*, that "we do not intend to give up, without a fight, constitutional, parental, religious, natural rights." This fight for parental and religious rights brought German Americans together with civil libertarians to challenge legislated loyalty in the nation's courts. The battle began in Nebraska, where the Nebraska State Council of Defense led the state's anti-German movements. In December 1917, the council banned teaching or using foreign languages in all private and denominational schools of the state. The next June, they extended the ban to include most religious services. Technically, these laws applied to all languages equally, but German was the only one directly targeted. Some of the congregations and their clergymen accepted these regulations, although resistance surfaced in heavily German pockets of the state.[53]

After Nebraska Republicans scored wide victory margins in the 1918 election, sweeping the Germans' political voice out of state government, the political drive to regulate German culture and language was unstoppable. That fall, Governor Keith Neville called a special session of the legislature to repeal the Mockett Law's protections for foreign-language education; Nebraska also adopted a state sedition law that forbade any enemy alien from acting "as lecturer, priest, preacher, minister, teacher, editor, publisher, or educator" without a permit from the state council. In April 1919, the Siman Act made it a misdemeanor to teach any subject in a foreign language, or any foreign language as a subject, to students not yet in the ninth grade. One legislator described the law as a wartime duty: "I would be ashamed to face my boy, when he returns from France, if I...had to tell him that I had done nothing to crush Kaiserism in this country."[54]

The Lutheran Church's Missouri Synod, together with a Polish Catholic parish in South Omaha, immediately challenged the Siman Act. Arthur Mullen, an Irish Catholic lawyer and prominent Nebraska Democrat, tried unsuccessfully to obtain an injunction on the grounds that the law infringed religious liberty and the authority of parents over their children. Mullen appealed to the Nebraska State Supreme Court, which denied the injunction in December 1919. "This tribunal understood the [Siman Act], not as an unconstitutional interference with religious liberty, but as an effort within the police power of the state to treat the language problem that had developed in the country because of the World War."[55]

On May 25, 1920, just after lunch, the Hamilton County Attorney stepped into Robert Meyer's classroom at the one-room schoolhouse of the Zion Lutheran Church in the town of Hampton, Nebraska. That day, Meyer was teaching the biblical story of Jacob's Ladder; fourth-grader Raymond Parpart was reading aloud from the Bible—in German. And Meyer was teaching in German, in violation of a 1919 law. Arrested, found guilty, and fined $25, Meyer launched an appeal.[56]

The Nebraska Supreme Court ruled on Robert Meyer's appeal in February 1922, voting 4 to 2 to uphold his conviction, persuaded by state lawyers that the law was crucial for keeping public order and Americanizing immigrants. "The salutary purpose of the statute is clear," they wrote. "The legislature had seen the baneful effects of permitting foreigners who had taken up residence in this country, to rear and educate their children in the language of their native land. The result of that condition was found to be inimical to our own safety." But a stinging dissent by Justice Charles Letton called the law a product of "crowd psychology."[57]

At the Zion Lutheran Church School in Hampton, Nebraska, local authorities fined Robert Meyer $25 in May 1920 for teaching a Bible lesson in German. Meyer's challenge to his arrest forced the U.S. Supreme Court to define the relationship between language and citizenship. (*Courtesy of the Nebraska State Historical Society, RG 2521-31*)

Undaunted, Arthur Mullen and his litigation team took Robert Meyer's case before the U.S. Supreme Court in February 1923, where in oral argument Mullen disparaged language restrictions as the product of "hatred, national bigotry and racial prejudice engendered by the World War" and argued that Nebraska's law violated the equal protection clause of the Fourteenth Amendment. Opposing counsel insisted that "it is the ambition of the State to have its entire population 100 per cent. American." That June, the Court handed down its decision in *Meyer v. Nebraska*. The majority opinion, authored by the conservative Justice James McReynolds, sidestepped the question of whether German posed a danger to the nation. It was likewise silent on matters of religious freedom; McReynolds and his fellow justices still believed the First Amendment applied only to Congress, not the states. He turned instead to obligation, noting in particular the "natural duty of the parent to give his children education suitable to their station in life."[58]

The Siman Act, reasoned McReynolds, interfered with German teachers' right to work, and further, it violated an implicit right of parents to control their children's education. These were old-fashioned liberties, the freedoms of contract and property that were the flip side of obligations to work or to obey a parent. Speaking for the Court, McReynolds also gave voice to a definition of the implicit rights that the Fourteenth Amendment protected for individuals against the power of the state, in a statement that would later serve as a bedrock for civil liberties movements throughout the twentieth century.

> Without doubt, [freedom] denotes not merely freedom from bodily restraint but also the right of the individual to contract, to engage in any of the common occupations of life, to acquire useful knowledge, to marry, establish a home and bring up children, to worship God according to the dictates of his own conscience, and generally to enjoy those privileges long recognized at common law as essential to the orderly pursuit of happiness by free men.[59]

McReynolds rejected the distinctions, all too common during the war, between the rights of citizens and aliens. "The protection of the Constitution extends to all, to those who speak other languages as well as to those born with English on the tongue. Perhaps it would be highly advantageous if all had ready understanding of our ordinary speech, but this cannot be coerced by methods which conflict with the Constitution—a desirable end cannot be promoted by prohibited means." Most important, McReynolds challenged the attempt to create a single national loyalty by legislative means. He acknowledged that "the desire of the Legislature to foster a homogeneous people with American ideals...is easy to appreciate. Unfortunate experiences during the late war and aversion toward every character of truculent adversaries were certainly enough to quicken that aspiration." But in a strident passage, he suggested limits to the state's efforts to remake the loyalty of its citizens. "That the state may do much, go very far, indeed, in order to improve the quality of its citizens, physically, mentally and morally, is clear; but the individual has certain fundamental rights which must be respected."[60]

Robert Meyer's case was a battle over whether the obligation of loyalty was singular or multiple, a question that would have interested Josiah Royce. Nebraska's legislators felt that alternative loyalties must be secondary to the duties of national citizenship. Meyer saw things differently, as he made clear when he told his attorney Arthur Mullen why he had continued teaching in German on that fateful day in 1920: "I knew that, if I changed into the English language, he would say nothing. If I went on in German, he would come in, and arrest me. I told myself that I must not flinch. And I did not flinch....It was my duty. I am not a pastor in my church. I am a teacher, but I have the same duty to uphold my religion. Teaching the children the religion of their fathers in the language of their fathers is part of that religion." Meyer groped toward the articulation of a duty to dissent, a notion of political obligation that would connect America's voluntarist culture of obligation with the individualism of a twentieth-century rights revolution that traced its roots to *Meyer*.[61]

Meyer invalidated language restrictions across the country, and the move to suppress private schools came to a screeching halt with the Supreme Court's later decision in *Pierce v. Society of Sisters* (1925). Hailed in the decades since as a victory for civil liberties, *Meyer* was, in and of itself, a deeply ambiguous precedent, one that protected rights that were closely tied to obligations, and deeply coercive ones at that. But simply because loyalty would not be monitored by direct legislation did not mean that the "desirable end" McReynolds sought would not be regulated through subtler means.[62]

★ The Obligation of Silence

For every Robert Meyer who learned during the war to speak out, there were many more German Americans who learned how to keep quiet. When Ohio considered adopting language restrictions, Governor James Cox insisted that Americanization was "a voluntary spiritual, and not a compulsory, process." Wartime events, however, showed that voluntarism and compulsion were not so easily distinguished. The suppression of German-American culture depended on the organized voluntary activity of German Americans themselves, as they worked out the terms of American citizenship in churches, clubs, newspapers, and even within households. The outcomes of these debates ranged from vigorous affirmations of loyalty to an eerie silence.[63]

German Americans often made noisy public displays of their American loyalty after the declaration of war, from the patriotic spring festival of the St. Louis *Turnvereine* in 1917 to a flag-waving rally of two thousand German Americans in Enid, Oklahoma, a year later. As the Selective Service Act drew in thousands of American citizens of German birth, these men highlighted their military service as evidence of national loyalty. A New York German newspaper proudly boasted of a long list of German-American patriots and assured readers that "German blood...will flow freely again if the Union again calls on its sons of the German race to be its sword and its buckler in its hour of danger." Religious leaders pointed out that more than 165,000 Lutherans wore the uniforms of the U.S. Army, and in Pocahontas, Arkansas, German-American Fred Gebhardt "beat the stuffing out of a blamed traitor" who worked next to him in a button factory.[64]

Some ethnic organizations turned themselves over to pro-war nationalism. The *Oklahoma Neuigkeiten* became a voice of strident American nationalism even as it continued to publish in German, and patriotic vigilance societies comprised of German Americans monitored their fellow citizens. The United States of America Loyalist Association counted members in every county in North Dakota; in Iowa, the German-American Patriotic Association dedicated itself to Americanizing the Lutheran Church. New York's Pro-American Society, which launched a boycott campaign against German newspapers, appears to have collaborated with the Committee of Investigations, a volunteer committee of the city's German Americans who kept an eye on the meetings of ethnic associations and paid "friendly visits" to outspoken German nationalists.[65]

German-American intellectuals were among the most vocal of anti-German wartime propagandists. Some were imbued with German culture and had close ties to organizations in Germany, but by 1917, most prominent intellectuals of German heritage had risen through the ranks of American professions and institutions, thoroughly embracing middle- and upper-class U.S. cultural norms along the way. Many were also bitter critics of the Prussian autocracy that had taken hold of their home country. Now they were uncomfortable to be singled out within their institutions as symbols of disloyalty, and some went to extreme lengths to affirm their loyalty. Otto Kahn, financier and philanthropist, called Germany "not a nation, but an evil spirit," and popular writer Hermann Hagedorn termed the hyphen "a disgrace" and called supporters of neutrality "emasculated arm-chair kickers, smug as eunuchs in a harem." Writing from Detroit, the young German Evangelical minister Reinhold Niebuhr published essays on "The Failure of German-Americanism" and ruthlessly pressed his reluctant congregation to switch its language of worship to English. Some even signed up for government service as translators and spent the war monitoring not the military cables of the imperial enemy but the small-town newspapers of the unassimilated German Americans they so eagerly wished to distance themselves from.[66]

The political crisis of the German-American churches that entangled Reinhold Niebuhr reflected conflicts among its members over the balance to strike between religious and political obligations. The Lutherans' Missouri Synod published its own anti-German tract as a way to show its members' dedication to the United States. But the German question split many congregations, often along generational lines that separated German immigrants and their American-born children. In Kingfisher, Oklahoma, younger and more acculturated German Americans wanted to switch the language of worship at the local German Evangelical Church to English but faced stubborn opposition from church leaders and from older parishioners. The young men got their way only after they beat the minister in the streets of town and forced his resignation.[67]

Many of the conflicts within churches turned on the use of German, and the debates within German-American churches were more common, more systematic, and far more decisive than the blustery decrees of the vigilance societies and Midwestern legislatures, which were only sporadically (if sometimes violently) enforced. In 1917, a sixth of the Missouri Synod Lutheran churches held at least one English service per month; by 1920, three quarters did so. German-American Catholics also changed the language of their homilies during the war. In October 1917, 30 percent of Mennonite schools taught German-language Bible classes. These were discontinued entirely by November 1918; the Mennonite-run Bethel College in Newton, Kansas, also dropped German from its curriculum. Such dilemmas faced German Americans of all ages, including Clara Jacobs, a western North Dakota farm girl who, at the age of seven, refused to speak German at home because she was embarrassed about being labeled a "pro-German" at school.[68]

Some retreated into a silent shell. University German instructors were regularly harassed, haunted by statements of German nationalism they had uttered between 1914 and 1917. After April 1917, the profession went into inner emigration: some left the field, and others who had published noisy political essays in the years of neutrality retreated into the havens of academicism and scholastic objectivity; in the pages of German literature journals after 1917, articles on philology and aesthetics took the place of earlier strident calls for pan-Germanic nationalism. Silence in German communities responded to legitimate fear, but it was also self-imposed. The *Oklahoma Vorwärts* lost eleven of its twenty-six local advertisers after the war's declaration; some of the paper's readers actually begged the editor to cancel their subscriptions for fear of being charged with disloyalty. New Haven Germans, forced by federal authorities to carry passes on public streets, now demanded them of one another; the Arbeiter Männerchor announced that "members much show their membership cards at the gates." In the most extreme case, a German teacher in Cincinnati, Ohio, was praised by his supervisor for censoring a textbook that he had written himself.[69]

Census figures tell a similar story. When the census takers came round for the 1920 count, they found 8.16 million native German speakers, a decrease of 5.6 percent in a decade, and the only language to show a decline. They also found that among all ethnic groups in 1920, Germans had the highest percentage of naturalized citizens, about 74 percent. Most remarkable was the suggestion that there had been a drop of 25.3 percent in the previous ten years in the number of people who were born in Germany. That they lied to their census takers is the only reasonable conclusion. Whether they lied to themselves, we cannot know.[70]

The transformation was not as complete as these events and figures may make it sound. German-American culture persisted and even thrived in many areas in the postwar years. The Steuben Society of America was founded after the war to give German-American culture a national presence, although it did not so much carry on the work of the National German-American Alliance as contribute a German voice to the fragile discourse of 1920s pluralism. It would never count more than twenty thousand members. Pro-German charity also quietly reemerged, through the organization of around three hundred relief collections for postwar reconstruction; some Germans withheld donations to the government-sanctioned European Relief Council, to which German Americans gave at a rate only about half that of Americans nationwide.[71]

One marker of the quiet burial of German culture came in Washington, D.C., on April 17, 1918, at a meeting of the Ladies Sewing Society of the German Orphan Asylum. As they recorded the club's minutes in broken English, they noted that "a motion was made and unanomisly carried, to conduct in the future our meetings, and write, the proceedings in the language of this the Land of our Choice, for the present and future." With a stiff upper lip, the secretary recorded that "we conform to this nescecity as good Citisens of this country, and it makes no diference to us which Language we use." But their regret shone through. "We only feel very sad that such a change had to take place, as it destroys the conecting link for those who may come to us, and do not understand the Language of this country: However we see this as our patirotic duty, and: 'start a new page.' "[72]

For confirmed Americanizers like Reinhold Niebuhr, the young Clara Jacobs, and the Lutheran thugs of Kingfisher, Oklahoma, switching from German to English included a swirling mix of pride, patriotism, embarrassment, and ambition. They renegotiated the terms of political obligation as they moved between German and American cultures, and as they spoke—increasingly in English—they gave voice to a new vision of German-American citizenship. But it was not always so easy to straddle the line. The structures of law, the threats of the councils, and pressures within German-American communities to prove national loyalty convinced older and less Americanized Germans that to speak German was somehow disloyal.

And so they were silent. If they could not speak German, they would not speak English either. Often, they simply didn't know how. As their grandchildren stubbornly refused to speak to them, their newspapers stopped coming, their Sunday sermons washed over them in familiar but indecipherable tones, and their clubrooms stood either cold and empty or burned to the ground, many Germans retreated into a shell of silence that offered little defense and even less comfort. In 1934, when sociologist Wentworth Eldredge circulated among New Haven's German immigrant community, he found his informants generally unhelpful. "The memory of the petty persecution and humiliation of those days seals the mouths of all the old timers," he noted. "Most informants withdrew into their shells as if the ban on free speech and snooping secret service agents were still the order of the day."[73]

The movement to legislate national loyalty could never have achieved the goals it set for these Germans, but it took them down in the fight. And it positioned the state squarely in the middle of these events, as German citizens stood before their local postmasters and registered as alien enemies of the nation. Their forms now rest in the archives, thousands upon thousands. The crabbed, Teutonic handwriting is nearly impenetrable, their dutifully submitted fingerprints a smudged row of inscrutable whorls. But it is the photographs that offer the most compelling images of their predicament. Dressed in grimy farmers' shirts or frilly Sunday best, the men and women in the photographs stare back at the watchful eyes of Uncle Sam with a silence excruciating to hear.

★ The Surveillance State

Thousands of those forms ended up on the desk of a twenty-three-year-old Washington clerk, hired by the Justice Department's Bureau of Investigation in July 1917. Fresh out of night law school at George Washington University, ambitious and aggressive, the young bureaucrat participated in a transformation of the American state as the wartime assault on enemy aliens laid the foundations of twentieth-century political surveillance. That summer, he still called himself by his first name, John, but he would soon begin signing his memos with the more distinctive J. Edgar.

Hoover's rise within the Bureau of Investigation was both the cause and the result of an important change in the institutions that regulated American loyalty as a political obligation. Ideas shifted, too, as concerns in the public press about enemy aliens became concerns about the "pro-German." The term was not synonymous with "enemy alien" but could include almost anyone whose actions or statements hindered the war effort. Striking workers, radical suffragists, and African-American migrants were all, at some point during the war, referred to as "pro-Germans." This was not an accident but a convergence of several factors: the institutional structures of the wartime state, preoccupied as they were with domestic subversion as well as international conspiracy; a heated and bifurcated political rhetoric that strictly divided "100 percent Americanism" from anything "pro-German"; finally, later in the war, the assumption widely held in the United States that Germany had deliberately fomented the Bolshevik Revolution to undermine the Russian war effort. The shift from "pro-German" to "Bolshevik" in the immediate aftermath of the war was seamless, then, because both culture and institutions had made the terms synonymous.[74]

Hoover helped make that transition institutional as well as intellectual. His initial position was as an aide to John Lord O'Brian, whom Attorney General Gregory had named as head of the War Emergency Division of the Justice Department. O'Brian handed his new assistant responsibility for regulating enemy aliens; Hoover's first big task was the mass registration of enemy alien women in April 1918. The young bureaucrat was efficient, but—despite his later reputation—Hoover was not always ruthless. When considering how to dispose of the case of Otto Mueller, an enemy alien who, when asked what he thought of America, responded, "fuck this god damned country," Hoover urged leniency, in contrast to senior colleagues who wanted Mueller interned for the duration.[75]

O'Brian, who found much of the day-to-day work of legal repression personally distasteful, resigned on Armistice Day, and he hurried to release enemy aliens still in captivity. Thomas Gregory resigned soon thereafter. But November 11th brought no letup in Hoover's activities or his preoccupations with radical subversion, and his new boss, Attorney General A. Mitchell Palmer, shared both his concerns about radicalism and his experience managing enemy aliens. Hoover was newly empowered, too, by the Alien Anarchist Act of October 1918, which asserted federal authority to deport any alien—or even any recently naturalized citizen—who believed in the violent overthrow of the government, even if that person had never actually acted on the belief. Bombings of the homes of prominent government officials in June 1919 stirred an outcry for immediate government action. In August 1919, Attorney General Palmer asked Hoover to head up a new General Intelligence Division. From this position, he gathered files on suspicious Americans (within four months, he had assembled two hundred thousand of them) and then masterminded the Palmer Raids, a series of radical roundups in November 1919 and January 1920 that, although they carried the name of his supervisor, bore the mark of Hoover's emerging vision. On January 2, 1920, ten thousand were arrested on a single day. Although a few thousand spent the night in the city jails (or on Ellis Island), most were released; only 556 were deemed deportable as radical aliens.[76]

The Palmer Raids had more than their share of critics. Francis Fisher Kane, a U.S. Attorney in Philadelphia, resigned in protest. Some of the newspapers and magazines that had cheered the slacker raids and applauded the intern-ment of enemy aliens looked askance at the Palmer Raids' excesses. January 1921 brought Senate hearings. Before Congress, Palmer defended himself. "I say that I was shouted at from every editorial sanctum in America from sea to sea. I was preached upon from every pulpit; I was urged—I could feel it dinned into my ears—throughout the country to do something and to do it now." Then, drawing on the rhetoric of vigilance that slacker raiders and home guards had found so persuasive, Palmer defended his agents. "If one or two of them, overzealous or perhaps outraged as patriotic American citizens—and all of them were—by the conduct of these aliens, stepped over the bounds and treated them a little roughly, I forgive them. I do not defend it, but I am not going to raise any row about it."[77]

Such language only further galvanized the civil liberties community in its fight against lawlessness and mob violence. Now they turned their guns on the state, challenging an attorney general who had displayed such an old-fashioned understanding of the law. "It appears by the public admission of the attorney general," harrumphed Harlan Fiske Stone, who would himself fill the attorney general's chair in the administration of President Calvin Coolidge, "that he has proceeded on the theory that such aliens are not entitled to the constitutional guaranty of due process of law." Stone was particularly concerned with the inaccessibility of the administrative state, writing in early 1920 to Columbia University President Nicholas Murray Butler that "the power to interfere with the liberty of the individual should never be committed to administrative offi-cers without some provision for review of their action by the courts." Given Stone's experience during the war with the Board of Inquiry, where he served as an administrative officer with plenty of power and no provision for review, his letter to Butler marked a dramatic reversal. In May 1920, the National Popular Government League, a coalition of prominent law professors—many of whom had stood quietly by during the war—published a damning pam-phlet that denounced the Bureau of Investigation as a threat to precisely the law and order that it claimed to protect. Then they followed up with court-room efforts to rein in the bureau. The next month, in *Colyer v. Skeffington*, federal judge George Anderson put the first brake on the bureau's efforts. On Capitol Hill, Montana Senator Thomas Walsh called the Palmer Raids "the lawless acts of a mob."[78]

The law professors believed that the state had failed to protect the American people; J. Edgar Hoover probably thought so, too. From the per-spective of ambitious state-builders, wartime federal enemy alien policy was a dismal failure. There was no mass internment of German Americans, and even registration had been a bust. By the end of the war, only 482,000 German enemy aliens had registered with the federal government, far below the 2.5 million German-born persons counted in the 1910 Census. But the wholesale assault on "pro-Germans" continued, and when those same people were aliens, they found the power of the wartime state, as well as the energies of its people, arrayed against them.[79]

This makes clear why Ellis Island operated as it did. During the war the number of German enemy aliens held there dwindled—most were gone from Ellis Island by April 1918—but the island's population steadily increased. "I became a jailer instead of a commissioner of immigration," reflected Frederic Howe, the island's administrator. The transition was nearly seamless: Hoover moved from regulating enemy aliens to radical ones; his colleague A. Mitchell Palmer finished up as alien property custodian and moved into the attorney general's office. Bureau of Investigation agents switched from slacker raiding to Palmer raiding. Congressional hearings about possible subversion by German brewing interests became investigations of Bolshevik conspiracies. Boston Symphony conductor Karl Muck departed Ellis Island—and radicals such as Emma Goldman and the 248 others who would be deported out of New York Harbor on the *Buford* in December 1919 moved in.[80]

★ *Schneider's Question*

Some time in 1917, fifteen-year-old John Stricklin Spratt traveled to the small coal-mining town of Mingus, Texas, from nearby Thurber for some Saturday shopping. Here a German immigrant by the name of Schneider had gone into business as a watchmaker. John Spratt remembered little about the German watchmaker, but he enjoyed looking into his shop and also fondly recalled a sleek black horse that Schneider kept out front.[81]

Spratt remembered one incident in particular. Schneider was a thrifty man, but his business had not made him rich; as a consequence he had no electricity in his home or shop. Instead, he built a large glass window in his shop front to provide natural light. "Passing his shop one day," Spratt would later recall, "I noticed him working on a watch and stopped and glued my nose to the plate glass to get a better view of his work. After a time, he asked me what I was doing. 'I'm just watching,' was my reply, to which he replied, 'Do I need watching?' "[82]

"Do I need watching?" That was the central question in the nation's wartime debate about loyalty. Plenty of Americans believed that people like

Schneider did need watching, and they attempted to enforce their loyalty through crowd actions or with stringent legislation. Others insisted, as Justice McReynolds did, that desirable ends could not be obtained by prohibited means. Direct attempts to coerce the political obligation of loyalty failed, but World War I succeeded in transforming political identities and political structures—and in turn, the very meaning of what it meant to be a loyal American. Loyalty legislation sought a visible marker of consent, but had it operated at full force, it would have made visible the state's coercive mechanisms, too. And so the coercions were masked under the guise of voluntarism and affirmations of loyalty. When even those could not be obtained, silence would suffice, adequate evidence of a tacit consent to the terms of political obligation. That for German Americans the assaults came to an end after the war does not mean that they did not endure elsewhere or have consequences.

Not long after young Spratt had his encounter with Schneider, rumors began to spread through town that the immigrant shopkeeper was a German spy. Spratt recalled little of the story, but noted that "threats followed" and that not long after, "Schneider closed his shop and left town." It is a plaintive story, the last chapter in the epic saga of the nineteenth-century American western, complete with a stranger riding his black horse out of town and onto the Texas plains. But the tale of the townspeople of Mingus is also one of the first stories of the twentieth century, the narrative contours of which remain less certain to us today. What should haunt us is what's missing from Spratt's tale, in that moment when two Americans locked eyes through a plate glass window in a dusty railroad town, as Schneider's question lingered in the air: "Do I need watching?" Spratt never answered the question.[83]

Conclusion: Armistice and After

★☆★☆★☆★☆★☆★☆★☆★☆★☆★☆★☆★☆★

Americans celebrated the Armistice twice. The first time, on Friday, November 8, 1918, rumors of the war's end triggered premature festivities. Church bells and factory whistles sounded their calls of triumph and relief— and then stopped just as suddenly, sending parishioners back to pray for peace and employees back to work for victory. November 11th, though, brought the real thing, and when it did, Americans celebrated the end of their first world war in as many ways as they had fought it. For some, the war's close meant little in light of the urgent political tasks of the day. Novelist Edith Wharton had spent the entire war in Paris, able at times to hear artillery fire from her apartment windows. After four years of dedicated voluntarism for humanitarian relief, she stood on her balcony listening to pealing church bells and reflected that her work was only beginning. "I do hope," she wrote to a friend, "that, amid all the rejoicing...my friends in America...will not forget...the desperate plight of the refugees." Carrie Chapman Catt, the president of the National American Woman Suffrage Association, treated the Armistice as just another moment in the struggle to win women the vote. She took no time off from her work that day and made only passing reference to the war's end when she wrote on November 12 in frustration to her colleague Maud Park Wood that "yesterday was such a wild bedlam that nothing could be done in the way of work."[1]

More common than the reactions of Wharton and Catt were the thousands of local celebrations in towns and cities across the nation and across the Atlantic. In New York City, crowds gathered in the chilly predawn hours to view the Statue of Liberty illuminated by floodlights. Grain traders at the Boston Chamber of

Commerce took it upon themselves to suspend wartime food conservation measures and started pelting each other with wheat, corn, oats, and rye. Savannah's drugstores reported a run on talcum powder after confetti ran out. From a canteen in Toul, near the front lines in France, Alice O'Brien, a volunteer worker with the American Fund for French Wounded, wrote to her family in Minnesota that "I have been crying with joy over the signing of the Armistice!...All the bells rang at eleven o'clock, the soldiers shouted, and everyone is so happy about it all."[2]

Americans also celebrated Armistice Day by burning things. In the small Midwestern city of Mishawaka, Indiana, populated largely by Belgian Americans whose homeland had been overrun and pillaged by German troops for four long years, townspeople gave speeches honoring both the Belgian people and American soldiers. Afterward the townspeople burned the German Kaiser in effigy. "A couple dozen Polanders" at the Glen Falls Mills in Moosup, Connecticut, "rigged up a 'kaiser' a-straddle a rail and marched through the mill," a sign, noted the local paper, "that no more work was to be done that day." Townspeople of all ethnic groups then organized a spontaneous parade in which Boy Scouts, Red Cross workers, the Moosup International Order of Odd Fellows, "citizens and business men," and even Uncle Sam himself all rode in borrowed automobiles through the streets of town with their capture. After the crowd had gathered, "with due solemnity, Bill Kaiser's carcass, weary with its long ride on a rail, was properly cremated."[3]

The Kaiser went on trial in Manhattan, where a crowd of two thousand marched through the German-American neighborhood of Yorkville behind the Kaiser's effigy, displayed in "a coffin made from the staves of a mackerel barrel." After the procession arrived at the building housing the New York Men's Night Court, a band played "The Star-Spangled Banner," and the procession entered the courtroom, determined to "bring to justice the despoiler of civilization." They demanded that the court's magistrate render punishment. "We want you to give the Kaiser fifty years." The crowd was disappointed to learn, however, that the toughest sentence handed down in the Men's Night Court was six months in a workhouse. "You leave him to us," a young woman told the judge. "We will take him to the street and attend to him." After dousing the Kaiser with kerosene and igniting him in the middle of Third Avenue, the crowd danced. A band struck up "There'll Be a Hot Time in the Old Town Tonight," while the judge resumed work in the courtroom upstairs.[4]

A trial of a different sort took place in Burrton, Kansas. John Schrag did not attend the Armistice celebrations, and townspeople wanted to know why. That night, a crowd of men filled five cars and drove to Schrag's farm eleven miles out of town, where they found the fifty-six-year-old Mennonite farmer hiding under his bed. The men brought Schrag back into town and demanded that he carry the American flag at the head of a makeshift victory parade. After Schrag refused, the crowd mocked him, beat him, and doused him in yellow paint. Someone, it was said, had gone to get a noose. Frustrated in their plan to lynch John Schrag, the crowd moved on, as a participant later remembered it, to burning "buggies and things."[5]

The Armistice's most peculiar burning took place in the tiny potato-farming community of Preston, Idaho, where eight of the town's three hundred men had given their lives in Uncle Sam's war. Preston was a progressive village that had installed a modern sewer system in the late summer of 1918, but because of the fall's influenza epidemic, local officials had forbidden town residents to remove their outhouses, for fear of illness. On the night of the Armistice, liberated from the twin plagues of war and flu, the people of Preston carried their obsolete outhouses into the town square, painted the names of German streets on them, and christened the new shantytown the "Schitty of Berlin." They then destroyed the shacks in a tremendous and angry bonfire.[6]

What did all the fires mean? For some, these were communal fires of festive celebration, and as they warmed their hands in front of the flames, they cheered the strength of the voluntary spirit that had brought the war to such a speedy end. But for others, these nighttime fires were thinly veiled threats: reminders of the episodes of hatred and bitterness that had enforced a vision of the war and cowed its opponents into silent acquiescence. The burnings of the Kaiser and his makeshift capital on the plains of Idaho erupted from a roil of conflicting emotions and political sentiments that the war had created but never resolved. What had it all been for? What, in fact, had it ever been against? In a country house outside Natick, Massachusetts, forty-four-year-old Helen Tufts Bailie laid her two young children to bed on the night of the false Armistice and grappled with these questions in her diary:

> The air is full of whistles and pealing bells. Better than Fourth of July.... I cannot feel compassion for the German people. Tho victims in a way, they...shd [*sic*] themselves have tasted more of the horrors of war.—It has been a mighty fine experience for us, braced to do our utmost, but to stop now is like running a racing automobile into a stone wall.—...My babies,—may they never know another war. That is what we have been fighting for. Many anxious hearts will leap tonight,—the carnage is over.[7]

For Bailie, as for many others, relief mixed with anger, trepidation, and the desire for revenge. The war still felt somehow unfinished.

The war had been exhausting. Moral resources, political capital, and the very flesh and bones of national citizens had been sacrificed on the Western Front. The war was also a crucial moment in the history of American political culture in the twentieth century, part of a massive and sometimes contradictory restructuring of the relationship between Americans and state power—indeed, of the basic terms of American citizenship itself. In their own way, Carrie Chapman Catt and Helen Tufts Bailie, along with the people of Moosup, Connecticut, and Preston, Idaho, knew that. That is why the political stakes were so high, why their political passions were, quite literally, inflamed.

The experience of war mobilization demonstrated the remarkable power of obligation to organize Americans' collective effort. "Men never before had so clear and moving a vision of duty. . . . There is a stimulating comradeship knitting us all together," President Wilson solemnly intoned, and he was not entirely wrong. Americans sacrificed, fought, and even died in World War I because they felt they owed something to their fellow citizens. They fought not only for themselves, their families, or privatized visions of the good life but also out of a shared sense of obligation that they had developed through their engagement with political ideas and their encounters with fellow Americans in families, schools, and community organizations. And in a sense, they were right. Obligations to the other people who made up the nation were sincere political commitments, particularly in the absence of a strong state. In practice, though, some people had more obligations than others, and creating the sense of duty that pushed Americans over the top at home or in France often had as much to do with coercion as it did with voluntarism.[8]

The history of Americans' wartime obligations brings several themes into focus: the changing relationship between individuals, voluntary associations, and the state; the connections between duties and rights in theory and political experience; the role of law and political violence in everyday life. It also helps explain some of the legacies of the wartime experience for later generations of Americans. American society had been transformed, although not always in visible ways. Viewed in a long-term perspective, America's first world war was less significant than the war endured in Europe. The United States lost some 126,000 soldiers, about 50,000 of them in combat; Germany, Russia, and France each counted their dead in the millions. The war left fewer scars on the American men who survived it: a few months in a dusty training camp was a far cry from four years in a muddy trench. Nor was the first world war as transformative as the second. World War II was longer and more intensive and did far more to reshape the structures of American politics, economics, and social relations.

The American Legion, which sponsored this 1921 parade in Kansas City, filled its ranks by drawing on America's wartime voluntarism and then mobilized that membership into the base of the nation's largest postwar lobby group. (*Courtesy of the Library of Congress Prints and Photographs Division*)

When Americans talked about wartime bureaucracy, they called it "Government," and they gave it a capital "G." Certainly "Government" got bigger during the war and, in some areas, stayed that way, with a standing army, a growing apparatus of surveillance and policing, a nascent welfare state, practice in managing the relations between labor and capital, and experience levying an income tax. The state had new concerns: some were global, as the postwar Red Scare's fear of Bolshevism blossomed into the twentieth century's Cold War. Others, particularly federal prohibition of alcohol, managed the boundary between federal and local, between the private citizen and the public good. The American polity had changed: the nation's voting rolls doubled as suffragists celebrated the ratification of the Nineteenth Amendment in 1920. Even the American people themselves had changed: submarine warfare had all but closed off transatlantic migration after 1914, a social fact codified into law by immigration restriction acts adopted in 1917, 1921, and 1924 that shaped the fundamental demographic character of American society for two generations.

During the war, the wishes of modernizing policy makers for expanded powers of coercion coincided with popular demands for voice and participation. Through countless actions, the bottom-up state-builders of wartime America blurred the line between state and civil society, creating an improvisational hybrid state that reconciled its coercive and voluntarist elements by

concealing the conflict between them. These processes did not disappear in the years after the war. In fact, voluntarism's central role in wartime political culture only furthered them.

And yet things changed. No group demonstrates this more clearly than the American Legion, the nation's largest postwar vigilance organization. Founded among American soldiers in France as a veterans' organization, it sought "to uphold and defend the Constitution...; to maintain law and order; to foster and perpetuate a one hundred per cent Americanism." It sought as well "to inculcate a sense of individual obligation to the community, state and nation;...to conse-crate and sanctify our comradeship by our devotion to mutual helpfulness." The American Legion put forward a stirring vision of obligation, articulated through comradeship and mutual devotion put in the service of the nation-state.[9]

The American Legion jumped wholeheartedly into the tumultuous conflicts of the postwar period, and Legionnaires frequently attempted to impose their vision of Americanism and social order through extralegal means. They worked closely with public and private espionage and surveillance organizations, as in Cleveland on May 1, 1919, when Legionnaires and former members of the American Protective League broke up the city's May Day parade and tore red flags from the hands of socialist veterans who dared march in their own uniforms. In the fall of 1919, Armistice Day commemorations brought violence to Centralia, Washington, where American Legion members stormed the local IWW hall and exchanged gunfire with the men inside; four Legionnaires were killed. They then captured local IWW leader Wesley Everest, killed him, and dragged his body through the city streets wrapped in an American flag.[10]

The American Legion's tumultuous postwar history demonstrates both the legacies and the dead ends of its vision. On the one hand, it continued to exercise considerable power, and it did so in conjunction with state institutions, as in November 1919, when Kansas Governor Arthur Capper called out the American Legion to break a coal strike in that state. "In time of need and emergency," announced National Commander Franklin D'Olier, "we stand ready...to support, strengthen, and speed up, if necessary, the civil authorities." Legionnaires continued to work as self-appointed state-builders, to reformulate institutions as they educated their fellow Americans into the obligations of citizenship. They made blustery intrusions into politics as they attempted to impose their vision, but they found it increasingly difficult to stamp their coercive work with the direct imprimatur of state power, as similar organizations had done during the war. In fact, American Legion leaders would soon go to great lengths to suppress vigilantism within the group's own ranks, efforts that contributed to the American Legion's transformation, by the mid-1920s, into the nation's most powerful lobby organization.[11]

Similar in its wartime origins, and yet divergent in outcome, was the postwar Ku Klux Klan. The organization had been active during the war in a few southern states (notably Georgia and Alabama), where its "secret-service men" appeared to have performed the same kinds of vigilance work undertaken elsewhere by the American Protective League. In Montgomery, the Klan delivered warnings to "immoral women" around Camp Sheridan; Birmingham's Klan was reported to be "on the lookout for alien enemies, for the disloyal, and for the fellow who is seeking to begin a strike." Unlike the APL, however, the war's end brought no letup in Klan activity, particularly as Klansmen confronted the social disorder and lawlessness that accompanied Prohibition. For the Klan, 1919 was a banner year. Klansmen made more than two hundred appearances in twenty-seven states and added perhaps a hundred thousand members to their ranks, mostly by drawing from the membership rolls of existing voluntary associations and fraternal lodges.[12]

The Klan, too, would enter politics, slowly turning from a disorganized wartime vigilance society preoccupied with lawlessness into what Imperial Wizard Hiram Wesley Evans boasted was "a great militant political organization." Within a few years, Klan candidates won elections in cities and states across the nation. Writing in 1924, during the Klan's heyday, anti-Klan reformer Horace Kallen insisted that "the Klan, indeed, is the concretion, sublimate, and gratification of the passions in play since the coming of the Great War." Social reformer Frank Tannenbaum attributed the Klan's growth to the fact that war had "intensified the habit of violence." John Moffatt Mecklin agreed. Born a preacher's son in central Mississippi in 1871, Mecklin was a sociologist at Dartmouth College. His description of the Klan's appeal to the "petty impotence of the small-town mind" was dismissive (and a sociologically inaccurate analysis of a diverse movement with a substantial urban presence), but the coalition of anti-Klan organizations and thinkers that he helped coordinate was plenty powerful. Opponents of the Klan increasingly responded to the Klan's rhetoric of obligation and community in the language of individual liberties. By 1925, internal squabbles and national opposition had decimated the Ku Klux Klan, a sign of the slowly declining power of coercive voluntarism to organize postwar civic life.[13]

If America's voluntary associations changed, the nation's citizens changed, too, and there seemed to be no going back for them either. The war created new categories of political obligation, most of them related directly to the state rather than to the people of the nation. As men carried draft registration cards and showed them to American Protective League operatives, as women told selective service boards details of their married lives in order to obtain allotments, as conscientious objectors articulated their religious beliefs to the Board of Inquiry, as women's clubs and vigilance societies transformed themselves into arms of the federal government, as German citizens submitted to surveillance as enemy aliens, and as small-town preachers found themselves in federal penitentiaries, they remade the relationship between Americans and their government. If World War I was a critical juncture in American history, political obligation was the switchman.

These days, some Americans wish for obligations, hoping to renew among Americans a sense of commitment toward our fellow citizens. Ninety years, they tell us, have put rights, and not obligations, at the center of our political life. Individualism has corroded our common culture and our civic associations; we even bowl alone. Given the collapse of Americans' trust not only in government but also in all our other public institutions; given our profound commitments to individual rights and self-fulfillment, expressed perhaps too easily through consumer culture; given how thoroughly our society has substituted the market for any other meaningful social bond; given all that, the citizens who fought America's first world war must seem far away indeed to those who still dream of a common good.[14]

From such a perspective, the sense of voluntarism and obligation in the political culture of early twentieth-century America must astound. People sacrificed, fought, and even died because of commitments to a common political life that Americans seem no longer to share. They created those obligations in their everyday institutions, places where they expressed their understandings of citizenship and fairness, of membership and belonging, where they came to consensus about their obligations in face-to-face meetings. It must have been comforting to see a familiar face at the draft board hearing or on the doorstep selling Liberty Bonds, to be able to negotiate the terms of political obligation in the lodge or club; it must even have been somewhat reassuring to those who registered as enemy aliens that they could do so at the local post office.

But how reassuring? Plenty of Americans feared and resisted draft board officials, Liberty Loan salesmen, and earnest clubwomen—just as they had resented and argued with them before the war. A historically informed analysis provides a critical perspective on our civic culture. Understanding American citizenship requires both the conceptual rigor of a democratic theory that can imagine citizens acting together and the empirical insights social history provides into the differences that have torn citizens apart. Those who seek something beyond the rights revolution must understand the political culture that existed before rights talk, when obligation still held sway. In a divided and unequal society, civil society could be an arena for negotiating political obligation; it could also be a weapon wielded against the weak.

The wartime state, especially as it exerted more and more authority over the legitimate exercise of force, did much to reshape the obligations of those who stood before it. When a young man appeared before a draft board and found his former boss across the table, now in a position of state authority, their new situation transformed the politics of everyday life. When that young man's wife later wrote a letter to the government demanding payment of her allotment as a soldier's dependent, or when she wrote a letter to the Justice Department turning in her neighbor's son as a slacker, she repositioned herself in the architecture of state power and the landscape of her local community, shifting their contours. What should really astound us is watching this generation of Americans act as political agents, building the modern nation-state, while also learning to live as political subjects—and sometimes even victims—under its powers. That state was not a thing but a process and a set of relationships—fragile, contested, unstable, even combustible. Those contests and combustions left postwar America with a fundamentally different state—and a fundamentally different political culture. Posters of Uncle Sam are still popular today. But the state the old man represents, and the citizens he now points to, he wouldn't even recognize.

Notes

Introduction

1. Willis Birchman, *Faces and Facts by and about 26 Contemporary Artists* (New Haven, Conn.: privately printed, 1937), n.p.; James Montgomery Flagg, *Roses and Buckshot* (New York: G. P. Putnam's Sons, [1946]), 156–58; Susan E. Meyer, *James Montgomery Flagg* (New York: Watson-Guptill, 1974), 37–42; "James Montgomery Flagg Dies; Illustrator and Author Was 82," *New York Times*, May 28, 1960.

2. Carlo Ginzburg, "'Your Country Needs You': A Case Study in Political Iconography," *History Workshop Journal* no. 52 (Autumn 2001): 1–22; W. J. T. Mitchell, *What Do Pictures Want? The Lives and Loves of Images* (Chicago: University of Chicago Press, 2005), 33–38.

3. Stephen Vaughn, *Holding Fast the Inner Lines: Democracy, Nationalism, and the Committee on Public Information* (Chapel Hill: University of North Carolina Press, 1980), 149. Flagg's original image for *Leslie's* used watercolors; the War Department poster was executed in ink and wash. Meyer, *James Montgomery Flagg*, 37, 42.

4. In his 1946 memoir, Flagg recalled having deliberately chosen to make a "new type" of Uncle Sam, "a handsome, dignified figure" less outlandish than the "circusy Uncle Sam with stars all over him." Flagg, *Roses and Buckshot*, 158.

5. "Ask Protection for War Posters," *Washington Post*, February 23, 1918.

6. My research owes much to the pioneering work on political obligation by Linda K. Kerber, *No Constitutional Right to Be Ladies: Women and the Obligations of Citizenship* (New York: Hill and Wang, 1998); Judith N. Shklar, *American Citizenship: The Quest for Inclusion* (Cambridge: Harvard University Press, 1991); and Robert B. Westbrook, *Why We Fought: Forging American Obligations in World War II* (Washington: Smithsonian Institution Press, 2004). See also Mark H. Leff, "The Politics of Sacrifice on the American Home Front in World War II," *Journal of American History* 77 (March 1991): 1296–1318; James M. McPherson, *For Cause*

and Comrades: Why Men Fought in the Civil War (New York: Oxford University Press, 1997); Cecilia O'Leary, To Die For: The Paradox of American Patriotism (Princeton, N.J.: Princeton University Press, 1997); and Rogers M. Smith, Civic Ideals: Conflicting Visions of Citizenship in U.S. History (New Haven, Conn.: Yale University Press, 1997). Elizabeth D. Samet explores matters of political obligation in American literary culture in Willing Obedience: Citizens, Soldiers, and the Progress of Consent in America, 1776–1898 (Stanford, Calif.: Stanford University Press, 2004).

7. Gerd Korman, Industrialization, Immigrants, and Americanizers: The View from Milwaukee, 1866–1921 (Madison: State Historical Society of Wisconsin, 1967), 144. In political philosophy and political theory, see George Klosko, Political Obligations (New York: Oxford University Press, 2005); Carole Pateman, The Problem of Political Obligation: A Critique of Liberal Theory (Berkeley: University of California Press, 1985); Michael Walzer, Obligations: Essays on Disobedience, War, and Citizenship (Cambridge: Harvard University Press, 1970). Investigations from the early twentieth century can be found in Thomas Hill Green, Lectures on the Principles of Political Obligation (London: Longmans Green, 1917 [1895]); Josiah Royce, The Philosophy of Loyalty (Nashville: Vanderbilt University Press, 1995 [1908]); Leonard Wood, The Military Obligation of Citizenship (Princeton, N.J.: Princeton University Press, 1915); and the annual Yale Lectures on the Responsibilities of Citizenship, beginning with David J. Brewer, American Citizenship (New York: Charles Scribner's Sons, 1907).

8. We cannot apply to this period Robert Westbrook's claims about World War II that since the United States, as a liberal society, lacked "a coherent conception of political obligation," wartime Americans "were not called upon to conceive of their obligation to participate in the war effort as an obligation to work, fight, or die for their country as a political community." Not only does the claim not apply to the civic culture of the World War I era but also it may not apply in any period, if we consider how Rogers Smith's persuasive articulation of the multiple traditions of American politics calls into question Westbrook's equation of American political culture with liberalism. See Robert B. Westbrook, "Fighting for the American Family: Private Interests and Political Obligation in World War II," in The Power of Culture: Critical Essays in American History, ed. Richard Wightman Fox and T. J. Jackson Lears (Chicago: University of Chicago Press, 1993), 195–221 (quotes from 198); Westbrook, Why We Fought; Rogers M. Smith, "Beyond Tocqueville, Myrdal, and Hartz: The Multiple Traditions in America," American Political Science Review 87 (September 1993): 549–66; and Alan Brinkley, "The Two World Wars and American Liberalism," in Liberalism and Its Discontents (Cambridge: Harvard University Press, 1998), 79–93.

9. American historians have recently become interested in the concept of citizenship, and for good reasons. Looking back at the political past through the lens of citizenship has allowed us to see ordinary people as political actors even when they were formally excluded from politics; citizenship has helped limn the nation's borders and its historical preoccupations with inclusion and exclusion. But citizenship can be an overly capacious term, subject to disparate definitions, including many

that wouldn't have made sense to Americans in 1917. Political obligation, too, had
plenty of definitions, but they were forged in their own times. As historians turn
increasingly to social and political theories to help make sense of the past, we ought
to begin with the theories that our own subjects used. William J. Novak offers a
forcefully overstated critique of current uses of "citizenship" in American historical literature, particularly as found in the work of Linda K. Kerber and Rogers
M. Smith, in "The Legal Transformation of Citizenship in Nineteenth-Century
America," in *The Democratic Experiment: New Directions in American Political
History*, ed. Meg Jacobs et al. (Princeton, N.J.: Princeton University Press, 2003),
85–119, esp. 85–87. Novak, though, focuses so exclusively on appearances of the
word "citizenship" that he ends up little closer to a reconstruction of nineteenth-
century American politics than those scholars with whom he quarrels. For an excellent reflection highlighting the interpretive possibilities of citizenship as a category
of analysis, see Kathleen Canning and Sonya O. Rose, "Gender, Citizenship, and
Subjectivity: Some Historical and Theoretical Considerations," *Gender and History*
13 (November 2001): 427–43. See also Candice Lewis Bredbenner, *A Nationality
of Her Own: Women, Marriage, and the Law of Citizenship* (Berkeley: University
of California Press, 1998); Nancy F. Cott, "Marriage and Women's Citizenship in
the United States, 1830–1934," *American Historical Review* 103 (December 1998):
1440–74; Smith, *Civic Ideals.*

10. John Dickinson, *The Building of an Army: A Detailed Account of Legislation,
Administration and Opinion in the United States, 1915–1920* (New York: Century,
1922), 86–91; Lettie Gavin, *American Women in World War I: They Also Served*
(Niwot: University Press of Colorado, 1997), x, 44; George Herbert Jones to Claude
Kitchin, August 10, 1918, Reel 26, Papers of Claude Kitchin, Southern Historical
Collection, Wilson Library, University of North Carolina, Chapel Hill, N.C.; Mrs.
Raynell Ryder to Marcus H. Holcomb, August 20, 1918, Box 254, Governor Marcus
Holcomb Papers, Record Group 5, Connecticut State Archives, Hartford, Conn.;
A. E. Black to State Defense Council, November 3, 1917, New York State Council
of Defense Records, Microfilm A4243, New York State Archives and Records
Administration, Albany, N.Y.

11. For interpretations that present the nineteenth-century American state as a dynamic
set of institutions, see Richard R. John, *Spreading the News: The American Postal
System from Franklin to Morse* (Cambridge: Harvard University Press, 1995), and
William J. Novak, *The People's Welfare: Law and Regulation in Nineteenth-Century
America* (Chapel Hill: University of North Carolina Press, 1996). Amy S. Greenberg,
Cause for Alarm: The Volunteer Fire Department in the Nineteenth-Century City
(Princeton, N.J.: Princeton University Press, 1998), gives an excellent account of
the relationship between voluntarist politics and state action.

12. My understanding of the relationship between language and political history has been
shaped by works such as Benjamin L. Alpers, *Dictators and Democracy in American
Public Culture: Envisioning the Totalitarian Enemy, 1920s–1950s* (Chapel Hill:
University of North Carolina Press, 2003); Terence Ball et al., eds., *Political Innovation
and Conceptual Change* (New York: Cambridge University Press, 1989); Thomas
Childers, "The Social Language of Politics in Germany: The Sociology of Discourse

in the Weimar Republic," *American Historical Review* 95 (April 1990): 331–58; Eric Foner, *The Story of American Freedom* (New York: Norton, 1998); Nancy Fraser and Linda Gordon, "A Genealogy of 'Dependency': Tracing a Keyword of the U.S. Welfare State," *Signs* 19 (Winter 1994): 309–36; Evelyn Brooks Higginbotham, "African-American Women's History and the Metalanguage of Race," *Signs* 17 (Winter 1992): 251–74; Jon Lawrence, *Speaking for the People: Party, Language, and Popular Politics in England, 1867–1914* (New York: Cambridge University Press, 1998); Daniel T. Rodgers, *Contested Truths: Keywords in American Politics since Independence* (New York: Basic Books, 1987); and Raymond Williams, *Keywords: A Vocabulary of Culture and Society* (New York: Oxford University Press, 1976).

13. "A Draft of a Proclamation," in Arthur S. Link et al., eds., *The Papers of Woodrow Wilson*, 69 vols. (Princeton, N.J.: Princeton University Press, 1966–94), vol. 42, p. 181 [hereafter PWW with volume number]. The words were originally drafted by Hugh Johnson, revised by Secretary of War Newton Baker, and revised again by the president. See ibid., 179–82; Edward M. Coffman, *The War to End All Wars: The American Military Experience in World War I* (New York: Oxford University Press, 1968), 28.

14. Woodrow Wilson, *The State: Elements of Historical and Practical Politics*, rev. ed. (Boston: D. C. Heath, 1899), 572–73; Niels Thorsen, *The Political Thought of Woodrow Wilson, 1875–1910* (Princeton, N.J.: Princeton University Press, 1988), 89–116.

15. Christopher C. Gibbs, *The Great Silent Majority: Missouri's Resistance to World War I* (Columbia: University of Missouri Press, 1988), 74–92, 109–34; Enoch H. Crowder, *Second Report of the Provost Marshal General to the Secretary of War on the Operations of the Selective Service System to December 20, 1918* (Washington, D.C.: Government Printing Office, 1919), 557; Meirion Harries and Susie Harries, *The Last Days of Innocence: America at War, 1917–1918* (New York: Vintage, 1997), 356–402.

16. "Editorial: Her Chance for Service," *Ladies' Home Journal* 34 (June 1917): 7.

17. Robert H. Ferrell, *Woodrow Wilson and World War I, 1917–1921* (New York: Harper and Row, 1985), 204. For attempts at a comprehensive catalogue of wartime violence, see National Civil Liberties Bureau, *War-Time Prosecutions and Mob Violence* (New York: NCLB, 1919), and H. C. Peterson and Gilbert C. Fite, *Opponents of War, 1917–1918* (Seattle: University of Washington Press, 1968 [1957]).

18. Hiram Johnson, quoted in Peterson and Fite, *Opponents of War*, 218; "Wants School 'Kept,'" *Washington Post*, May 2, 1917; Norman Thomas, "Justice to War's Heretics," *Nation* 107 (November 9, 1918): 547; Thorstein Veblen, "Dementia Praecox," *Freeman* 5 (June 21, 1922): 344–47. Central texts on violence in American history include Richard Maxwell Brown, *No Duty to Retreat: Violence and Values in American History and Society* (New York: Oxford University Press, 1991); Richard Hofstadter and Michael Wallace, comps., *American Violence: A Documentary History* (New York: Knopf, 1970); Rhodri Jeffreys-Jones, *Violence and Reform in American History* (New York: Viewpoints, 1978); and Mark Mazower, "Violence and the State in the Twentieth Century," *American Historical Review* 107 (October 2002): 1158–78.

19. Walton Rawls, *Wake Up, America! World War I and the American Poster* (New York: Abbeville Press, 1988), 196; Katherine Anne Porter, *Pale Horse, Pale Rider* (New York: New American Library, 1962 [1939]), 116; William Henry Thomas Jr., "The United States Department of Justice and Dissent during the First World War" (Ph D. dissertation, University of Iowa, 2002), 42.

20. Henry Litchfield West, *Federal Power: Its Growth and Necessity* (New York: George H. Doran, 1918); W. F. Willoughby, *An Introduction to the Government of Modern States* (New York: Century, 1919). Robert H. Wiebe, *The Search for Order, 1877–1920* (New York: Hill and Wang, 1967) suggests that state expansion was a necessary response to the developments of modern society. Morton Keller, *Affairs of State: Public Life in Late Nineteenth Century America* (Cambridge: Harvard University Press, 1977) finds little evidence of state expansion in the late nineteenth century, whereas Stephen Skowronek, *Building a New American State: The Expansion of National Administrative Capacities, 1877–1920* (New York: Cambridge University Press, 1982), sees a transition from a late nineteenth-century "patchwork" of state action to a "reconstitution" of state power in the early twentieth century. Richard Bensel, *Yankee Leviathan: The Origins of Central State Authority in America, 1859–1877* (New York: Cambridge University Press, 1990), dates the same patterns to an earlier period. Theda Skocpol locates the state-building impulse in contests over the provision of social services in *Protecting Soldiers and Mothers: The Political Origins of Social Policy in the United States* (Cambridge: Harvard University Press, 1992); Marc Allen Eisner, *From Warfare State to Welfare State: World War I, Compensatory State Building, and the Limits of the Modern Order* (University Park: Pennsylvania State University Press, 2000), locates these shifts in the interwar period, where Ellis Hawley, *The Great War and the Search for a Modern Order: A History of the American People and Their Institutions, 1917–1933* (New York: St. Martin's Press, 1979) explores their consequences. Rodgers, *Contested Truths*, 144–75, places theories of the state in the context of changing relations between intellectuals and democratic politics in this period.

21. Randolph S. Bourne, "The State," in *War and the Intellectuals: Collected Essays, 1915–1919*, ed. Carl Resek (New York: Harper and Row, 1964), 69. Complementing Bourne are Ira Katznelson, "Rewriting the Epic of America," in *Shaped by War and Trade: International Influences on American Political Development*, ed. Ira Katznelson and Martin Shefter (Princeton, N.J.: Princeton University Press, 2002), 3–23, and Charles Tilly, "War Making and State Making as Organized Crime," in *Bringing the State Back In*, ed. Peter Evans et al. (New York: Cambridge University Press, 1985), 169–91.

22. John Dewey, "Force, Violence and Law" (1916) and "Force and Coercion" (1916), in Dewey, *The Middle Works, 1899–1924*, ed. Jo Ann Boydston (Carbondale: Southern Illinois University Press, 1980), 211–15 and 244–51. The "immense moral wrench" is from Dewey, "Conscience and Compulsion" (1917), in ibid., 260–64. Bourne, "War and the Intellectuals," in *War and the Intellectuals*, 3–14.

23. Max Weber, quoted in Dirk Käsler, *Max Weber: An Introduction to His Life and Work*, trans. Philippa Hurd (Cambridge, U.K.: Polity, 1988), 16; Weber, "Politics as a Vocation," in *From Max Weber: Essays in Sociology*, ed. and trans. H. H. Gerth and C. Wright Mills (New York: Oxford University Press, 1946), 78.

24. William Bayard Hale to Joseph Patrick Tumulty, April 18, 1918, in PWW, vol. 47, pp. 362–63.

25. Green, *Lectures*, 143; Brewer, *American Citizenship*, 106; Moorfield Storey, *Obedience to the Law: An Address at the Opening of Petigru College in Columbia, South Carolina* (Boston: Geo. H. Ellis, 1919), 3. For more on Brewer, see Linda Przybyszewski, "Judicial Conservatism and Protestant Faith: The Case of Justice David J. Brewer," *Journal of American History* 91 (September 2004): 471–96. For more recent theorizations of legal obligation, see John Rawls, "Legal Obligation and the Duty of Fair Play," in *Law and Philosophy: A Symposium*, ed. Sidney Hook (New York: New York University Press, 1964), 3–18; and *A Theory of Justice* (Cambridge: Harvard University Press, 1971), esp. 333–91.

26. Theda Skocpol et al., "Patriotic Partnerships: Why Great Wars Nourished American Civic Voluntarism," in *Shaped by War and Trade*, ed. Katznelson and Shefter, 134–80, demonstrates that World War I contributed to substantial increases in the membership of voluntary associations, particularly those that supported the war effort. Although the 1920s was in many ways an era of voluntarist politics, as Nancy F. Cott, *The Grounding of Modern Feminism* (New Haven, Conn.: Yale University Press, 1987), 85–114, similarly argues, the participation of voluntary associations in violence and policing had begun to change, as the spectacular rise and fall of the postwar Ku Klux Klan and the quiet transformation of the American Legion in the same period suggest.

27. Mary Parker Follett, *The New State: Group Organization the Solution of Popular Government* (University Park: Pennsylvania State University Press, 1998 [1918]), 173. For more on Follett, see Kevin Mattson, *Creating a Democratic Public: The Struggle for Urban Participatory Democracy during the Progressive Era* (University Park: Pennsylvania State University Press, 1998), 87–104, and Joan C. Tonn, *Mary P. Follett: Creating Democracy, Transforming Management* (New Haven, Conn.: Yale University Press, 2003).

28. Walter Lippmann, *Liberty and the News* (New York: Harcourt, Brace and Howe, 1920), 5, 62; *The Phantom Public* (New York: Harcourt, Brace, 1925). For more on Lippmann, see Ronald Steel, *Walter Lippmann and the American Century* (Boston: Little Brown, 1980), esp. 171–85. For two attempts to place consent in a historical framework for modern American politics, see William Graebner, *The Engineering of Consent: Democracy and Authority in Twentieth-Century America* (Madison: University of Wisconsin Press, 1987) and Margaret C. Levi, *Consent, Dissent, and Patriotism* (New York: Cambridge University Press, 1997).

Chapter 1

1. "Eighteen to Forty-Five," *New York Times,* September 15, 1918.

2. Ibid.

3. Ibid.; Enoch H. Crowder, *Second Report of the Provost Marshal General to the Secretary of War on the Operations of the Selective Service System to December 20, 1918* (Washington, D.C.: Government Printing Office, 1919), 557.

4. "Eighteen to Forty-Five," *New York Times,* September 15, 1918; Alfred Cornebise, *War as Advertised: The Four Minute Men and America's Crusade, 1917–1918* (Philadelphia: American Philosophical Society, 1984), 62.

5. Theodore Roosevelt, quoted in Jack McCallum, *Leonard Wood: Rough Rider, Surgeon, Architect of American Imperialism* (New York: New York University Press, 2006), 263.

6. Leonard Wood, *Universal Military Training* (New York: Collier Classics, 1917), 118; Hugh Scott, quoted in *The Draft and Its Enemies: A Documentary History,* ed. John O'Sullivan and Alan M. Meckler (Urbana: University of Illinois Press, 1974), 121; William Howard Taft, "The Crisis," *Yale Review* 6 (April 1917): 455. For more on the preparedness movement, see John Patrick Finnegan, *Against the Specter of a Dragon: The Campaign for American Military Preparedness, 1914–1917* (Westport, Conn.: Greenwood, 1974); Michael Pearlman, *To Make Democracy Safe for America: Patricians and Preparedness in the Progressive Era* (Urbana: University of Illinois Press, 1984); Barbara J. Steinson, *American Women's Activism in World War I* (New York: Garland, 1982), 114–62, 299–349; Wood, *The Military Obligation of Citizenship* (Princeton, N.J.: Princeton University Press, 1915), 40–49.

7. Robert H. Ferrell, *Woodrow Wilson and World War I, 1917–1921* (New York: Harper and Row, 1985), 16; Wood, *Universal Military Training*, 118; Edward M. Coffman, *The War to End All Wars: The American Military Experience in World War I* (New York: Oxford University Press, 1968), 24. The movement to professionalize the American armed forces is traced in Jerry M. Cooper, *The Rise of the National Guard: The Evolution of the American Militia, 1865–1920* (Lincoln: University of Nebraska Press, 1997) and Stephen Skowronek, *Building a New American State: The Expansion of National Administrative Capacities, 1877–1920* (New York: Cambridge University Press, 1982), 212–47.

8. Randolph S. Bourne, "A Moral Equivalent for Universal Military Service," in Randolph S. Bourne, *War and the Intellectuals: Collected Essays, 1915–1919*, ed. Carl Resek (New York: Harper Torchbooks, 1964), 144, 146.

9. Robert W. Dubay, "The Opposition to Selective Service, 1916–1918," *Southern Quarterly* 7 (April 1969): 301–322; Anthony Gaughan, "Woodrow Wilson and the Rise of Militant Interventionism in the South," *Journal of Southern History* 65 (November 1999): 771–808; Jeanette Keith, *Rich Man's War, Poor Man's Fight: Race, Class, and Power in the Rural South during the First World War* (Chapel Hill: University of North Carolina Press, 2004), 13–56; George Brown Tindall, *The Emergence of the New South, 1913–1945* (Baton Rouge: Louisiana State University Press, 1967), 33–69.

10. Woodrow Wilson to Newton Baker, May 3, 1917, in Arthur S. Link et al., eds., *The Papers of Woodrow Wilson*, 69 vols. (Princeton, N.J.: Princeton University Press, 1966–94), vol. 42, p. 201 [hereafter PWW with volume number]; Wilson to Edward W. Pou, April 13, 1917, in ibid., 52; John Whiteclay Chambers II, *To Raise an Army: The Draft Comes to Modern America* (New York: Free Press, 1987), 136–41, 167–71; David M. Kennedy, *Over Here: The First World War and American Society* (New York: Oxford University Press, 1980), 146–48; William H. Crawford, "He Risked Disgrace to Speed the Draft," *New York Times Magazine,* June 9, 1918.

11. "Lodge Knocks Down Pacifist Assailant," *New York Times*, April 3, 1917; Kennedy, *Over Here*, 15; Lillian Wald, quoted in Raymond B. Fosdick, *Chronicle of a Generation: An Autobiography* (New York: Harper and Bros., 1958), 143.

12. Stanley T. Rice to Claude Kitchin, March 19, 1917, Reel 16, Papers of Claude Kitchin, Southern Historical Collection, Wilson Library, University of North

Carolina, Chapel Hill, N.C.; Jessica Whitcomb to Henry A. Cooper, April 11, 1917, in *Draftees or Volunteers? A Documentary History of the Debate over Military Conscription in the United States, 1787–1973*, ed. John Whiteclay Chambers II (New York: Garland, 1975), 265; Thomas Gore, quoted in Monroe Billington, "Thomas P. Gore and Oklahoma Public Opinion, 1917–1918," *Journal of Southern History* 27 (August 1961): 347; Champ Clark, quoted in Kennedy, *Over Here*, 18.

13. Chambers, *To Raise an Army*, 125–51; Coffman, *War to End All Wars*, 21; "Churlish Guests," *New York Times*, June 10, 1917.

14. Thomas D. Snyder, ed., *120 Years of American Education: A Statistical Portrait* (Washington, D.C.: National Center for Education Statistics, 1993), 76; Newton D. Baker, "A Draft of a Proclamation," in PWW, vol. 42, p. 181. The characterization of Newton Baker appears in Meirion Harries and Susie Harries, *The Last Days of Innocence: America at War, 1917–1918* (New York: Vintage, 1997), 50; that of Frederick Keppel can be found in Rufus M. Jones, *A Service of Love in War Time: American Friends Relief Work in Europe, 1917–1919* (New York: Macmillan, 1920), 50. David A. Lockmiller, *Enoch H. Crowder: Soldier, Lawyer, and Statesman* (Columbia: University of Missouri Studies, 1955), 152–78.

15. Baker, "Draft of a Proclamation," 181. Enoch H. Crowder, *The Spirit of Selective Service* (New York: Century, 1920). On polling places, see Ferrell, *Woodrow Wilson and World War I*, 17. Philadelphia War History Committee, *Philadelphia in the World War, 1914–1919* (New York: Wynkoop Hallenbeck Crawford, 1922), 127, notes that board regions in that city followed election ward boundaries, and poll officials were recruited as draft board volunteers.

16. Quoted in Cornebise, *War as Advertised*, 66.

17. Philadelphia War History Committee, *Philadelphia in the World War*, 127.

18. Baker, "Draft of a Proclamation," 180; Chambers, *To Raise an Army*, 184–85; Cornebise, *War as Advertised*, 61–64 (quote on 62). Three further registration days followed, on June 5, August 24, and September 12, 1918.

19. Thomas Gregory, quoted in Homer Cummings and Carl McFarland, *Federal Justice: Chapters in the History of Justice and the Federal Executive* (New York: Macmillan, 1937), 419.

20. Fred D. Ragan, "An Unlikely Alliance: Tom Watson, Harry Weinberger, and the World War I Draft," *Atlanta Historical Journal* 25 (Fall 1981): 19–36; *Jones v. Perkins*, 243 Fed. 997 (1917); "Judge Speer to Hear Watson Cases Today," *Atlanta Constitution*, August 18, 1917; "Speer Reserves Watson Decisions," *Atlanta Constitution*, August 19, 1917. Watson's radical influence reached far and wide, including a group of forty men who were arrested in the fall of 1917 on Bumble Bee Island near Cedar Key, Florida. Charged with conspiracy to avoid the draft, they claimed to have gathered to raise campaign funds for Watson. The case against the men was dismissed after a hung jury. Kermit L. Hall and Eric W. Rise, *From Local Courts to National Tribunals: The Federal District Courts of Florida, 1821–1990* (Brooklyn, N.Y.: Carlson, 1991), 72.

21. *Arver v. United States*, 245 U.S. 366 (1918), at 378. See also Alexander M. Bickel, *The Judiciary and Responsible Government, 1910–1921* (New York: Macmillan, 1984), 519–22; "Draft Law Upheld by Supreme Court," *New York Times*, January 8, 1918.

22. Crowder, *Second Report*, 199–212; Harries and Harries, *Last Days of Innocence*, 97; James F. Willis, "The Cleburne County Draft War," *Arkansas Historical Quarterly* 26 (Spring 1967): 24–39; Thomas A. Britten, *American Indians in World War I: At Home and at War* (Albuquerque: University of New Mexico Press, 1997), 51–72; Britten, "The Creek Draft Rebellion of 1918: Wartime Hysteria and Indian Baiting in WWI Oklahoma," *Chronicles of Oklahoma* 79 (Summer 2001): 200–15; Erik Zissu, "Conscription, Sovereignty, and Land: American Indian Resistance during World War I," *Pacific Historical Review* 64 (November 1995): 537–66. Among the best works on the Green Corn Rebellion are Jim Bissett, *Agrarian Socialism in America: Marx, Jefferson, and Jesus in the Oklahoma Countryside, 1904–1920* (Norman: University of Oklahoma Press, 1999); James R. Green, *Grass-Roots Socialism: Radical Movements in the Southwest, 1895–1943* (Baton Rouge: Louisiana State University Press, 1978), esp. 345–95; and Nigel Anthony Sellars, *Oil, Wheat, and Wobblies: The Industrial Workers of the World in Oklahoma, 1905–1930* (Norman: University of Oklahoma Press, 1998), 77–92.

23. Buchanan County, Iowa, Report, Box 1, Chronicles of the Draft Files, Records of the Selective Service System (World War I), Record Group 163, National Archives and Records Administration, Washington, D.C. [hereafter RG 163, NARA]. Crowder, *Second Report*, 557, gives the official figure; Chambers, *To Raise an Army*, 211, concludes the higher number based on internal Selective Service System documents that suggested a 10 to 15 percent failure rate for the registration process. The actual number is probably closer to the lower number than the higher one. Many men marked as delinquents had merely registered in the wrong place or fallen through the cracks of an improvisational bureaucracy.

24. The term "slacker" had already entered the language of American slang by 1917. Its use for draft evaders was so immediate and so widespread that it is difficult to point to a single individual as the originator of the term. Robert L. Chapman, ed., *American Slang*, 2nd ed. (New York: Harper Perennial, 1998), 462, dates its first appearance to 1898. See also Mary Paxton Keeley, "A.E.F. English: Some Delimitations," *American Speech* 5 (June 1930): 385.

25. "Watertown Girls Will Bait Slackers," *Boston Globe*, May 17, 1918; "The Ladies' Auxiliary," *Masses* 9 (July 1917): 29; Leslie Midkiff DeBauche, *Reel Patriotism: The Movies and World War I* (Madison: University of Wisconsin Press, 1997), 148.

26. Quoted in Clark T. Irwin Jr., "Portland Supports 'War to End Wars,'" in *Greater Portland Celebration 350*, comp. and ed. Albert F. Barnes (Portland, Me.: Gannett, 1984), 136. Much was made at the time, and since, about the return of European immigrants to fight for their home countries during the early years of World War I. Their numbers were far lower than the historical literature might suggest, however, and so I do not deal with them here. See Philip A. Bean, "The Great War and Ethnic Nationalism in Utica, New York, 1914–1920," *New York History* 74 (October 1993): 382–413; Chambers, *To Raise an Army*, 226–32; Nancy Gentile Ford, *Americans All! Foreign-Born Soldiers in World War I* (College Station: Texas A&M University Press, 2001), 16–44; Lucy E. Salyer, "Baptism by Fire: Race, Military Service, and U.S. Citizenship Policy, 1918–1935," *Journal of American History* 91 (December 2004): 847–76; Richard Slotkin, *Lost Battalions: The Great War and the Crisis of*

American Nationality (New York: Henry Holt, 2005); Christopher M. Sterba, *Good Americans: Italian and Jewish Immigrants during the First World War* (New York: Oxford University Press, 2003).

27. Lewis P. Brown, "The Jew Is Not a Slacker," *North American Review* 207 (June 1918): 857; "Opposes Jewish Brigade," *New York Times*, April 3, 1917; Faith Rogow, *Gone to Another Meeting: The National Council of Jewish Women, 1893–1993* (Tuscaloosa: University of Alabama Press, 1993), 168; Sterba, *Good Americans*, esp. 53–81.

28. Quoted in Yumei Sun, "San Francisco's *Chung Sai Yat Po* and the Transformation of Chinese Consciousness, 1900–1920," in *Print Culture in a Diverse America*, ed. James P. Danky and Wayne A. Wiegand (Urbana: University of Illinois Press, 1998), 94–95; James Brown Scott, "The Amendment of the Naturalization and Citizenship Acts with Respect to Military Service," *American Journal of International Law* 12 (July 1918): 613–19; Salyer, "Baptism by Fire."

29. Gary Gerstle notes that some Canadian immigrants in Woonsocket, Rhode Island, distanced themselves from the popular anticonscription movement north of the border and even took to calling themselves "Franco-American" more often than "French Canadian" during this period. Gerstle, *Working-Class Americanism: The Politics of Labor in a Textile City, 1914–1960* (New York: Cambridge University Press, 1989), 45.

30. Worcester, Massachusetts, Report, Box 2, Chronicles of the Draft Files, RG 163, NARA.

31. National Civil Liberties Bureau, *War-Time Prosecutions and Mob Violence* (New York: NCLB, 1918), 5; "Mob Attack Kills Colored Preacher," *Washington Post*, August 24, 1917; New York *Sun*, quoted in Mark Ellis, *Race, War, and Surveillance: African Americans and the United States Government during World War I* (Bloomington: Indiana University Press, 2001), 4. Generally, see Arthur E. Barbeau and Florette Henri, *The Unknown Soldiers: African-American Troops in World War I* (New York: DaCapo, 1996 [1974]), esp. 33–55; Stephen L. Harris, *Harlem's Hell Fighters: The African-American 369th Infantry in World War I* (Washington, D.C.: Brassey's, 2003); Theodore Kornweibel Jr., "Apathy and Dissent: Black America's Negative Responses to World War I," *South Atlantic Quarterly* 80 (Summer 1981): 322–38; Kornweibel, *"Investigate Everything": Federal Efforts to Compel Black Loyalty during World War I* (Bloomington: Indiana University Press, 2002), 76–117; Chad Louis Williams, "Torchbearers of Democracy: The First World War and the Figure of the African-American Soldier" (Ph.D. dissertation, Princeton University, 2004), esp. 31–123.

32. E. D. Anderson, quoted in Jennifer D. Keene, *Doughboys, the Great War, and the Remaking of America* (Baltimore: Johns Hopkins University Press, 2001), 40; Lewis B. Moore, *How the Colored Race Can Help in the Problems Issuing from the War*, 2nd ed. (New York: National Security League, 1919), 5, 7, 19.

33. Harris, *Harlem's Hell Fighters*, 82, 104; Sidney Wilson, quoted in Ellis, *Race, War, and Surveillance*, 90.

34. "Close Ranks," *Crisis* 16 (July 1918): 111; William Monroe Trotter, quoted in Stephen R. Fox, *The Guardian of Boston: William Monroe Trotter* (New York: Atheneum, 1971), 215, 219; New York *News*, quoted in David Levering Lewis, *W. E. B. Du Bois: Biography of a Race, 1868–1919* (New York: Henry Holt, 1993),

556. For more on the controversy surrounding "Close Ranks," see Ellis, *Race, War, and Surveillance*, 141–82; Lewis, *W. E. B. Du Bois*, 552–59; and William Jordan, "'The Damnable Dilemma': African-American Accommodation and Protest in World War I," *Journal of American History* 81 (March 1995): 1562–83.

35. James Vardaman, quoted in William F. Holmes, *The White Chief: James Kimble Vardaman* (Baton Rouge: Louisiana State University Press, 1970), 326–27, and Ellis, *Race, War, and Surveillance*, 75; Enoch Crowder, quoted in W. Allison Sweeney, *History of the American Negro in the Great World War* (New York: Johnson Reprint, 1970 [1919]), 113.

36. Louis S. Epes to Carter Glass, August 27, 1917, in Box 100, Folder 1, Papers of Carter Glass, MSS 2913, Special Collections, University of Virginia Library, Charlottesville, Va. [hereafter UVA].

37. Carter Glass to Louis S. Epes, September 1, 1917, in ibid.

38. Sweeney, *History of the American Negro*, 116; Chambers, *To Raise an Army*, 194–202; Paula Giddings, *When and Where I Enter: The Impact of Black Women on Race and Sex in America* (New York: William Morrow, 1984), 140–41; Edward Harry Hauenstein, *A History of Wayne County in the World War and in the Wars of the Past* (Wooster, Ohio: Wayne County History Co., 1919), 182; Tera W. Hunter, *To 'Joy My Freedom: Southern Black Women's Lives and Labors after the Civil War* (Cambridge: Harvard University Press, 1997), 227–32; Gerald E. Shenk, *"Work or Fight!": Race, Gender, and the Draft in World War One* (New York: Palgrave Macmillan, 2005), 41–43 (quote on 42); Walter F. White, "Work or Fight in the South," *New Republic* 18 (March 1, 1919): 144–46.

39. Chambers, *To Raise an Army*, 222–26; Crowder, *Second Report*, 191–97; K. Walter Hickel, "'Justice and the Highest Kind of Equality Require Discrimination': Citizenship, Dependency, and Conscription in the South, 1917–1919," *Journal of Southern History* 66 (November 2000): 749–80; Keith, *Rich Man's War*, 120–34; Paul T. Murray, "Blacks and the Draft: A History of Institutional Racism," *Journal of Black Studies* 2 (September 1971): 57–76.

40. Buchanan County, Iowa, Report, Chronicles of the Draft Files, RG 163, NARA. For more on the makeup of the draft boards, see Chambers, *To Raise an Army*, 179–82; Christopher C. Gibbs, *The Great Silent Majority: Missouri's Resistance to World War I* (Columbia: University of Missouri Press, 1988), 93–108. Small-town boards could include some dense social connections. In Avery County, North Carolina, for example, the draft board appears to have included two brothers and a husband-and-wife team. Horton Cooper, *History of Avery County, North Carolina* (Asheville, N.C.: Biltmore, 1964), 72.

41. Mrs. R. K. Dooley to Carter Glass, n.d. [before December 4, 1917], in Box 100, Folder 1, Papers of Carter Glass, UVA.

42. Buchanan County, Iowa, Report, Chronicles of the Draft Files, RG 163, NARA; Emma W. Wolschendorf to Enoch Crowder, Box 158, Folder Mass. 17 (81–100), in States Files, RG 163, NARA.

43. K. Walter Hickel, "War, Region, and Social Welfare: Federal Aid to Servicemen's Dependents in the South, 1917–1921," *Journal of American History* 87 (March 2001): 1362–91; Samuel Lindsay, quoted in Frances H. Early, *A World without*

War: How U.S. Feminists and Pacifists Resisted World War I (Syracuse, N.Y.: Syracuse University Press, 1997), 74.

44. Edna Shaw to Enoch Crowder, Box 179, Folder Missouri 17 (41–60), and Emma W. Wolschendorf to Enoch Crowder, Box 158, Folder Mass. 17 (81–100), both in States Files, RG 163, NARA.

45. H. Wayne Morgan and Anne Hodges Morgan, *Oklahoma: A Bicentennial History* (New York: Norton, 1977), 101; John Hope Franklin and Alfred A. Moss Jr., *From Slavery to Freedom: A History of African Americans*, 8th ed. (Boston: McGraw-Hill, 2000), 361; Early, *World without War*, 64, 84–85; David Alan Corbin, *Life, Work and Rebellion in the Coal Fields: The Southern West Virginia Miners, 1880–1922* (Urbana: University of Illinois Press, 1982), 186.

46. Early, *World without War*, 64, 67; Luther H. Gulick, "Legal Advice for Selectives," *Annals of the American Academy of Political and Social Science* 79 (September 1918): 235–38; Henry W. Taft, "The Bar in the War," in Taft, *Occasional Papers and Addresses of an American Lawyer* (New York: Macmillan, 1920), 53–67; J.H.W. [John H. Wigmore], "The Lawyer's Honor in War-Time," *Illinois Law Review* 12 (June 1917): 117–18.

47. Woodrow Wilson, quoted in Kennedy, *Over Here*, 150; "893 Men Register," *Moosup Journal*, September 29, 1918, clipping in Scrapbook, Plainfield Historical Society, Box 1, Record Group 112, Records of the Plainfield Historical Society, Connecticut State Archives, Hartford, Conn. [hereafter Plainfield Historical Society Scrapbook, CSA].

48. "For National Army," *Moosup Journal*, November 22, 1917; "Questionnaires Being Returned," *Moosup Journal*, December 24, 1917; "Sixty Men Registered from Plainfield," *Moosup Journal*, June 13, 1918; and "Drafted Men in Exams," *Moosup Journal*, August 1, 1918, clippings in Plainfield Historical Society Scrapbook, CSA. For another example, see "District Boards Decide 181 Cases," *Providence Journal*, January 19, 1918.

49. "New Draft Men," *Moosup Journal*, April 18, 1918; "Entrain Today," *Moosup Journal*, July 25, 1918, clippings in Plainfield Historical Society Scrapbook, CSA. Daniel McDougall also went on to camp as an alternate in August 1918. "Eighty Boys Leave for Camp," *Moosup Journal*, August 29, 1918, clipping in ibid. Entrainment could also be a moment of resistance to the draft, as when a group of women in Brooklyn, New York, stopped a train car and called military officials "murderers." Early, *World without War*, 65.

50. "Service Flags," *Moosup Journal*, February 7, 1918, and "Uncle Sam's Men on Honor Roll," *Moosup Journal*, February 21, 1918, clippings in Plainfield Historical Society Scrapbook, CSA.

51. Cummings and McFarland, *Federal Justice*, 421; Emerson Hough, *The Web: The Authorized History of the American Protective League* (Chicago: Reilly and Lee, 1919), 29–30; Joan M. Jensen, *The Price of Vigilance* (Chicago: Rand-McNally, 1968); Max Lowenthal, *The Federal Bureau of Investigation* (New York: William Sloane Associates, 1950), 22–36. On January 8, 1918, Fred T. Frazer wrote to the American Protective League headquarters in Washington and requested " 3 [membership badges] for ladies." Fred T. Frazer to American Protective League, Box 5,

Records of the Federal Bureau of Investigation: American Protective League, Record Group 65, National Archives and Records Administration [hereafter APL Records, RG 65, NARA]; see also Hough, *The Web*, 189. Although almost no women joined the APL, they worked closely with the league through organizations such as the National League for Woman's Service, which had reconfigured itself as a quasi-military force by mid-1918. Ida Clyde Clarke, *American Women and the World War* (New York: D. Appleton, 1918), 181–89.

52. John Sharp Williams, quoted in H. C. Peterson and Gilbert C. Fite, *Opponents of War, 1917–1918* (Seattle: University of Washington Press, 1968 [1957]), 209.

53. Membership files in Box 4, APL Records, RG 65, NARA. Hough, *The Web*, 191, gives an account of "foreign-born" APL chapters in Chicago and other cities.

54. "The A. P. L. Badge," *Spy Glass,* June 4, 1918; Hough, *The Web*, 180; Hauenstein, *History of Wayne County*, 185.

55. Hough, *The Web*, 28, 143. The small body of literature on Hough focuses entirely on his Western writings, providing almost no background on his wartime activities. See Richard Hopkins Gray, "A Dedication to the Memory of Emerson Hough, 1857–1923," *Arizona and the West* 17 (Spring 1975): 1–4; Delbert E. Wylder, *Emerson Hough* (Boston: Twayne, 1981), 56–62.

56. "The League's Job: How to Start Work," *Spy Glass,* July 25, 1918.

57. Willis, "Cleburne County Draft War," 25–26. Gibbs, *Great Silent Majority*, 84, 106, describes raids on saloons and pool halls in Missouri in the fall of 1917 and notes that Boy Scouts participated in "slacker hunts" to encourage people to buy Liberty Bonds.

58. Major Roscoe B. Conkling to Colonel J. C. Easby-Smith, May 1, 1918, and Colonel J. C. Easby-Smith to Major Roscoe Conkling, May 1, 1918, both in Correspondence Files, General 17–329, RG 163, NARA.

59. Hough, *The Web*, 144, 314; Crowder, *Second Report*, 201.

60. "4,000 A. P. L. Members in Slacker Drive," *Spy Glass*, July 25, 1918; "A. P. L. Valuable Aid in Draft Roundup," *Chicago Tribune*, September 24, 1918; "Roundup at Ball Park," *New York Times*, July 12, 1918; "Round up 10,000 in Chicago," *New York Times*, July 14, 1918. The APL's own account of the Chicago raid can be found in Hough, *The Web*, 141–47, 179–198.

61. "4,000 A. P. L. Members in Slacker Drive," *Spy Glass*, July 25, 1918.

62. "Get 653 Slackers at Coney," *New York Times*, July 22, 1918; "Arrest 300 in Trenton in Slacker Round-Up," *New York Times*, August 3, 1918; "Slacker Raid at Seashore," *New York Times*, August 16, 1918; "Slacker Roundup in Atlantic City," *New York Times*, August 17, 1918; "Two Drives in Galveston," *Spy Glass*, September 7, 1918; "20,000 Caught at Beach by Draft Raiders," *San Francisco Chronicle*, September 2, 1918; "Government to Use Armory as Draft Station," *San Francisco Chronicle*, September 5, 1918; George B. Catlin, *The Story of Detroit* (Detroit: Detroit News, 1926), 732.

63. Hough, *The Web*, 458–59; Aram Goudsouzian, "All Gods Dead: Babe Ruth and Boston, 1918–1920," in *The Rock, the Curse, and the Hub: A Random History of Boston Sports*, ed. Randy Roberts (Cambridge: Harvard University Press, 2005), 8–33.

64. "Net for Slackers to Be Nation-Wide," *New York Times*, September 2, 1918; "Agents Search Offices of Liberties Bureau," *New York Times*, September 1, 1918.

65. "Start Drive Today for Draft Slackers," *New York Times*, September 3, 1918; S. S. Doty to E. H. Rushmore, September 30, 1918, in Box 5, APL Records, RG 65, NARA; "Civil Liberty Dead," *Nation* 107 (September 14, 1918): 282. Hough, *The Web*, 204, gives the low number; Congressional debates quoted the higher number. No systematic count was ever made.

66. "Second Day Nets Few Slackers Here," *New York Times*, September 5, 1918. The newspaper happily reported that the man in question was released into the custody of his wife by that evening.

67. Ibid.; "Seize 20,000 Here in Slacker Search," *New York Times*, September 4, 1918.

68. "Second Day Nets Few Slackers Here," *New York Times*, September 5, 1918; Lowenthal, *Federal Bureau of Investigation*, 25.

69. "Seize 20,000 Here in Slacker Search," *New York Times*, September 4, 1918; Lawrence Bergreen, *As Thousands Cheer: The Life of Irving Berlin* (New York: Viking, 1990), 149–63.

70. "Second Day Nets Few Slackers Here," *New York Times*, September 5, 1918; "Get 1,500 Slackers in 3-Day Roundup," *New York Times*, September 6, 1918.

71. "Get 1,500 Slackers in 3-Day Roundup," *New York Times*, September 6, 1918; "War Comes to Wall Street," *New York Evening Post*, September 5, 1918, clipping in Box 5, APL Records, RG 65, NARA; "Round up Half Regiment," *Spy Glass*, September 7, 1918; "Wilson Asks Full Report on New York Draft Raids," *San Francisco Chronicle*, September 6, 1918; "Seize 20,000 Here in Slacker Search," *New York Times*, September 4, 1918.

72. "Get 1,500 Slackers in 3-Day Roundup," *New York Times*, September 6, 1918; "Hidden for 5 Days in Subway, Slacker Caught by Policeman," unidentified clipping in Box 5, APL Records, RG 65, NARA.

73. "Few Slackers, Says Conboy," *New York Times*, September 13, 1918.

74. "Get 653 Slackers at Coney," *New York Times*, July 22, 1918; "Arrest 300 in Trenton in Slacker Round-Up," *New York Times*, August 3, 1918; Lowenthal, *Federal Bureau of Investigation*, 30.

75. "More Bitter on Raids," *Washington Post*, September 7, 1918, clipping in Box 5, APL Records, RG 65, NARA; "Draft Raids Here Anger Senators," *New York Times*, September 6, 1918.

76. "Senators Denounce Raid on 'Slackers,'" *Washington Star*, undated clipping in Box 5, APL Records, RG 65, NARA; "Draft Raids Here Anger Senators," *New York Times*, September 6, 1918.

77. "Draft Raids Here Anger Senators," *New York Times*, September 6, 1918; "Inquiry by Wilson," *Washington Post*, unidentified clipping in Box 5, APL Records, RG 65, NARA.

78. "Draft Raids Here Anger Senators," *New York Times*, September 6, 1918.

79. "Halt Senate Action upon Slacker Raids," *New York Times*, September 7, 1918.

80. "Raid Critics and Defender," *New York Herald*, undated clipping, and "The Slacker Raids," September 12, 1918, unidentified clipping, both in Box 5, APL Records, RG 65, NARA; New York *Evening World*, September 6, 1917, quoted in Cummings and McFarland, *Federal Justice*, 426.

81. "Slacker Is Doused in Barrel of Paint," *San Francisco Chronicle*, September 7, 1918; "Militarism in America," *San Francisco Chronicle*, September 7, 1918; "Hunting the Slacker," *New York Times*, September 6, 1918.

82. Frank Irving Cobb to Joseph Patrick Tumulty, September 5, 1918, and Joseph Patrick Tumulty to Frank Irving Cobb, September 5, 1918, in PWW, vol. 49, p. 451; Woodrow Wilson to Thomas Watt Gregory, September 5, 1918, in ibid., 452; Josephus Daniels diary entry, September 10, 1918, in ibid., 513. When Wilson first learned of the existence of the American Protective League in June 1917, he told Attorney General Gregory it "sounds dangerous." Woodrow Wilson, quoted in Donald Johnson, *The Challenge to American Freedoms* (Lexington: University of Kentucky Press, 1963), 65.

83. Thomas Watt Gregory to Woodrow Wilson, September 9, 1918, in PWW, vol. 49, pp. 499–503; "Investigated Draft Raids," *New York Times*, September 7, 1918; "Get 1,500 Slackers in 3-Day Roundup," *New York Times*, September 6, 1918.

84. "Debs in Slacker Raid," *New York Times*, September 9, 1918. Although the APL formally disbanded in February 1919, volunteers continued to offer their services to local law enforcement agencies. Agents assisted the Bureau of Investigation in its raids on the Industrial Workers of the World in Seattle in the spring of 1919 and helped Attorney General A. Mitchell Palmer deport radicals and Bolshevists to the Soviet Union in 1920. Eliot Asinof, *1919: America's Loss of Innocence* (New York: Donald I. Fine, 1990), 132; John Higham, *Strangers in the Land: Patterns of American Nativism, 1860–1925* (New Brunswick, N.J.: Rutgers University Press, 1955), 220, 289, 294; Jensen, *Price of Vigilance*, 235–56.

85. E. H. Rushmore to Captain Charles D. Frey, September 25, 1918, in Box 7, APL Records, RG 65, NARA.

86. Rushmore to APL Directors, September 12, 1918, and Rushmore to Frey, October 7, 1918, in Box 7, APL Records, RG 65, NARA.

87. Rushmore to Frey, October 4, 1918, Box 7, APL Records, RG 65, NARA; Cummings and McFarland, *Federal Justice*, 422.

88. Coffman, *War to End All Wars*, 28; Ferrell, *Woodrow Wilson and World War I*, 18; "Government Preparations for a Big Round-Up of Draft Dodgers," *Literary Digest* 65 (June 26, 1920): 58–59; Stephen M. Kohn, *Jailed for Peace: The History of American Draft Law Violators, 1658–1985* (Westport, Conn.: Greenwood, 1986), 29–38; "Now for the Draft-Dodgers and Deserters," *Literary Digest* 65 (April 3, 1920): 69–70; Mark Sullivan, *Our Times: The United States, 1900–1925* (New York: Scribners, 1933), vol. 5, p. 359.

89. "Leigh May Succeed Bielaski," *New York Times*, December 9, 1918; "Retain Mr. Bielaski," *Washington Post*, December 11, 1918.

90. "Proclamation, September 6, 1918," Box 189, Mayor John Hylan Papers, New York Municipal Archives and Record Center, New York, N.Y.

91. Ibid. In Alabama, members of the National League for Woman's Service publicized the names of those they had witnessed violating the "Gasless Sunday" rules. National League for Woman's Service, *Annual Report for the Year 1918 with a Summary of the Year 1917* (New York: National League for Woman's Service, n.d. [1919]), 58. In Chicago, operatives of the American Protective League recorded 129,000 license plates of those violating "Gasless Sunday." Hough, *The Web*, 185. Emily

Frankenstein, the daughter of a Chicago doctor, noted that local children harassed her father in his car on "Gasless Sundays," despite his permit. Emily Frankenstein Diary, December 9, 1918 entry, Papers of Emily Frankenstein, Chicago Historical Society, Chicago.

92. Hough, *The Web*, 425.

93. William Jennings Bryan to Louis F. Post, April 1, 1920, Box 1, Papers of Louis F. Post, Library of Congress Manuscript Division, Washington, D.C.; Chambers, *To Build an Army*, 239, 240–48; John Dickinson, *The Building of an Army: A Detailed Account of Legislation, Administration and Opinion in the United States, 1915–1920* (New York: Century, 1922), 323–77.

Chapter 2

1. Norman Thomas, *The Conscientious Objector in America* (New York: B. W. Huebsch, 1923), 191–92; W. A. Swanberg, *Norman Thomas: The Last Idealist* (New York: Scribner's, 1976), 68–69.

2. Philip Grosser, *Uncle Sam's Devil's Island: Experiences of a Conscientious Objector in America during the World War* (Boston: Excelsior, 1933); Winthrop D. Lane, *Uncle Sam: Jailer: A Study of the Conditions of Federal Prisoners in Kansas Jails* (New York: National Civil Liberties Bureau, [1919]).

3. Edward M. Coffman, *The War to End All Wars: The American Military Experience in World War I* (New York: Oxford University Press, 1968), 74; H. C. Peterson and Gilbert C. Fite, *Opponents of War, 1917–1918* (Seattle: University of Washington Press, 1968 [1957]), 123. Of the 2,600, some 1,300 accepted noncombatant positions within the armed forces, 1,200 obtained agricultural furloughs, and a small detachment of men went to France with the Quakers to do reconstruction work. For accounts sympathetic to the military's handling of conscientious objectors, see Enoch H. Crowder, *Second Report of the Provost Marshal General to the Secretary of War on the Operations of the Selective Service System to December 20, 1918* (Washington, D.C.: Government Printing Office, 1919), 56–60; John Dickinson, *The Building of an Army: A Detailed Account of Legislation, Administration and Opinion in the United States, 1915–1920* (New York: Century, 1922), 136–45; and United States Department of War, *Statement concerning the Treatment of Conscientious Objectors in the Army* (Washington, D.C.: Government Printing Office, 1919).

4. For general histories of conscientious objection, see John Whiteclay Chambers II, "Conscientious Objectors and the American State from Colonial Times to the Present," in *The New Conscientious Objection: From Sacred to Secular Resistance*, ed. Charles C. Moskos and John Whiteclay Chambers II (New York: Oxford University Press, 1993), 23–46; Charles Chatfield, *For Peace and Justice: Pacifism in America, 1914–1941* (Knoxville: University of Tennessee Press, 1971); C. Roland Marchand, *The American Peace Movement and Social Reform, 1898–1918* (Princeton, N.J.: Princeton University Press, 1972). Rich collections of primary materials can be found in Melanie Springer Mock, *Writing Peace: The Unheard Voices of Great War Mennonite Objectors* (Scottdale, Pa.: Herald, 2003); Lillian Schlissel, ed., *Conscience in America: A Documentary History of Conscientious Objection in America, 1757–1967* (New York: Dutton, 1968), 128–75; and Thomas, *Conscientious Objector*.

5. Harlan F. Stone, "The Conscientious Objector," *Columbia University Quarterly* 21 (October 1919): 253–72.

6. Newton Baker, quoted in Coffman, *War to End All Wars*, 74. The term "conscientious objector" first entered the English language in the late nineteenth century to describe opponents of mandatory vaccination. Martin Kaufman, "The American Anti-Vaccinationists and Their Arguments," *Bulletin of the History of Medicine* 41 (September–October 1967): 463–78; Nadja Durbach, "Class, Gender, and the Conscientious Objector to Vaccination, 1898–1907," *Journal of British Studies* 41 (January 2002): 58–83. Forthcoming work by Michael Willrich will do much to situate conscientious objectors within nascent civil liberties movements of the early twentieth century. See Michael Willrich, "'The Least Vaccinated of Any Civilized Country': Personal Liberty and Public Health in the Progressive Era," *Journal of Policy History* 20 (January 2008).

7. "War Objectors Call on Baker," *Washington Post*, November 8, 1917; Rufus M. Jones, *A Service of Love in War Time: American Friends Relief Work in Europe, 1917–1919* (New York: Macmillan, 1920), 50–51. On the Selective Service Act regulations, see Arthur S. Link et al., eds., *Papers of Woodrow Wilson*, 69 vols. (Princeton, N.J.: Princeton University Press, 1966–94), vol. 42, p. 179 n. 2 [hereafter PWW with volume number]. The War Department's list of "well-recognized creeds" appears in Crowder, *Second Report*, 56–61. Arlyn John Parish, *Kansas Mennonites during World War I* (Fort Hays, Kan.: Fort Hays Studies, 1968), 23–24, notes that some Mennonites refused to lobby Congress because of their religious beliefs.

8. Walter Guest Kellogg, *The Conscientious Objector* (New York: Boni and Liveright, 1919), 33; Newton D. Baker to Woodrow Wilson, September 20, 1917, in PWW, vol. 44, p. 225.

9. William Dunham, quoted in Thomas, *Conscientious Objector*, 270. John F. Piper Jr., *The American Churches in World War I* (Athens: Ohio University Press, 1985), 16, 144–45. Patricia McNeal counts four Catholics in "Catholic Pacifism in America," in *Catholics in America, 1776–1976*, ed. Robert Trisco (Washington, D.C.: National Conference of Catholic Bishops, 1976), 265; Mark A. May, "The Psychological Examination of Conscientious Objectors," *American Journal of Psychology* 31 (April 1920): 154, counts nine. For critical studies of the Protestant churches and the conscientious objector, see Ray H. Abrams, *Preachers Present Arms* (Scottdale, Pa.: Herald, 1969 [1933]), 143–57, and Thomas, *Conscientious Objector*, 264–70. The General Conference Mennonites left the Federal Council of Churches in 1917 over the issue of conscientious objection. Parish, *Kansas Mennonites*, 54.

10. Stone, "Conscientious Objector," 254; "The Conscientious Objector," *Biblical World* 50 (December 1917): 329.

11. "Roosevelt Attacks Objectors to War," *New York Times*, January 31, 1918.

12. "Questions Hard to Answer," *New York Times*, January 24, 1919; "Roosevelt Attacks Objectors to War," *New York Times*, January 31, 1918. On the Canadian case, see Kellogg, *Conscientious Objector*, 117–18, and Levi, *Consent, Dissent, and Patriotism* (New York: Cambridge University Press, 1997), 134–64.

13. Marvin King, quoted in "Eyewitness Accounts," *Mennonite Life* 30 (September 1975): 22.

14. Sidney Webb, "Conscience and the 'Conscientious Objector,'" *North American Review* 205 (March 1917), 412. For more on Webb, see Lisanne Radice, *Beatrice and*

Sidney Webb: Fabian Socialists (New York: St. Martin's, 1984). Webb frequently collaborated with his wife, Beatrice Webb. I have been unable to determine if Beatrice Webb contributed to this essay, but in a diary entry written after she attended an anticonscription rally in London in April 1916, she expressed many of the same views. See Norman MacKenzie and Jeanne MacKenzie, eds., *The Diary of Beatrice Webb*, vol. 3 (London: Virago, 1984), 253–54.

15. Parish, *Kansas Mennonites*, 3–4, 7, 14–15, 18; D. Aidan McQuillan, *Prevailing over Time: Ethnic Adjustment on the Kansas Prairies, 1875–1925* (Lincoln: University of Nebraska Press, 1990), 90–92; H. W. Berky, quoted in "Eyewitness Accounts," 19.

16. *Gospel Herald*, May 31, 1917, quoted in Parish, *Kansas Mennonites*, 27. See ibid., 29, 36–37; Gerald E. Shenk, *"Work or Fight!": Race, Gender, and the Draft in World War One* (New York: Palgrave Macmillan, 2005), 58–60.

17. "Anti-Drafters Fill the Jail," *Los Angeles Times*, June 10, 1917; "Molokans Who Wouldn't Register Sent to Prison," *Los Angeles Times*, August 9, 1917; Nancy Gentile Ford, *Americans All! Foreign-Born Soldiers in World War I* (College Station: Texas A&M University Press, 2001), 66; William Haas Moore, "Prisoners in the Promised Land: The Molokans in World War I," *Journal of Arizona History* 14 (Winter 1973): 281, 284–85; Pauline V. Young, *The Pilgrims of Russian-Town* (Chicago: University of Chicago Press, 1932), 131, 134.

18. Edward Harry Hauenstein, *A History of Wayne County in the World War and in the Wars of the Past* (Wooster, Ohio: Wayne County History Co., 1919), 181. The five Kansas counties were Butler, Harvey, Marion, McPherson, and Reno.

19. R. B. Quinn, quoted in James C. Juhnke, "Mob Violence and Kansas Mennonites in 1918," *Kansas Historical Quarterly* 43 (August 1977): 334; Parish, *Kansas Mennonites*, 51–52; Frederick C. Luebke, "Legal Restrictions on Foreign Languages in the Great Plains States, 1917–1923," in *Languages in Conflict: Linguistic Acculturation on the Great Plains*, ed. Paul Schach (Lincoln: University of Nebraska Press, 1980), 10.

20. James C. Juhnke, "John Schrag Espionage Case," *Mennonite Life* 22 (July 1967): 121; Rufus M. Franz, "It Happened in Montana," *Mennonite Life* 7 (October 1952): 182.

21. "Religious Intolerance: Pastor Russell's Followers Persecuted Because They Tell the People the Truth," *Kingdom News*, March 15, 1918; Emerson Hough, *The Web: The Authorized History of the American Protective League* (Chicago: Reilly and Lee, 1919), 191; "Mob Takes Four Men from Prison to Tar and Feather Them," *New York Evening Call*, April 30, 1918; "Sedition Brings Whipping and Tar Coat to Four Men," *Memphis Press*, April 30, 1918; "Four Tarred and Feathered," *St. Louis Republican*, May 1, 1918; clippings in Reel 8, Volume 70, American Civil Liberties Union Archives, microfilm ed. (Wilmington, Del.: Scholarly Resources, 1996). Even the relatively respectable Quakers were not exempt from wartime pressure. See Hugh Barbour, "The Woods of Mt. Kisco," *Quaker History* 87 (Spring 1998): 9; Philip S. Benjamin, *The Philadelphia Quakers in the Industrial Age, 1865–1920* (Philadelphia: Temple University Press, 1976), 192–215; Helen Lefkowitz Horowitz, *The Power and Passion of M. Carey Thomas* (New York: Knopf, 1994), 430–31; Allan Kohrman, "Respectable Pacifists: Quaker Response to World War I," *Quaker History* 75 (Spring 1986): 35–53.

22. Kellogg, *Conscientious Objector*, 48–51, 264; Paula F. Pfeffer, *A. Philip Randolph, Pioneer of the Civil Rights Movement* (Baton Rouge: Louisiana State University Press, 1990), 10. See also John H. Stanfield II, "The Dilemma of Conscientious Objection for Afro-Americans," in *New Conscientious Objection*, ed. Moskos and Chambers, 47–56.

23. "Mason Makes Denial," *Memphis Commercial Appeal*, April 2, 1918; "German Money Used Freely in Mississippi," *Memphis Commercial Appeal*, April 2, 1918; "Jail Pastor for Obstructing Draft," *Chicago Defender*, June 29, 1918; "German Money," New York *Age*, April 6, 1918; Theodore Kornweibel Jr., "Race and Conscientious Objection in World War I: The Story of the Church of God in Christ," in *Proclaim Peace: Christian Pacifism from Unexpected Quarters*, ed. Theron F. Schlabach and Richard T. Hughes (Urbana: University of Illinois Press, 1997), 58–81.

24. Thomas, *Conscientious Objector*, 21, 149; Frances H. Early, *A World without War: How U.S. Feminists and Pacifists Resisted World War I* (Syracuse, N.Y.: Syracuse University Press, 1997), 219 n. 38.

25. Adam Mumaw, quoted in "Eyewitness Accounts," 24; Sheldon Smith, quoted in Peterson and Fite, *Opponents of War*, 127, 135; Ferdinand Schroeder, quoted in "Eyewitness Accounts," 22. Thomas, *Conscientious Objector*, 143–64, provides a full inventory of coercions in military camps. Sarah D. Shields, "The Treatment of Conscientious Objectors during World War I: Mennonites at Camp Funston," *Kansas History* 4 (Winter 1987): 255–69, argues that there was no "systematic abuse" (269) but drastically understates unofficial harassment. Moore, "Prisoners in the Promised Land," 293–94, questions the authenticity of some of the evidence included in Norman Thomas's book.

26. Newton Baker in Kellogg, *Conscientious Objector*, xiv; Theodore Roosevelt, quoted in Peterson and Fite, *Opponents of War*, 136; Bruno Grunzig, quoted in Early, *World without War*, 103, 106.

27. Leonard Wood, quoted in Hermann Hagedorn, *Leonard Wood: A Biography* (New York: Harper and Bros., 1931), vol. 2, p. 310; C. E. Kilbourne, quoted in Shields, "Treatment of Conscientious Objectors," 256; Stone, "Conscientious Objector," 263. On variation, see Coffman, *War to End All Wars*, 75; Joan Jensen, *The Price of Vigilance* (Chicago: Rand-McNally, 1968), 84–85.

28. Newton Baker to Woodrow Wilson, October 1, 1917, in PWW, vol. 44, pp. 288–89; Wilson to Baker, October 2, 1917, in ibid., 293; Josephus Daniels diary entry, October 12, 1917, in ibid., 370–71; Newton Baker in Kellogg, *Conscientious Objector*, xv. Secretary Daniels did not have to deal with issues of conscientious objection in the navy, which did not include drafted men in its ranks during World War I.

29. Newton Baker to Woodrow Wilson, September 19, 1917, in PWW, vol. 44, p. 221.

30. Harlan F. Stone, quoted in Alpheus Thomas Mason, *Harlan Fiske Stone: Pillar of the Law* (New York: Viking, 1956), 114; Baker in Kellogg, *Conscientious Objector*, xv–xvi.

31. Alvin C. York, "Sergeant York's Own Story, A Lecture," in *Sergeant York: An American Hero*, ed. David D. Lee (Lexington: University Press of Kentucky, 1985), 17. The lecture was not transcribed by York, but by an unidentified listener, who added its unorthodox spelling and punctuation.

32. Lee, *Sergeant York*, ix, 14–26. For a sampling of popular accounts, see Joseph Cummings Chase, "Corporal York, General Pershing, and Others," *World's Work*

37 (April 1919): 636–54; A. M. Jungmann, "What Did Alvin C. York Do?" *Ladies' Home Journal* 36 (October 1919): 64; "Conscience Plus Red Hair Are Bad for Germans," *Literary Digest* 61 (June 14, 1919): 42–48. York's story was made into a highly popular film starring Gary Cooper in 1941, just as the United States instituted its first peacetime draft in anticipation of World War II. See Lee, ed., *Sergeant York*, 92–115. Even Harlan Stone got caught up in the myths surrounding Alvin York. In a letter to Arthur Basse in the spring of 1940, Stone claimed that it was at a hearing of the Board of Inquiry that York had been persuaded to renounce his objector status; York, in fact, was in France before the board ever began its work. See Mason, *Harlan Fiske Stone*, 106.

33. "Eyewitness Accounts," 23, 25.

34. Parish, *Kansas Mennonites*, 35, 38, 40, 43–45; Enos Stutzman, quoted in "Eyewitness Accounts," 19.

35. Stone, "Conscientious Objector," 258; Webb, "Conscience and the 'Conscientious Objector,'" 412.

36. John Nevin Sayre to Woodrow Wilson, April 27, 1917, in PWW, vol. 42, p. 159; Charles F. Howlett, "John Nevin Sayre and the American Fellowship of Reconciliation," *Pennsylvania Magazine of History and Biography* 114 (July 1990): 399–421; Swanberg, *Norman Thomas*, 52–53. Margaret Levi has rightly rejected the insistence by liberal states on principled objection to all war, pointing out that in actual historical practice no objection to "war in general" has ever occurred without at least some context of criticism of "this war in particular," because no war in history has ever gone unopposed. Levi, *Consent, Dissent, and Patriotism*, 165.

37. Sayre to Wilson, April 27, 1917, in PWW, vol. 42, pp. 159–60; Wilson to Sayre, May 1, 1917, in ibid., 179.

38. Coffman, *War to End All Wars*, 74.

39. Newton Baker, quoted in Parish, *Kansas Mennonites*, 31. Matters were just as difficult for secular objectors. Although many of them were avowed individualists, they nevertheless depended in practice on support from socialist or civil liberties organizations, groups that during the war the federal government did not just exclude from draft board hearing rooms, but actively tried to destroy.

40. "Defines Service for War Objectors," *New York Times*, March 22, 1918; Gerlof D. Homan, "Mennonites and Military Justice in World War I," *Mennonite Quarterly Review* 66 (July 1992): 366–67; Parish, *Kansas Mennonites*, 32–33, 42. The term "furlough," although used throughout the war, was not technically accurate, because men on agricultural detail remained members of the U.S. military liable to the dictates of military law.

41. Norman Thomas, quoted in *The Politics of Conscience: The Historic Peace Churches and America at War, 1917–1955*, ed. Albert N. Keim and Grant M. Stolzfus (Scottdale, Pa.: Herald, 1988), 37; Josephus Daniels diary entry, October 12, 1917, in PWW, vol. 44, p. 371.

42. Newton Baker to Woodrow Wilson, August 27, 1917, in PWW, vol. 44, p. 74; see also Wilson to Baker, August 16, 1917, in PWW, vol. 43, p. 492; Wilson to R. M. Jones, August 28, 1917, in PWW, vol. 44, p. 75; Jones, *Service of Love*, 49, 55. For more on the AFSC, see John Forbes, *The Quaker Star under Seven Flags*

(Philadelphia: University of Pennsylvania Press, 1962), 31–47; J. William Frost, "'Our Deeds Carry Our Message': The Early History of the American Friends Service Committee," *Quaker History* 81 (Spring 1992): 1–51; and Lester M. Jones, *Quakers in Action: Recent Humanitarian and Reform Activities of the American Quakers* (New York: Macmillan, 1929).

43. "Setting the Pacifists at Work," *New York Times*, March 23, 1918; Kellogg, *Conscientious Objector*, 77, 80.

44. "Draft Objectors to Be Segregated," *New York Times*, June 1, 1918; Mason, *Harlan Fiske Stone*, 100–114; Mason, "Harlan Fiske Stone: In Defense of Individual Freedom, 1918–1920," *Columbia Law Review* 51 (February 1951): 147–69; Herbert Wechsler, "Harlan Fiske Stone," *New York History* 69 (April 1988): 154–62; Harry Barnard, *The Forging of an American Jew: The Life and Times of Judge Julian W. Mack* (New York: Herzl, 1974).

45. Stone, "Conscientious Objector," 258; Newton Baker to Woodrow Wilson, August 22, 1917, in PWW, vol. 44, p. 29; "Draft Objectors to Be Segregated," *New York Times*, June 1, 1918; "600 Draft Objectors," *New York Times*, June 2, 1918.

46. Kellogg, *Conscientious Objector*, 127–30; Mason, *Harlan Fiske Stone*, 103; "Draft Objectors to Be Segregated," *New York Times*, June 1, 1918; "Sifts Draft Objectors," *New York Times*, June 28, 1918. The remaining sixteen objectors at Camp Gordon either were transferred to Fort Leavenworth for further examination, were determined to be enemy aliens not subject to the draft, or were in the hospital and unavailable for interview.

47. Kellogg, *Conscientious Objector*, 30; Newton Baker to Woodrow Wilson, October 1, 1917, in PWW, vol. 44, p. 288; May, "Psychological Examination"; Stone, "Conscientious Objector," 267. For similar events in Germany, see Peter Brock, "Confinement of Conscientious Objectors as Psychiatric Patients in World War I Germany," *Peace and Change* 23 (July 1998): 247–64.

48. Mrs. Edward Johnson to William Morgan, October 6, 1918, in Stephen M. Kohn, *American Political Prisoners: Prosecutions under the Espionage and Sedition Acts* (Westport, Conn.: Praeger, 1994), 45–48.

49. Winthrop D. Lane, "Who Are the Conscientious Objectors?" *New Republic* 22 (April 14, 1920): 216–17. See also May, "Psychological Examination," 152–65; "Testing the Conscience of the Conscientious Objector," *Literary Digest* 61 (April 5, 1919): 66–71.

50. Kellogg, *Conscientious Objector*, 38, 51; Newton Baker to Woodrow Wilson, October 1, 1917, in PWW, vol. 44, p. 288; "'Objector' Gets 20 Years," *New York Times*, July 31, 1918. Robinson's punishment was actually a reduced term; he had originally been sentenced to life in prison.

51. "15,000 Appeal to Baker," *New York Times*, December 24, 1918; "Pleads with Baker to Free Objectors," *New York Times*, December 25, 1918; Kellogg, *Conscientious Objector*, 105; Stone, "Conscientious Objector," 260, 264–65; Roger Nash Baldwin, "The Faith of a Heretic," *Nation* 107 (November 9, 1918): 549; Forbes, *Quaker Star*, 43.

52. "Setting the Pacifists at Work," *New York Times*, March 23, 1918.

53. Carl Haessler, *Statement by Carl Haessler* (Milwaukee, Wis.: Milwaukee Committee on Amnesty for Political Prisoners, 1919), 3.

54. David Jantzen, quoted in "Eyewitness Accounts," 25; Norman Thomas, "Justice to War's Heretics," *Nation* 107 (November 9, 1918): 547; U.S. Department of War, *Statement*, 41.

55. Coffman, *War to End All Wars*, 76; Homan, "Mennonites and Military Justice," 368, 372-73; Parish, *Kansas Mennonites*, 41; Peterson and Fite, *Opponents of War*, 131. Objectors were a small minority of those subjected to military justice; more than eleven thousand soldiers faced court martial during World War I. Frederick Paul Keppel, *Some War-Time Lessons* (New York: Columbia University Press, 1920), 17. Only after the war, because of the pressure of civil liberties organizations and reformers within the military itself, did the army overhaul the military justice system. Jennifer D. Keene, *Doughboys, the Great War, and the Remaking of America* (Baltimore: Johns Hopkins University Press, 2001), 35-61, 161-178; John M. Lindley, *"A Soldier Is Also a Citizen": The Controversy over Military Justice, 1917-1920* (New York: Garland, 1990).

56. Erling H. Lunde, *Defense of Erling H. Lunde, Conscientious Objector to War* (Chicago: American Industrial, n.d.), 11; Haessler, *Statement*; "Court Martial 1918: Pvt. Ura V. Aschliman (420382)," *Mennonite Life* 31 (September 1976): 18-21.

57. David A. Lockmiller, *Enoch H. Crowder: Soldier, Lawyer, and Statesman* (Columbia: University of Missouri Studies, 1955), 133-41, 149; George V. Strong, "The Administration of Military Justice at the United States Disciplinary Barracks, Fort Leavenworth, Kansas," *Journal of the American Institute of Criminal Law and Criminology* 8 (September 1917): 420-27.

58. Ethel Thornburg to Thomas Walsh, October 23, 1919, and Mr. and Mrs. S. S. Croy to Thomas Walsh, November 3, 1919, both in Series I, Box 162, Papers of Thomas J. Walsh, Library of Congress Manuscript Division, Washington, D.C. See also Forbes, *Quaker Star*, 38, 43; Donald Johnson, *The Challenge to American Freedoms: World War I and the Rise of the American Civil Liberties Union* (Lexington: University of Kentucky Press, 1963), 49-54; Kohn, *American Political Prisoners*, 28. Federal amnesty provisions didn't reach everyone, though, because only those who had officially been classified as COs could claim amnesty. Peter Slyngstad, confined in a Mendocino, California, hospital after the Adjutant General's Office ruled him "mentally unbalanced," never qualified. S. Bartens to Thomas Walsh, March 10, 1919, Series I, Box 162, Papers of Thomas J. Walsh, ibid.

59. "Not Cruel to Slackers," *New York Times*, November 20, 1918; Kennedy, *Over Here*, 165; Parish, *Kansas Mennonites*, 39, 42; Thomas, *Conscientious Objector*, 162.

60. Kansas legislature quoted in James C. Juhnke, "The Agony of Civic Isolation: Mennonites in World War I," *Mennonite Life* 25 (January 1970): 32; "Legion Caucus Ends Cheering Young T.R.," *Boston Globe*, May 11, 1919; C. H. Cramer, *Newton D. Baker: A Biography* (Cleveland: World, 1961), 107; Jensen, *Price of Vigilance*, 281; William Pencak, *For God and Country: The American Legion, 1919-1941* (Boston: Northeastern University Press, 1989), 59. Almost all objectors were released by December 1920, but the last World War I conscientious objector was not freed until Franklin Roosevelt took office in 1933. See Milford Q. Sibley and Philip E. Jacob, *Conscription of Conscience: The American State and the Conscientious Objector, 1940-1947* (Ithaca, N.Y.: Cornell University Press, 1952), 16.

61. Shields, "Treatment of Conscientious Objectors," 268; H. W. Berky, quoted in "Eyewitness Accounts," 20; Franz, "It Happened in Montana," 184; Romans 12:19. Some COs were dishonorably discharged, depending on whether their CO status had been confirmed as sincere by the board, and whether they had been court-martialed. See John D. Unruh, "The Hutterites during World War I," *Mennonite Life* 24 (July 1969): 134.

62. John Dewey, "Conscience and Compulsion," in Dewey, *The Middle Works, 1899–1924*, ed. Jo Ann Boydston (Carbondale: Southern Illinois University Press, 1980), 260–64; Stone, "Conscientious Objector," 261; Kellogg, *Conscientious Objector*, 106.

63. In re *Roeper*, 274 Fed. 490 (1921), at 491; In re *D—*, 290 Fed. 863 (1923), at 865; Homan, "Mennonites and Military Justice," 369; "Aliens—Naturalization—'Conscientious Objector' Denied Citizenship," *Michigan Law Review* 22 (December 1923): 152–53; Young, *Pilgrims of Russian-Town*, 129.

64. Baldwin, "Faith of a Heretic," 549.

65. Harlan Fiske Stone to Fred Briehl, in Mason, *Harlan Fiske Stone*, 105. On World War II, see Sibley and Jacob, *Conscription of Conscience*; Rachel Waltner Goossen, *Women against the Good War: Conscientious Objection and Gender on the American Home Front, 1941–1947* (Chapel Hill: University of North Carolina Press, 1997); Shawn Francis Peters, *Judging Jehovah's Witnesses: Religious Persecution and the Dawn of the Rights Revolution* (Lawrence: University Press of Kansas, 2000).

Chapter 3

1. Mrs. C. Douglass Smith, quoted in Jo Ann Ruckman, "'Knit, Knit, and Then Knit': The Women of Pocatello and the War Effort of 1917–1918," *Idaho Yesterdays* 26 (Spring 1982): 28; W. H. Lightfoot, ed. and comp., *Our Heroes in Our Defense: Labette County, Kansas* (Parsons, Kan.: Commercial, 1921), n.p.; Amey Aldrich, *Fifty Years Ago: Early Days of the Cosmopolitan Club* (Stamford, Conn.: Overbrook, 1959), 15. More generally, see Anne S. MacDonald, *No Idle Hands: The Social History of American Knitting* (New York: Ballantine, 1988), 199–238.

2. Lester Stephens, ed., "A Righteous Aim: Emma LeConte Furman's 1918 Diary," *Georgia Historical Quarterly* 62 (Fall 1978): 217; Ruckman, "'Knit, Knit,'" 32; Myra M. Sampson, "Surgical Dressings," March 25, 1918, Box 130, War Service Files, 1914–1918, Smith College Archives, Northampton, Mass.

3. "Women in Wartime," *Chicago Tribune*, January 28, 1918; "Efforts to Disparage Work of Red Cross," *Atlanta Constitution*, October 13, 1917; "Scandal Mongering," *Chicago Tribune*, October 27, 1917; "Mice, Not Spies, Injured Sweaters," *Atlanta Constitution*, November 12, 1917; MacDonald, *No Idle Hands*, 217; *State v. Freerks*, 140 Minn. 349 (1918), at 350; *State v. Holm*, 139 Minn. 267 (1918).

4. Ruckman, "'Knit, Knit,'" 32; MacDonald, *No Idle Hands*, 218. Hand-knitting accounted for the majority of soldiers' socks, but uniforms were more of an indus-trial affair. See "The American Soldier's Uniform," *Review of Reviews* 64 (November 1921): 542–43; Rachel Maines, "Wartime Allocation of Textiles and Apparel Resources: Emergency Policy in the Twentieth Century," *Public Historian* 7 (Winter 1985): 29–51.

5. Mrs. Coffin Van Rensselaer, "The National League for Woman's Service," *Annals of the American Academy of Political and Social Science* 79 (September 1918): 280. On women's voluntarism and unpaid labor, see Jeanie Attie, *Patriotic Toil: Northern Women and the American Civil War* (Ithaca, N.Y.: Cornell University Press, 1998), 19–49, and Doris B. Gold, "Women and Voluntarism," in *Woman in Sexist Society: Studies in Power and Powerlessness*, ed. Vivian Gornick and Barbara K. Moran (New York: Basic Books, 1971), 384–400.

6. Molly Matson, ed., *An Independent Woman: The Autobiography of Edith Guerrier* (Amherst: University of Massachusetts Press, 1992), 98; Philadelphia War History Committee, *Philadelphia in the World War, 1914–1919* (New York: Wynkoop Hallenbeck Crawford, 1922), 545–46, 693; "Uniforms from Sweatshops," *Survey* 38 (September 15, 1917): 519; *New York Tribune*, August 26, 1917, quoted in Eileen Boris, "Tenement Homework on Army Uniforms: The Gendering of Industrial Democracy during World War I," *Labor History* 32 (Spring 1991): 242; "Negro Women Workers," *New York Times*, July 21, 1918; Judith Weisenfeld, *African American Women and Christian Activism: New York's Black YWCA, 1905–1945* (Cambridge: Harvard University Press, 1997), 146.

7. For more on voluntarism in American political culture from the perspectives of the social sciences, see Brian J. Glenn, "Fraternal Rhetoric and the Development of the U.S. Welfare State," *Studies in American Political Development* 15 (Fall 2001): 220–33; Jason Kaufman, *For the Common Good? American Civic Life and the Golden Age of Fraternity* (New York: Oxford University Press, 2002); Robert D. Putnam, "Bowling Alone: America's Declining Social Capital," *Journal of Democracy* 6 (January 1995): 65–78; Putnam, *Bowling Alone: The Collapse and Revival of American Community* (New York: Simon & Schuster, 2000); and Theda Skocpol and Morris P. Fiorina, eds., *Civic Engagement in American Democracy* (Washington, D.C.: Brookings Institution Press, 1999), esp. 1–80. Excellent case studies of the relationship between voluntary associations and American political culture include Lynn Dumenil, *Freemasonry and American Culture, 1880–1930* (Princeton, N.J.: Princeton University Press, 1984); Stuart McConnell, *Glorious Contentment: The Grand Army of the Republic, 1865–1900* (Chapel Hill: University of North Carolina Press, 1992); and Francesca Morgan, *Women and Patriotism in Jim Crow America* (Chapel Hill: University of North Carolina Press, 2005).

8. William J. Novak analyzes the structural foundation in "The American Law of Association: The Legal-Political Construction of Civil Society," *Studies in American Political Development* 15 (Fall 2001): 163–88. Putnam, *Bowling Alone*, 367–401 surveys late nineteenth- and early twentieth-century voluntarism and finds in voluntary associations a vibrant alternative to state institutions; Theda Skocpol et al., "A Nation of Organizers: The Institutional Origins of Civic Voluntarism in the United States," *American Political Science Review* 94 (September 2000): 527–46, traces the synergy between voluntary associations and state institutions.

9. Lettie Gavin, *American Women in World War I: They Also Served* (Niwot: University Press of Colorado, 1997), x, 44. Gavin also accounts for the wide range of military and quasi-military positions in which women served. Susan Zeiger, *In Uncle Sam's Service: Women Workers with the American Expeditionary Force, 1917–1919* (Ithaca,

N.Y.: Cornell University Press, 1999), explores the political and cultural implications of service.

10. In the vast literature on clubwomen's political participation at the turn of the century, see Karen J. Blair, *The Clubwoman as Feminist: True Womanhood Redefined, 1868–1914* (New York: Holmes and Meier, 1980); Elisabeth S. Clemens, "Securing Political Returns to Social Capital: Women's Associations in the United States, 1880s–1920s," *Journal of Interdisciplinary History* 29 (Spring 1999): 613–38; Nancy F. Cott, *The Grounding of Modern Feminism* (New Haven, Conn.: Yale University Press, 1987), 85–114; Glenda Elizabeth Gilmore, *Gender and Jim Crow: Women and the Politics of White Supremacy in North Carolina, 1896–1920* (Chapel Hill: University of North Carolina, 1996); Anne Firor Scott, *Natural Allies: Women's Associations in American History* (Urbana: University of Illinois Press, 1991); and Theda Skocpol, *Protecting Soldiers and Mothers: The Political Origins of Social Policy in the United States* (Cambridge: Belknap Press of Harvard University Press, 1992), 321–72.

11. Numbers from Ida Clyde Clarke, *American Women and the World War* (New York: D. Appleton, 1918), 189. For more on the history of the General Federation of Women's Clubs, see Sophonisba P. Breckinridge, *Women in the Twentieth Century: A Study of Their Political, Social and Economic Activities* (New York: Arno, 1972 [1933]); Mary Jean Houde, *Reaching Out: A Story of the General Federation of Women's Clubs* (Chicago: Mobium, 1989). On women's participation in turn-of-the-century politics, even—or perhaps despite—their exclusion from the polls, see Paula Baker, "The Domestication of Politics: Women and American Political Society, 1780–1920," *American Historical Review* 89 (June 1984): 620–47; Rebecca Edwards, *Angels in the Machinery: Gender in American Party Politics from the Civil War to the Progressive Era* (New York: Oxford University Press, 1997); Liette Gidlow, *The Big Vote: Gender, Consumer Culture, and the Politics of Exclusion, 1890s-1920s* (Baltimore: Johns Hopkins University Press, 2004); Melanie Susan Gustafson, *Women and the Republican Party, 1854–1924* (Urbana: University of Illinois Press, 2001); and Robyn Muncy, *Creating a Female Dominion in American Reform, 1890–1935* (New York: Oxford University Press, 1991).

12. The richest and fullest study of African-American clubwomen in this period is Nikki Brown, *Private Politics and Public Voices: Black Women's Activism from World War I to the New Deal* (Bloomington: Indiana University Press, 2006). See Elizabeth Lindsay Davis, *Lifting as They Climb* (New York: G. K. Hall, 1996 [1933]); Gilmore, *Gender and Jim Crow*; Evelyn Brooks Higginbotham, *Righteous Discontent: The Women's Movement in the Black Baptist Church* (Cambridge: Harvard University Press, 1993); Higginbotham, "Clubwomen and Electoral Politics in the 1920s," in *African American Women and the Vote, 1837–1965*, ed. Ann D. Gordon et al. (Amherst: University of Massachusetts Press, 1997), 134–55; Maude T. Jenkins, "The History of the Black Woman's Club Movement in America" (Ph.D. dissertation, Teachers College, Columbia University, 1984), esp. 33–64; Anne Firor Scott, "Most Invisible of All: Black Women's Voluntary Associations," *Journal of Southern History* 56 (February 1990): 5–22; Stephanie J. Shaw, "Black Club Women and the Creation of the National Association of Colored Women," *Journal of Women's History* 3 (Fall 1991): 10–25; Deborah Gray White, *Too Heavy a Load: Black Women in Defense of*

Themselves, 1894–1994 (New York: Norton, 1999), 1–109. Numerous pathbreaking articles are included in Darlene Clark Hine, ed., *Black Women in American History: The Twentieth Century*, 4 vols. (Brooklyn, N.Y.: Carlson, 1990–1995).

13. Virginia Scharff, *Taking the Wheel: Women and the Coming of the Motor Age* (New York: Free Press, 1991), 93, 99; "Women Now Have Opportunity to Become Wireless Operators," *New York Times*, April 1, 1917; "Prepare to Mobilize Women," *New York Times*, April 2, 1917; Clarke, *American Women*, 181–88; Barbara J. Steinson, *American Women's Activism in World War I* (New York: Garland, 1982), 300–308; Theodora Dunham to Mother, October 24, 1916, and February 9, 1917, in Box 30, Bodman Family Papers, Sophia Smith Collection, Smith College, Northampton, Mass. [hereafter Sophia Smith Collection]; Van Rensselaer, "National League," 277. The NLWS, which drew heavily from conservative women, included probably the most explicitly militarist of clubwomen. See National League for Woman's Service, *Annual Report for the Year 1918 with a Summary of the Year 1917* (New York: National League for Woman's Service, n.d. [1919]), 8–13.

14. Quotes from Houde, *Reaching Out*, 150, 155. "Clubwomen May Make Munitions," *New York Times*, April 25, 1917; Aldrich, *Fifty Years Ago*, 13; Minutes, November 19, 1917, Minutes of the Meetings of the Board of Directors of the New York City Federation of Women's Clubs, Item 1306–03–1, Local Club Records (Record Group 13), General Federation of Women's Clubs Archives, Washington, D.C. [hereafter GFWC Archives]; Faith Rogow, *Gone to Another Meeting: The National Council of Jewish Women, 1893–1993* (Tuscaloosa: University of Alabama Press, 1993), 178. On women's prewar peace work in voluntary associations, see Harriet Hyman Alonso, *Peace as a Women's Issue: A History of the U.S. Movement for World Peace and Women's Rights* (Syracuse, N.Y.: Syracuse University Press, 1993), 56–84; Marie Louise Degen, *The History of the Woman's Peace Party* (New York: Burt Franklin's Reprints, 1974 [1939]); Linda K. Schott, *Reconstructing Women's Thoughts: The Women's International League for Peace and Freedom before World War II* (Stanford, Calif.: Stanford University Press, 1997).

15. "History of the Worcester Branch," typescript (1945), in Box 1, Folder 1; Executive Committee Minutes, September 6, 1917, in Box 1, Folder 3; and "Twenty-First Annual Report of the Secretary, March 23, 1918," in Box 1, Folder 5, American Association of University Women, Worcester Branch Records, Sophia Smith Collection.

16. "Editorial: The Woman 'Slacker,'" *Ladies' Home Journal* 34 (July 1917): 7.

17. A. D. S. [Anna Davenport Sparks], "Editor's Table," *Smith College Monthly* 24 (May 1917): 381; "Editorial: Her Chance for Service," *Ladies' Home Journal* 34 (June 1917): 7. For a fictional example, see Edith Wharton, *The Marne* (New York: D. Appleton, 1918), 33–34.

18. NLWS, *Annual Report*, 14; Mrs. Walter A. Hall et al., comps., *Progress and Achievement: A History of the Massachusetts State Federation of Women's Clubs, 1893–1931* (Norwood, Mass.: Plimpton, 1932), 85; Houde, *Reaching Out*, 150–51; Weisenfeld, *African American Women and Christian Activism*, 145; "Prepare to Mobilize Women," *New York Times*, April 2, 1917; Mrs. Henry Schmidt, quoted in Virginia R. Boynton, "'Even in the Remotest Parts of the State': Downstate 'Woman's Committee' Activities on the Illinois Home Front during World War I," *Journal of*

the Illinois State Historical Society 96 (Winter 2003–04): 321–22; "Editorial," *Smith College Monthly* 24 (June 1917): 436.

19. Quoted in Mary Jean Houde, *The Clubwoman: A Story of the Illinois Federation of Women's Clubs* (Chicago: Illinois Federation of Women's Clubs, 1970), 87. The speaker is unnamed. See also David Zonderman, "Over Here: The Wisconsin Homefront during World War I," *Wisconsin Magazine of History* 77 (Summer 1994): 297. The NLWS vigorously debated whether their wartime uniforms should consist of a skirt or "knickerbockers." The women reached a compromise, allowing field volunteers at military camps to wear pants while insisting on skirts for regular volunteers. See "Khaki for Woman's League," *New York Times*, April 7, 1917.

20. On the wartime work of the YMCA and YWCA, see YMCA of the USA, *Service with Fighting Men* (New York: Association Press, 1922); Dorothea Browder, "A 'Christian Solution of the Labor Situation': How Workingwomen Reshaped the YWCA's Religious Mission and Politics," *Journal of Women's History* 19 (Summer 2007): 85–110; Nina Mjagkij, *Light in the Darkness: African Americans and the YMCA, 1852–1946* (Lexington: University Press of Kentucky, 1994), 86–100; and Weisenfeld, *African American Women and Christian Activism*, 121–55. On the Woman's Committee of the Council of National Defense, see William J. Breen, *Uncle Sam at Home: Civilian Mobilization, Wartime Federalism, and the Council of National Defense* (Westport, Conn.: Greenwood, 1984), 115–56; Penelope Noble Brownell, "The Women's Committees of the First World War: Women in Government, 1917–1919" (Ph.D. dissertation, Brown University, 2003). For the American Library Association, see Arthur P. Young, *Books for Sammies: The American Library Association and World War I* (Pittsburgh, Pa.: Beta Phi Mu, 1981). Theda Skocpol et al., "Patriotic Partnerships: Why Great Wars Nourished American Civic Voluntarism," in *Shaped by War and Trade: International Influences on American Political Development*, ed. Ira Katznelson and Martin Shefter (Princeton, N.J.: Princeton University Press, 2002), 154–69, traces the war's impact on the membership and public voice of national organizations.

21. Raymond B. Fosdick, *Chronicle of a Generation: An Autobiography* (New York: Harper and Brothers, 1958), 149; Harriot Stanton Blatch and Alma Lutz, *Challenging Years: The Memoirs of Harriot Stanton Blatch* (New York: G. P. Putnam's Sons, 1940), 290. See also Maurice Francis Egan, *The Knights of Columbus in Peace and War* (New Haven, Conn.: Knights of Columbus, 1920); Christopher J. Kauffman, *Faith and Fraternalism: The History of the Knights of Columbus, 1882–1982* (New York: Harper and Row, 1982); Elizabeth McKeown, *War and Welfare: American Catholics and World War I* (New York: Garland, 1988); National Jewish Welfare Board, *Final Report of War Emergency Activities* (New York: National Jewish Welfare Board, 1920); Christopher M. Sterba, *Good Americans: Italian and Jewish Immigrants during the First World War* (New York: Oxford University Press, 2003), 86–129; Michael Williams, *American Catholics in the World War: The National Catholic War Council, 1917–1921* (New York: Macmillan, 1921); Young, *Books for Sammies*, 34–35, 126 n. 49.

22. James J. Kenneally, *The History of American Catholic Women* (New York: Crossroad, 1990), 140–42; Philadelphia War History Committee, *Philadelphia in the World*

War, 355; Florida Ruffin Ridley, quoted in Weisenfeld, *African American Women and Christian Activism*, 142, 145; Brown, *Private Politics and Public Voices*, 66–107; Alice Dunbar-Nelson, "Negro Women in War Work," in Emmett J. Scott, *The American Negro in the World War* (Chicago: Homewood, 1919), 374–97; Paula Giddings, *When and Where I Enter: The Impact of Black Women on Race and Sex in America* (New York: William Morrow, 1984), 155–58; "The Negro and the Red Cross," *Crisis* 16 (August 1918): 167; Jacqueline Anne Rouse, *Lugenia Burns Hope: Black Southern Reformer* (Athens: University of Georgia Press, 1989), 1–3, 94–96; Weisenfeld, *African American Women and Christian Activism*, 123, 142, 145, 148.

23. Ena L. Farley, "Caring and Sharing since World War I: The League of Women for Community Service—A Black Volunteer Organization in Boston," in Hine, ed., *Black Women in American History*, vol. 5, pp. 317–28; Dorothy B. Porter, "Maria Louise Baldwin, 1856–1922," in ibid., vol. 8, pp. 1017–19; Nannie Burroughs, quoted in Higginbotham, *Righteous Discontent*, 225; Ada Thoms, quoted in Weisenfeld, *African American Women and Christian Activism*, 144.

24. For biographical information, see Houde, *Reaching Out*, 150; Newton Baker to Carrie Chapman Catt, April 24, 1917, Reel 2, Papers of Carrie Chapman Catt, Library of Congress Manuscript Division, Washington, D.C. [hereafter LCMD]; Mrs. Thomas G. Winter, "A Gallant Leader Passes," undated clipping from *The Clubwoman GFWC*, and Dr. Arthur E. Bestor, *A Tribute to Mrs. Percy V. Pennybacker* (Chautauqua, N.Y.: Chautauqua Institute, 1938), both in file 020703-1-2, Papers of Anna H. Pennybacker (Memorials), 1938, Presidents' Papers (Record Group 2), GFWC Archives; "Federation Matriarch Active Today," clipping from *General Federation News* (December 1929): 15, 24, file 020601-1-1, Papers of Eva P. Moore (Biographical Information), 1908–1912, Presidents' Papers (Record Group 2), GFWC Archives. For local examples, see Houde, *Reaching Out*, 151, 153; The National Society of New England Women, *Tidings from Far and Near* (Chicago: Dunwell and Ford, March 1918), 23, in Box 23, Folder 3, National Society of New England Women Records, Sophia Smith Collection; Maude G. Palmer, comp., *The History of the Illinois Federation of Women's Clubs, 1894–1928* (n.p.: Illinois Federation of Women's Clubs, 1928), 91; Carrie Niles Whitcomb, *Reminiscences of the Springfield Women's Club, 1884–1924* (n.p.: n.d. [1924]), 127.

25. On the draft, see Ione V. H. Cowles to State Presidents, circular letter, May 30, 1917, file 020806-1-4, Papers of Ione V. H. Cowles (Correspondence, Outgoing), 1917, Presidents' Papers (Record Group 2), GFWC Archives; "Women Help Recruiting," *New York Times*, April 2, 1917; "Call to New York Women to Aid in Military Census," *New York Times*, April 10, 1917; NLWS, *Annual Report*, 21; United States Council of National Defense, *Third Annual Report of the United States Council of National Defense* (Washington, D.C.: Government Printing Office, 1919), 35. On bonds, see Walter E. Whitaker, *Centennial History of Alamance County, 1849–1949* (Burlington, N.C.: Burlington Chamber of Commerce, 1949), 248. But see Caroline Ruutz-Rees, "The Mobilization of American Women," *Yale Review* 7 (July 1918): 809; and Ruckman, "'Knit, Knit,'" 31, who notes that women war volunteers in Pocatello, Idaho, never spoke publicly in front of mixed-sex audiences and were excluded from all but clerical tasks in the Liberty Loan drives.

26. Matson, ed., *An Independent Woman*, 97; Emily Newell Blair, *Bridging Two Eras: The Autobiography of Emily Newell Blair, 1877–1951*, ed. Virginia Jeans Laas (Columbia: University of Missouri Press, 1999), 179–84.

27. Anna Gordon, quoted in Joseph R. Gusfield, *Symbolic Crusade: Status Politics and the American Temperance Movement* (Urbana: University of Illinois Press, 1963), 123; Clarke, *American Women and the World War*, 198; Helen E. Tyler, *Where Prayer and Purpose Meet: The WCTU Story, 1874–1949* (Evanston, Ill.: Signal, 1949); Frances W. Graham, *A History of Sixty Years' Work of the Woman's Christian Temperance Union of the State of New York, 1874–1934* (Lockport, N.Y.: WCTU, 1934), 120–21; David M. Kennedy, *Over Here: The First World War and American Society* (New York: Oxford University Press, 1980), 185; Skocpol, "Patriotic Partnerships," 167.

28. The best introduction to wartime prohibition is Richard F. Hamm, *Shaping the 18th Amendment: Temperance Reform, Legal Culture, and the Polity, 1880–1920* (Chapel Hill: University of North Carolina Press, 1995). K. Austin Kerr, *Organized for Prohibition: A New History of the Anti-Saloon League* (New Haven, Conn.: Yale University Press, 1985), 185–210, and Thomas R. Pegram, *Battling Demon Rum: The Struggle for a Dry America, 1800–1933* (Chicago: Ivan R. Dee, 1998), 136–64, both focus primarily on the Anti-Saloon League.

29. Anna Howard Shaw, quoted in Marsha Gordon, "Onward Kitchen Soldiers: Mobilizing the Domestic during World War I," *Canadian Review of American Studies* 29, no. 2 (1999): 61–87; Ruutz-Rees, "Mobilization of American Women," 808, 817–18. Kennedy, *Over Here*, 286, questions the wartime significance of the Woman's Committee of the Council of National Defense; Breen, *Uncle Sam at Home*, agrees.

30. Anna Howard Shaw, quoted in Gordon, "Kitchen Soldiers," 64–65; Meg Jacobs, *Pocketbook Politics: Economic Citizenship in Twentieth-Century America* (Princeton, N.J.: Princeton University Press, 2005), 53–66. Belinda J. Davis explores the European experience with wartime food rationing in *Home Fires Burning: Food, Politics, and Everyday Life in World War I Berlin* (Chapel Hill: University of North Carolina Press, 2000).

31. Herbert Hoover, quoted in Robert D. Cuff, "Herbert D. Hoover, the Ideology of Voluntarism and War Organization during the Great War," *Journal of American History* 64 (September 1977): 361–62. After the war, in an oddly mistitled volume called *American Individualism* (1922), Hoover would suggest American voluntary association as the cure for the postwar ills of radical Bolshevism. Hoover, *American Individualism* (Garden City, N.Y.: Doubleday, Page, 1922). For the impact of voluntarism on the mobilization of political economy, see Valerie Jean Conner, *The National War Labor Board: Stability, Social Justice, and the Voluntary State in World War I* (Chapel Hill: University of North Carolina Press, 1983); Ellis W. Hawley, *The Great War and the Search for a Modern Order: A History of the American People and Their Institutions, 1917–1933* (New York: St. Martin's, 1979), 52–55, 66–71, 100–117; Kennedy, *Over Here*, 142–53.

32. Woodrow Wilson, quoted in Alfred Cornebise, *War as Advertised: The Four Minute Men and America's Crusade, 1917–1918* (Philadelphia: American Philosophical Society, 1984), 87; poster in Joseph Carruth, "World War I Propaganda and Its Effects in Arkansas," *Arkansas Historical Quarterly* 56 (Winter 1997): 391; Herbert

Hoover, *The Memoirs of Herbert Hoover: Years of Adventure, 1874–1920* (New York: Macmillan, 1951), 244.

33. Herbert Hoover, quoted in Ivan L. Pollock, *The Food Administration in Iowa* (Iowa City: State Historical Society of Iowa, 1923), vol. 1, p. 127; Jane Addams, "The World's Food Supply and Woman's Obligation," typescript, c. 1918, pp. 11, 13–14, in Box 1, Folder 22, Papers of Jane Addams, Sophia Smith Collection. See also Addams, *Peace and Bread in Time of War* (Urbana: University of Illinois Press, 2002 [1922]); Addams, *The Second Twenty Years at Hull-House* (New York: Macmillan, 1930), 144–46.

34. Houde, *Reaching Out*, 154; "Women's Convention Ends," *New York Times*, November 17, 1917; Members of the Past Presidents Association of the Dallas Federation of Women's Clubs, eds., *History of the Dallas Federation of Women's Clubs, 1898–1936* (Dallas, Tex.: Clyde C. Cockrell and Son, 1936), 81.

35. Numbers from William Clinton Mullendore, *History of the United States Food Administration, 1917–1919* (Stanford, Calif.: Stanford University Press, 1941), 12; Matson, ed., *An Independent Woman*, 105, 141 n. 3; NLWS, *Annual Report*, 18; Gordon, "Kitchen Soldiers," 76. See also Hoover, *Memoirs*, 240–80. The text of the Hoover Pledge was substantially different, however: "I am glad to join you in the service of food conservation in our United States and I hereby accept membership in the United States Food Administration, pledging myself to carry out the direction and advice of the Food Administrator in the conduct of my household in so far as my circumstances permit." Pollock, *Food Administration in Iowa*, vol. 1, p. 128. In fact, a wide array of food pledges circulated on the home front, including one in which a reader of *Good Housekeeping* who pledged to "enlist as a Kitchen Soldier" received a certificate from the magazine. It is perhaps telling that, as Marsha Gordon notes, the editors of *Good Housekeeping* felt compelled in November 1918 "to correct rumours that it was in fact a government publication." Gordon, "Kitchen Soldiers," 68.

36. Lura Harris Craighead, *History of the Alabama Federation of Women's Clubs* (Montgomery: Paragon, 1936), vol. 1, pp. 431–34; Pollock, *Food Administration in Iowa*, vol. 1, pp. 36, 54, 77, 103. I have encountered little evidence that men ever participated in the house-to-house work of pledge collection, nor that they signed pledge cards, even when there were no women in their households.

37. Matson, ed., *An Independent Woman*, 101; David Alan Corbin, *Life, Work, and Rebellion in the Coal Fields: The Southern West Virginia Miners, 1880–1922* (Urbana: University of Illinois Press, 1982), 182; Christopher C. Gibbs, *The Great Silent Majority: Missouri's Resistance to World War I* (Columbia: University of Missouri Press, 1988), 126, 130; Lou Hoover, quoted in Nancy Beck Young, *Lou Henry Hoover: Activist First Lady* (Lawrence: University Press of Kansas, 2004), 28; Meirion Harries and Susie Harries, *The Last Days of Innocence: America at War, 1917–1918* (New York: Vintage, 1997), 163; Pollock, *Food Administration in Iowa*, vol. 1, pp. 152–53. Food conservation's most violent incident occurred in April 1918 near Grannis, Arkansas, where Henry Dafforn, a German-American farmer, shot and killed A. D. Boatner when he came around to collect pledges from farmers for the U.S. Food Administration. See Carruth, "World War I Propaganda," 397.

38. Pollock, *Food Administration in Iowa*, vol. 1, pp. 133–34, 137, 145; Philadelphia War History Committee, *Philadelphia in the World War*, 353; Melanie Rich, " 'She

Would Raise Hens to Aid War': The Contributions of Oklahoma Women during World War I," *Chronicles of Oklahoma* 91 (Fall 2003): 336; Mary Kingsbury Simkhovitch, *Neighborhood: My Story of Greenwich House* (New York: Norton, 1938), 186–87, 193; Herbert Hoover to Rev. Dr. Rudolph Muenzinger, June 18, 1917, in Rudolf Muenzinger Papers, Bentley Historical Library, University of Michigan, Ann Arbor, Mich.

39. Charles N. Herreid, "The Federal Food Administration in South Dakota during the World War," *South Dakota Historical Collections* 10 (1920): 309; "Public Hearings for Food Rule Violators," *Vicksburg Daily Herald*, April 3, 1918; Stephens, ed., "A Righteous Aim," 222; Mary Aldis, "For the Homemaker: Housekeeping in War Time," *Journal of Home Economics* 10 (February 1918): 73; Gordon, "Kitchen Soldiers," 72–74.

40. Gibbs, *Great Silent Majority*, 109–34. On the contested modernization of rural women's food production, see Joan M. Jensen, "Canning Comes to New Mexico: Women and the Agricultural Extension Service, 1914–1919," *New Mexico Historical Review* 57, no. 4 (1982): 361–86; Lynne A. Rieff, " 'Go Ahead and Do All You Can': Southern Progressives and Alabama Home Demonstration Clubs, 1914–1940," in *Hidden Histories of Women in the New South*, ed. Virginia Bernhard et al. (Columbia: University of Missouri Press, 1994), 134–49. In the households of World War II, another generation of industrial development had shifted the terrain of politics from food preparation to food consumption. See Amy Bentley, *Eating for Victory: Food Rationing and the Politics of Domesticity* (Urbana: University of Illinois Press, 1998); Meg Jacobs, " 'How About Some Meat?' The Office of Price Administration, Consumption Politics, and State Building from the Bottom Up, 1941–1946," *Journal of American History* 84 (December 1997): 910–41.

41. Martha Lavinia Hunter, *A Quarter of a Century History of the Dallas Woman's Forum, 1906–1931* (Dallas, Tex.: Clyde C. Cockrell, 1932), 61; Craighead, *History of the Alabama Federation of Women's Clubs*, vol. 1, p. 431; Pollock, *Food Administration in Iowa*, vol. 1, pp. 78–83. Sometimes middle-class volunteers and working-class women worked together, as in the case of the Food Reserve Battalion, which traveled Long Island presenting to housewives and factory girls. "Senate Takes Up Food Census Bill," *New York Times*, May 24, 1917.

42. Tera W. Hunter, *To 'Joy My Freedom: Southern Black Women's Lives and Labors after the Civil War* (Cambridge: Harvard University Press, 1997), 225.

43. Elizabeth Reis, "The AFL, the IWW, and Bay Area Cannery Workers," *California History* 64 (Summer 1985): 186–87; NLWS, *Annual Report*, 29, 30; "Women Wanted for Farms and Canneries," *Boston Globe*, July 18, 1917.

44. Bentley, *Eating for Victory*, 20–21; Cornebise, *War as Advertised*, 98.

45. "Red Cross Bandages Poisoned by Spies," *New York Times*, March 29, 1917; Simkhovitch, *Neighborhood*, 192; *A History of the New Jersey State Federation of Women's Clubs, 1894–1958* (Caldwell, N.J.: Progress, 1958), 54.

46. Scharff, *Taking the Wheel*, 99–100; NLWS, *Annual Report*, 61.

47. "Women Open Fight to Bar German Toys," *New York Times*, October 26, 1918; "Refuse to Accept German-Made Toys," *New York Times*, October 27, 1918; Emerson Hough, *The Web* (Chicago: Reilly and Lee, 1919), 464.

48. E. Marguerite Lindley, "Greetings to Patriotic New England Women," in The National Society of New England Women, *Tidings from Far and Near*, 18.

49. C. E. Clark to Committee on Public Information, September 13, 1917, in Box 10, Papers of Joseph P. Tumulty, LCMD; Mrs. Clarence Rainwater, quoted in Houde, *Reaching Out*, 87.

50. Cott, *Grounding of Modern Feminism*, 1–81; Eleanor Flexner, *Century of Struggle: The Woman's Rights Movement in the United States*, rev. ed. (Cambridge: Harvard University Press, 1975), 235–345; Sara Hunter Graham, *Woman Suffrage and the New Democracy* (New Haven, Conn.: Yale University Press, 1996); Ida Husted Harper, ed., *The History of Woman Suffrage* (New York: National American Woman Suffrage Association, 1922), vol. 5, pp. 513–682, 720–40; Rosalyn Terborg-Penn, *African American Women in the Struggle for the Vote, 1850–1920* (Bloomington: Indiana University Press, 1998), 159–66; Terborg-Penn, "Discontented Black Feminists: Prelude and Postscript to the Passage of the Nineteenth Amendment," in *Decades of Discontent: The Women's Movement, 1920–1940*, ed. Lois Scharf and Joan M. Jensen (Westport, Conn.: Greenwood, 1983), 261–78.

51. Susan B. Anthony, quoted in Doris Stevens, *Jailed for Freedom* (New York: Liveright, 1920), 73. Flexner, *Century of Struggle*, 256–70; Wil A. Linkugel and Martha Solomon, eds., *Anna Howard Shaw: Suffrage Orator and Social Reformer* (New York: Greenwood, 1991); Steinson, *American Women's Activism*.

52. On antisuffrage, see Anne M. Benjamin, *History of the Anti-Suffrage Movement in the United States from 1895 to 1920: Women against Equality* (Lewiston, N.Y.: Edwin Mellen, 1991); Jane Jerome Camhi, *Women against Women: American Anti-Suffragism, 1880–1920* (Brooklyn, N.Y.: Carlson, 1994); Flexner, *Century of Suffrage*, 304–18; Manuela Thurner, " 'Better Citizens without the Ballot': American Antisuffrage Women and Their Rationale during the Progressive Era," *Journal of Women's History* 5 (Spring 1993): 33–60.

53. The League for the Civic Education of Women, *Special Announcement and Preliminary Program, 1912–1913* (n.p., n.d.), in Box 2, Folder 50, Organizations (Small Files), Sophia Smith Collection; Lanham Study Club, Minutes, September 1917, item 1310–03–2, Study Club of Lanham Minute Book, Local Club Records (Record Group 13), GFWC Archives; Sorosis, Minutes, October 15, 1917, pp. 168–71, Sorosis Minute Book, Papers of Sorosis, Sophia Smith Collection.

54. Benjamin, *History of the Anti-Suffrage Movement*, 285–95; Rogow, *Gone to Another Meeting*, 80; May Ellis Nichols, *A History of the Meridian* (Brooklyn, N.Y.: n.p., 1934), 13, 17, 80.

55. "Excerpts from Correspondence with Esther Allen Gaw, relating to Her Mother," undated typescript, in Box 1, Folder 2, Elizabeth J. Hauser, "Florence E. Allen— Lawyer," *The Woman Citizen*, September 6, 1919, and Mildred Adams, "Can Women Make Good Judges?" *Christian Advocate*, December 10, 1925, clippings in Box 1, Folder 3, Papers of Florence Ellinwood Allen, Sophia Smith Collection; Ida Joyce Jackson to Mary Church Terrell, October 3, 1917, Reel 4, Papers of Mary Church Terrell, LCMD; [Ida Husted Harper] to Editor, *Dallas Evening Journal*, June 4, 1917, Reel 3, Papers of Carrie Chapman Catt, LCMD; "Antis Report Rush to Join New League," *New York Times*, November 17, 1917.

56. Blatch and Lutz, *Challenging Years*, 284.

57. Carrie Chapman Catt, quoted in Harper, ed., *History of Woman Suffrage*, vol. 5, p. 721.

58. Jean H. Baker, *Sisters: The Lives of America's Suffragists* (New York: Hill and Wang, 2005), 221; Harper, ed., *History of Woman Suffrage*, vol. 5, pp. 723 (quote), 730, 732; Ronald Schaffer, *America in the Great War: The Rise of the War Welfare State* (New York: Oxford University Press, 1991), 92; Jacqueline Van Voris, *Carrie Chapman Catt: A Public Life* (New York: Feminist Press, 1987), 117–65.

59. "Suffragists Aid Drive for Recruits," *New York Times*, April 14, 1917; "'Antis' Pledge Aid to Loan," *New York Times*, October 5, 1917; "Antis Will Open Fight on Pacifism," *New York Times*, November 16, 1917; *The Woman Patriot*, quoted in Benjamin, *History of the Anti-Suffrage Movement*, 217; Mrs. A. J. George, quoted in ibid., 219; Carrie Chapman Catt, quoted in Harper, ed., *History of Woman Suffrage*, vol. 5, p. 736. Catt and her allies gave as good as they got, frequently pointing out the antisuffragists' ties to the German-dominated brewing industry, which opposed suffrage because of women's leadership in the prohibition movement. The war and its masculinization of politics also gave new political arguments to antisuffragist men, who argued that women were incapable of handling the manly burdens of political life. For an example, see Schaffer, *America in the Great War*, 91.

60. "Declares Pacifists Helped Women to Win," *New York Times*, November 8, 1917; "Antis Will Open Fight on Pacifism," *New York Times*, November 16, 1917; "Antis Start Fight to Lose the Vote," *New York Times*, January 29, 1918; "Anti-German Anti-Suffragists," *New York Times*, November 17, 1917. For more on conservative women during and after the war, see Kathleen Kennedy, *Disloyal Mothers and Scurrilous Citizens: Women and Subversion during World War I* (Bloomington: Indiana University Press, 1999); Morgan, *Women and Patriotism*, 101–26; Kim E. Nielsen, *Un-American Womanhood: Antiradicalism, Antifeminism, and the First Red Scare* (Columbus: Ohio State University Press, 2001), 1–10.

61. Stevens, *Jailed for Freedom*, 72; Carrie Chapman Catt, quoted in Schaffer, *America in the Great War*, 91–92; Louise Michele Newman, *White Women's Rights: The Racial Origins of Feminism in the United States* (New York: Oxford University Press, 1999), 56–85.

62. Harold Marshall to Mary Church Terrell, March 1, 1917; draft copy of Mary Church Terrell to *Baltimore American*, June 22, 1917, both in Reel 4, Papers of Mary Church Terrell, LCMD; Beverly Washington Jones, *Quest for Equality: The Life and Writings of Mary Eliza Church Terrell, 1863–1954* (Brooklyn, N.Y.: Carlson, 1990). The NACW was not invited to participate in NAWSA's 1920 Victory Celebration. Jenkins, "History of the Black Woman's Club Movement," 115. Alice Paul and the NWP were just as outspokenly racist as any other white women's suffrage group. Giddings, *When and Where I Enter*, 159–70.

63. Woodrow Wilson, quoted in Baker, *Sisters*, 204, 205. A feisty—and, to my mind, not yet concluded—debate specifically over Wilson's decision for suffrage can be found in Christine A. Lunardini and Thomas J. Knock, "Woodrow Wilson and Woman Suffrage: A New Look," *Political Science Quarterly* 95 (Winter 1980–81): 655–71, and Sally Hunter Graham, "Woodrow Wilson, Alice Paul, and the Woman Suffrage Movement," *Political Science Quarterly* 98 (Winter 1983–84): 665–79.

64. Alice Paul, quoted in Baker, *Sisters*, 212. On the inauguration, see Lucy G. Barber, *Marching on Washington: The Forging of an American Political Tradition* (Berkeley: University of California Press, 2002), 44–74; Baker, *Sisters*, 183–185; Edward Keating, *The Gentleman from Colorado: A Memoir* (Denver: Sage, 1964), 288–89. For more on Paul and the radical suffragists, see Baker, *Sisters*, 183–230; Christine A. Lunardini, *From Equal Suffrage to Equal Rights: Alice Paul and the National Woman's Party, 1910–1928* (New York: New York University Press, 1986); Stevens, *Jailed for Freedom*.

65. NWP official, quoted in Graham, "Wilson and Woman Suffrage," 667; Stevens, *Jailed for Freedom*, 123; Blatch and Lutz, *Challenging Years*, 278.

66. "Suffrage and Sedition," *Masses* 9 (August 1917): 42; Senator quoted in Schaffer, *America in the Great War*, 93; Alice Paul, quoted in Graham, "Woodrow Wilson, Alice Paul," 668; "Advice to a Suffragist," *New York Times*, September 16, 1917; Baker, *Sisters*, 218; Susan Ware, *Modern American Women: A Documentary History* (Chicago: Dorsey, 1989), 150–56.

67. Alice Paul, quoted in Robert S. Gallagher, "'I Was Arrested, of Course…,'" *American Heritage* 25 (February 1974): 20; Baker, *Sisters*, 214; Blatch and Lutz, *Challenging Years*, 279; Dudley Field Malone, *Unaccustomed as I Am: Miscellaneous Speeches* (New York: J. J. Little and Ives, 1929), 72.

68. Stevens, *Jailed for Freedom*, 65, 67, 76–77, 139.

69. "Crowd Destroys Suffrage Banner," *New York Times*, June 21, 1917; Stevens, *Jailed for Freedom*, 123–26.

70. "Crowd Destroys Suffrage Banner," *New York Times*, June 21, 1917; Graham, "Woodrow Wilson, Alice Paul," 668.

71. "Pickets Turn Lawyers," *New York Times*, July 6, 1917; Graham, "Woodrow Wilson, Alice Paul," 676; Malone, *Unaccustomed*, 69.

72. Baker, *Sisters*, 216; Graham, "Woodrow Wilson, Alice, Paul," 670; Stevens, *Jailed for Freedom*, 122.

73. "Hunger Striker Forcibly Fed," *New York Times*, November 9, 1917. Later, in *Hunter v. D.C.*, 47 App. D.C. 406 (1918), the NWP won a victory over the use of traffic regulations to regulate speech.

74. Malone, "Letter to President Wilson Resigning as Collector of the Port of New York," in *Unaccustomed*, 53; "Malone Resigns as Collector to Aid Suffrage," *New York Times*, September 8, 1917; "Occoquan Probe Plan," *Washington Post*, September 29, 1917.

75. "Decry the Militants," *New York Times*, August 13, 1918; Stevens, *Jailed for Freedom*, 71.

76. Michael Francis Doyle, quoted in Graham, "Woodrow Wilson, Alice Paul," 676; "Crowd Destroys Suffrage Banner," *New York Times*, June 21, 1917; "Seize Suffragists near White House," *New York Times*, August 13, 1918; Blatch and Lutz, *Challenging Years*, 281.

77. Woodrow Wilson, "An Address to the Senate," September 30, 1918, in Arthur S. Link et al., eds., *The Papers of Woodrow Wilson*, 69 vols. (Princeton, N.J.: Princeton University Press, 1966–94), vol. 51, p. 158. Graham, "Woodrow Wilson, Alice Paul," 677–78, makes the strongest case for the significance of Lawrence's visit, supported by Stevens, *Jailed for Freedom*, 226, and "Antis Make Apology," *New York*

Times, January 27, 1918. In Gallagher, "I Was Arrested," 92, Alice Paul gives a cagily evasive account of the night's events; David Lawrence, *The True Story of Woodrow Wilson* (New York: George H. Doran, 1924), is silent on the matter.

78. "Charge of Sedition Stirs Club Women," *New York Times*, February 2, 1918.
79. Ibid.
80. Ibid.

Chapter 4

1. Quoted in Carl Weinberg, "The Tug of War: Labor, Loyalty, and Rebellion in the Southwestern Illinois Coalfields, 1914–1920" (Ph.D. dissertation, Yale University, 1995), 484. The richest account of the Prager killing can be found in Carl R. Weinberg, *Labor, Loyalty, and Rebellion: Southwestern Illinois Coalminers and World War I* (Carbondale: Southern Illinois University Press, 2005), esp. 112–53; see also "German Is Lynched by Illinois Mob," *New York Times*, April 5, 1918; Donald R. Hickey, "The Prager Affair: A Study in Wartime Hysteria," *Journal of the Illinois State Historical Society* 62 (Summer 1969): 117–34; Frederick C. Luebke, *Bonds of Loyalty: German-Americans and World War I* (DeKalb: Northern Illinois University Press, 1974), 3–26; and E. A. Schwartz, "The Lynching of Robert Prager, the United Mine Workers, and the Problems of Patriotism in 1918," *Journal of the Illinois State Historical Society* 96 (Winter 2003): 414–37. One official German response can be found in "Germany Protests Prager Lynching," *New York Times*, June 13, 1918.

2. Weinberg, *Labor, Loyalty, and Rebellion*, 127. Richard Hofstadter memorably argued that the United States "has a history but not a tradition of domestic violence." Hofstadter, "Reflections on Violence in the United States," in *American Violence: A Documentary History*, comp. Richard Hofstadter and Michael Wallace (New York: Knopf, 1970), 3. See also Richard Maxwell Brown, *No Duty to Retreat: Violence and Values in American History and Society* (New York: Oxford University Press, 1991); Brown, "Western Violence: Structure, Values, Myth," *Western Historical Quarterly* 24 (February 1993): 5–20; Gary Gerstle, "Liberty, Coercion, and the Making of Americans," *Journal of American History* 84 (September 1997): 524–58; "What We See and Can't See in the Past: A Round Table," *Journal of American History* 83 (March 1997): 1217–72.

3. Woodrow Wilson, "A Statement to the American People," July 26, 1918, in Arthur S. Link et al., eds., *The Papers of Woodrow Wilson*, 69 vols. (Princeton, N.J.: Princeton University Press, 1966–94), vol. 49, pp. 97, 98 [hereafter PWW with volume number].

4. Quotes from "Thanks Wilson for Words," *Washington Post*, July 29, 1918; "Mr. Wilson on the Mob Spirit," *New York Times*, July 27, 1918; John Lord O'Brian to Thomas Gregory, April 18, 1918, in PWW, vol. 47, p. 364. Press accounts include "Wilson on Mob Law," *Atlanta Constitution*, July 27, 1918; "Indorsement by Negroes," *Christian Science Monitor*, July 27, 1918; George Creel, "Unite and Win," *Independent* 94 (April 6, 1918): 5–6. Most historians agree that Wilson's statement offered too little, too late. See Henry Blumenthal, "Woodrow Wilson and the Race Question," *Journal of Negro History* 48 (January 1963): 4, 10–12; Robert L. Allen, with the collaboration of Pamela P. Allen, *Reluctant Reformers: Racism and Social Reform Movements in the United States* (Washington, D.C.: Howard University

Press, 1974), 98. When James Weldon Johnson and a delegation from the NAACP asked Wilson to make a public statement denouncing racial violence, he "demurred, saying that he did not think any word from him would have special effect." James Weldon Johnson, *Along This Way: The Autobiography of James Weldon Johnson* (New York: Viking, 1933), 324. In private correspondence, Wilson was at times more forthright. See Woodrow Wilson to Otto C. Butz, April 12, 1918, Woodrow Wilson Papers, Chicago Historical Society, Chicago.

5. Richard Maxwell Brown, "The History of Vigilantism in America," in *Vigilante Politics*, ed. H. Jon Rosenbaum and Peter C. Sederberg (Philadelphia: University of Pennsylvania Press, 1976), 103–104; Christian Fritz, "Popular Sovereignty, Vigilantism, and the Constitutional Right of Revolution," *Pacific Historical Review* 63 (February 1994): 39–66; David A. Johnson, "Vigilance and the Law: The Moral Authority of Popular Justice in the Far West," *American Quarterly* 33 (Winter 1981): 558–86; Pauline Maier, "Popular Uprisings and Civil Authority in Eighteenth-Century America," *William and Mary Quarterly*, 3rd ser. 27 (January 1970): 3–35; Gordon S. Wood, *The Creation of the American Republic, 1776–1787* (New York: Norton, 1967), 319–28.

6. Figures from Brown, "History of Vigilantism," 80–81. For definitions, see Ray Abrahams, *Vigilant Citizens: Vigilantism and the State* (Cambridge, U.K.: Polity, 1998), 4–10; Richard Maxwell Brown, *Strain of Violence: Historical Studies of American Violence and Vigilantism* (New York: Oxford University Press, 1975), 95–96; and H. Jon Rosenbaum and Peter C. Sederberg, "Vigilantism: An Analysis of Establishment Violence," in *Vigilante Politics*, ed. Rosenbaum and Sederberg, 3–29. *The Oxford English Dictionary*, 2nd ed. (Oxford: Clarendon, 1989), vol. 19, p. 624, defines a vigilance committee as "a self-appointed committee for the maintenance of justice and order in an imperfectly ordered community," highlighting the role of voluntarism, the organized nature of its undertaking, and its relationship to institutions of law. Brown, "History of Vigilantism," 85 n. 19, notes that the term "vigilante" entered American discourse after the Virginia City movement in the Montana Territory in 1863–65.

7. T. W. Gregory, *Reconstruction and the Ku Klux Klan: A Paper Read before the Arkansas and Texas Bar Associations, July 10, 1906* (Austin, Tex.: n.p., [1906]); Theodore Roosevelt, quoted in Brown, "History of Vigilantism," 105. Martin Alan Greenberg, *Citizens Defending America: From Colonial Times to the Age of Terrorism* (Pittsburgh, Pa.: University of Pittsburgh Press, 2005), esp. 73–108; Sidney L. Harring, *Policing a Class Society: The Experience of American Cities, 1865–1915* (New Brunswick, N.J.: Rutgers University Press, 1983); Eric H. Monkkonen, *The Police in Urban America, 1860–1920* (New York: Cambridge University Press, 1981). Another future U.S. Attorney General, Charles J. Bonaparte, argued in 1890 that the point of vigilantism "is not to violate, but to vindicate, the law." Bonaparte, quoted in David M. Kennedy, *Over Here: The First World War and American Society* (New York: Oxford University Press, 1980), 79.

8. On private policing, see Rhodri Jeffreys-Jones, *Violence and Reform in American History* (New York: New Viewpoints, 1978), 6. Even the Department of Justice relied on Pinkertons as its investigators prior to 1893; see Joan M. Jensen, *The*

Price of igilance (Chicago: Rand-McNally, 1968), 12; Frank Morn, *"The Eye That Never Sleeps": A History of the Pinkerton National Detective Agency* (Bloomington: Indiana University Press, 1982), esp. 164–91. On citizen voluntarism in the maintenance of industrial order, see Melvyn Dubofsky, *We Shall Be All: A History of the Industrial Workers of the World*, 2nd ed. (Urbana: University of Illinois Press, 1988), 376–97; Eugene E. Leach, "The Literature of Riot Duty: Managing Class Conflict in the Streets, 1877–1927," *Radical History Review* no. 56 (Spring 1993): 23–50; and Steven C. Levi, *Committee of Vigilance: The San Francisco Chamber of Commerce Law and Order Committee, 1916–1919: A Case Study in Official Hysteria* (Jefferson, N.C.: McFarland, 1983). The cooperation of the federal government in the suppression of strikes is outlined in Jerry M. Cooper, *The Army and Civil Disorder: Federal Military Intervention in Labor Disputes, 1877–1900* (Westport, Conn.: Greenwood, 1980).

9. Maude E. Miner, *Slavery of Prostitution: A Plea for Emancipation* (New York: Macmillan, 1916), 288, 290. Ruth Rosen suggests that antivice activity reached its peak in the 1910s in *The Lost Sisterhood: Prostitution in America, 1900–1918* (Baltimore: Johns Hopkins University Press, 1982), 12–15. See also Timothy J. Gilfoyle, *City of Eros: New York City, Prostitution, and the Commercialization of Sex, 1790–1920* (New York: Norton, 1992), 185–96; Miner, *Slavery of Prostitution*, esp. 125–61, 223–49. For campaigns against prostitution, see Mark Thomas Connelly, *The Response to Prostitution in the Progressive Era* (Chapel Hill: University of North Carolina Press, 1980), and David J. Langum, *Crossing over the Line: Legislating Morality and the Mann Act* (Chicago: University of Chicago Press, 1994). Battles against legal regulation of morality galvanized late nineteenth-century movements for civil liberties; see Helen Lefkowitz Horowitz, *Rereading Sex: Battles over Sexual Knowledge and Suppression in Nineteenth-Century America* (New York: Knopf, 2002). Sarah Mercer Judson, "'Leisure Is a Foe to Any Man': The Pleasures and Dangers of Leisure in Atlanta during World War I," *Journal of Women's History* 15 (Spring 2003): 92–115, examines the experiences of some of the working-class women who ended up in the wartime net. Estelle B. Freedman, *Their Sisters' Keepers: Women's Prison Reform in America, 1830–1930* (Ann Arbor: University of Michigan Press, 1981), and Michael Willrich, *City of Courts: Socializing Justice in Progressive Era Chicago* (New York: Cambridge University Press, 2003) explore progressives' involvement in moral vigilance and social reform.

10. W. Fitzhugh Brundage, *Lynching in the New South: Georgia and Virginia, 1880–1930* (Urbana: University of Illinois Press, 1993); Brundage, ed., *Under Sentence of Death: Lynching in the South* (Chapel Hill: University of North Carolina Press, 1997); William D. Carrigan, *The Making of a Lynching Culture: Violence and Vigilantism in Central Texas, 1836–1916* (Urbana: University of Illinois Press, 2004); J. William Harris, "Etiquette, Lynching, and Racial Boundaries in Southern History: A Mississippi Example," *American Historical Review* 100 (April 1995): 387–410; Robert P. Ingalls, *Urban Vigilantes in the New South: Tampa, 1882–1936* (Knoxville: University of Tennessee Press, 1988); Leon F. Litwack, *Trouble in Mind: Black Southerners in the Age of Jim Crow* (New York: Knopf, 1998); Michael J. Pfeifer, *Rough Justice: Lynching and American Society, 1874–1947* (Urbana: University of Illinois Press, 2004); and the

extremely valuable Christopher Waldrep, *The Many Faces of Judge Lynch: Extralegal Violence and Punishment in America* (New York: Palgrave Macmillan, 2004).

11. Conference Committee on National Preparedness, "The Advance Agents of the Hun," undated broadside [1917], portfolio 315, no. 2, and New Hampshire Committee of Public Safety, "People of New Hampshire, Wake Up! We Are at War!" undated broadside [1917], portfolio 98, no. 3, both in Broadside Collection, Rare Book Division, Library of Congress, Washington, D.C.; Wilson, "A Flag Day Address," June 14, 1917, in PWW, vol. 42, pp. 499, 504.

12. "Citizens May Arrest Disloyal Persons," *Albany Journal*, April 17, 1918, clipping enclosed with Dudley Paul Babcock to American Union against Militarism, April 17, 1918, reel 5, volume 35, American Civil Liberties Union Archives, microfilm ed. (Wilmington, Del.: Scholarly Resources, 1996) [hereafter ACLU Archives]. The Albany editorialist's claim is somewhat oversimplified, in that a citizen's arrest could be made only if a felony had been committed. Espionage Act violations were felonies; breaches of peace or outrages of public decency were misdemeanors. Few vigilant Americans bothered with such procedural distinctions, however, and even civil libertarians such as Roger Baldwin did not apparently understand or insist on them until very late in the war.

13. Philadelphia War History Committee, *Philadelphia in the World War, 1914–1919* (New York: Wynkoop Hallenbeck Crawford, 1922), 55–56; Rockwell D. Hunt, *California and Californians* (Chicago: Lewis, 1926), vol. 2, p. 516; H. C. Peterson and Gilbert C. Fite, *Opponents of War, 1917–1918* (Seattle: University of Washington Press, 1968 [1957]), 18.

14. Rollin G. Osterweis, *Three Centuries of New Haven, 1638–1938* (New Haven, Conn.: Yale University Press, 1953), 404. Portland *Telegram*, quoted in Clark T. Irwin Jr., "From a Gilded Age onto a World War," in *Greater Portland Celebration 350*, comp. and ed. Albert F. Barnes (Portland, Me.: Gannett, 1984), 124.

15. Edward F. Alexander to Roger N. Baldwin, September 16, 1918, reel 12, volume 72, ACLU Archives; *A History of the New Jersey State Federation of Women's Clubs, 1894–1958* (Caldwell, N.J.: Progress, 1958), 54; Kimberly S. Jensen, "Minerva on the Field of Mars: American Women, Citizenship, and Military Service in the First World War" (Ph.D. dissertation, University of Iowa, 1992), chap. 1.

16. "An Act concerning the Home Guard," reprinted in Connecticut Home Guard, *Regulations for the Connecticut Home Guard* (Hartford: Connecticut Military Emergency Board, 1917), 1; Connecticut Military Emergency Board, *Report to the Governor: November 1, 1918* (Hartford: Connecticut Military Emergency Board, 1918), 1. On Home Guards nationally, see Barry M. Stentiford, *The American Home Guard: The State Militia in the Twentieth Century* (College Station: Texas A&M University Press, 2002), 21–51. For more on the makeup of the Connecticut Home Guard, see Bruce Fraser, "Yankees at War: Social Mobilization on the Connecticut Homefront, 1917–1918" (Ph.D. dissertation, Columbia University, 1976), 97–99, 351–60; Connecticut Home Guard, *Register of Officers* ([Hartford]: Military Emergency Board, 1917). Two cities, Hartford and New Haven, had reserve units in which all the officers had Italian surnames. See Christopher M. Sterba, *Good Americans: Italian and Jewish Immigrants during the First World War* (New York: Oxford University Press, 2003), 47.

17. Charles W. Burpee, *Burpee's The Story of Connecticut* (New York: American Historical, 1939), 958; "An Act concerning the Militia," reprinted in Connecticut Home Guard, *Regulations*, 3. For other local activities, see Roy Eddins, ed., *History of Falls County, Texas* (n.p.: Old Settlers and Veterans Association of Falls County, Texas, 1947), 212–13; Irwin, "WWI Galvanizes Region's Activities," 136; Hugh T. Lovin, "World War I Vigilantes in Idaho, 1917–1918," *Idaho Yesterdays* 18 (Summer 1974): 2–11; Maryland War Records Commission, *Maryland in the World War, 1917–1919: Military and Naval Service Records* (Baltimore: Maryland War Records Commission, 1933), 99–101; and Mrs. Ralph E. Randel, ed., *A Time to Purpose: A Chronicle of Carson County* (n.p.: Pioneer, 1966), vol. 1, p. 280, vol. 4, p. 293. The Texas Rangers, perhaps the best known vigilance organization in American history, spent most of World War I along the Mexican border, where another debate about lawlessness and vigilantism played out. See Richard Henry Ribb, "José Tomas Canales and the Texas Rangers: Myth, Identity, and Power in South Texas, 1900–1920" (Ph.D. dissertation, University of Texas, 2002); Charles M. Robinson III, *The Men Who Wear the Star: The Story of the Texas Rangers* (New York: Random House, 2000), 269–79.

18. "Connecticut's Military Census," *Review of Reviews* 55 (May 1917): 534; Marcus H. Holcomb, "Connecticut in the Van," *Review of Reviews* 57 (May 1918): 520; Connecticut Military Emergency Board, *Report*, 3–4. The report notes that the tip came from the U.S. Secret Service, but it probably came from the volunteer operatives of the American Protective League instead.

19. Charles Burpee, quoted in Fraser, "Yankees at War," 307; Burpee, "Connecticut in the Wars," in *History of Connecticut in Monographic Form*, ed. Norris Galpin Osborn (New York: States History, 1925), vol. 5, p. 127; "Socialist Meeting Packed by Patriots," *New York Tribune*, April 8, 1918, and "Home Guards Break Up Socialist Rally," *New York Call*, April 8, 1918, clippings in reel 8, vol. 70, ACLU Archives; "Home Guard Invades Socialist Meeting," *Christian Science Monitor*, April 8, 1918; "Seize Socialists' Hall," *Washington Post*, April 8, 1918.

20. Fraser, "Yankees at War," 107; Burpee, "Connecticut in the Wars," 127.

21. William B. Wilson, quoted in Samuel Morse, "The Truth about Bisbee: An Account Compiled from Legal Evidence and Other Authenticated Documents of the I.W.W. Deportation on July 12, 1917, from Bisbee, Arizona, and Its Aftermath," typescript, Special Collections, University of Arizona Library, Tucson; Carlos A. Schwantes, "Toil and Trouble: Rhythms of Work Life," in *Bisbee: Urban Outpost on the Frontier,* ed. Carlos A. Schwantes (Tucson: University of Arizona Press, 1992), 121. Dubofsky, *We Shall Be All*, 370, suggests that even the IUMMSW was IWW-dominated by the summer of 1917. Bisbee was an ethnically diverse mix of northern, southern, and eastern European immigrant workers, as well as African Americans, Mexicans, and some Chinese, who were excluded from the town of Bisbee itself. See Katherine Benton-Cohen, "Docile Children and Dangerous Revolutionaries: The Racial Hierarchy of Manliness and the Bisbee Deportation of 1917," *Frontiers: A Journal of Women Studies* 24, nos. 2–3 (2003): 30–50; Charles S. Sargent, "Copper Star of the Arizona Urban Firmament," in Schwantes, *Bisbee*, 35–36; and Tom Vaughan, "Everyday Life in a Copper Camp," in Schwantes, *Bisbee*, 59–61.

22. Harry Wheeler, quoted in Morse, "Truth about Bisbee," 14, 16, 24; Bill O'Neal, "Captain Harry Wheeler, Arizona Lawman," *Journal of Arizona History* 27 (Autumn 1986): 308.

23. Walter Douglas, quoted in John H. Lindquist and James Fraser, "A Sociological Interpretation of the Bisbee Deportation," *Pacific Historical Review* 37 (November 1968): 417; "Arizona Sheriff Ships 1,000 I.W.W.'s Out in Cattle Cars," *New York Times*, July 13, 1917. The Citizens' Protective League had hoped to deliver the deportees to the U.S. Army camp in Columbus, New Mexico, but angry civilians in the town refused the shipment. The most extensive source on the Bisbee deportations is James W. Byrkit, *Forging the Copper Collar: Arizona's Labor-Management War of 1901–1921* (Tucson: University of Arizona Press, 1982), although Katherine A. Benton, "What about Women in the White Man's Camp? Gender, Nation, and the Redefinition of Race in Cochise County, Arizona, 1853–1941" (Ph.D. dissertation, University of Wisconsin, 2002), 397–496, usefully reframes the deportation around issues of gender, race, and national identity. See also Vernon H. Jensen, *Heritage of Conflict: Labor Relations in the Nonferrous Metals Industry up to 1930* (Ithaca, N.Y.: Cornell University Press, 1950), 381–410; Lindquist and Fraser, "Sociological Interpretation," 401–22; Philip J. Mellinger, *Race and Labor in Western Copper: The Fight for Equality, 1896–1918* (Tucson: University of Arizona Press, 1995), 174–203; and Colleen O'Neill, "Domesticity Deployed: Gender, Race, and the Construction of Class Struggle in the Bisbee Deportation," *Labor History* 34 (Spring-Summer 1993): 256–73. Accounts sympathetic to Wheeler and the deportation include Pamela Mayhall, "Bisbee's Response to Civil Disorder," *American West* 9 (May 1972): 22–31; and O'Neal, "Captain Harry Wheeler," 297–314. On the privately hired detectives, see Robert W. Bruere, "Copper Camp Patriotism," *Nation* 106 (February 21, 1918): 202.

24. Bruere, "Copper Camp Patriotism," 203, 235; Lindquist and Fraser, "Sociological Interpretation," 405–407. Passes could also be issued by the chief of police or the chamber of commerce in El Paso or Tucson. Although the league's decisions were final, further historical research by Katherine Benton-Cohen will shed light on how many people were interviewed, the results of their deliberation, and the extent of compliance with those decisions.

25. Harry Wheeler, quoted in Morse, "Truth about Bisbee," 21, 29; telegram from Thomas E. Campbell to Woodrow Wilson, July 12, 1917, in PWW, vol. 43, p. 157; Wheeler, quoted in Dubofsky, *We Shall Be All*, 386; *Los Angeles Times*, July 15, 1917; Theodore Roosevelt, quoted in Peterson and Fite, *Opponents of War*, 55–56.

26. J. Sheik, "Autocracy in Arizona," *Public* 21 (February 16, 1918): 216–17; Samuel Gompers to Woodrow Wilson, July 20, 1917, in PWW, vol. 43, p. 231. Some writers used the events of the Bisbee deportations to attack other government policies, as when Georgia editor Tom Watson wrote that "the Conscription Act … is every bit as lawless as the action of the Phelps-Dodge Copper Company." Watson, quoted in Peterson and Fite, *Opponents of War*, 99.

27. Bruere, "Copper Camp Patriotism," 202, 235; "Diversions of the I.W.W.," *New York Times*, July 14, 1917.

28. William Wilson to Newton Baker, June 22, 1917, in PWW, vol. 42, p. 563; telegram from Woodrow Wilson to Thomas Campbell, July 12, 1917, in PWW, vol. 43, p. 158.

29. Clifford C. Faires, "I.W.W. Patriotism in Globe," *Nation* 106 (March 21, 1918): 320.

30. Bruere, "Copper Camp Patriotism," 202; United States Department of Labor, *Report on the Bisbee Deportations Made by the President's Mediation Commission to the President of the United States* (Washington, D.C.: Government Printing Office, 1918). For more on the PMC, see Jensen, *Heritage of Conflict*, 411–29, and Joseph A. McCartin, *Labor's Great War: The Struggle for Industrial Democracy and the Origins of Modern American Labor Relations, 1912–1921* (Chapel Hill: University of North Carolina Press, 1997), 77–80.

31. Thomas Campbell, quoted in Morse, "Truth about Bisbee," 33; Theodore Roosevelt, quoted in Helen Shirley Thomas, *Felix Frankfurter: Scholar on the Bench* (Baltimore: Johns Hopkins Press, 1960), 16–17; Joseph P. Lash, *From the Diaries of Felix Frankfurter: With a Biographical Essay and Notes* (New York: Norton, 1975), 24.

32. Harry Wheeler, quoted in Lindquist and Fraser, "Sociological Interpretation," 408; George Soule, "Law and Necessity in Bisbee," *Nation* 113 (August 31, 1921): 225–27; *United States v. Wheeler*, 254 U.S. 281 (1920).

33. Newton Baker, quoted in George J. Anderson, "Making the Camps Safe for the Army," *Annals of the American Academy of Political and Social Science* 79 (September 1918): 143; Baker, quoted in Penn Borden, *Civilian Indoctrination of the Military: World War I and Future Implications for the Military-Industrial Complex* (Westport, Conn.: Greenwood, 1989), 105; Baker, quoted in Raymond B. Fosdick, *Chronicle of a Generation: An Autobiography* (New York: Harper and Bros., 1958), 145.

34. D. J. Poynter to Newton Baker, August 6, 1917, quoted in Nancy K. Bristow, *Making Men Moral: Social Engineering during the Great War* (New York: New York University Press, 1996), 135.

35. Anderson, "Making the Camps Safe," 144; Mary Macey Dietzler, *Detention Houses and Reformatories as Protective Social Agencies in the Campaign of the United States Government Against Venereal Diseases* (Washington, D.C.: Government Printing Office, 1922), 15; Fosdick, *Chronicle*, 145; David J. Pivar, "Cleansing the Nation: The War on Prostitution, 1917–1921," *Prologue* 12 (Spring 1980): 30.

36. Martha P. Falconer, "The Segregation of Delinquent Women and Girls as a War Problem," *Annals of the American Academy of Political and Social Science* 79 (September 1918): 165. See also Henrietta S. Additon, "Work among Delinquent Women and Girls," *Annals of the American Academy of Political and Social Science* 79 (September 1918): 152–60; "Plan to Safeguard Girls in Wartime," *Chicago Tribune*, November 17, 1917; "Women in Wartime," *Chicago Tribune*, December 22, 1917; "Protective Work for Girls Takes Systematic Form," *Atlanta Constitution*, January 20, 1918. For more on the government's wartime attack on prostitution, see Donnelly, *Response to Prostitution*, 136–50; Fosdick, *Chronicle*, 142–52; Pivar, "Cleansing the Nation," 29–40.

37. Gloria E. Myers, *A Municipal Mother: Portland's Lola Greene Baldwin, America's First Policewoman* (Corvallis: Oregon State University Press, 1995), 128; Additon, "Work among Delinquent Women and Girls," 155–56; Anderson, "Making the Camps Safe," 145.

38. Maude Miner, "Probation Work," Lectures under the Auspices of the War Work Council of the YWCA, 52, 63–64, Box 28a, YWCA of the USA National Board

Records, Sophia Smith Collection, Smith College, Northampton, Mass. The General Federation of Women's Clubs and the National Association of Colored Women were active nationwide in antivice activities. See California Federation of Women's Clubs, *Diamond Jubilee History Highlights* (n.p.: California Federation of Women's Clubs, 1975), 16; Sallie Southall Cotten, *History of the North Carolina Federation of Women's Clubs, 1901–1925* (Raleigh: Edwards and Broughton, 1925), 110; Mary Jean Houde, *The Clubwoman: A Story of the Illinois Federation of Women's Clubs* (Chicago: Illinois Federation of Women's Clubs, 1970), 92; Martha Lavinia Hunter, *A Quarter of a Century History of the Dallas Woman's Forum, 1906–1931* (Dallas, Tex.: Clyde C. Cockrell, 1932), 67; Maude T. Jenkins, "The History of the Black Woman's Club Movement in America" (Ph.D. dissertation, Teachers College, Columbia University, 1984), 81, 97; Members of the Past Presidents Association of the Dallas Federation of Women's Clubs, eds., *History of the Dallas Federation of Women's Clubs, 1898–1936* (Dallas, Tex.: Clyde C. Cockrell and Son, 1936), 81; Maude G. Palmer, comp., *The History of the Illinois Federation of Women's Clubs, 1894–1928* (n.p.: Illinois Federation of Women's Clubs, 1928), 91; Rosen, *The Lost Sisterhood*, 52, 116; Judith Weisenfeld, *African American Women and Christian Activism: New York's Black YWCA, 1905–1945* (Cambridge: Harvard University Press, 1997), 134; Carrie Niles Whitcomb, *Reminiscences of the Springfield Women's Club, 1884–1924* (n.p.: n.d. [1924]), 137.

39. Fosdick, *Chronicle*, 147; Barbara Meil Hobson, *Uneasy Virtue: The Politics of Prostitution and the American Reform Tradition* (Chicago: University of Chicago Press, 1990), 177; Captain Paul Popenoe, quoted in Bristow, *Making Men Moral*, 130.

40. Bristow, *Making Men Moral*, 118–19, 124; Dietzler, *Detention Houses*, 64; Freedman, *Their Sisters' Keepers*, 147; Hobson, *Uneasy Virtue*, 176; Pivar, "Cleansing the Nation," 34; "Houses of Detention Planned for All Camps," *Atlanta Constitution*, April 2, 1918. Myers, *Municipal Mother*, 130, 134, details the harsh punishments at some of the detention facilities. Falconer, "Segregation of Women and Girls," 160, went so far as to suggest a national internment camp system for the women who were "a menace to the men in training." Women were the only targets of the wartime raids on prostitution; in the context of war mobilization, authorities ignored the calls of some reformers to crack down on their male solicitors.

41. Hobson, *Uneasy Virtue*, 168–71; Pivar, "Cleansing the Nation," 34.

42. John O. Cobb, quoted in "Army Now Takes Hand in Inquiry into City's Vice," *Chicago Tribune*, September 22, 1918; Anderson, "Making the Camps Safe," 150; Dietzler, *Detention Houses*, 3–4, 47, 56; Jessie D. Hodder, "The Next Step in the Treatment of Girl and Women Offenders," *Mental Hygiene* 2 (July 1918): 443–47; Rosen, *Lost Sisterhood*, 22–23; figures from Allan M. Brandt, *No Magic Bullet: A Social History of Venereal Disease in the United States since 1880*, expanded ed. (New York: Oxford University Press, 1987), 234 n. 118. Hobson, *Uneasy Virtue*, 176–77, suggests that no more than one third of interned women were actually commercial prostitutes. Falconer, "Segregation of Delinquent Women and Girls," 161, notes that psychological testing procedures were borrowed from the U.S. Army; on the problematic nature of these tests, see Daniel J. Kevles, "Testing the Army's Intelligence: Psychologists and the Military in World War I," *Journal of American History* 55 (December 1968):

565–81. Additon, "Work among Delinquent Women and Girls," 156, reports that in one study a whopping forty-two of eighty-eight women examined were found to be feebleminded. John D'Emilio and Estelle B. Freedman, *Intimate Matters: A History of Sexuality in America* (New York: Harper and Row, 1988), 215; Hobson, *Uneasy Virtue*, 191–92. On clubwomen's advocacy of sterilization laws, see Vernetta Murchison Hogsett, *The Golden Years: A History of the Idaho Federation of Women's Clubs, 1905–1955* (Caldwell, Idaho: Caxton, 1955), 82.

43. "Hotel Roof for Women's Rifle Club," *New York Times*, April 8, 1917; The National Society of New England Women, *Tidings from Far and Near* (Chicago: Dunwell and Ford, March 1918), 14, in Box 23, Folder 3, National Society of New England Women Records, Sophia Smith Collection; "Bayonne Women Hit Target," *New York Times*, April 15, 1917.

44. Osterweis, *Three Centuries of New Haven*, 405; Caroline Ruutz-Rees, "The Mobilization of American Women," *Yale Review* 7 (July 1918): 810; James C. Juhnke, "Mob Violence and Kansas Mennonites in 1918," *Kansas Historical Quarterly* 60 (Autumn 1977): 348; Schwantes, "Toil and Trouble," 127; Lindquist and Fraser, "Sociological Interpretation," 408 n. 43; National Society of New England Women, *Tidings from Far and Near*, 26; Ann Barton, *Mother Bloor* (New York: Workers Library, 1935), 16–17.

45. Quote from Stephen H. Norwood, "Bogalusa Burning: The War against Biracial Unionism in the Deep South, 1919," *Journal of Southern History* 63 (August 1997): 609; Philadelphia War History Committee, *Philadelphia in the War*, 58; Vincent P. Franklin, "The Philadelphia Race Riot of 1918," *Pennsylvania Magazine of History and Biography* 99 (July 1975): 336–50.

46. Statistics from John Hope Franklin and Alfred A. Moss Jr., *From Slavery to Freedom: A History of African Americans*, 8th ed. (Boston: McGraw-Hill, 2000), 385. See also William M. Tuttle, *Race Riot: Chicago in the Red Summer of 1919* (New York: Atheneum, 1970); James C. Olson and Ronald C. Naugle, *History of Nebraska*, 3rd ed. (Lincoln: University of Nebraska Press, 1997), 289–92.

47. *Tenth Annual Report of the NAACP for the Year 1919* (1920), in *Civil Rights and the American Negro: A Documentary History*, ed. Albert P. Blaustein and Robert L. Zangrando (New York: Trident, 1968), 339; W. S. Scarborough, "Race Riots and Their Remedy," *Independent* 99 (August 16, 1919): 223; Jeffreys-Jones, *Violence and Reform in American History*, 151; John R. Shillady to Woodrow Wilson, July 21, 1919, in PWW, vol. 61, pp. 576–77. On the opposition to lynching, see Gail Bederman, *Manliness and Civilization: A Cultural History of Gender and Race in the United States, 1880–1917* (Chicago: University of Chicago Press, 1995), 45–76; Crystal Nicole Feimster, " 'Ladies and Lynching': The Gendered Discourse of Mob Violence in the New South, 1880–1930" (Ph.D. dissertation, Princeton University, 2000); 164–234; Claudine L. Ferrell, *Nightmare and Dream: Antilynching in Congress, 1917–1922* (New York: Garland, 1986); Jacquelyn Dowd Hall, *Revolt against Chivalry: Jessie Daniel Ames and the Women's Campaign against Lynching*, rev. ed. (New York: Columbia University Press, 1993); Rosalyn Terborg-Penn, "African-American Women's Networks in the Anti-Lynching Crusade," in *Gender, Class, Race, and Reform in the Progressive Era*, ed. Noralee Frankel and Nancy S. Dye

(Lexington: University Press of Kentucky, 1991), 148–61; and Robert Zangrando, *The NAACP Crusade against Lynching, 1909–1950* (Philadelphia: Temple University Press, 1980). Glenn Feldman "Conservative Progressivism: Antivigilantism in Post–World War I Alabama," *Alabama Review* 50 (Spring 1997): 18–36, and Lawrence Edward Kight, "'The State Is on Trial': Governor Edmund F. Noel and the Defense of Mississippi's Legal Institutions against Mob Violence," *Journal of Mississippi History* 60 (Fall 1998): 191–222, explore tensions among white Southerners over violence.

48. The oath is quoted in Walter F. White, "'Massacring Whites' in Arkansas," *Nation* 109 (December 6, 1919): 715. The two fullest accounts of the events in Elaine in 1919 are Richard C. Cortner, *A Mob Intent on Death: The NAACP and the Arkansas Riot Cases* (Middletown, Conn.: Wesleyan University Press, 1988), and Grif Stockley, *Blood in Their Eyes: The Elaine Race Massacres of 1919* (Fayetteville: University of Arkansas Press, 2001). Other good studies include Kieran Taylor, "'We Have Just Begun': Black Organizing and White Response in the Arkansas Delta, 1919," *Arkansas Historical Quarterly* 58 (Autumn 1999): 265–84; Jeannie M. Whayne, "Low Villains and Wickedness in High Places: Race and Class in the Elaine Riots," *Arkansas Historical Quarterly* 58 (Autumn 1999): 285–313; and Nan Elizabeth Woodruff, "African-American Struggles for Citizenship in the Arkansas and Mississippi Deltas in the Age of Jim Crow," *Radical History Review* no. 55 (Winter 1993): 33–51. Contemporary press accounts include "Bloody Race Riots in Arkansas County; 9 Men Reported Killed," *Atlanta Constitution*, October 2, 1919; "Arkansas Riot-Torn," *Los Angeles Times*, October 2, 1919; "Planned Massacre of Whites Today," *New York Times*, October 6, 1919; "The Real Causes of Two Race Riots," *Crisis* 19 (December 1919): 56–62.

49. The official death toll of the Committee of Seven was thirty people, but few scholars believe that number. See White, "'Massacring Whites,'" 715; William B. Hixson Jr., *Moorfield Storey and the Abolitionist Tradition* (New York: Oxford University Press, 1972), 183; Carolyn Wedin, *Inheritors of the Spirit: Mary White Ovington and the Founding of the NAACP* (New York: John Wiley and Sons, 1998), 190. The "mob spirit" inside the courtroom could also be seen in the trial of Robert Prager's killers, all of whom were acquitted in June 1918. "Prager's Lynchers Quickly Acquitted," *New York Times*, June 2, 1918.

50. National Association for the Advancement of Colored People, *Thirty Years of Lynching in the United States, 1889–1918* (New York: NAACP, 1919); Zangrando, *NAACP Crusade against Lynching*, 23–50; Ida B. Wells, *Crusade for Justice: The Autobiography of Ida B. Wells,* ed. Alfreda M. Duster (Chicago: University of Chicago Press, 1970), 397–404; Moorfield Storey, *Obedience to the Law: An Address at the Opening of Petigru College in Columbia, South Carolina* (Boston: Geo. H. Ellis, 1919), 3–5, 7. See also George E. Haynes, "What Negroes Think of the Race Riots," *Public* 22 (August 9, 1919): 848–49. The NAACP's legal campaign is chronicled in Cortner, *Mob Intent on Death*, 106–184.

51. Moorfield Storey, quoted in Hixson, *Moorfield Storey*, 184; *Moore v. Dempsey*, 261 U.S. 86 (1923), at 91. But see Justice McReynolds's dissent at 93: "The delays incident to enforcement of our criminal laws have become a national scandal and give serious alarm to those who observe." Similarly, just two years before, the Court in *Brown v. United*

States, 256 U.S. 335 (1921), upheld the general principle of self-defense that Richard Maxwell Brown has called "no duty to retreat." Brown, "Western Violence," 15.

52. For more on the law as a weapon against lynching and the rise of legal consciousness among African-American Southerners, see Pfeifer, *Rough Justice*. William D. Carrigan and Clive Webb, "The Lynching of Persons of Mexican Origin or Descent in the United States, 1848 to 1928," *Journal of Social History* 37 (Winter 2003): 423–29, credit the decline in lynchings both to the rise of Tejano/a legal consciousness and diplomatic pressures from post-Revolutionary Mexico.

53. Taylor, "'We Have Just Begun,'" 283.

54. Connecticut Military Emergency Board, *Report*, 7; "Two Men Shot as 5,000 Mob Yale Students," *New York Tribune*, May 28, 1919, clipping in reel 8, volume 70, ACLU Archives.

55. "Omaha," *Literary Digest* 63 (October 11, 1919): 16.

56. E. D. Verink, quoted in Juhnke, "Mob Violence," 347; Edda Bilger, "The 'Oklahoma Vorwärts': The Voice of German-Americans in Oklahoma during World War I," *Chronicles of Oklahoma* 54 (Summer 1976): 252.

57. Mark Ellis, "Joel Spingarn's 'Constructive Programme' and the Wartime Antilynching Bill of 1918," *Journal of Policy History* 4, no. 2 (1992): 134–61; Barbara Holden-Smith, "Lynching, Federalism, and the Intersection of Race and Gender in the Progressive Era," *Yale Journal of Law and Feminism* 8 (1996): 31–78; Christopher Waldrep, "War of Words: The Controversy over the Definition of Lynching, 1899–1940," *Journal of Southern History* 66 (February 2000): 75–100. On the Canales Commission, see Evan Anders, *Boss Rule in South Texas: The Progressive Era* (Austin: University of Texas Press, 1982), 235–52; Patrick L. Cox, "'An Enemy Closer to Us than Any European Power': The Impact of Mexico on Texan Public Opinion before World War I," *Southwestern Historical Quarterly* 105 (July 2001): 41–80; Benjamin Heber Johnson, *Revolution in Texas: How a Forgotten Rebellion and Its Bloody Suppression Turned Mexicans into Americans* (New Haven, Conn.: Yale University Press, 2003), esp. 144–75; Michael J. Lynch III, "The Role of J.T. Canales in the Development of Tejano Identity and Mexican American Integration in Twentieth Century South Texas," *Journal of South Texas* 13 (Fall 2000): 220–39.

58. Richard C. Rohrs, *The Germans in Oklahoma* (Norman: University of Oklahoma Press, 1980), 45; E. H. Rushmore to Captain Charles D. Frey, October 4, 1918, in Box 7, American Protective League Correspondence with Field Offices, 1917–1919, Record Group 65, National Archives and Records Administration, Washington, D.C.; "The Washington Riots," *Independent* 99 (August 2, 1919): 147; "The May Day Rioting," *Nation* 108 (May 10, 1919): 726.

59. For just one example of a range of publications issuing from the NCLB at this time, see Everett Dean Martin, *The Mob Mind vs. Civil Liberty* (New York: American Civil Liberties Union, 1920).

60. "Racial Tension and Race Riots," *Outlook* 122 (August 6, 1919): 533.

61. Allan Nevins, "Crowds and Crowd-Psychology," *Dial* 60 (May 11, 1916): 465–66; Walter Lippmann, *Liberty and the News* (New York: Harcourt, Brace and Howe, 1920), 56. See also Walter Lippmann, *The Phantom Public* (New York: Harcourt Brace, 1925), and, for a contrasting view, John Dewey, *The Public and*

Its Problems (New York: Henry Holt, 1927). For an extended consideration of Lippmann and Dewey on "the public," see Robert B. Westbrook, *John Dewey and American Democracy* (Ithaca, N.Y.: Cornell University Press, 1991), 275–318.

62. Excusing the crowd actions of "gentlemen of property and standing" historically helped elites distinguish their own political coercions from those that threatened their social privileges. See Feimster, " 'Ladies and Lynching' "; Paul A. Gilje, *Rioting in America* (Bloomington: Indiana University Press, 1996); Eugene E. Leach, "Chaining the Tiger: The Mob Stigma and the Working Class, 1863–1894," *Labor History* 35 (Spring 1994): 187–215; and Leonard L. Richards, *Gentlemen of Property and Standing: Anti-Abolitionist Mobs in Jacksonian America* (New York: Oxford University Press, 1970).

63. Bruere, "Copper Camp Patriotism," 203.

64. "Mob Violence," *Public* 22 (May 10, 1919): 481.

Chapter 5

1. Philadelphia War History Committee, *Philadelphia in the World War, 1914–1919* (New York: Wynkoop Hallenbeck Crawford, 1922), 130; "The Illness of the Liberty Bell," *Literary Digest* 50 (March 13, 1915): 542–43; "Shall We Mend the Liberty Bell?" *Literary Digest* 65 (June 26, 1920): 29–30; "Liberty Bell Still Unmended," *Literary Digest* 66 (September 11, 1920): 136–38. See also Eric Foner, *The Story of American Freedom* (New York: Norton, 1998), 89–90; David Kimball, *Venerable Relic: The Story of the Liberty Bell* (Philadelphia: Eastern National Park and Monument Association, 1989), 69; Victor Rosewater, *The Liberty Bell: Its History and Significance* (New York: D. Appleton, 1926), 189–90.

2. The literature on the origins of civil liberties is vast. Some of the most important works include Zechariah Chafee Jr., *Free Speech in the United States* (New York: Atheneum, 1969 [1941]), 1–281; Robert C. Cottrell, *Roger Nash Baldwin and the American Civil Liberties Union* (New York: Columbia University Press, 2000), 46–134; Foner, *Story of American Freedom*, 163–93; Donald Johnson, *The Challenge to American Freedoms* (Lexington: University of Kentucky Press, 1963); Paul L. Murphy, *World War I and the Origins of Civil Liberties in the United States* (New York: Norton, 1979); Richard Polenberg, *Fighting Faiths: The Abrams Case, the Supreme Court, and Free Speech* (New York: Viking, 1987); David M. Rabban, *Free Speech in Its Forgotten Years* (New York: Cambridge University Press, 1997); Harry N. Scheiber, *The Wilson Administration and Civil Liberties, 1917–1921* (Ithaca, N.Y.: Cornell University Press, 1960); Geoffrey R. Stone, *Perilous Times: Free Speech in Wartime from the Sedition Act of 1798 to the War on Terrorism* (New York: Norton, 2004); Samuel Walker, *In Defense of American Liberties: A History of the ACLU,* 2nd ed. (New York: Oxford University Press, 1999), 3–47; John Fabian Witt, *Patriots and Cosmopolitans: Hidden Histories of American Law* (Cambridge: Harvard University Press, 2007), esp. 157–208.

3. On Wells's editorship of the *Free Speech and Headlight* and its suppression in 1892, see Ida B. Wells, *Crusade for Justice: The Autobiography of Ida B. Wells,* ed. Alfreda M. Duster (Chicago: University of Chicago Press, 1970), 35–67. Rabban, *Free Speech in Its Forgotten Years,* presents the most thorough overview of prewar speech

debates. See also Linda Cobb-Reiley, "Not an Empty Box with Beautiful Words on It: The First Amendment in Progressive Era Scholarship," *Journalism Quarterly* 69 (Spring 1992): 37–47; Rochelle Gurstein, *The Repeal of Reticence: A History of America's Cultural and Legal Struggles over Free Speech, Obscenity, Sexual Liberation, and Modern Art* (New York: Hill and Wang, 1996); Helen Lefkowitz Horowitz, *Rereading Sex: Battles over Sexual Knowledge and Suppression in Nineteenth-Century America* (New York: Knopf, 2002); Norman L. Rosenberg, *Protecting the Best Men: An Interpretive History of the Law of Libel* (Chapel Hill: University of North Carolina Press, 1986); Christine Stansell, *American Moderns: Bohemian New York and the Creation of a New Century* (New York: Metropolitan Books, 2000); Sandra F. VanBurkleo, "Words as Hard as Cannon-Balls: Women's Rights Agitation and Liberty of Speech in Nineteenth-Century America," in *Constitutionalism and American Culture: Writing the New Constitutional History*, ed. Sandra F. VanBurkleo et al. (Lawrence: University Press of Kansas, 2002), 307–58.

4. Rabban, *Free Speech in Its Forgotten Years*, 44–57.

5. "Free Speech," *Outlook* 117 (October 17, 1917): 239. For histories of the suppression and regulation of speech in the era before World War I, see Michael Kent Curtis, *Free Speech, the People's Darling Privilege: Struggles for Freedom of Expression in American History* (Durham, N.C.: Duke University Press, 2000); Joanne B. Freeman, "Explaining the Unexplainable: The Cultural Context of the Sedition Act," in *The Democratic Experiment: New Directions in American Political History*, ed. Meg Jacobs et al. (Princeton, N.J.: Princeton University Press, 2003), 20–49; Marc Lendler, "'Equally Proper at All Times and Equally Necessary': Civility, Bad Tendency, and the Sedition Act," *Journal of the Early Republic* 24 (Fall 2004): 419–44; Leonard Williams Levy, *Legacy of Suppression: Freedom of Speech and Press in Early American History* (Cambridge: Harvard University Press, 1960).

6. Halbert Gardner, quoted in Clark T. Irwin Jr., "WWI Galvanizes Region's Activities," in *Greater Portland Celebration 350*, comp. and ed. Albert F. Barnes (Portland, Me.: Gannett, 1984), 137; George Morehouse, "Kansas as a State of Extremes and Its Attitude during the World War," *Collections of the Kansas State Historical Society* 15 (1923): 21.

7. "Pacifists Routed by Baltimoreans," *Washington Post*, April 2, 1917; Anne Klejment, "The Radical Origins of Catholic Pacifism: Dorothy Day and the Lyrical Left during World War I," in *American Catholic Pacifism: The Influence of Dorothy Day and the Catholic Worker Movement*, ed. Anne Klejment and Nancy L. Roberts (Westport, Conn.: Praeger, 1996), 17; Kenneth G. Guthrie, "A Pacifist Plea to Clergymen," *New York Times*, January 25, 1918.

8. Jane Addams, *Peace and Bread in Time of War* (New York: Macmillan, 1922); Addams, *The Second Twenty Years at Hull-House* (New York: Macmillan, 1930), 113–52; Allen F. Davis, *American Heroine: The Life and Legend of Jane Addams* (New York: Oxford University Press, 1973), 212–50; James Weber Linn, *Jane Addams: A Biography* (New York: Greenwood, 1968 [1935]), 284–351; Susan Zeiger, "She Didn't Raise Her Boy to Be a Slacker: Motherhood, Conscription, and the Culture of the First World War," *Feminist Studies* 22 (Spring 1996): 15–16.

9. Linn, *Jane Addams*, 330–32; "Chief Justice Rebukes Miss Jane Addams," *New York Times*, June 11, 1917; "Carter Dissents to Jane Addams' Views on War," *Chicago*

Tribune, June 11, 1917; Mrs. Lawrence B. Perkins, *One Hundred Years of Christian Service* (Evanston, Ill.: First Congregational Church of Evanston, 1970), 18; Michael Willrich, *City of Courts: Socializing Justice in Progressive Era Chicago* (New York: Cambridge University Press, 2003), 67, 88.

10. Unidentified clipping from *Club Fellow*, May 7, 1919, in Box 1, Folder 6, Papers of Jane Addams, Sophia Smith Collection, Smith College, Northampton, Mass. [hereafter Sophia Smith Collection]; Robert Morss Lovett, *Jane Addams and The Women's International League for Peace and Freedom* (Chicago: WILPF, 1946), 17; Linn, *Jane Addams*, 329–30; Kim E. Nielsen, *Un-American Womanhood: Antiradicalism, Antifeminism, and the First Red Scare* (Columbus: Ohio State University, 2001), 83.

11. Lillian Wald, quoted in "Free Speech and Peaceable Assembly," *Survey* 38 (May 12, 1917): 144. On the American Union against Militarism and the founding of the National Civil Liberties Bureau, see Charles Chatfield, "World War I and the Liberal Pacifist in the United States," *American Historical Review* 75 (December 1970): 1920–37; Johnson, *Challenge to American Freedoms*, 1–25.

12. "A.F. of L. Organizer's Home Is Dynamited," *New York Evening Call*, May 7, 1919, clipping in reel 8, volume 70, American Civil Liberties Union Archives, microfilm ed. (Wilmington, Del.: Scholarly Resources, 1996).

13. Edda Bilger, "The 'Oklahoma Vorwärts': The Voice of German-Americans in Oklahoma during World War I," *Chronicles of Oklahoma* 54 (Summer 1976): 258–59.

14. Woodrow Wilson, "An Address in Buffalo to the American Federation of Labor," in Arthur S. Link et al., eds., *The Papers of Woodrow Wilson,* 69 vols. (Princeton, N.J.: Princeton University Press, 1966–94), vol. 45, p. 14 [hereafter PWW with volume number]; O. A. Hilton, "The Oklahoma Council of Defense and the First World War," *Chronicles of Oklahoma* 20 (March 1942): 34 n. 38; David Alan Corbin, *Life, Work, and Rebellion in the Coal Fields: The Southern West Virginia Miners, 1880–1922* (Urbana: University of Illinois Press, 1982), 188; "Free Speech and Peaceable Assembly," 145; H. C. Peterson and Gilbert C. Fite, *Opponents of War, 1917–1918* (Seattle: University of Washington Press, 1968 [1957]), 213.

15. 40 Stat. 217 (1917). Rabban, *Free Speech in Its Forgotten Years*, 248–98, and Peterson and Fite, *Opponents of War*, 92–101, provide thorough histories of the Espionage Act.

16. William H. Lamar, "The Government's Attitude toward the Press," *Forum* 59 (February 1918): 132. For a sampling of commentary, see "Congress Fights Censorship," *Independent* 90 (May 12, 1917): 275–76; "The Censorship Muddle," *Nation* 104 (May 31, 1917): 648–49; George Creel, "The Censorship Myth," in *Rebel at Large: Recollections of Fifty Crowded Years* (New York: G. P. Putnam's Sons, 1947), 156–65; Stephen Vaughn, *Holding Fast the Inner Line: Democracy, Nationalism, and the Committee on Public Information* (Chapel Hill: University of North Carolina Press, 1980).

17. Adrian Anderson, "President Wilson's Politician: Albert Sidney Burleson of Texas," *Southwestern Historical Quarterly* 72 (January 1974): 339–54.

18. Thomas Gregory, quoted in Gene Sessions, "Espionage in Windsor: Clarence H. Waldron and Patriotism in World War I," *Vermont History* 61 (Summer 1993): 151; Oswald Garrison Villard to Joseph Tumulty, September 26, 1917, in PWW, vol. 44,

p. 272; Henry R. Martinson, "Some Memoirs of a Nonpartisan League Organizer," *North Dakota History* 42 (Spring 1975): 19; Bilger, "The 'Oklahoma Vorwärts,'" 257–58; Lillian Wald et al. to Woodrow Wilson, August 10, 1917, in PWW, vol. 43, p. 423.

19. Albert S. Burleson, *Address at a Conference of Representatives of Business Organizations and the Postal Service at Washington, D.C., April 1, 1919* (Washington, D.C.: Government Printing Office, 1919), 5; Lamar, "Government's Attitude," 132.

20. Albert Burleson, quoted in Donald Johnson, "Wilson, Burleson, and Censorship in the First World War," *Journal of Southern History* 28 (February 1962): 48; Homer Cummings and Carl McFarland, *Federal Justice: Chapters in the History of Justice and the Federal Executive* (New York: Macmillan, 1937), 420; David M. Kennedy, *Over Here: The First World War and American Society* (New York: Oxford University Press, 1980), 61–62.

21. On the suppression of the publications, see "Watson's Paper Suspended," *New York Times*, June 29, 1917; Leslie Fishbein, *Rebels in Bohemia: The Radicals of The Masses, 1911–1917* (Chapel Hill: University of North Carolina Press, 1982), 24; C. Vann Woodward, *Tom Watson: Agrarian Rebel* (New York: Oxford University Press, 1963 [1938]), 458. Several other papers were also suppressed at this time; see the list in Volume 20, Item 3208, Papers of Albert Sidney Burleson, Library of Congress Manuscript Division, Washington, D.C. [hereafter LCMD].

22. "Watson Is Scored by Atlanta Pastor," *Atlanta Constitution*, June 25, 1917; Woodward, *Tom Watson*, 451–86.

23. "Socialist Papers Stopped by Lucas," *Atlanta Constitution*, July 1, 1917; "Watson's Case Being Considered," *Atlanta Constitution*, July 29, 1917; Woodward, *Tom Watson*, 454, 457–58.

24. Fred D. Ragan, "An Unlikely Alliance: Tom Watson, Harry Weinberger, and the World War I Draft," *Atlanta Historical Journal* 25 (Fall 1981): 23–27; Harry Weinberger, "A Rebel's Interrupted Autobiography," *American Journal of Economics and Sociology* 2 (October 1942): 114.

25. Josephus Daniels diary entry, August 7, 1917, in PWW, vol. 43, p. 389. Quotes from "Speer Decision Hits Anti-Draft Papers," *New York Times*, September 2, 1917; Ragan, "Unlikely Alliance," 23. See also "Watson's 'Jeffersonian' Is Barred from Mails at Second-Class Rates," *Atlanta Constitution*, August 14, 1917; "Watson Asks Speer to Enjoin Postmaster," *Atlanta Constitution*, August 15, 1917; "Speer Reserves Watson Decisions," *Atlanta Constitution*, August 19, 1917; *Jeffersonian Publishing Co. v. West*, 245 Fed. 585, at 589. For Burleson's defense of the Post Office Department in the case against the *Jeffersonian*, see his untitled typescript, May 13, 1918, Volume 20, Item 3223, Papers of Albert Sidney Burleson, LCMD.

26. "Memorandum of Post Office Department Inspector in Atlanta," September 25, 1917, Box 3, Case File 47404, Records of the Post Office Department, Office of the Solicitor, Records Relating to the Espionage Act, World War I, 1917–1921, Record Group 28, National Archives and Records Administration, Washington, D.C. [hereafter RG 28, NARA]; "Tom Watson Buys Another Weekly," *Atlanta Constitution*, September 7, 1917; "Watson to Suspend Papers," *New York Times*, September 23, 1917.

27. "What Happened to the August Masses," *Masses* 9 (September 1917): 3; Fishbein, *Rebels in Bohemia*, 24–29.

28. Johnson, *Challenge*, 60; Max Eastman et al. to Woodrow Wilson, July 12, 1917, in PWW, vol. 43, p. 165; Amos Pinchot to Joseph Tumulty, July 14, 1917, in ibid., 175; Amos Pinchot to Woodrow Wilson, July 25 1917, in ibid., 277.

29. Gerald Gunther, *Learned Hand: The Man and the Judge* (Cambridge: Harvard University Press, 1994), 151–61; Polenberg, *Fighting Faiths*, 70–72; *Masses Publishing Company v. Patten*, 244 Fed. 535 (S.D.N.Y., 1917), at 543; *Masses Publishing Company v. Patten*, 245 Fed. 102 (C.C.A. 2d.,1917); *Masses Publishing Company v. Patten*, 246 Fed. 24 (C.C.A. 2d., 1917).

30. All misspellings in the Kahn quotation are reproduced from the original document. Isaï T. Kahn to Albert S. Burleson, August 21, 1917, Box 7, Case File 47445; J. H. Maddox to Albert S. Burleson, March 11, 1919, Box 3, Case File 47404, RG 28, NARA.

31. Woodward, *Tom Watson*, 461–74 (quote from 463).

32. Ibid., 473; Tom Watson, quoted in Ragan, "Unlikely Alliance," 25; Charles P. Sweeney, "Bigotry in the South: Anti-Catholic Prejudice," *Nation* 111 (November 24, 1920): 585.

33. Ray H. Abrams, *Preachers Present Arms* (Scottdale, Pa.: Herald, 1969 [1933]), 205; "Negro Preacher Tarred," *Memphis Commercial Appeal*, April 18, 1918. See also John F. Piper Jr., *The American Churches in World War I* (Athens: Ohio University Press, 1985); Peterson and Fite, *Opponents of War*, 115.

34. Sessions, "Espionage in Windsor," 133–55. See also Chafee, *Free Speech*, 55–56; Stephen M. Kohn, *American Political Prisoners: Prosecutions under the Espionage and Sedition Acts* (Westport, Conn.: Praeger, 1994), 137; Peterson and Fite, *Opponents of War*, 117–18.

35. Clarence Waldron, quoted in Sessions, "Espionage in Windsor," 142; *Christian Register*, quoted in Abrams, *Preachers Present Arms*, 216. "Testimony Given in Sedition Case," *Christian Science Monitor*, January 10, 1918; "Vermont's Sedition Trial," *New York Evening Post*, February 4, 1918; "Prison Term for Preacher," *New York Times*, March 22, 1918; "Sedition Penalty Severe," *New York Times*, March 24, 1918; "Waldron Taken to Prison," *New York Times*, March 31, 1918.

36. "Russellites Guilty of Hindering Draft," *New York Times*, June 21, 1918; "Freedom Is Not Unlimited," *New York Times*, June 22, 1918; Kohn, *American Political Prisoners*, 95; Herbert Hewitt Stroup, *The Jehovah's Witnesses* (New York: Columbia University Press, 1945), 17.

37. "Free Speech and Peaceable Assembly," 144; Shirley Burton, "The Espionage and Sedition Acts of 1917 and 1918: Sectional Interpretations in the United States District Courts of Illinois," *Illinois Historical Journal* 87 (Spring 1994): 48, 49; Joseph Carruth, "World War I Propaganda and Its Effects in Arkansas," *Arkansas Historical Quarterly* 56 (Winter 1997): 394; "Our Ferocious Sentences," *Nation* 107 (November 2, 1918): 504.

38. John Lord O'Brian, quoted in Cummings and McFarland, *Federal Justice*, 426; Arnon Gutfeld, "The Ves Hall Case, Judge Bourquin, and the Sedition Act of 1918," *Pacific Historical Review* 37 (May 1968): 163–78; *United States v. Hall*, 248 Fed. 150 (1918), at 152.

39. Memorandum from Roger Baldwin to Edward M. House, January 24, 1918, in PWW, vol. 46, p. 382. The best source on the founding of the National Civil

Liberties Bureau is Walker, *In Defense of American Liberties*. See also Cottrell, *Roger Nash Baldwin*; Peggy Lamson, *Roger Baldwin: Founder of the American Civil Liberties Union* (Boston: Houghton Mifflin, 1976), 67–137. Frances H. Early, "Feminism, Peace, and Civil Liberties: Women's Role in the Origins of the World War I Civil Liberties Movement," *Women's Studies* 18, nos. 1–2 (1990): 95–115, is particularly valuable for the war years. For early NAACP activities, see Charles Flint Kellogg, *NAACP: A History of the National Association for the Advancement of Colored People* (Baltimore: Johns Hopkins University Press, 1967), vol. 1, pp. 209–75; Steven A. Reich, "Soldiers of Democracy: Black Texans and the Fight for Democracy, 1917–1921," *Journal of American History* 82 (March 1996): 1478–1504; Carolyn Wedin, *Inheritors of the Spirit: Mary White Ovington and the Founding of the NAACP* (New York: John Wiley and Sons, 1998), 155–98.

40. R. Lockey to Thomas J. Walsh, April 17, 1918, in Series I, Box 269, Papers of Thomas Walsh, LCMD; Peterson and Fite, *Opponents of War,* 212; "The Bigelow Incident," *New Republic* 13 (November 10, 1917): 37.

41. Woodrow Wilson, quoted in Johnson, "Wilson, Burleson," 47, 56.

42. Woodrow Wilson to Lillian Wald, in PWW, vol. 42, p. 153; Wilson to Albert Burleson, September 4, 1917, in ibid., vol. 44, p. 147; Wilson to Burleson, October 11, 1917, in ibid., vol. 44, p. 358; "'The Nation' and the Post Office," *Nation* 107 (September 28, 1918): 336–37.

43. Cummings and McFarland, *Federal Justice*, 425–26; Peterson and Fite, *Opponents of War*, 208–21; Rabban, *Free Speech in Its Forgotten Years*, 267.

44. Hugh T. Lovin, "World War Vigilantes in Idaho, 1917–1918," *Idaho Yesterdays* 18 (Summer 1974): 9. On the Nonpartisan League, see Carol E. Jenson, *Agrarian Pioneer in Civil Liberties: The Nonpartisan League in Minnesota during World War I* (New York: Garland, 1986); Robert L. Morlan, *Political Prairie Fire: The Nonpartisan League, 1915–1922* (Minneapolis: University of Minnesota Press, 1955).

45. On the NPL's often-overlooked support for the war, see Douglas Bakken, "NPL in Nebraska, 1917–1920," *North Dakota History* 39 (Spring 1972): 30, and Jenson, *Agrarian Pioneer in Civil Liberties*, 168. The story of the Liberty Bond and *The New Freedom* comes from Martinson, "Some Memoirs," 19.

46. James C. Olson and Ronald C. Naugle, *History of Nebraska*, 3rd ed. (Lincoln: University of Nebraska Press, 1997), 281–82; Martinson, "Some Memoirs," 20; Keith Neville, quoted in Bakken, "NPL in Nebraska," 30–31. For more on NPL use of the press, see Morlan, *Political Prairie Fire*, 234–36, 251–52; Paul C. Schmidt, "The Press in North Dakota," *North Dakota History* 31 (October 1964): 220.

47. *Gilbert v. State of Minnesota*, 254 U.S. 325 (1920), at 333, 331; Jenson, *Agrarian Pioneer in Civil Liberties*, 1–5, 170, 177–82; Morlan, *Political Prairie Fire*, 172–73, 290–92.

48. Chafee, *Free Speech*, 160, 162, 163. John Fabian Witt, "Crystal Eastman and the Internationalist Beginnings of American Civil Liberties," *Duke Law Journal* 54, no. 3 (2004): 710, 750–52, makes a similar argument about the ways that Roger Baldwin's nationalist rhetoric diverted and suppressed the internationalist impulses that motivated civil libertarians such as Crystal Eastman, but Witt overlooks the multiple origins of civil liberties through the work of Tom Watson, the Nonpartisan League, and others who can hardly be considered internationalists.

49. Diane Garey, *Defending Everybody: A History of the American Civil Liberties Union* (New York: TV Books, 1998), 27–29.

50. "Pacifist Professor Gets Year in Prison," *New York Times*, October 31, 1918; Staughton Lynd, ed., *Nonviolence in America: A Documentary History* (Indianapolis, Ind.: Bobbs-Merrill, 1966), 176–77.

51. Thomas Gregory, quoted in Jenson, *Agrarian Pioneer in Civil Liberties,* 167; *State v. Lowery*, 177 Pac. 355 (Wash. 1918), at 356. On the wartime prosecution of IWW members, see William Preston Jr., *Aliens and Dissenters: Federal Suppression of Radicals, 1903–1933*, 2nd ed. (Urbana: University of Illinois Press, 1994), 88–207.

52. On Wald's resignation from the AUAM, see Doris Groshen Daniels, *Always a Sister: The Feminism of Lillian D. Wald* (New York: Feminist Press, 1989), 125–40, and Edward Wagenknecht, *Daughters of the Covenant: Portraits of Six Jewish Women* (Amherst: University of Massachusetts Press, 1983), 97–117.

53. "Bigelow Tells of Beating," *New York Times*, January 14, 1918; Peterson and Fite, *Opponents of War*, 79.

54. The literature on the doctrinal evolution of the law in the postwar speech cases is vast. In addition to general works cited previously, see also Sheldon M. Novick, "The Unrevised Holmes and Free Expression," *Supreme Court Review* (1991): 303–390; Polenberg, *Fighting Faiths*, 197–242; Fred D. Ragan, "Justice Oliver Wendell Holmes, Jr., Zechariah Chafee, Jr., and the Clear and Present Danger Test for Free Speech: The First Year, 1919," *Journal of American History* 58 (June 1971): 24–45; and G. Edward White, *Justice Oliver Wendell Holmes: Law and the Inner Self* (New York: Oxford University Press, 1993), 412–54.

55. *Schenck v. U.S.*, 249 U.S. 47 (1919), at 51; Ragan, "Justice Oliver Wendell Holmes," 33; Polenberg, *Fighting Faiths*, 207–218.

56. *Schenck v. U.S.*, at 51–52.

57. Zechariah Chafee Jr., "Freedom of Speech," *New Republic* 17 (November 16, 1918): 66–69; Ernst Freund, "The Debs Case and Freedom of Speech," *New Republic* 19 (May 3, 1919): 13–15. *Frohwerk v. U.S.*, 249 U.S. 204 (1919), at 207; *Schaefer v. U.S.*, 251 U.S. 466 (1920).

58. Quoted in *Abrams v. U.S.,* 250 U.S. 616 (1919), at 623. A careful history of the pamphlets appears in Polenberg, *Fighting Faiths*, 49–55.

59. *Abrams v. U.S.*, at 618–619, 621, 622; Polenberg, *Fighting Faiths*, 228–35; "Our Ferocious Sentences," 504.

60. *Abrams v. U.S.*, at 627, 630. Polenberg, *Fighting Faiths*, 218–228, 236–42, persuasively argues that Holmes's stance in *Abrams* represented a distinct shift in the justice's views, rather than the application of the "clear and present danger" test to a slightly changed situation, as argued in Novick, "Unrevised Holmes," 303–90.

61. *Abrams v. U.S.*, at 628, 629.

62. Eugene Debs, quoted in Nick Salvatore, *Eugene V. Debs: Citizen and Socialist* (Urbana: University of Illinois Press, 1982), 292–93; *Abrams v. U.S.*, at 630.

63. Arthur P. Young, *Books for Sammies: The American Library Association and World War I* (Pittsburgh, Pa.: Beta Phi Mu, 1981), 24; Wayne A. Wiegand, *An Active Instrument for Propaganda: The American Public Library during World War I* (Westport, Conn.: Greenwood, 1989); and for a later period, Christopher P. Loss, "Reading between

Enemy Lines: Armed Services Editions and World War II," *Journal of Military History* 67 (July 2003): 811–34. Of course, not all American soldiers could read; perhaps a quarter of soldiers were illiterate, although an exact measure is difficult to sift out through the cultural and language bias of officers. Jennifer D. Keene, *Doughboys, the Great War, and the Remaking of America* (Baltimore: Johns Hopkins University Press, 2001), 28.

64. Thomas Cripps, *Slow Fade to Black: The Negro in American Film, 1900–1942* (New York: Oxford University Press, 1977), 41–70; "The Story of the Branches for 1918," *Crisis* 17 (April 1919): 283.

65. Dorothy Weyer Creigh, *Nebraska: A Bicentennial History* (New York: Norton, 1977), 171–72; Frederick C. Luebke, "Legal Restrictions on Foreign Languages in the Great Plains States, 1917–1923," in *Languages in Conflict: Linguistic Acculturation on the Great Plains,* ed. Paul Schach (Lincoln: University of Nebraska Press, 1980), 5; Carl Wittke, *German-Americans and the World War* (Columbus: Ohio State Archaeological and Historical Society, 1936), 182; "To Throw Out Teuton Books," *Washington Post,* August 10, 1917; "Condemns German Libraries," *New York Times,* November 14, 1917; "Raid School; Burn German Books Found," *Chicago Tribune,* March 6, 1918.

66. Young, *Books for Sammies,* 52.

67. Bruce E. Ford, "The Newark Public Library," in *A History of New Jersey Libraries, 1750–1996,* ed. Edwin Beckerman (Lanham, Md.: Scarecrow, 1997), 75; Kevin Mattson, "The Librarian as Secular Minister to Democracy: The Life and Ideas of John Cotton Dana," *Libraries and Culture* 35 (Fall 2000): 514–34; Wiegand, *Active Instrument for Propaganda,* 96–99; Young, *Books for Sammies,* 6. For more on the Vigilantes, see John Carver Edwards, "America's Vigilantes and the Great War," *Army Quarterly and Defence Journal* 106 (July 1976): 277–86.

68. "In the Libraries," *Christian Science Monitor,* September 5, 1917; John Cotton Dana, "Public Libraries as Censors," *Bookman* 49 (April 1919): 147–52; Dana, "The Librarian as Censor," *Library Journal* 44 (November 1919): 728.

69. W. E.[?] Gifford to the Several State Councils of Defense, June 28, 1918, in Box 56, Record Group 30, Connecticut Council of Defense Records, Connecticut State Archives, Hartford, Conn.

70. Dotha Stone Pinneo to A. B. Sands, July 16, 1918, and Grace A. Child to Sands, September 6, 1918, in ibid.

71. All misspellings in the Clark quotation are reproduced from the original document. Alice E. Coffin to Connecticut State Council of Defense, July 16, 1918; A. M. Clark to CSCD, n.d.; Margery Abell to A. B. Sands, July 24, 1918; and Andrew Keough to A. B. Sands, July 16, 1918, in ibid.

72. Woodrow Wilson to Albert Burleson, November 27, 1918, in PWW, vol. 53, p. 214; Wilson to Burleson, February 28, 1919, in ibid., vol. 55, p. 327; "Wilson Commutes Espionage Terms," *New York Times,* March 6, 1919; "Burleson and the Call," *New Republic* 21 (January 7, 1920): 158; Max Eastman, "The Post Office Censorship," *Masses* 9 (September 1917): 24; Milwaukee *Leader,* May 23, 1918, quoted in Peterson and Fite, *Opponents of War,* 22; *U.S. ex rel. Milwaukee Social Democratic Pub. Co. v. Burleson,* 255 U.S. 407 (1921), at 413.

73. Burleson, *Address*, 8; Lowes Dickinson, quoted in Walter Nelles, "In the Wake of the Espionage Act," *Nation* 111 (December 15, 1920): 684; George Creel, quoted in Peterson and Fite, *Opponents of War*, 95.
74. Burleson, *Address*, 8.

Chapter 6

1. "All Hail France in Mighty Tribute on Bastile [*sic*] Day," *New York Times*, July 15, 1918.
2. William Preston Jr., *Aliens and Dissenters: Federal Suppression of Radicals, 1903– 1933*, 2nd ed. (Urbana: University of Illinois Press, 1994), traces increasing regula- tion of political radicals against the backdrop of an aggressively expansive Bureau of Investigation in the Justice Department. Richard Polenberg, *Fighting Faiths: The Abrams Case, The Supreme Court, and Free Speech* (New York: Viking, 1987), 154–96, connects events in wartime courts to institutions of surveillance. David Cole, *Enemy Aliens: Double Standards and Constitutional Freedoms in the War on Terrorism* (New York: New Press, 2003), argues that restrictions on the rights of aliens have typically been extended to citizens in times of crisis. Recent work on the regulation of immigrants likewise demonstrates that the process of early twentieth- century state-building took place at the border itself. See Erika S. Lee, *At America's Gates: Chinese Immigration during the Exclusion Era* (Chapel Hill: University of North Carolina Press, 2003); Mae M. Ngai, *Impossible Subjects: Illegal Aliens and the Making of Modern America* (Princeton, N.J.: Princeton University Press, 2004). Modern philosophical inquiries include Hannah Arendt, *The Origins of Totalitari- anism* (New York: Harcourt, Brace, 1951) and Seyla Benhabib, *The Rights of Others: Aliens, Residents, and Citizens* (New York: Cambridge University Press, 2004). Linda K. Kerber, "Toward a History of Statelessness in America," *American Quarterly* 57 (September 2005): 727–49, and Kerber, "The Stateless as the Citizen's Other: A View from the United States," *American Historical Review* 112 (February 2007): 1–34, situate the history of citizenship in the context of its opposites.
3. On the linkage of national citizenship and identity, see Rogers M. Smith's expli- cation of the "ascriptive" tradition in American history in "Beyond Tocqueville, Myrdal, and Hartz: The Multiple Traditions in America," *American Political Science Review* 87 (September 1993): 549–66.
4. For an introduction to intellectual and cultural responses to modernization in the early twentieth-century United States, see Casey Nelson Blake, *Beloved Community: The Cultural Criticism of Randolph Bourne, Van Wyck Brooks, Waldo Frank, and Lewis Mumford* (Chapel Hill: University of North Carolina Press, 1990), and David B. Danbom, *"The World of Hope": Progressives and the Search for an Ethical Public Life* (Philadelphia: Temple University Press, 1987).
5. Josiah Royce, *The Philosophy of Loyalty* (Nashville: Vanderbilt University Press, 1995 [1908]), 9, 56; Josiah Royce, *The Duties of Americans in the Present War: Address Delivered at Tremont Temple, Sunday January 30, 1916* (Boston: Citizens' League for America and the Allies, 1916), 2. On Royce, see Robert V. Hine, *Josiah Royce: From Grass Valley to Harvard* (Norman: University of Oklahoma Press, 1992), 186– 90, and Bruce Kuklick, *Josiah Royce: An Intellectual Biography* (Indianapolis, Ind.: Bobbs-Merrill, 1972), esp. 211–40. For a thoughtful reflection from a friend (and

rival), see John Dewey, "Voluntarism in the Roycean Philosophy" (1916), in Dewey, *The Middle Works, 1899–1924,* ed. Jo Ann Boydston (Carbondale: Southern Illinois University Press, 1980), 79–88.

6. "Dr. Josiah Royce, Philosopher, Dies," *New York Times,* September 16, 1916; "Commencement Exercises Held at Bowdoin," *Christian Science Monitor,* June 15, 1916; Josiah Royce, "The Hope of the Great Community," in Royce, *The Hope of the Great Community* (Freeport, N.Y.: Books for Libraries Press, 1967 [1916]), 31.

7. Louis Brandeis, quoted in Melvin I. Urofsky, *Louis D. Brandeis and the Progressive Tradition* (Boston: Little Brown, 1981), 93. See also Randolph S. Bourne, "Trans-National America," in Bourne, *War and the Intellectuals: Collected Essays, 1915–1919,* ed. Carl Resek (New York: Harper Torchbooks, 1964), 107–23; Horace Kallen, "Democracy versus the Melting-Pot," in *Culture and Democracy in the United States* (New Brunswick, N.J.: Transaction, 1998 [1924]), 59–117.

8. Tony Smollok, quoted in Constantine M. Panunzio, *The Deportation Cases of 1919–1920* (New York: Federal Council of the Churches of Christ in America, 1921), 75.

9. John Perkins Field, *Halo over Hoboken: The Memoirs of John Perkins Field as Told to John Leroy Bailey* (New York: Exposition, 1955), 62; Meirion Harries and Susan Harries, *The Last Days of Innocence: America at War, 1917–1918* (New York: Random House, 1997), 31–32; Tracie Lynn Provost, "The Great Game: Imperial German Sabotage and Espionage against the United States, 1914–1917" (Ph.D. dissertation, University of Toledo, 2003); Mary L. Medley, *History of Anson County North Carolina, 1750–1976* (Wadesboro, N.C.: Anson County Historical Society, 1976), 150; Jules Witcover, *Sabotage at Black Tom: Imperial Germany's Secret War in America, 1914–1917* (Chapel Hill, N.C.: Algonquin, 1989); "Munitions Explosions Cost Loss of $20,000,000," *New York Times,* July 31, 1916.

10. "President's Proclamation of a State of War, and Regulations Governing Alien Enemies," *New York Times,* April 7, 1917. Assistant Attorney General Charles Warren was responsible for resuscitating the Alien Enemy Act of 1798 as part of his crusade for greater control over the German population in the United States. See Jörg Nagler, "Victims of the Home Front: Enemy Aliens in the United States during the First World War," in *Minorities in Wartime: National and Racial Groupings in Europe, North America, and Australia during the Two World Wars,* ed. Panikos Panayi (Providence, R.I.: Berg, 1993), 196–97. By contrast, the German government did not immediately move against U.S. citizens in Germany. "Won't Molest Americans," *New York Times,* April 7, 1917. Regulations against Austro-Hungarian enemy aliens were much less restrictive, merely forbidding them to enter or leave the country, and allowing for the possibility of internment. Nor were they required to register. Josephus Daniels diary entry, February 1, 1918, in *The Cabinet Diaries of Josephus Daniels, 1913–1921,* ed. E. David Cronon (Lincoln: University of Nebraska Press, 1963), 275.

11. "President's Proclamation of a State of War, and Regulations Governing Alien Enemies," *New York Times,* April 7, 1917; "Mayor Asks Everyone to Help Keep Peace," *New York Times,* April 7, 1917; "Warns Enemy Aliens," *New York Times,* April 7, 1917.

12. Frances H. Early, *A World without War: How U.S. Feminists and Pacifists Resisted World War I* (Syracuse, N.Y.: Syracuse University Press, 1997), 80–81; Frederick

C. Luebke, *Bonds of Loyalty: German-Americans in World War I* (DeKalb, Ill.: Northern Illinois University Press, 1974), 255–56; Harry N. Scheiber, *The Wilson Administration and Civil Liberties, 1917–1921* (Ithaca, N.Y.: Cornell University Press, 1960), 14; Office of the Judge Advocate General of the Army, *Compilation of the War Laws of the Various States and Insular Possessions* (Washington, D.C.: Government Printing Office, 1919), 9–17.

13. "Eight Taken Here as German Spies," *New York Times*, April 7, 1917; Jörg Nagler, *Nationale Minoritäten im Krieg: Feindliche Ausländer und die Amerikanische Heimatfront während des Ersten Weltkriegs* (Hamburg: Hamburger Edition, 2000), 199, 209–11. Brückner was later released, although I have not been able to determine when. See Herman Brückner to Pastor Knubel, June 21, 1918, Series 2, Box 7, National Lutheran Commission for Soldiers' and Sailors' Welfare Papers, Archives of the Evangelical Lutheran Church of the United States, Elk Grove Village, Ill. [hereafter ELCA].

14. Rogers Brubaker, *Citizenship and Nationhood in France and Germany* (Cambridge: Harvard University Press, 1992), 115; John Higham, *Strangers in the Land: Patterns of American Nativism, 1860–1925* (New Brunswick, N.J.: Rutgers University Press, 1955), 214; Luebke, *Bonds of Loyalty*, 255; Eli Nathans, *The Politics of Citizenship in Germany: Ethnicity, Utility and Nationalism* (New York: Berg, 2004), 169–98; Gustavus Ohlinger, *The German Conspiracy in American Education* (New York: George H. Doran, 1919), 18–19; Rogers M. Smith, *Civic Ideals: Conflicting Visions of Citizenship in U.S. History* (New Haven, Conn.: Yale University Press, 1997), 446–48; Leon E. Aylsworth, "The Passing of Alien Suffrage," *American Political Science Review* 25 (February 1931): 114–116; Office of the Judge Advocate General of the Army, *Compilation of War Laws*, § 42.

15. Ohlinger, *German Conspiracy*, 107–108; Morgan Barclay and Charles N. Glaab, *Toledo: Gateway to the Great Lakes* (Tulsa: Continental Heritage, 1982), 64, 71, 75–77. Ohlinger later emerged as a leading figure in the movement to destroy the National German-American Alliance. See Charles Thomas Johnson, *Culture at Twilight: The National German-American Alliance* (New York: Peter Lang, 1999), 119–20, 149–51.

16. Edda Bilger, "The 'Oklahoma Vorwärts': The Voice of German-Americans in Oklahoma during World War I," *Chronicles of Oklahoma* 54 (Summer 1976): 245–46; Clifford L. Nelson, *German-American Political Behavior in Nebraska and Wisconsin, 1916–1920* (Lincoln: University of Nebraska–Lincoln Publication, 1972), 3; James C. Olson and Ronald C. Naugle, *History of Nebraska*, 3rd ed. (Lincoln: University of Nebraska Press, 1997), 278; LaVern J. Rippley, "Ameliorated Americanization: The Effect of World War I on German-Americans in the 1920s," in *America and the Germans: An Assessment of a Three-Hundred-Year History*, ed. Frank Trommler and Joseph McVeigh (Philadelphia: University of Pennsylvania Press, 1983), vol. 2, pp. 218, 222; Henry J. Schmidt, "The Rhetoric of Survival: The Germanist in America from 1900 to 1925," in ibid., vol. 2, p. 204.

17. Bilger, "'Oklahoma Vorwärts,'" 245–46; Steven L. Schlossman, "Is There an American Tradition of Bilingual Education? German in the Public Elementary Schools, 1840–1919," *American Journal of Education* 92 (February 1983): 139–86;

Schmidt, "Rhetoric of Survival," 204. The best histories of German Americans in this period are Russell A. Kazal, *Becoming Old Stock: The Paradox of German-American Identity* (Princeton, N.J.: Princeton University Press, 2004), esp. 171–94, and Luebke, *Bonds of Loyalty.*

18. Bilger, "'Oklahoma Vorwärts,'" 248–49; Nelson, *German-American Political Behavior*, 8–9; Elliott Shore et al., eds., *The German-American Radical Press: The Shaping of a Left Political Culture, 1850–1940* (Urbana: University of Illinois Press, 1992); Johnson, *Culture at Twilight*, 57–58; Rippley, "Ameliorated Americanization," 221; Mack Walker, "The Old Homeland and the New," in *German Culture in Texas: A Free Earth*, ed. Glen E. Lich and Dona B. Reeves (Boston: Twayne, 1980), 78. Quotes from Matthew Frye Jacobson, *Whiteness of a Different Color: European Immigrants and the Alchemy of Race* (Cambridge: Harvard University Press, 1998), 47; H. Wentworth Eldredge, "Enemy Aliens: New Haven Germans during the World War," in *Studies in the Science of Society: Presented to Albert Galloway Keller in Celebration of His Completion of Thirty Years as Professor of the Science of Society in Yale University*, ed. George Peter Murdock (New Haven, Conn.: Yale University Press, 1937), 202.

19. La Vern J. Rippley with Robert J. Paulson, *German-Bohemians: The Quiet Immigrants* (Northfield, Minn.: St. Olaf College Press, 1995), 203–204; Arlyn John Parish, *Kansas Mennonites during World War I* (Fort Hays, Kan.: Fort Hays Studies, 1968), 20.

20. On prewar opinion of Germany, see Luebke, *Bonds of Loyalty*, 64–66; Peter Novick, *That Noble Dream: The "Objectivity Question" and the American Historical Profession* (New York: Cambridge University Press, 1988), 112; Daniel T. Rodgers, *Atlantic Crossings: Social Politics in a Progressive Age* (Cambridge: Harvard University Press, 1998), 87–89, 141–44, 271–76. Stanhope W. Sprigg, "A Word of Explanation," in Theodore Roosevelt, *Why America Should Join the Allies* (London: C. Arthur Pearson, n.d. [1915]), 8–9, 15; Billy Sunday, quoted in Paul Finkelman, "German Victims and American Oppressors: The Cultural Background and Legacy of *Meyer v. Nebraska*," in *Law and the Great Plains: Essays on the Legal History of the Heartland*, ed. John R. Wunder (Westport, Conn.: Greenwood, 1996), 37; Frederick C. Luebke, "Legal Restrictions on Foreign Languages in the Great Plains States, 1917–1923," in *Languages in Conflict: Linguistic Acculturation on the Great Plains,* ed. Paul Schach (Lincoln: University of Nebraska Press, 1980), 5.

21. Stories of German atrocities in Belgium were widely discredited in the decades after the war but have been more carefully documented in John Horne and Alan Kramer, *German Atrocities, 1914: A History of Denial* (New Haven, Conn.: Yale University Press, 2001). Regardless of the actual record of events in Belgium, on the American home front the stories of German atrocities functioned as lurid and voyeuristic propaganda, even if they included more truths than postwar historians would admit. See Brett Gary, *The Nervous Liberals: Propaganda Anxieties from World War I to the Cold War* (New York: Columbia University Press, 1999), 15–53.

22. Josiah Royce, "The Duties of Americans in the Present War," in *Hope of the Great Community*, 10; "Is Hatred of the German in the Present Crisis a Duty?" *Current Opinion* 65 (December 1918): 384; Horace J. Bridges, "The Duty of Hatred," *Atlantic Monthly* 122 (October 1918): 464–66.

23. Hermann Hagedorn, *Where Do You Stand? An Appeal to Americans of German Origin* (New York: Macmillan, 1918), 1.

24. Johnson, *Culture at Twilight,* 157; Michael J. McNally, *Catholic Parish Life on Florida's West Coast, 1860–1968* (n.p.: Catholic Media Ministries, 1996), 78; Rippley, "Ameliorated Americanization," 224. Frank Perry Olds was particularly virulent in his attacks on German newspapers. For a typical example, see Olds, "Disloyalty of the German-American Press," *Atlantic Monthly* 120 (July 1917): 136–40.

25. American Defense Society, quoted in Finkelman, "German Victims and American Oppressors," 39; Dorothy Weyer Creigh, *Nebraska: A Bicentennial History* (New York: Norton, 1977), 170; Miss Jefferson Bell to Woodrow Wilson, March 11, 1918, in Arthur S. Link et al., eds., *The Papers of Woodrow Wilson,* 69 vols. (Princeton, N.J.: Princeton University Press, 1966–94), vol. 46, p. 604; Carl Wittke, *German-Americans and the World War* (Columbus: Ohio State Archaeological and Historical Society, 1936), 191–92. By contrast, Glen E. Lich claims that of all the singing societies in Texas during the war, not a single one shut down during the war. Lich, *The German Texans* (San Antonio: University of Texas Institute of Texan Cultures, 1981), 149.

26. Wittke, *German-Americans,* 183; "Dr. Muck Resigns, Then Plays Anthem," *New York Times,* November 3, 1917; "Director Muck Taken in East as Enemy Alien," *Chicago Tribune,* March 26, 1918; "Arrest Karl Muck as Enemy Alien," *New York Times,* March 26, 1918. On Muck and wartime German music generally, see Bliss Perry, *Life and Letters of Henry Lee Higginson* (Freeport, N.Y.: Books for Libraries Press, 1972 [1921]), 462–527; Barbara L. Tischler, "One Hundred Percent Americanism and Music in Boston during World War I," *American Music* 4 (Summer 1986): 164–76; J. E. Vacha, "When Wagner Was Verboten: The Campaign against German Music in World War I," *New York History* 64 (April 1983): 171–88. Muck's citizenship claims were ultimately rejected by the Swiss legation in Washington; "Decides Dr. Muck Is German," *Washington Post,* April 25, 1918.

27. Finkelman, "German Victims," 39; Wittke, *German-Americans,* 171.

28. Luebke, "Legal Restrictions," 9–10; Creigh, *Nebraska,* 170; Mark Ellis, "German-Americans in World War I," in *Enemy Images in American History,* ed. Ragnhild Fiebig-von Hase and Ursula Lehmkuhl (Providence, R.I.: Berghahn, 1997), 204 n. 77; Wittke, *German-Americans,* 193; Finkelman, "German Victims," 38–39; Carl R. Weinberg, *Labor, Loyalty, and Rebellion: Southwestern Illinois Coal Miners and World War I* (Carbondale: Southern Illinois University Press, 2005), 112–53.

29. Richard C. Rohrs, *The Germans in Oklahoma* (Norman: University of Oklahoma Press, 1980), 44; Bilger, " 'Oklahoma Vorwärts,' " 253; Luebke, "Legal Restrictions," 9; Office of the Judge Advocate General, *Compilation of War Laws,* § 16.

30. Telegram from Harry W. Walker to Joseph P. Tumulty, July 12, 1917, in Box 10, Papers of Joseph P. Tumulty, Library of Congress Manuscript Division, Washington, D.C. [hereafter LCMD]; Velma Brundage to Secret Service Department, November 27, 1915, Old German File 605 and D. H. Rittenhouse to Attorney General, June 28, 1918, Old German File 574, both on Reel 275, Microfilm M1085, Record Group 65, Records of the Department of Justice, National Archives and Records Administration, College Park, Md.

31. Homer Cummings and Carl McFarland, *Federal Justice: Chapters in the History of Justice and the Federal Executive* (New York: Macmillan, 1937), 416–18, 427; Nagler, *Nationale Minoritäten*, 536–669; Allan Kent Powell, *Splinters of a Nation: German Prisoners of War in Utah* (Salt Lake City: University of Utah Press, 1989), 14; "Eight Taken Here as German Spies," *New York Times*, April 7, 1917; "Escape from Ellis Island," *New York Times*, June 3, 1917.

32. National Committee on Prisons and Prison Labor Committee of Internment of Alien Enemies in the United States, *Plan for the Internment of Aliens of Enemy Nationality in the United States* (New York: n.p., n.d. [1917]), 1. The group publicized its work in a pamphlet that circulated relatively widely during the war. National Committee on Prisons and Prison Labor, *German Subjects within Our Gates* (New York: Division of Intelligence and Publicity of Columbia University, 1917).

33. National Committee, *Plan for the Internment*, 40, 72; Nagler, "Victims of the Home Front," 202; Josephus Daniels diary entry, November 13, 1917, in *Cabinet Diaries*, ed. Cronon, 236. Representative J. Walter Kehoe of Florida introduced legislation that would have required enemy aliens to wear a button with the words "registered alien enemy" on it. Nagler, ibid. By contrast, during World War II, the government could draw on the institutional structures of the New Deal state—a state that knew how to classify citizens, move them around the country, and even house and feed them—experiences that the government did not have in 1917. Jason Scott Smith, "New Deal Policy Works at War: The WPA and Japanese American Internment," *Pacific Historical Review* 72 (February 2003): 63–92.

34. United States Department of Labor, *Reports of the Department of Labor, 1917* (Washington, D.C.: Government Printing Office, 1918), 103–7, 132–37, 148–52; Powell, *Splinters of a Nation*, 14–15.

35. Powell, *Splinters of a Nation*, 24–31.

36. "Camp Pastors–Reports and Correspondence," Box 13, Folder 28, Papers of the National Lutheran Commission for Soldiers' and Sailors' Welfare, ELCA.

37. "Enemy Alien Women Must Register Now," *New York Times*, April 20, 1918; Cummings and McFarland, *Federal Justice*, 427; Thomas Gregory, quoted in H. C. Peterson and Gilbert C. Fite, *Opponents of War, 1917–1918* (Seattle: University of Washington Press, 1968 [1957]), 86; Harries and Harries, *Last Days of Innocence*, 75–76; Edward Harry Hauenstein, *A History of Wayne County in the World War and in the Wars of the Past* (Wooster, Ohio: Wayne County History Co., 1919), 180. A small number of women were interned following Wilson's proclamation. "Women to Be Interned," *New York Times*, July 4, 1918. Sample forms are included in R. Wayne Jennings and Ruth A. Armstrong, comps., *Registration of Axis Aliens in Kansas, January, 1918 thru June, 1918* (Overland Park, Kan.: Kansas Statistical Publications, 1992).

38. Cummings and McFarland, *Federal Justice*, 427; Eldredge, "Enemy Aliens," 204, 210–11; Luebke, *Bonds of Loyalty*, 255–56; Rollin G. Osterweis, *Three Centuries of New Haven, 1638–1938* (New Haven, Conn.: Yale University Press, 1953), 403–404; Scheiber, *Wilson Administration and Civil Liberties*, 14.

39. Field, *Halo over Hoboken*, 62–72; George Long Moller, *The Hoboken of Yesterday* (Hoboken, N.J.: G. L. Moller, 1964), vol. 1, pp. 27–28.

40. H. Brett Melendy, *Walter Francis Dillingham, 1875–1963: Hawaiian Entrepreneur and Statesman* (Lewiston, N.Y.: Edwin Mellen, 1996), 65–75; John S. Whitehead, "Western Progressives, Old South Planters, or Colonial Oppressors: The Enigma of Hawai'i's 'Big Five,' 1898–1940," *Western Historical Quarterly* 30 (Autumn 1999): 307; Ruth Tabrah, *Hawaii: A Bicentennial History* (New York: Norton, 1980), 135.

41. Royce, *Philosophy of Loyalty*, 108; "Hatred of the German," 384.

42. William Borah, quoted in Weinberg, *Labor, Loyalty, and Rebellion*, 137; Thomas W. Gregory to Dr. W. D. Jones, April 28, 1917, in Box 1, Papers of Thomas Watt Gregory, LCMD.

43. "Loyalty and Language," *Century* 92 (September 1916): 792; H. Miles Gordy, "The German Language in Our Schools," *Educational Review* 56 (October 1918): 261.

44. Finkelman, "German Victims," 40; Luebke, "Legal Restrictions," 3; Ohlinger, *German Conspiracy*, 24–25, 63–65; *State* ex rel. *Thayer v. School District*, 99 Neb. 338 (1916).

45. Luebke, "Legal Restrictions," 1, 7–8, 10; "German in Schools Is Prohibited," *Christian Science Monitor*, February 23, 1918; South Dakota State Council of Defense, *Report of South Dakota State Council of Defense* (n.p.: n.d. [1919]), 51.

46. Benjamin Paul Hegi, "'Old Time Good Germans': German-Americans in Cooke County, Texas, during World War I," *Southwestern Historical Quarterly* 109 (October 2005): 244; Bilger, "'Oklahoma Vorwärts,'" 254; Luebke, "Legal Restrictions," 8–9; Rohrs, *Germans in Oklahoma*, 46. A. R. Buechler and R. J. Barr, eds., *History of Hall County, Nebraska* (Lincoln, Neb.: Western Publishing and Engraving, 1920), 449, notes that the language changes there were "voluntarily taken." Policies toward the use of German on the telephone were attempted on a statewide basis in Nebraska and South Dakota; in Hillsboro, Kansas, it was not the local Council of Defense but the telephone company that took the lead, through a policy directive that instructed operators to cut off any phone users using German when the operator deemed it unnecessary. Parish, *Kansas Mennonites*, 52; South Dakota State Council, *Report*, 72, 110–11.

47. Finkelman, "German Victims," 41–42; Hegi, "'Old Time Good Germans,'" 242; Luebke, "Legal Restrictions," 11. For summaries of immediate postwar laws, see Charles Kettleborough, ed., "Legislative Notes and Reviews," *American Political Science Review* 14 (September 1920): 113–14; "Recent Legislation Forbidding Teaching of Foreign Languages in Public Schools," *Minnesota Law Review* 4 (May 1920): 449–51.

48. Bilger, "'Oklahoma Vorwärts,'" 255; Giles R. Hoyt, "Germans," in *Peopling Indiana: The Ethnic Experience*, ed. Robert M. Taylor Jr. and Connie A. McBirney (Indianapolis: Indiana Historical Society, 1996), 171. On Smith-Towner, see Lynn Dumenil, "'The Insatiable Maw of Bureaucracy': Antistatism and Education Reform in the 1920s," *Journal of American History* 77 (September 1990): 499–524; Thomas T. McAvoy, "The Catholic Church in the United States between Two Wars," *Review of Politics* 4 (October 1942): 419; and Frank V. Thompson, *Schooling of the Immigrant* (New York: Harper and Bros., 1920), 292–301.

49. Frederick S. Allen et al., *The University of Colorado, 1876–1976: A Centennial Publication of the University of Colorado* (New York: Harcourt, Brace, Jovanovich,

1976), 81; Finkelman, "German Victims," 42; Luebke, "Legal Restrictions," 6; Rohrs, *Germans in Oklahoma*, 46.

50. "Does the Devil Hate the Tongue of Luther?" *Literary Digest* 63 (October 4, 1919): 34; Bilger, "'Oklahoma Vorwärts,'" 250, 253; Peter A. Speek, *A Stake in the Land* (New York: Harper and Bros., 1921), 161.

51. "Lutherans Clinging to German," *Literary Digest* 61 (June 28, 1919): 33; Alan Graebner, *Uncertain Saints: The Laity in the Lutheran Church—Missouri Synod, 1900–1970* (Westport, Conn.: Greenwood, 1975), 39–41; Nagler, *Nationale Minoritäten*, 518–29; South Dakota Council, *Report*, 72–74; "Language Order Checks Sedition," *Christian Science Monitor*, June 5, 1918. Battles back and forth in South Dakota can be traced in "German Language Order to Stand," *Christian Science Monitor*, September 2, 1918; "Anti-German Rule Change Protested," *Christian Science Monitor*, October 8, 1918; "No Change in Use of German Order," *Christian Science Monitor*, October 17, 1918. For the Nebraska case, see "Order to Drop German Opposed," *Christian Science Monitor*, August 17, 1918.

52. George Schottenhamel, "How Big Bill Thompson Won Control of Chicago," *Journal of the Illinois State Historical Society* 45 (Spring 1952): 30–49; Charles E. Morris, *Progressive Democracy of James M. Cox* (Indianapolis, Ind.: Bobbs-Merrill, 1920), 76–78; R. A. Burchell, "Did the Irish and German Voters Desert the Democrats in 1920? A Tentative Statistical Answer," *Journal of American Studies* 6 (August 1972): 153–64; Rippley and Paulson, *German-Bohemians*, 253; Nelson, *German-American Political Behavior*, 3, 14–17.

53. "Does the Devil," 34; Luebke, "Legal Restrictions," 7–8; Jack W. Rodgers, "The Foreign Language Issue in Nebraska, 1918–1923," *Nebraska History* 39 (March 1958): 7.

54. Thomas O'Brien Hanley, "A Western Democrat's Quarrel with the Language Laws," *Nebraska History* 50 (Summer 1969): 154; Paul I. Johnston, "Freedom of Speech Means Freedom to Teach: The Constitutional Battle in Nebraska, 1919–1923," *Concordia Historical Institute Quarterly* 52 (Fall 1979): 119; Luebke, "Legal Restrictions," 11–13; Arthur F. Mullen, *Western Democrat* (New York: Wilfred Funk, 1940); 182; Rodgers, "Foreign Language Issue," 7–13. For the text of the Siman Act, see Nebraska Laws, 1919, chap. 249.

55. Luebke "Legal Restrictions," 13; Rodgers, "Foreign Language Issue," 14–17; *Nebraska District of Evangelical Lutheran Synod of Missouri v. McKelvie*, 104 Neb. 93 (1919), at 98. Known since 1947 as the Lutheran Church–Missouri Synod, the church was then officially called the Evangelical Lutheran Synod of Missouri, Ohio, and Other States.

56. The key text on *Meyer v. Nebraska* is William G. Ross, *Forging New Freedoms: Nativism, Education, and the Constitution, 1917–1927* (Lincoln: University of Nebraska Press, 1994). See also Finkelman, "German Victims"; Hanley, "Western Democrat's Quarrel"; Johnston, "Freedom of Speech"; Luebke, "Legal Restrictions"; Mullen, *Western Democrat*; and Rodgers, "Foreign Language Issue in Nebraska."

57. *Meyer v. State*, 107 Neb. 657 (1922), at 661, 669.

58. Arthur Mullen, quoted in Hanley, "Western Democrat's Quarrel," 155; *Meyer v. Nebraska*, 262 U.S. 390 (1923), at 400; "Hold Nebraska Law Is Curb on Religion,"

New York Times, February 24, 1923; "Alien Tongue May Be Used in Any School," *New York Times*, June 5, 1923.

59. *Meyer v. Nebraska*, 262 U.S. 390 (1923), at 399. The appeal to property rights explains in part why Justices George Sutherland and Oliver Wendell Holmes dissented, unwilling to imagine that such liberty interests required protection at the expense of police power. Holmes's dissent accompanies the companion case *Bartels v. State of Iowa*, 262 U.S. 404 (1923), at 412.

60. *Meyer v. Nebraska*, 262 U.S. 390 (1922), at 401, 402.

61. Robert Meyer, quoted in Mullen, *Western Democrat*, 218.

62. Finkelman, "German Victims," 33; *Pierce v. Society of Sisters*, 268 U.S. 510 (1925).

63. Morris, *Progressive Democracy of James M. Cox*, 78.

64. Wittke, *German-Americans*, 141–42; Rohrs, *Germans in Oklahoma*, 47; Jacobson, *Whiteness of a Different Color*, 48; Joseph Carruth, "World War I Propaganda and Its Effects in Arkansas," *Arkansas Historical Quarterly* 56 (Winter 1997): 396.

65. Lucretia L. Blankenburg, *The Blankenburgs of Philadelphia* (Chicago: John C. Winston, 1929), 174–75; Rohrs, *Germans in Oklahoma*, 47; Wittke, *German-Americans*, 141–42; Gustav Scholer to Carl L. Schurz, May 23, 1917, Box 2, Gustav Scholer Papers, New York Public Library. In Philadelphia, the North American Civic League for Immigrants—which had few immigrants as members—collected "suspicious literature." Philadelphia War History Committee, *Philadelphia in the World War, 1914–1919* (New York: Wynkoop Hallenbeck Crawford, 1922), 715.

66. Otto H. Kahn, *Right above Race* (New York: Century, 1918), 65; Hagedorn, *Where Do You Stand?* 45, 49; Richard Wightman Fox, *Reinhold Niebuhr, A Biography* (Ithaca, N.Y.: Cornell University Press, 1996 [1985]), 41–61; Reinhold Niebuhr, "The Failure of German-Americanism," *Atlantic Monthly* 118 (July 1916): 13–18; Niebuhr, "Nation's Crime against the Individual," *Atlantic Monthly* 118 (November 1916): 609–14. See also Phyllis Keller, *States of Belonging: German-American Intellectuals and the First World War* (Cambridge: Harvard University Press, 1979).

67. Jon Gjerde, *The Minds of the West: Ethnocultural Evolution in the Rural Middle West, 1830–1917* (Chapel Hill: University of North Carolina Press, 1997), 324; Rohrs, *Germans in Oklahoma*, 46. The irony, of course, is that the Lutheran churches were probably, as G. H. Geberding noted in 1914, "the most polyglot Protestant church in America," including a wide array of European immigrant communities. E. Clifford Nelson, *Lutheranism in North America, 1914–1970* (Minneapolis: Augsburg, 1972), 8.

68. Rippley, "Ameliorated Americanization," 224; McNally, *Catholic Parish Life*, 166; Mary Neth, *Preserving the Family Farm: Women, Community, and the Foundations of Agribusiness in the Midwest, 1900–1940* (Baltimore: Johns Hopkins University Press, 1995), 84; Parish, *Kansas Mennonites*, 53–54.

69. Schmidt, "Rhetoric of Survival," 209–10; Bilger, "'Oklahoma Vorwärts,'" 257–58; Eldredge, "Enemy Aliens," 214. For an example of changing German literary criticism, see *German-American Annals*, vols. 15–17 (1917–1919).

70. Rippley, "Ameliorated Americanization," 224.

71. Ibid., 225; Wittke, *German-Americans*, 171; Rippley, "Gift Cows for Germany," *North Dakota History* 40 (Summer 1973): 4–15; Ellis, "German-Americans in

World War I," 208; Jonathan Zimmerman, "Ethnics against Ethnicity: European Immigrants and Foreign-Language Instruction, 1890–1940," *Journal of American History* 88 (March 2002): 1383–1404; Kazal, *Becoming Old Stock*, 197–260.

72. All misspellings in the quotations from the society are reproduced from the original document. Minutes, May 14, 1918, in Box 1, Volume 1, Papers of the Ladies Sewing Society of the German Orphan Asylum, MC 214, Schlesinger Library, Radcliffe Institute, Harvard University, Cambridge, Mass.

73. Eldredge, "Enemy Aliens," 211 n. 46.

74. Robert K. Murray, *Red Scare: A Study in National Hysteria, 1919–1920* (Minneapolis: University of Minnesota Press, 1955); Polenberg, *Fighting Faiths*, 178–89; Regin Schmidt, *Red Scare: FBI and the Origins of Anticommunism in the United States, 1919–1943* (Copenhagen: Museum Tusculanum Press, 2000); Athan G. Theoharis, *The FBI and American Democracy: A Brief Critical History* (Lawrence: University Press of Kansas, 2004), 14–37; David Williams, "The Bureau of Investigation and Its Critics, 1919–1921: The Origins of Federal Political Surveillance," *Journal of American History* 68 (December 1981): 560–79.

75. Richard Gid Powers, *Secrecy and Power: The Life of J. Edgar Hoover* (New York: Free Press, 1987), 50–54, quote on 53; Athan G. Theoharis and John Stuart Cox, *The Boss: J. Edgar Hoover and the Great American Inquisition* (Philadelphia: Temple University Press, 1988), 48–49.

76. Cummings and McFarland, *Federal Justice*, 429; Jay Robert Nash, *Citizen Hoover: A Critical Study of the Life and Times of J. Edgar Hoover and His FBI* (Chicago: Nelson-Hall, 1972), 18–19; Powers, *Secrecy and Power*, 55; Theoharis and Cox, *The Boss*, 49, 53, 56, 64; "Gregory Out March 4," *Washington Post*, January 13, 1919. The passage in May 1918 of a law requiring "hostile aliens" to obtain passports added another feature to America's surveillance state. See John Torpey, "The Great War and the Birth of the Modern Passport System," in *Documenting Individual Identity: The Development of State Practices in the Modern World*, ed. Jane Caplan and John Torpey (Princeton, N.J.: Princeton University Press, 2001), 256–70, esp. 264.

77. A. Mitchell Palmer, quoted in Nash, *Citizen Hoover*, 22. Theoharis and Cox, *The Boss*, 64; Cummings and McFarland, *Federal Justice*, 429–30. On resistance to the Red Scare, see W. Anthony Gengarelly, *Distinguished Dissenters and Opposition to the 1919–1920 Red Scare* (Lewiston, N.Y.: Edwin Mellen, 1996); Schmidt, *Red Scare*, 300–323.

78. Harlan F. Stone, quoted in Nash, *Citizen Hoover*, 22; Stone to Nicholas Murray Butler, January 21, 1920, in Box 45, Papers of Harlan Fiske Stone, LCMD; Thomas Walsh, quoted in Theoharis and Cox, *The Boss*, 70; National Popular Government League, *To the American People: Report upon the Illegal Practices of the United States Department of Justice* (Washington, D.C.: The League, 1920); *Colyer v. Skeffington*, 265 Fed. 17 (1920). The National Popular Government League included such figures as Felix Frankfurter, Ernst Freund, Roscoe Pound, and its leader, Zechariah Chafee Jr. Hoover, intent on destroying Chafee's initiatives, nearly succeeded in pushing Chafee off the Harvard Law School faculty. Theoharis and Cox, *The Boss*, 64, 68–69.

79. United States Department of Justice, *Annual Report of the Attorney General of the United States, 1919* (Washington, D.C.: Government Printing Office, 1920), 25; Wittke, *German-Americans*, 162.

80. August C. Bolino, *The Ellis Island Source Book* (Washington, D.C.: Kensington Historical, 1985), 31; Frederic Howe, quoted in David M. Brownstone et al., *Island of Hope, Island of Tears* (New York: Rawson, Wade, 1979), 283; United States Senate Committee on the Judiciary, *Brewing and Liquor Interests and German and Bolshevik Propaganda* (Washington, D.C.: Government Printing Office, 1919).

81. The reconstruction of wartime Thurber in this and subsequent paragraphs comes from John S. Spratt Sr., *Thurber, Texas: The Life and Death of a Company Coal Town*, ed. Harwood P. Hinton (Austin: University of Texas Press, 1986). Spratt composed this memoir sporadically between the mid-1960s and his death in 1976.

82. Ibid., 73.

83. Ibid.

Conclusion

1. Edith Wharton to Miss Bartol, November 20, 1918, in Papers of Edith Wharton, MSS 6909, Clifton Waller Barrett Library of American Literature, Special Collections, University of Virginia Library, Charlottesville, Va.; William M. Morgan, *Questionable Charity: Gender, Humanitarianism, and Complicity in U.S. Literary Realism* (Hanover, N.H.: University Press of New England, 2004), 146–65; Alan Price, *The End of the Age of Innocence: Edith Wharton and the First World War* (New York: St. Martin's, 1996), 164; Carrie Chapman Catt to Maud Park Wood, November 12, 1918, Papers of Carrie Chapman Catt, Box 4, Sophia Smith Collection, Smith College, Northampton, Mass.

2. Meirion Harries and Susie Harries, *The Last Days of Innocence: America at War, 1917–1918* (New York: Vintage, 1997), 421; "Commercial Markets Closed," *Boston Globe*, November 12, 1918; "Savannah Has Early Start in Celebration," *Atlanta Constitution*, November 12, 1918; Alice O'Brien, quoted in Eileen Manning Michels, "Alice O'Brien: Volunteer and Philanthropist," in *Women of Minnesota: Selected Biographical Essays*, rev. ed., ed. Barbara Stuhler and Gretchen Kreuter (St. Paul: Minnesota Historical Society Press, 1998), 143–44.

3. Robert P. Swierenga, "The Low Countries," in *Peopling Indiana: The Ethnic Experience*, ed. Robert M. Taylor Jr. and Connie A. McBirney (Indianapolis: Indiana Historical Society, 1996), 363; "The War Ends, November 11, 1918," in Scrapbook, Plainfield Historical Society, Box 1, Record Group 112, Records of the Plainfield Historical Society, Connecticut State Archives, Hartford, Conn. At Harvard, "effigies of the Kaiser were treated most disrespectfully." "Harvard Goes Wild," *Boston Globe*, November 12, 1918.

4. "How Peace Struck Man in the Street," *New York Times*, November 12, 1918.

5. James C. Juhnke, "Mob Violence and Kansas Mennonites in 1918," *Kansas Historical Quarterly* 43 (Autumn 1977): 344–45; Juhnke, "John Schrag Espionage Case," *Mennonite Life* 22 (July 1967): 121–22; Gregory J. Stucky, "Fighting against War: The Mennonite *Vorwaerts* from 1914 to 1919," *Kansas Historical Quarterly* 38 (Summer 1972): 183–84.

6. Newell Hart, ed., *Hometown Album: A Pictorial History of Franklin County, Idaho— Horse and Buggy Days and Early Auto Era* (Preston, Idaho: Cache Valley Newsletter, 1986 [1973]), item 627.

7. Helen Tufts Bailie Diary, November 7, 1918 entry, Papers of Helen Tufts Bailie, Sophia Smith Collection.

8. "Full Text of President Wilson's Address to the Houses of Congress in Joint Session," *New York Times*, May 28, 1918.

9. Quoted in W. H. Lightfoot, ed. and comp., *Our Heroes in Our Defense: Labette County, Kansas* (Parsons, Kan.: Commercial, 1921), 55.

10. "The May Day Rioting," *Nation* 108 (May 10, 1919): 726; Tom Copeland, *The Centralia Tragedy of 1919: Elmer Smith and the Wobblies* (Seattle: University of Washington Press, 1993); and Melvyn Dubofsky, *We Shall Be All: A History of the Industrial Workers of the World*, 2nd ed. (Urbana: University of Illinois Press, 1988), 455–56.

11. Franklin D'Olier, quoted in William Pencak, *For God and Country: The American Legion, 1919–1941* (Boston: Northeastern University Press, 1989), 213. For more on the American Legion, vigilantism, and postwar political culture, see Pencak, *For God and Country*, 144–69; Lynn Dumenil, *The Modern Temper: American Culture and Society in the 1920s* (New York: Hill and Wang, 1994), 40–55; Christopher Nehls, "A Grand and Glorious Feeling: The American Legion and American Nationalism between the Two World Wars" (Ph.D. dissertation, University of Virginia, 2007); Thomas A. Rumer, *The American Legion: An Official History, 1919–1989* (New York: M. Evans, 1990); and Theda Skocpol et al., "Patriotic Partnerships: Why Great Wars Nourished American Civic Voluntarism," in *Shaped by War and Trade: International Influences on American Political Development*, ed. Ira Katznelson and Martin Shefter (Princeton, N.J.: Princeton University Press, 2002), 154–69.

12. Littell McClung, "Ku Klux Klan again in the South," *New York Times*, September 1, 1918; John Hope Franklin and Alfred A. Moss Jr., *From Slavery to Freedom: A History of African Americans*, 8th ed. (Boston: McGraw-Hill, 2000), 384. For the rise of the Second Klan, see David Chalmers, *Hooded Americanism: The History of the Ku Klux Klan* (Chicago: Quadrangle, 1968); Kathleen M. Blee, *Women of the Klan: Racism and Gender in the 1920s* (Berkeley: University of California Press, 1991); Nancy MacLean, *Behind the Mask of Chivalry: The Making of the Second Ku Klux Klan* (New York: Oxford University Press, 1994); and Leonard J. Moore, *Citizen Klansmen: The Ku Klux Klan in Indiana, 1921–1928* (Chapel Hill: University of North Carolina Press, 1991).

13. Horace M. Kallen, *Culture and Democracy in the United States* (New Brunswick, N.J.: Transaction, 1998 [1924]), 4–5; Frank Tannenbaum, *Darker Phases of the South* (New York: G. P. Putnam's Sons, 1924), 13; John Moffatt Mecklin, *The Ku Klux Klan: A Study of the American Mind* (New York: Harcourt, Brace, 1924), 120–25; Mecklin, *My Quest for Freedom* (New York: Charles Scribner's Sons, 1945), 209–12. Other early studies of the Klan that identified it as an organization with roots in wartime politics include Frederick Lewis Allen, *Only Yesterday: An Informal History of the Nineteen-Twenties* (New York: Harper and Bros., 1931), 65–69; Stanley Frost, *The Challenge of the Klan* (Indianapolis, Ind.: Bobbs-Merrill, 1924); and Henry P. Fry, *The Modern Ku Klux Klan* (Boston: Small, Maynard, 1922). On the relationship between voluntary associations and Klan recruitment, see Charles O. Jackson, "William J. Simmons: A Career in Ku Kluxism," *Georgia Historical Quarterly* 50

(December 1966): 351–65, and Leonard J. Moore, "Historical Interpretations of the 1920s Klan: The Traditional View and Recent Revisions," in *The Invisible Empire in the West: Toward a New Historical Appraisal of the Ku Klux Klan of the 1920s*, ed. Shawn Lay (Urbana: University of Illinois Press, 1992), 30.

14. For a brief introduction to the contours of the debate over the rights revolution, see Benjamin R. Barber, *Strong Democracy: Participatory Politics for a New Age*, 20th anniversary ed. (Berkeley: University of California Press, 2003); Robert N. Bellah et al., *Habits of the Heart: Individualism and Commitment in American Life* (Berkeley: University of California Press, 1985); Mary Ann Glendon, *Rights Talk: The Impoverishment of Political Discourse* (New York: Free Press, 1991); Jedediah Purdy, *For Common Things: Irony, Trust, and Commitment in America Today* (New York: Knopf, 1999); Michael J. Sandel, *Democracy's Discontent: America in Search of a Public Philosophy* (Cambridge: Harvard University Press, 1996); and Michael Walzer, *Obligations: Essays on Disobedience, War, and Citizenship* (Cambridge: Harvard University Press, 1970).

Bibliography

Manuscript Collections

Special Collections Library, University of Arizona, Tucson, Ariz.
    Bisbee Deportation of 1917 Collection.
Connecticut State Archives, Connecticut State Library, Hartford, Conn.
    Record Group 5. Governor Marcus Holcomb Papers.
    Record Group 30. Records of the Connecticut Council of Defense.
    Record Group 107. Records of the Hartford Woman's Club.
    Record Group 112. Records of the Plainfield Historical Society.
General Federation of Women's Clubs Archives, Washington, D.C.
    Record Group 2. Presidents' Papers.
    Record Group 3. Convention Records.
    Record Group 7. Program Records.
    Record Group 8. National Club Records.
    Record Group 13. Local Club Records.
    Record Group 18. Resolutions and Legislations Records.
Manuscript Division, Library of Congress, Washington, D.C.
    Papers of Newton D. Baker.
    Papers of Edward Bok.
    Papers of William E. Borah.
    Papers of Albert Sidney Burleson.
    Papers of Carrie Chapman Catt.
    Papers of William Rufus Day.
    Papers of Thomas Watt Gregory.
    Papers of Oliver Wendell Holmes, Jr.
    Papers of Robert M. La Follette, Sr.
    Papers of Robert McNutt McElroy.

Papers of the National Association for the Advancement of Colored People.
Papers of the National Association for Universal Military Training.
Papers of Louis F. Post.
Papers of A. Philip Randolph.
Papers of Elihu Root.
Papers of Harlan Fiske Stone.
Papers of Moorfield Storey.
Papers of Mary Church Terrell.
Papers of Joseph P. Tumulty.
Papers of Willis P. Van Devanter.
Papers of Thomas Walsh.
Papers of John Sharp Williams.
Papers of Edith Bolling Wilson.
Papers of Woodrow Wilson.
Papers of Owen Wister.
Papers of Leonard Wood.
Rare Books Division, Library of Congress, Washington, D.C.
Broadside Collection.
National Archives and Records Administration, Washington, D.C.
Record Group 4. Records of the United States Food Administration.
Record Group 28. Records of the Post Office Department.
Record Group 60. General Records of the Department of Justice.
Record Group 62. Records of the Council of National Defense.
Record Group 65. Records of the Federal Bureau of Investigation.
Record Group 163. Records of the Selective Service System (World War I).
Chicago Historical Society, Chicago, Ill.
Papers of Emily Frankenstein.
Papers of Woodrow Wilson.
Archives of the Evangelical Lutheran Church in America, Elk Grove Village, Ill.
Papers of the National Lutheran Commission for Soldiers' and Sailors' Welfare.
Schlesinger Library, Radcliffe Institute, Harvard University, Cambridge, Mass.
Papers of Fannie Fern Andrews.
Papers of Erin-Go-Bragh.
Papers of the Fragment Society.
Papers of Alice Hamilton.
Papers of the Ladies Sewing Society of the German Orphan Asylum.
Papers of the Mothers' Discussion Club.
Papers of the Mothers' Study Club.
Papers of the United States Council of National Defense, Women's Committee.
Smith College Archives, Smith College, Northampton, Mass.
Distinguished Visitors Files.
Office of the President: William Allan Neilson Presidential Papers.
War Service Files.
Sophia Smith Collection, Smith College, Northampton, Mass.
Papers of Jane Addams.

Papers of Florence Ellinwood Allen.
American Association of University Women, Worcester Branch Records.
Papers of Helen Tufts Bailie.
Papers of Ella Reeve Bloor.
Bodman Family Papers.
Papers of Carrie Chapman Catt.
Consumers' League of Kentucky Records.
Papers of Madeleine Zabriskie Doty.
Papers of Ethel Eyre Dreier.
Dunham Family Papers.
Papers of Harriet Chalmers Ford.
Papers of Emma Goldman.
International Organizations Files.
Papers of Alma Lutz.
National Society of New England Women Records.
New England Hospital Records.
Organizations (Small Files).
Papers of Vida Dutton Scudder.
Papers of Sorosis.
Papers of Ida Minerva Tarbell.
Temperance Collection.
Papers of Florence Guertin Tuttle.
Women's Clubs Collection.
YWCA of the USA National Board Records.
Bentley Historical Library, University of Michigan, Ann Arbor, Mich.
Papers of Harold Studley Gray.
Papers of the Home Guard of Ironwood.
Papers of Rudolf Muenzinger.
Carl Ernest Schmidt Scrapbooks.
New York State Archives, Albany, N.Y.
New York State Council of Defense Records.
Rare Book and Manuscript Library, Columbia University, New York, N.Y.
Harlan Fiske Stone Collection.
New York Municipal Archives and Record Center, New York, N.Y.
Mayor John Hylan Papers.
Manuscripts and Archives Division, New York Public Library, New York, N.Y.
Papers of Newton D. Baker.
Papers of Gustav Scholer.
World War I Collection.
Special Collections Research Center, Syracuse University, Syracuse, N.Y.
Emmanuel Evangelical United Brethren Church, Binghamton, N.Y., Records.
Goodwill Congregational Church, Syracuse, N.Y., Records.
Grace Episcopal Church, Syracuse, N.Y., Records.
Methodist Episcopal Church, Groton, N.Y., Records.
Oak Street Methodist Church, Binghamton, N.Y., Records.

Southern Historical Collection, Wilson Library, University of North Carolina, Chapel Hill, N.C.
    Papers of Claude Kitchin.
South Caroliniana Library, University of South Carolina, Columbia, S.C.
    Papers of John Kinard Aull.
    Papers of W. P. Beard.
    Coleman Blease Scrapbook.
    Papers of David R. Coker.
    Horton Family Papers.
    Papers of W. H. Mears.
    Papers of Mendel Lafayette Smith.
    Papers of A. D. Williams.
Special Collections, University of Virginia Library, Charlottesville, Va.
    Papers of Kate Flanagan Coles.
    Papers of Carter Glass.
    Papers of the University of Virginia Student Army Training Corps.
    Papers of Edith Wharton.
    Papers of the Women's Christian Temperance Union of Virginia.

Published Primary Sources

Included in this list are books and articles published during the World War I era, as well as memoirs, oral histories, local wartime service records, and edited document collections published after the war. General local histories and club histories are listed with secondary sources.

Addams, Jane. *Peace and Bread in Time of War*. Urbana: University of Illinois Press, 2002 [1922].
———. *The Second Twenty Years at Hull-House*. New York: Macmillan, 1930.
Additon, Henrietta S. "Work among Delinquent Women and Girls." *Annals of the American Academy of Political and Social Science* 79 (September 1918): 152–60.
Aldis, Mary. "For the Homemaker: Housekeeping in War Time." *Journal of Home Economics* 10 (February 1918): 73–79.
"Aliens—Naturalization—'Conscientious Objector' Denied Citizenship." *Michigan Law Review* 22 (December 1923): 152–53.
American Civil Liberties Union. *American Civil Liberties Union Archives: The Roger Baldwin Years, 1917–1950*, microfilm ed., 293 reels. Wilmington, Del.: Scholarly Resources, 1996.
"The American Soldier's Uniform." *Review of Reviews* 64 (November 1921): 542–43.
Anderson, George J. "Making the Camps Safe for the Army." *Annals of the American Academy of Political and Social Science* 79 (September 1918): 143–51.
"Another Menace to the Press." *Nation* 104 (February 22, 1917): 205–6.
Baldwin, Roger Nash. "The Faith of a Heretic." *Nation* 107 (November 9, 1918): 549.
Blair, Emily Newell. *Bridging Two Eras: The Autobiography of Emily Newell Blair, 1877–1951*, ed. Virginia Jeans Laas. Columbia: University of Missouri Press, 1999.
Blatch, Harriot Stanton, and Alma Lutz. *Challenging Years: The Memoirs of Harriot Stanton Blatch*. New York: G. P. Putnam's Sons, 1940.

Blaustein, Albert P., and Robert L. Zangrando, eds. *Civil Rights and the American Negro: A Documentary History*. New York: Trident, 1968.

Bourne, Randolph S. *War and the Intellectuals: Collected Essays, 1915–1919*, ed. Carl Resek. New York: Harper Torchbooks, 1964.

Brewer, David J. *American Citizenship*. New York: Charles Scribner's Sons, 1907.

Bridges, Horace J. "The Duty of Hatred." *Atlantic Monthly* 122 (October 1918): 464–66.

Brown, Lewis P. "The Jew Is Not a Slacker." *North American Review* 207 (June 1918): 857–62.

Bruere, Robert W. "Copper Camp Patriotism." *Nation* 106 (February 21, 1918): 202–3.

——. "Copper Camp Patriotism: An Interpretation." *Nation* 106 (February 28, 1918): 235–36.

Burleson, Albert S. *Address at a Conference of Representatives of Business Organizations and the Postal Service at Washington, D.C., April 1, 1919*. Washington, D.C.: Government Printing Office, 1919.

"The Censorship Muddle." *Nation* 104 (May 31, 1917): 648–49.

Chafee, Zechariah, Jr. "Freedom of Speech." *New Republic* 17 (November 16, 1918): 66–69.

Chambers, John Whiteclay, II, ed. *Draftees or Volunteers? A Documentary History of the Debate over Military Conscription in the United States, 1787–1973*. New York: Garland, 1975.

Chase, Joseph Cummings. "Corporal York, General Pershing, and Others." *World's Work* 37 (April 1919): 636–54.

"Civil Liberty Dead." *Nation* 107 (September 14, 1918): 282.

Clarke, Ida Clyde. *American Women and the World War*. New York: D. Appleton, 1918.

"Congress Fights Censorship." *Independent* 90 (May 12, 1917): 275–76.

Connecticut Home Guard. *Register of Officers*. [Hartford]: Connecticut Military Emergency Board, 1917.

——. *Regulations for the Connecticut Home Guard*. Hartford: Connecticut Military Emergency Board, 1917.

Connecticut Military Emergency Board. *Report to the Governor: November 1, 1918*. Hartford: Connecticut Military Emergency Board, 1918.

"Connecticut's Military Census." *Review of Reviews* 55 (May 1917): 533–35.

"Conscience Plus Red Hair Are Bad for Germans." *Literary Digest* 61 (June 14, 1919): 42–48.

"The Conscientious Objector." *Biblical World* 50 (December 1917): 329.

"Court Martial 1918: Pvt. Ura V. Aschliman (420382)." *Mennonite Life* 31 (September 1976): 18–21.

Creel, George. *Rebel at Large: Recollections of Fifty Crowded Years*. New York: G. P. Putnam's Sons, 1947.

——. "Unite and Win." *Independent* 94 (April 6, 1918): 5–6.

Crowder, Enoch H. *Second Report of the Provost Marshal General to the Secretary of War on the Operations of the Selective Service System to December 20, 1918*. Washington, D.C.: Government Printing Office, 1919.

——. *The Spirit of Selective Service*. New York: Century, 1920.

Dana, John Cotton. "The Librarian as Censor." *Library Journal* 44 (November 1919): 728.

——. "Public Libraries as Censors." *Bookman* 49 (April 1919): 147–52.

Daniels, Josephus. *The Cabinet Diaries of Josephus Daniels, 1913–1921*, ed. E. David Cronon. Lincoln: University of Nebraska Press, 1963.

Dewey, John. *The Middle Works, 1899–1924*, ed. Jo Ann Boydston. Carbondale: Southern Illinois University Press, 1980.

——. *The Public and Its Problems*. New York: Henry Holt, 1927.

Dietzler, Mary Macey. *Detention Houses and Reformatories as Protective Social Agencies in the Campaign of the United States against Venereal Diseases*. Washington, D.C.: Government Printing Office, 1922.

"Does the Devil Hate the Tongue of Luther?" *Literary Digest* 63 (October 4, 1919): 34.

[Du Bois, W. E. B.] "Close Ranks." *Crisis* 16 (July 1918): 111.

Dunbar-Nelson, Alice. "Negro Women in War Work." In *The American Negro in the World War*, ed. Emmett J. Scott. Chicago: Homewood, 1919.

Eastman, Max. "The Post Office Censorship." *Masses* 9 (September 1917): 24.

"Editorial." *Smith College Monthly* 24 (June 1917): 436.

"Editorial: Her Chance for Service." *Ladies' Home Journal* 34 (June 1917): 7.

"Editorial: The Woman 'Slacker.' " *Ladies' Home Journal* 34 (July 1917): 7.

Egan, Maurice Francis. *The Knights of Columbus in Peace and War*. New Haven, Conn.: Knights of Columbus, 1920.

"Eyewitness Accounts." *Mennonite Life* 30 (September 1975): 19–25.

Faires, Clifford C. "I.W.W. Patriotism in Globe." *Nation* 106 (March 21, 1918): 319–20.

Falconer, Martha P. "The Segregation of Delinquent Women and Girls as a War Problem." *Annals of the American Academy of Political and Social Science* 79 (September 1918): 160–66.

Field, John Perkins. *Halo over Hoboken: The Memoirs of John Perkins Field as Told to John Leroy Bailey*. New York: Exposition, 1955.

Flagg, James Montgomery. *Roses and Buckshot*. New York: G. P. Putnam's Sons, n.d. [1946].

Follett, Mary Parker. *The New State: Group Organization the Solution of Popular Government*. University Park: Pennsylvania State University Press, 1998 [1918].

Fosdick, Raymond B. *Chronicle of a Generation: An Autobiography*. New York: Harper and Bros., 1958.

"Free Speech." *Outlook* 117 (October 17, 1917): 238–39.

"Free Speech and Peaceable Assembly." *Survey* 38 (May 12, 1917): 144–45.

Freund, Ernst. "The Debs Case and Freedom of Speech." *New Republic* 19 (May 3, 1919): 13–15.

Frost, Stanley. *The Challenge of the Klan*. Indianapolis, Ind.: Bobbs-Merrill, 1924.

Fry, Henry P. *The Modern Ku Klux Klan*. Boston: Small, Maynard, 1922.

Gallagher, Robert S. " 'I Was Arrested, of Course....' " *American Heritage* 25 (February 1974): 16–24, 92–94.

Gordy, H. Miles. "The German Language in Our Schools." *Educational Review* 56 (October 1918): 257–63.

"Government Preparations for a Big Round-Up of Draft Dodgers." *Literary Digest* 65 (June 26, 1920): 58–59.

Green, Thomas Hill. *Lectures on the Principles of Political Obligation*. London: Longmans Green, 1917 [1895].

Gregory, T. W. *Reconstruction and the Ku Klux Klan: A Paper Read before the Arkansas and Texas Bar Associations, July 10, 1906.* Austin, Tex.: n.p. [1906].

Grosser, Philip. *Uncle Sam's Devil's Island: Experiences of a Conscientious Objector in America during the World War.* Boston: Excelsior, 1933.

Gulick, Luther H. "Legal Advice for Selectives." *Annals of the American Academy of Political and Social Science* 79 (September 1918): 235–38.

Haessler, Carl. *Statement by Carl Haessler.* Milwaukee, Wis.: Milwaukee Committee on Amnesty for Political Prisoners, 1919.

Hagedorn, Hermann. *Where Do You Stand? An Appeal to Americans of German Origin.* New York: Macmillan, 1918.

Harper, Ida Husted, ed. *The History of Woman Suffrage.* New York: National American Woman Suffrage Association, 1922.

Hauenstein, Edward Harry. *A History of Wayne County in the World War and in the Wars of the Past.* Wooster, Ohio: Wayne County History Co., 1919.

Haynes, George E. "What Negroes Think of the Race Riots." *Public* 22 (August 9, 1919): 848–49.

Herreid, Charles N. "The Federal Food Administration in South Dakota during the World War." *South Dakota Historical Collections* 10 (1920): 295–314.

Hofstadter, Richard, and Michael Wallace, comps. *American Violence: A Documentary History.* New York: Knopf, 1970.

Holcomb, Marcus H. "Connecticut in the Van." *Review of Reviews* 57 (May 1918): 520–21.

Hoover, Herbert. *American Individualism.* Garden City, N.Y.: Doubleday, Page, 1922.

———. *The Memoirs of Herbert Hoover: Years of Adventure, 1874–1920.* New York: Macmillan, 1951.

Hough, Emerson. *The Web: The Authorized History of the American Protective League.* Chicago: Reilly and Lee, 1919.

"The Illness of the Liberty Bell." *Literary Digest* 50 (March 13, 1915): 542–43.

"Is Hatred of the German in the Present Crisis a Duty?" *Current Opinion* 65 (December 1918): 383–84.

Jennings, R. Wayne, and Ruth A. Armstrong, comps. *Registration of Axis Aliens in Kansas, January, 1918 thru June, 1918.* Overland Park, Kan.: Kansas Statistical Publications, 1992.

Johnson, James Weldon. *Along This Way: The Autobiography of James Weldon Johnson.* New York: Viking, 1933.

Jungmann, A. M. "What Did Alvin C. York Do?" *Ladies' Home Journal* 36 (October 1919): 64.

Kahn, Otto H. *Right above Race.* New York: Century, 1918.

Kallen, Horace M. *Culture and Democracy in the United States.* New Brunswick, N.J.: Transaction, 1998 [1924].

Keating, Edward. *The Gentleman from Colorado: A Memoir.* Denver: Sage, 1964.

Kellogg, Walter Guest. *The Conscientious Objector.* New York: Boni and Liveright, 1919.

Keppel, Frederick Paul. *Some War-Time Lessons.* New York: Columbia University Press, 1920.

Kettleborough, Charles, ed. "Legislative Notes and Reviews." *American Political Science Review* 14 (September 1920): 113–14.

"The Ladies' Auxiliary." *Masses* 9 (July 1917): 29.

Lamar, William H. "The Government's Attitude toward the Press." *Forum* 59 (February 1918): 129–40.

Lane, Winthrop D. *Uncle Sam: Jailer: A Study of the Conditions of Federal Prisoners in Kansas Jails*. New York: National Civil Liberties Bureau, n.d. [1919].

———. "Who Are the Conscientious Objectors?" *New Republic* 22 (April 14, 1920): 215–17.

Lash, Joseph P. *From the Diaries of Felix Frankfurter: With a Biographical Essay and Notes*. New York: Norton, 1975.

Lawrence, David. *The True Story of Woodrow Wilson*. New York: George H. Doran, 1924.

"Liberty Bell Still Unmended." *Literary Digest* 66 (September 11, 1920): 136–38.

Lightfoot, W. H., ed. and comp. *Our Heroes in Our Defense: Labette County, Kansas*. Parsons, Kan.: Commercial, 1921.

Link, Arthur S., et al., eds. *The Papers of Woodrow Wilson*. 69 vols. Princeton, N.J.: Princeton University Press, 1966–94.

Linkugel, Wil A., and Martha Solomon, eds. *Anna Howard Shaw: Suffrage Orator and Social Reformer*. New York: Greenwood, 1991.

Lippmann, Walter. *Liberty and the News*. New York: Harcourt, Brace and Howe, 1920.

———. *The Phantom Public*. New York: Harcourt, Brace, 1925.

"Loyalty and Language." *Century* 92 (September 1916): 792.

Lunde, Erling H. *Defense of Erling H. Lunde, Conscientious Objector to War*. Chicago: American Industrial, n.d.

"Lutherans Clinging to German." *Literary Digest* 61 (June 28, 1919): 33.

Lynd, Staughton, ed. *Nonviolence in America: A Documentary History*. Indianapolis, Ind.: Bobbs-Merrill, 1966.

MacKenzie, Norman, and Jeanne MacKenzie, eds. *The Diary of Beatrice Webb*. London: Virago, 1984.

Malone, Dudley Field. *Unaccustomed as I Am: Miscellaneous Speeches*. New York: J. J. Little and Ives, 1929.

Martin, Everett Dean. *The Mob Mind vs. Civil Liberty*. New York: American Civil Liberties Union, 1920.

Martinson, Henry R. "Some Memoirs of a Nonpartisan League Organizer." *North Dakota History* 42 (Spring 1975): 18–21.

Maryland War Records Commission. *Maryland in the World War, 1917–1919: Military and Naval Service Records*. Baltimore: Maryland War Records Commission, 1933.

Matson, Molly, ed. *An Independent Woman: The Autobiography of Edith Guerrier*. Amherst: University of Massachusetts Press, 1992.

"The May Day Rioting." *Nation* 108 (May 10, 1919): 726.

May, Mark A. "The Psychological Examination of Conscientious Objectors." *American Journal of Psychology* 31 (April 1920): 152–65.

Mecklin, John Moffatt. *The Ku Klux Klan: A Study of the American Mind*. New York: Harcourt, Brace, 1924.

———. *My Quest for Freedom*. New York: Charles Scribner's Sons, 1945.

Miner, Maude E. *Slavery of Prostitution: A Plea for Emancipation*. New York: Macmillan, 1916.

"Mob Violence." *Public* 22 (May 10, 1919): 481–82.

Mock, Melanie Springer. *Writing Peace: The Unheard Voices of Great War Mennonite Objectors.* Scottdale, Pa.: Herald, 2003.

Moore, Lewis B. *How the Colored Race Can Help in the Problems Issuing from the War,* 2nd ed. New York: National Security League, 1919.

Morehouse, George. "Kansas as a State of Extremes and Its Attitude during the World War." *Collections of the Kansas State Historical Society* 15 (1923): 15–28.

Morris, Charles E. *Progressive Democracy of James M. Cox.* Indianapolis, Ind.: Bobbs-Merrill, 1920.

Mullen, Arthur F. *Western Democrat.* New York: Wilfred Funk, 1940.

National Association for the Advancement of Colored People. *Thirty Years of Lynching in the United States, 1889–1918.* New York: NAACP, 1919.

National Civil Liberties Bureau. *War-Time Prosecutions and Mob Violence.* New York: NCLB, 1919.

National Committee on Prisons and Prison Labor. *German Subjects within Our Gates.* New York: Division of Intelligence and Publicity of Columbia University, 1917.

National Committee on Prisons and Prison Labor Committee of Internment of Alien Enemies in the United States. *Plan for the Internment of Aliens of Enemy Nationality in the United States.* New York: n.p., n.d. [1917].

National Jewish Welfare Board. *Final Report of War Emergency Activities.* New York: National Jewish Welfare Board, 1920.

National League for Woman's Service. *Annual Report for the Year 1918 with a Summary of the Year 1917.* New York: National League for Woman's Service, n.d. [1919].

National Popular Government League. *To the American People: Report upon the Illegal Practices of the United States Department of Justice.* Washington, D.C.: The League, 1920.

"The Negro and the Red Cross." *Crisis* 16 (August 1918): 167.

Nelles, Walter. "In the Wake of the Espionage Act." *Nation* 111 (December 15, 1920): 684–86.

Nevins, Allan. "Crowds and Crowd-Psychology." *Dial* 60 (May 11, 1916): 465–66.

Niebuhr, Reinhold. "The Failure of German-Americanism." *Atlantic Monthly* 118 (July 1916): 13–18.

——. "The Nation's Crime against the Individual." *Atlantic Monthly* 118 (November 1916): 609–14.

"Now for the Draft-Dodgers and Deserters." *Literary Digest* 65 (April 3, 1920): 69–70.

Office of the Judge Advocate General of the Army. *Compilation of War Laws of the Various States and Insular Possessions.* Washington, D.C.: Government Printing Office, 1919.

Ohlinger, Gustavus. *The German Conspiracy in American Education.* New York: George H. Doran, 1919.

Olds, Frank Perry. "Disloyalty of the German-American Press." *Atlantic Monthly* 120 (July 1917): 136–40.

"Omaha." *Literary Digest* 63 (October 11, 1919): 16.

O'Sullivan, John, and Alan M. Meckler, eds. *The Draft and Its Enemies: A Documentary History.* Urbana: University of Illinois Press, 1974.

"Our Ferocious Sentences." *Nation* 107 (November 2, 1918): 504.

Panunzio, Constantine M. *The Deportation Cases of 1919–1920.* New York: Federal Council of the Churches of Christ in America, 1921.

Philadelphia War History Committee. *Philadelphia in the World War, 1914–1919.* New York: Wynkoop Hallenbeck Crawford, 1922.

Pollock, Ivan L. *The Food Administration in Iowa.* Iowa City: State Historical Society of Iowa, 1923.

Porter, Katherine Anne. *Pale Horse, Pale Rider.* New York: New American Library, 1962 [1939].

"Racial Tension and Race Riots." *Outlook* 122 (August 6, 1919): 532–34.

"The Real Causes of Two Race Riots." *Crisis* 19 (December 1919): 56–62.

"Recent Legislation Forbidding Teaching of Foreign Languages in Public Schools." *Minnesota Law Review* 4 (May 1920): 449–51.

Roosevelt, Theodore. *Why America Should Join the Allies.* London: C. Arthur Pearson, n.d. [1915].

Royce, Josiah. *The Duties of Americans in the Present War: Address Delivered at Tremont Temple, Sunday, January 30, 1916.* Boston: Citizens' League for America and the Allies, 1916.

———. *The Hope of the Great Community.* Freeport, N.Y.: Books for Libraries Press, 1967 [1916].

———. *The Philosophy of Loyalty.* Nashville: Vanderbilt University Press, 1995 [1908].

Ruutz-Rees, Caroline. "The Mobilization of American Women." *Yale Review* 7 (July 1918): 801–18.

Scarborough, W. S. "Race Riots and Their Remedy." *Independent* 99 (August 16, 1919): 223.

Schlissel, Lillian, ed. *Conscience in America: A Documentary History of Conscientious Objection in America, 1757–1967.* New York: E. P. Dutton, 1968.

Scott, James Brown. "The Amendment of the Naturalization and Citizenship Acts with Respect to Military Service." *American Journal of International Law* 12 (July 1918): 613–19.

"Shall We Mend the Liberty Bell?" *Literary Digest* 65 (June 26, 1920): 29–30.

Sheik, J. "Autocracy in Arizona." *Public* 21 (February 16, 1918): 216–17.

Simkhovitch, Mary Kingsbury. *Neighborhood: My Story of Greenwich House.* New York: Norton, 1938.

Soule, George. "Law and Necessity in Bisbee." *Nation* 113 (August 31, 1921): 225–27.

South Dakota State Council of Defense. *Report of South Dakota State Council of Defense.* N.p.: n.d. [1919].

[Sparks, Anna Davenport.] "Editor's Table." *Smith College Monthly* 24 (May 1917): 381.

Speek, Peter A. *A Stake in the Land.* New York: Harper and Bros., 1921.

Stephens, Lester, ed. "A Righteous Aim: Emma LeConte Furman's 1918 Diary." *Georgia Historical Quarterly* 62 (Fall 1978): 213–24.

Stevens, Doris. *Jailed for Freedom.* New York: Boni and Liveright, 1920.

Stone, Harlan F. "The Conscientious Objector." *Columbia University Quarterly* 21 (October 1919): 253–72.

Storey, Moorfield. *Obedience to the Law: An Address at the Opening of Petigru College in Columbia, South Carolina.* Boston: Geo. H. Ellis, 1919.

"The Story of the Branches for 1918." *Crisis* 17 (April 1919): 283.

Strong, George V. "The Administration of Military Justice at the United States Disciplinary Barracks, Fort Leavenworth, Kansas." *Journal of the American Institute of Criminal Law and Criminology* 8 (September 1917): 420–27.

"Suffrage and Sedition." *Masses* 9 (August 1917): 42.

Sweeney, Charles P. "Bigotry in the South: Anti-Catholic Prejudice." *Nation* 111 (November 24, 1920): 585–86.

Sweeney, W. Allison. *History of the American Negro in the Great World War.* New York: Johnson Reprint, 1970 [1919].

Taft, Henry W. *Occasional Papers and Addresses of an American Lawyer.* New York: Macmillan, 1920.

Taft, William Howard. "The Crisis." *Yale Review* 6 (April 1917): 449–58.

Tannenbaum, Frank. *Darker Phases of the South.* New York: G. P. Putnam's Sons, 1924.

"Testing the Conscience of the Conscientious Objector." *Literary Digest* 61 (April 5, 1919): 66–71.

Thomas, Norman. *The Conscientious Objector in America.* New York: B. W. Huebsch, 1923.

———. "Justice to War's Heretics." *Nation* 107 (November 9, 1918): 547.

Thompson, Frank V. *Schooling of the Immigrant.* New York: Harper and Bros., 1920.

"Uniforms from Sweatshops." *Survey* 38 (September 15, 1917): 519.

United States Council of National Defense. *Third Annual Report of the United States Council of National Defense.* Washington, D.C.: Government Printing Office, 1919.

United States Department of Justice. *Annual Report of the Attorney General of the United States, 1919.* Washington, D.C.: Government Printing Office, 1920.

United States Department of Labor. *Report on the Bisbee Deportations Made by the President's Mediation Committee to the President of the United States.* Washington, D.C.: Government Printing Office, 1918.

———. *Reports of the Department of Labor, 1917.* Washington, D.C.: Government Printing Office, 1918.

United States Department of War. *Statement concerning the Treatment of Conscientious Objectors in the Army.* Washington, D.C.: Government Printing Office, 1919.

United States Senate Committee on the Judiciary. *Brewing and Liquor Interests and German and Bolshevik Propaganda.* Washington, D.C.: Government Printing Office, 1919.

Van Rensselaer, Mrs. Coffin. "The National League for Woman's Service." *Annals of the American Academy of Political and Social Science* 79 (September 1918): 275–82.

Veblen, Thorstein. "Dementia Praecox." *Freeman* 5 (June 21, 1922): 344–47.

Ware, Susan. *Modern American Women: A Documentary History.* Chicago: Dorsey Press, 1989.

"The Washington Riots." *Independent* 99 (August 2, 1919): 147.

Webb, Sidney. "Conscience and the 'Conscientious Objector.'" *North American Review* 205 (March 1917): 403–20.

Weber, Max. "Politics as a Vocation." In *From Max Weber: Essays in Sociology*, ed. and trans. H. H. Gerth and C. Wright Mills. New York: Oxford University Press, 1946.

Weinberger, Harry. "A Rebel's Interrupted Autobiography." *American Journal of Economics and Sociology* 2 (October 1942): 111–22.

Wells, Ida B. *Crusade for Justice: The Autobiography of Ida B. Wells*, ed. Alfreda M. Duster. Chicago: University of Chicago Press, 1970.

West, Henry Litchfield. *Federal Power: Its Growth and Necessity.* New York: George H. Doran, 1918.

Wharton, Edith. *The Marne.* New York: D. Appleton, 1918.

"What Happened to the August Masses." *Masses* 9 (September 1917): 3.

White, Walter F. "'Massacring Whites' in Arkansas." *Nation* 109 (December 6, 1919): 715.

———. "Work or Fight in the South." *New Republic* 18 (March 1, 1919): 144–46.

[Wigmore, John H.] "The Lawyer's Honor in War-Time." *Illinois Law Review* 12 (June 1917): 117–18.

Williams, Michael. *American Catholics in the World War: The National Catholic War Council, 1917–1921.* New York: Macmillan, 1921.

Willoughby, W. F. *An Introduction to the Government of Modern States.* New York: Century, 1919.

Wilson, Woodrow. *The State: Elements of Historical and Practical Politics*, rev. ed. Boston: D. C. Heath, 1899.

Wood, Leonard. *The Military Obligation of Citizenship.* Princeton N.J.: Princeton University Press, 1915.

———. *Universal Military Training.* New York: Collier Classics, 1917.

YMCA of the USA. *Service with Fighting Men.* New York: Association Press, 1922.

Legal Opinions

Abrams v. U.S., 250 U.S. 616 (1919).

Arver v. United States, 245 U.S. 366 (1918).

Bartels v. State of Iowa, 262 U.S. 404 (1923).

Brown v. U.S., 250 U.S. 335 (1921).

Colyer v. Skeffington, 265 Fed. 17 (1920).

Frohwerk v. U.S., 249 U.S. 204 (1919).

Gilbert v. State of Minnesota, 254 U.S. 325 (1920).

Hunter v. D.C., 47 App. D.C. 406 (1918).

In re *D—*, 290 Fed. 863 (1923).

In re *Roeper*, 274 Fed. 490 (1921).

Jeffersonian Publishing Co. v. West, 245 Fed. 585.

Jones v. Perkins, 243 Fed. 997 (1917).

Masses Publishing Company v. Patten, 244 Fed. 535 (S.D.N.Y., 1917).

Masses Publishing Company v. Patten, 245 Fed. 102 (C.C.A. 2d., 1917).

Masses Publishing Company v. Patten, 246 Fed. 24 (C.C.A. 2d., 1917).

Meyer v. Nebraska, 262 U.S. 390 (1923).

Meyer v. State, 107 Neb. 657 (1922).

Moore v. Dempsey, 261 U.S. 86 (1923).

Nebraska District of Evangelical Lutheran Synod of Missouri v. McKelvie, 104 Neb. 93 (1919).

Pierce v. Society of Sisters, 268 U.S. 510 (1925).

Schaefer v. U.S., 251 U.S. 466 (1920).

Schenck v. U.S., 249 U.S. 47 (1919).

State ex rel. *Thayer v. School District*, 99 Neb. 338 (1916).

State v. Freerks, 140 Minn. 349 (1918).

State v. Holm, 139 Minn. 267 (1918).

State v. Lowery, 177 Pac. 355 (Wash. 1918).

United States ex rel. *Milwaukee Social Democratic Pub. Co. v. Burleson*, 255 U.S. 407 (1921).

United States v. Hall, 248 Fed. 150 (1918).

United States v. Wheeler, 254 U.S. 281 (1920).

Newspapers

Atlanta Constitution

Boston Globe

Chicago Defender

Chicago Tribune

Christian Science Monitor

Kingdom News

Los Angeles Times

Memphis Commercial Appeal

New York Age

New York Evening Post

New York Times

Providence Journal

San Francisco Chronicle

Spy Glass

Vicksburg Daily Herald

Washington Post

Secondary Sources

Books and Articles

Abrahams, Ray. *Vigilant Citizens: Vigilantism and the State*. Cambridge, U.K.: Polity, 1998.

Abrams, Ray H. *Preachers Present Arms*. Scottdale, Pa.: Herald, 1969 [1933].

Aldrich, Amey. *Fifty Years Ago: Early Days of the Cosmopolitan Club*. Stamford, Conn.: Overbrook, 1959.

Allen, Frederick Lewis. *Only Yesterday: An Informal History of the Nineteen-Twenties*. New York: Harper and Bros., 1931.

Allen, Frederick S., et al. *The University of Colorado, 1876–1976: A Centennial Publication of the University of Colorado*. New York: Harcourt, Brace, Jovanovich, 1976.

Allen, Robert L., with the collaboration of Pamela P. Allen. *Reluctant Reformers: Racism and Social Reform Movements in the United States*. Washington, D.C.: Howard University Press, 1974.

Alonso, Harriet Hyman. *Peace as a Woman's Issue: A History of the U.S. Movement for World Peace and Women's Rights*. Syracuse, N.Y.: Syracuse University Press, 1993.

Alpers, Benjamin L. *Dictators and Democracy in American Public Culture: Envisioning the Totalitarian Enemy, 1920s–1950s*. Chapel Hill: University of North Carolina Press, 2003.

Anders, Evan. *Boss Rule in South Texas: The Progressive Era*. Austin: University of Texas Press, 1982.

Anderson, Adrian. "President Wilson's Politician: Albert Sidney Burleson of Texas." *Southwestern Historical Quarterly* 72 (January 1974): 339–54.

Arendt, Hannah. *The Origins of Totalitarianism*. New York: Harcourt, Brace, 1951.

Asinof, Eliot. *1919: America's Loss of Innocence*. New York: Donald I. Fine, 1990.

Attie, Jeanie. *Patriotic Toil: Northern Women and the American Civil War*. Ithaca, N.Y.: Cornell University Press, 1998.

Aylsworth, Leon E. "The Passing of Alien Suffrage." *American Political Science Review* 25 (February 1931): 114–16.

Baker, Jean H. *Sisters: The Lives of America's Suffragists*. New York: Hill and Wang, 2005.

Baker, Paula. "The Domestication of Politics: Women and American Political Society, 1780–1920." *American Historical Review* 89 (June 1984): 620–47.

Bakken, Douglas. "NPL in Nebraska, 1917–1920." *North Dakota History* 39 (Spring 1972): 26–31.

Ball, Terence, et al., eds. *Political Innovation and Conceptual Change*. New York: Cambridge University Press, 1989.

Barbeau, Arthur E., and Florette Henri. *The Unknown Soldiers: African-American Troops in World War I*. New York: DaCapo, 1996 [1974].

Barber, Benjamin R. *Strong Democracy: Participatory Politics for a New Age*, 20th anniversary ed. Berkeley: University of California Press, 2003.

Barber, Lucy G. *Marching on Washington: The Forging of an American Political Tradition*. Berkeley: University of California Press, 2002.

Barbour, Hugh. "The Woods of Mt. Kisco." *Quaker History* 87 (Spring 1998): 1–34.

Barclay, Morgan, and Charles N. Glaab. *Toledo: Gateway to the Great Lakes*. Tulsa: Continental Heritage, 1982.

Barnard, Harry. *The Forging of an American Jew: The Life and Times of Judge Julian W. Mack*. New York: Herzl, 1974.

Barnes, Albert F., comp. and ed. *Greater Portland Celebration 350*. Portland, Maine: Gannett, 1984.

Barton, Ann. *Mother Bloor*. New York: Workers Library, 1935.

Bean, Philip A. "The Great War and Ethnic Nationalism in Utica, New York, 1914–1920." *New York History* 74 (October 1993): 382–413.

Beckerman, Edwin, ed. *A History of New Jersey Libraries, 1750–1996*. Lanham, Md.: Scarecrow, 1997.

Bederman, Gail. *Manliness and Civilization: A Cultural History of Gender and Race in the United States, 1880–1917*. Chicago: University of Chicago Press, 1995.

Bellah, Robert N., et al. *Habits of the Heart: Individualism and Commitment in American Life*. Berkeley: University of California Press, 1985.

Benhabib, Seyla. *The Rights of Others: Aliens, Residents, and Citizens*. New York: Cambridge University Press, 2004.

Benjamin, Anne M. *A History of the Anti-Suffrage Movement in the United States from 1895 to 1920: Women against Equality*. Lewiston, N.Y.: Edwin Mellen, 1991.

Benjamin, Philip S. *The Philadelphia Quakers in the Industrial Age, 1865–1920*. Philadelphia: Temple University Press, 1976.

Bensel, Richard. *Yankee Leviathan: The Origins of Central State Authority in America, 1859–1877*. New York: Cambridge University Press, 1990.

Bentley, Amy. *Eating for Victory: Food Rationing and the Politics of Domesticity*. Urbana: University of Illinois Press, 1998.

Benton-Cohen, Katherine. "Docile Children and Dangerous Revolutionaries: The Racial Hierarchy of Manliness and the Bisbee Deportation of 1917." *Frontiers: A Journal of Women Studies* 24, nos. 2–3 (2003): 30–50.

Bergreen, Lawrence. *As Thousands Cheer: The Life of Irving Berlin.* New York: Viking, 1990.

Bickel, Alexander M. *The Judiciary and Responsible Government, 1910–1921.* New York: Macmillan, 1984.

Bilger, Edda. "The 'Oklahoma Vorwärts': The Voice of German-Americans in Oklahoma during World War I." *Chronicles of Oklahoma* 54 (Summer 1976): 245–60.

Billington, Monroe. "Thomas P. Gore and Oklahoma Public Opinion, 1917–1918." *Journal of Southern History* 27 (August 1961): 344–53.

Birchman, Willis. *Faces and Facts by and about 26 Contemporary Artists.* New Haven, Conn.: privately printed, 1937.

Bissett, Jim. *Agrarian Socialism in America: Marx, Jefferson, and Jesus in the Oklahoma Countryside, 1904–1920.* Norman: University of Oklahoma Press, 1999.

Blair, Karen J. *The Clubwoman as Feminist: True Womanhood Redefined, 1868–1914.* New York: Holmes and Meier, 1980.

Blake, Casey Nelson. *Beloved Community: The Cultural Criticism of Randolph Bourne, Van Wyck Brooks, Waldo Frank, and Lewis Mumford.* Chapel Hill: University of North Carolina Press, 1990.

Blankenburg, Lucretia L. *The Blankenburgs of Philadelphia.* Chicago: John C. Winston, 1929.

Blee, Kathleen M. *Women of the Klan: Racism and Gender in the 1920s.* Berkeley: University of California Press, 1991.

Blumenthal, Henry. "Woodrow Wilson and the Race Question." *Journal of Negro History* 48 (January 1963): 1–21.

Bolino, August C. *The Ellis Island Source Book.* Washington, D.C.: Kensington Historical, 1985.

Borden, Penn. *Civilian Indoctrination of the Military: World War I and Future Implications for the Military-Industrial Complex.* Westport, Conn.: Greenwood, 1989.

Boris, Eileen. "Tenement Homework on Army Uniforms: The Gendering of Industrial Democracy during World War I." *Labor History* 32 (Spring 1991): 231–52.

Boynton, Virginia R. " 'Even in the Remotest Parts of the State': Downstate 'Woman's Committee' Activities on the Illinois Home Front during World War I." *Journal of the Illinois State Historical Society* 96 (Winter 2003–04): 318–46.

Brandt, Allan M. *No Magic Bullet: A Social History of Venereal Disease in the United States since 1880,* expanded ed. New York: Oxford University Press, 1987.

Breckinridge, Sophonisba P. *Women in the Twentieth Century: A Story of Their Political, Social and Economic Activities.* New York: Arno, 1972 [1933].

Bredbenner, Candice Lewis. *A Nationality of Her Own: Women, Marriage, and the Law of Citizenship.* Berkeley: University of California Press, 1998.

Breen, William J. *Uncle Sam at Home: Civilian Mobilization, Wartime Federalism, and the Council of National Defense.* Westport, Conn.: Greenwood, 1984.

Brinkley, Alan. "The Two World Wars and American Liberalism." In *Liberalism and Its Discontents.* Cambridge: Harvard University Press, 1998.

Bristow, Nancy K. *Making Men Moral: Social Engineering during the Great War*. New York: New York University Press, 1997.

Britten, Thomas A. *American Indians in World War I: At Home and at War*. Albuquerque: University of New Mexico Press, 1997.

——. "The Creek Draft Rebellion of 1918: Wartime Hysteria and Indian Baiting in WWI Oklahoma." *Chronicles of Oklahoma* 79 (Summer 2001): 200–215.

Brock, Peter. "Confinement of Conscientious Objectors as Psychiatric Patients in World War I Germany." *Peace and Change* 23 (July 1998): 247–64.

Browder, Dorothea. "A 'Christian Solution of the Labor Situation': How Workingwomen Reshaped the YWCA's Religious Mission and Politics." *Journal of Women's History* 19 (Summer 2007): 85–110.

Brown, Nikki. *Private Politics and Public Voices: Black Women's Activism from World War I to the New Deal*. Bloomington: Indiana University Press, 2006.

Brown, Richard Maxwell. "The History of Vigilantism in America." In *Vigilante Politics*, ed. H. Jon Rosenbaum and Peter C. Sederberg. Philadelphia: University of Pennsylvania Press, 1976.

——. *No Duty to Retreat: Violence and Values in American History and Society*. New York: Oxford University Press, 1991.

——. *Strain of Violence: Historical Studies of American Violence and Vigilantism*. New York: Oxford University Press, 1975.

——. "Western Violence: Structure, Values, Myth." *Western Historical Quarterly* 24 (February 1993): 5–20.

Brownstone, David M., et al. *Island of Hope, Island of Tears*. New York: Rawson, Wade, 1979.

Brubaker, Rogers. *Citizenship and Nationhood in France and Germany*. Cambridge: Harvard University Press, 1992.

Brundage, W. Fitzhugh. *Lynching in the New South: Georgia and Virginia, 1880–1930*. Urbana: University of Illinois Press, 1993.

——, ed. *Under Sentence of Death: Lynching in the South*. Chapel Hill: University of North Carolina Press, 1997.

Buechler, A. R., and R. J. Barr, eds. *History of Hall County, Nebraska*. Lincoln, Neb.: Western Publishing and Engraving, 1920.

Burchell, R. A. "Did the Irish and German Voters Desert the Democrats in 1920? A Tentative Statistical Answer." *Journal of American Studies* 6 (August 1972): 153–64.

Burpee, Charles W. *Burpee's The Story of Connecticut*. New York: American Historical, 1939.

Burton, Shirley. "The Espionage and Sedition Acts of 1917 and 1918: Sectional Interpretations in the United States District Courts of Illinois." *Illinois Historical Journal* 87 (Spring 1994): 41–50.

Byrkit, James W. *Forging the Copper Collar: Arizona's Labor-Management War of 1901–1921*. Tucson: University of Arizona Press, 1982.

California Federation of Women's Clubs. *Diamond Jubilee Highlights*. N.p.: California Federation of Women's Clubs, 1975.

Camhi, Jane Jerome. *Women against Women: American Anti-Suffragism, 1880–1920*. Brooklyn, N.Y.: Carlson, 1994.

Canning, Kathleen, and Sonya O. Rose. "Gender, Citizenship, and Subjectivity: Some Historical and Theoretical Considerations." *Gender and History* 13 (November 2001): 427–43.

Carrigan, William D. *The Making of a Lynching Culture: Violence and Vigilantism in Central Texas, 1836–1916*. Urbana: University of Illinois Press, 2004.

——, and Clive Webb. "The Lynching of Persons of Mexican Origin or Descent in the United States, 1848 to 1928." *Journal of Social History* 37 (Winter 2003): 411–38.

Carruth, Joseph. "World War I Propaganda and Its Effects in Arkansas." *Arkansas Historical Quarterly* 56 (Winter 1997): 385–98.

Catlin, George B. *The Story of Detroit*. Detroit: Detroit News, 1926.

Chafee, Zechariah, Jr. *Free Speech in the United States*. New York: Atheneum, 1969 [1941].

Chalmers, David. *Hooded Americanism: The History of the Ku Klux Klan*. Chicago: Quadrangle, 1968.

Chambers, John Whiteclay, II. "Conscientious Objectors and the American State from Colonial Times to the Present." In *The New Conscientious Objection: From Sacred to Secular Resistance*, ed. Charles C. Moskos and John Whiteclay Chambers II (New York: Oxford University Press, 1993).

——. *To Raise an Army: The Draft Comes to Modern America*. New York: Free Press, 1987.

Chatfield, Charles. *For Peace and Justice: Pacifism in America, 1914–1941*. Knoxville: University of Tennessee Press, 1971.

——. "World War I and the Liberal Pacifist in the United States." *American Historical Review* 75 (December 1970): 1920–37.

Childers, Thomas. "The Social Language of Politics in Germany: The Sociology of Discourse in the Weimar Republic." *American Historical Review* 95 (April 1990): 331–58.

Clemens, Elisabeth S. "Securing Political Returns to Social Capital: Women's Associations in the United States, 1880s–1920s." *Journal of Interdisciplinary History* 29 (Spring 1999): 613–38.

Cobb-Reiley, Linda. "Not an Empty Box with Beautiful Words on It: The First Amendment in Progressive Era Scholarship." *Journalism Quarterly* 69 (Spring 1992): 37–47.

Coffman, Edward M. *The War to End All Wars: The American Military Experience in World War I*. New York: Oxford University Press, 1968.

Cole, David. *Enemy Aliens: Double Standards and Constitutional Freedoms in the War on Terrorism*. New York: New Press, 2003.

Connelly, Mark Thomas. *The Response to Prostitution in the Progressive Era*. Chapel Hill: University of North Carolina Press, 1980.

Conner, Valerie Jean. *The National War Labor Board: Stability, Social Justice, and the Voluntary State in World War I*. Chapel Hill: University of North Carolina Press, 1983.

Cooper, Horton. *History of Avery County, North Carolina*. Asheville, N.C.: Biltmore, 1964.

Cooper, Jerry M. *The Army and Civil Disorder: Federal Military Intervention in Labor Disputes, 1877–1900*. Westport, Conn.: Greenwood, 1980.

——. *The Rise of the National Guard: The Evolution of the American Militia, 1865–1920*. Lincoln: University of Nebraska Press, 1997.

Copeland, Tom. *The Centralia Tragedy of 1919: Elmer Smith and the Wobblies.* Seattle: University of Washington Press, 1993.

Corbin, David Alan. *Life, Work, and Rebellion in the Coal Fields: The Southern West Virginia Miners, 1880–1922.* Urbana: University of Illinois Press, 1982.

Cornebise, Alfred. *War as Advertised: The Four Minute Men and America's Crusade, 1917–1918.* Philadelphia: American Philosophical Society, 1984.

Cortner, Richard C. *A Mob Intent on Death: The NAACP and the Arkansas Riot Cases.* Middletown, Conn.: Wesleyan University Press, 1988.

Cott, Nancy F. *The Grounding of Modern Feminism.* New Haven, Conn.: Yale University Press, 1987.

——. "Marriage and Women's Citizenship in the United States, 1830–1934." *American Historical Review* 103 (December 1998): 1440–74.

Cotten, Sallie Southall. *History of the North Carolina Federation of Women's Clubs, 1901–1925.* Raleigh: Edwards and Broughton, 1925.

Cottrell, Robert C. *Roger Nash Baldwin and the American Civil Liberties Union.* New York: Columbia University Press, 2000.

Cox, Patrick L. " 'An Enemy Closer to Us than Any European Power': The Impact of Mexico on Texan Public Opinion before World War I." *Southwestern Historical Quarterly* 105 (July 2001): 41–80.

Craighead, Lura Harris. *History of the Alabama Federation of Women's Clubs.* Montgomery: Paragon, 1936.

Cramer, C. H. *Newton D. Baker: A Biography.* Cleveland: World, 1961.

Creigh, Dorothy Weyer. *Nebraska: A Bicentennial History.* New York: Norton, 1977.

Cripps, Thomas. *Slow Fade to Black: The Negro in American Film, 1900–1942.* New York: Oxford University Press, 1977.

Cuff, Robert C. "Herbert D. Hoover, the Ideology of Voluntarism, and War Organization during the Great War." *Journal of American History* 64 (September 1977): 358–72.

Cummings, Homer, and Carl McFarland. *Federal Justice: Chapters in the History of Justice and the Federal Executive.* New York: Macmillan, 1937.

Curtis, Michael Kent. *Free Speech, the People's Darling Privilege: Struggles for Freedom of Expression in American History.* Durham, N.C.: Duke University Press, 2000.

Danbom, David B. *"The World of Hope": Progressives and the Search for an Ethical Public Life.* Philadelphia: Temple University Press, 1987.

Daniels, Doris Groshen. *Always a Sister: The Feminism of Lillian D. Wald.* New York: Feminist Press, 1989.

Davis, Allen F. *American Heroine: The Life and Legend of Jane Addams.* New York: Oxford University Press, 1973.

Davis, Belinda J. *Home Fires Burning: Food, Politics, and Everyday Life in World War I Berlin.* Chapel Hill: University of North Carolina Press, 2000.

Davis, Elizabeth Lindsay. *Lifting as They Climb.* New York: G. K. Hall, 1996 [1933].

DeBauche, Leslie Midkiff. *Reel Patriotism: The Movies and World War I.* Madison: University of Wisconsin Press, 1997.

Degen, Mary Louise. *The History of the Woman's Peace Party.* New York: Burt Franklin's Reprints, 1974 [1939].

D'Emilio, John, and Estelle B. Freedman. *Intimate Matters: A History of Sexuality in America.* New York: Harper and Row, 1988.

Dickinson, John. *The Building of an Army: A Detailed Account of Legislation, Administration and Opinion in the United States, 1915–1920.* New York: Century, 1922.

Dubay, Robert W. "The Opposition to Selective Service, 1916–1918." *Southern Quarterly* 7 (April 1969): 301–22.

Dubofsky, Melvyn. *We Shall Be All: A History of the Industrial Workers of the World,* 2nd ed. Urbana: University of Illinois Press, 1988.

Dumenil, Lynn. *Freemasonry and American Culture, 1880–1930.* Princeton, N.J.: Princeton University Press, 1984.

———. " 'The Insatiable Maw of Bureaucracy': Antistatism and Education Reform in the 1920s." *Journal of American History* 77 (September 1990): 499–524.

———. *The Modern Temper: American Culture and Society in the 1920s.* New York: Hill and Wang, 1994.

Durbach, Nadja. "Class, Gender, and the Conscientious Objector to Vaccination, 1898–1907." *Journal of British Studies* 41 (January 2002): 58–83.

Early, Frances H. "Feminism, Peace, and Civil Liberties: Women's Role in the Origins of the World War I Civil Liberties Movement." *Women's Studies* 18, nos. 1–2 (1990): 95–115.

———. *A World without War: How U.S. Feminists and Pacifists Resisted World War I.* Syracuse, N.Y.: Syracuse University Press, 1997.

Eddins, Roy, ed. *History of Falls County, Texas.* N.p.: Old Settlers and Veterans Association of Falls County, Texas, 1947.

Edwards, John Carver. "America's Vigilantes and the Great War." *Army Quarterly and Defence Journal* 106 (July 1976): 277–86.

Edwards, Rebecca. *Angels in the Machinery: Gender in American Party Politics from the Civil War to the Progressive Era.* New York: Oxford University Press, 1997.

Eisner, Marc Allen. *From Warfare State to Welfare State: World War I, Compensatory State Building, and the Limits of the Modern Order.* University Park: Pennsylvania State University Press, 2000.

Eldredge, H. Wentworth. "Enemy Aliens: New Haven Germans during the World War." In *Studies in the Science of Society: Presented to Albert Galloway Keller in Celebration of His Completion of Thirty Years as Professor of the Science of Society in Yale University,* ed. George Peter Murdock. New Haven, Conn.: Yale University Press, 1937.

Ellis, Mark. "German-Americans in World War I." In *Enemy Images in American History,* ed. Ragnhild Fiebig-von Hase and Ursula Lehmkuhl. Providence, R.I.: Berghahn, 1997.

———. "Joel Spingarn's 'Constructive Programme' and the Wartime Antilynching Bill of 1918." *Journal of Policy History* 4, no. 2 (1992): 134–61.

———. *Race, War, and Surveillance: African Americans and the United States Government during World War I.* Bloomington: Indiana University Press, 2001.

Feldman, Glenn. "Conservative Progressivism: Antivigilantism in Post–World War I Alabama." *Alabama Review* 50 (Spring 1997): 18–36.

Ferrell, Claudine L. *Nightmare and Dream: Antilynching in Congress, 1917–1922.* New York: Garland, 1986.

Ferrell, Robert H. *Woodrow Wilson and World War I, 1917–1921.* New York: Harper and Row, 1985.

Finkelman, Paul. "German Victims and American Oppressors: The Cultural Background and Legacy of *Meyer v. Nebraska.*" In *Law and the Great Plains: Essays on the Legal History of the Heartland,* ed. John R. Wunder. Westport, Conn.: Greenwood, 1996.

Finnegan, John Patrick. *Against the Specter of a Dragon: The Campaign for American Military Preparedness, 1914–1917.* Westport, Conn.: Greenwood, 1974.

Fishbein, Leslie. *Rebels in Bohemia: The Radicals of The Masses, 1911–1917.* Chapel Hill: University of North Carolina Press, 1982.

Flexner, Eleanor. *Century of Struggle: The Woman's Rights Movement in the United States,* rev. ed. Cambridge: Harvard University Press, 1975.

Foner, Eric. *The Story of American Freedom.* New York: Norton, 1998.

Forbes, John. *The Quaker Star under Seven Flags.* Philadelphia: University of Pennsylvania Press, 1962.

Ford, Nancy Gentile. *Americans All! Foreign-Born Soldiers in World War I.* College Station: Texas A&M University Press, 2001.

Fox, Richard Wightman. *Reinhold Niebuhr: A Biography.* Ithaca, N.Y.: Cornell University Press, 1996 [1985].

Fox, Stephen R. *The Guardian of Boston: William Monroe Trotter.* New York: Atheneum, 1971.

Franklin, John Hope, and Alfred A. Moss Jr. *From Slavery to Freedom: A History of African Americans,* 8th ed. New York: McGraw-Hill, 2000.

Franklin, Vincent P. "The Philadelphia Race Riot of 1918." *Pennsylvania Magazine of History and Biography* 99 (July 1975): 336–50.

Franz, Rufus M. "It Happened in Montana." *Mennonite Life* 7 (October 1952): 181–82.

Fraser, Nancy, and Linda Gordon. "A Genealogy of 'Dependency': Tracing a Keyword of the U.S. Welfare State." *Signs* 19 (Winter 1994): 309–36.

Freedman, Estelle B. *Their Sisters' Keepers: Women's Prison Reform in America, 1830–1930.* Ann Arbor: University of Michigan Press, 1981.

Freeman, Joanne B. "Explaining the Unexplainable: The Cultural Context of the Sedition Act." In *The Democratic Experiment: New Directions in American Political History,* ed. Meg Jacobs et al. Princeton, N.J.: Princeton University Press, 2003.

Fritz, Christian. "Popular Sovereignty, Vigilantism, and the Constitutional Right of Revolution." *Pacific Historical Review* 63 (February 1994): 39–66.

Frost, J. William. "'Our Deeds Carry Our Message': The Early History of the American Friends Service Committee." *Quaker History* 81 (Spring 1992): 1–51.

Garey, Diane. *Defending Everybody: A History of the American Civil Liberties Union.* New York: TV Books, 1998.

Gary, Brett. *The Nervous Liberals: Propaganda Anxieties from World War I to the Cold War.* New York: Columbia University Press, 1999.

Gaughan, Anthony. "Woodrow Wilson and the Rise of Militant Interventionism in the South." *Journal of Southern History* 65 (November 1999): 771–808.

Gavin, Lettie. *American Women in World War I: They Also Served.* Niwot: University Press of Colorado, 1997.

Gengarelly, W. Anthony. *Distinguished Dissenters and Opposition to the 1919–1920 Red Scare.* Lewiston, N.Y.: Edwin Mellen, 1996.

Gerstle, Gary. "Liberty, Coercion, and the Making of Americans." *Journal of American History* 84 (September 1997): 524–58.

——. *Working-Class Americanism: The Politics of Labor in a Textile City, 1914–1960.* New York: Cambridge University Press, 1989.

Gibbs, Christopher C. *The Great Silent Majority: Missouri's Resistance to World War I.* Columbia: University of Missouri Press, 1988.

Giddings, Paula. *When and Where I Enter: The Impact of Black Women on Race and Sex in America.* New York: William Morrow, 1984.

Gidlow, Liette. *The Big Vote: Gender, Consumer Culture, and the Politics of Exclusion, 1890s–1920s.* Baltimore: Johns Hopkins University Press, 2004.

Gilfoyle, Timothy J. *City of Eros: New York City, Prostitution, and the Commercialization of Sex, 1790–1920.* New York: Norton, 1992.

Gilje, Paul A. *Rioting in America.* Bloomington: Indiana University Press, 1996.

Gilmore, Glenda Elizabeth. *Gender and Jim Crow: Women and the Politics of White Supremacy in North Carolina, 1896–1920.* Chapel Hill: University of North Carolina Press, 1996.

Ginzburg, Carlo. "'Your Country Needs You': A Case Study in Political Iconography." *History Workshop Journal* no. 52 (Autumn 2001): 1–22.

Gjerde, Jon. *The Minds of the West: Ethnocultural Evolution in the Rural Middle West, 1830–1917.* Chapel Hill: University of North Carolina Press, 1997.

Glendon, Mary Ann. *Rights Talk: The Impoverishment of Political Discourse.* New York: Free Press, 1991.

Glenn, Brian J. "Fraternal Rhetoric and the Development of the U.S. Welfare State." *Studies in American Political Development* 15 (Fall 2001): 220–33.

Gold, Doris B. "Women and Voluntarism." In *Woman in Sexist Society: Studies in Power and Powerlessness*, ed. Vivian Gornick and Barbara K. Moran. New York: Basic Books, 1971.

Goossen, Rachel Waltner. *Women against the Good War: Conscientious Objection and Gender on the American Home Front, 1941–1947.* Chapel Hill: University of North Carolina Press, 1997.

Gordon, Marsha. "Onward Kitchen Soldiers: Mobilizing the Domestic during World War I." *Canadian Review of American Studies* 29, no. 2 (1999): 61–87.

Goudsouzian, Aram. "All Gods Dead: Babe Ruth and Boston, 1918–1920." In *The Rock, the Curse, and the Hub: A Random History of Boston Sports*, ed. Randy Roberts. Cambridge: Harvard University Press, 2005.

Graebner, Alan. *Uncertain Saints: The Laity in the Lutheran Church—Missouri Synod, 1900–1970.* Westport, Conn.: Greenwood, 1975.

Graebner, William. *The Engineering of Consent: Democracy and Authority in Twentieth-Century America.* Madison: University of Wisconsin Press, 1987.

Graham, Frances W. *A History of Sixty Years' Work of the Women's Christian Temperance Union of the State of New York, 1874–1934.* Lockport, N.Y.: WCTU, 1934.

Graham, Sally Hunter. "Woodrow Wilson, Alice Paul, and the Woman Suffrage Movement." *Political Science Quarterly* 98 (Winter 1983–84): 665–79.

Graham, Sarah Hunter. *Woman Suffrage and the New Democracy.* New Haven, Conn.: Yale University Press, 1996.

Gray, Richard Hopkins. "A Dedication to the Memory of Emerson Hough, 1857–1923." *Arizona and the West* 17 (Spring 1975): 1–4.

Green, James R. *Grass-Roots Socialism: Radical Movements in the Southwest, 1895–1943.* Baton Rouge: Louisiana State University Press, 1978.

Greenberg, Amy S. *Cause for Alarm: The Volunteer Fire Department in the Nineteenth-Century City.* Princeton, N.J.: Princeton University Press, 1998.

Greenberg, Martin Alan. *Citizens Defending America: From Colonial Times to the Age of Terrorism.* Pittsburgh, Pa.: University of Pittsburgh Press, 2005.

Gunther, Gerald. *Learned Hand: The Man and the Judge.* Cambridge: Harvard University Press, 1994.

Gurstein, Rochelle. *The Repeal of Reticence: A History of America's Cultural and Legal Struggles over Free Speech, Obscenity, Sexual Liberation, and Modern Art.* New York: Hill and Wang, 1996.

Gusfield, Joseph R. *Symbolic Crusade: Status Politics and the American Temperance Movement.* Urbana: University of Illinois Press, 1963.

Gustafston, Melanie Susan. *Women and the Republican Party, 1854–1924.* Urbana: University of Illinois Press, 2001.

Gutfeld, Arnon. "The Ves Hall Case, Judge Bourquin, and the Sedition Act of 1918." *Pacific Historical Review* 37 (May 1968): 163–78.

Hagedorn, Hermann. *Leonard Wood: A Biography.* New York: Harper and Bros., 1931.

Hall, Jacquelyn Dowd. *Revolt against Chivalry: Jessie Daniel Ames and the Women's Campaign against Lynching,* rev. ed. New York: Columbia University Press, 1993.

Hall, Kermit L., and Eric W. Rise. *From Local Courts to National Tribunals: The Federal District Courts of Florida, 1821–1990.* Brooklyn, N.Y.: Carlson, 1991.

Hall, Mrs. Walter A., et al., comps. *Progress and Achievement: A History of the Massachusetts State Federation of Women's Clubs, 1893–1931.* Norwood, Mass.: Plimpton, 1932.

Hamm, Richard F. *Shaping the Eighteenth Amendment: Temperance Reform, Legal Culture, and the Polity, 1880–1920.* Chapel Hill: University of North Carolina Press, 1995.

Hanley, Thomas O'Brien. "A Western Democrat's Quarrel with the Language Laws." *Nebraska History* 50 (Summer 1969): 151–71.

Harries, Meirion, and Susie Harries. *The Last Days of Innocence: America at War, 1917–1918.* New York: Vintage, 1997.

Harring, Sidney L. *Policing a Class Society: The Experience of American Cities, 1865–1915.* New Brunswick, N.J.: Rutgers University Press, 1983.

Harris, Stephen L. *Harlem's Hell Fighters: The African-American 369th Infantry in World War I.* Washington, D.C.: Brassey's, 2003.

Harris, William. "Etiquette, Lynching, and Racial Boundaries in Southern History: A Mississippi Example." *American Historical Review* 100 (April 1995): 387–410.

Hart, Newell, ed. *Hometown Album: A Pictorial History of Franklin County, Idaho—Horse and Buggy Days and Early Auto Era.* Preston, Idaho: Cache Valley Newsletter, 1986 [1973].

Hawley, Ellis W. *The Great War and the Search for a Modern Order: A History of the American People and Their Institutions, 1917–1933.* New York: St. Martin's, 1979.

Hegi, Benjamin Paul. "'Old Time Good Germans': German-Americans in Cooke County, Texas, during World War I." *Southwestern Historical Quarterly* 109 (October 2005): 234–57.

Hickel, K. Walter. "'Justice and the Highest Kind of Equality Require Discrimination': Citizenship, Dependency, and Conscription in the South, 1917–1919." *Journal of Southern History* 66 (November 2000): 749–80.

———. "War, Region, and Social Welfare: Federal Aid to Servicemen's Dependents in the South, 1917–1921." *Journal of American History* 87 (March 2001): 1362–91.

Hickey, Donald R. "The Prager Affair: A Study in Wartime Hysteria." *Journal of the Illinois State Historical Society* 62 (Summer 1969): 117–34.

Higginbotham, Evelyn Brooks. "African-American Women's History and the Metalanguage of Race." *Signs* 17 (Winter 1992): 251–74.

———. "Clubwomen and Electoral Politics in the 1920s." In *African American Women and the Vote, 1837–1965*, ed. Ann D. Gordon et al. Amherst: University of Massachusetts Press, 1997.

———. *Righteous Discontent: The Women's Movement in the Black Baptist Church*. Cambridge: Harvard University Press, 1993.

Higham, John. *Strangers in the Land: Patterns of American Nativism, 1860–1925*. New Brunswick, N.J.: Rutgers University Press, 1955.

Hilton, O. A. "The Oklahoma Council of Defense and the First World War." *Chronicles of Oklahoma* 20 (March 1942): 18–42.

Hine, Darlene Clark, ed. *Black Women in United States History*. 17 vols. Brooklyn, N.Y.: Carlson, 1990–95.

Hine, Robert V. *Josiah Royce: From Grass Valley to Harvard*. Norman: University of Oklahoma Press, 1992.

A History of the New Jersey State Federation of Women's Clubs, 1894–1958. Caldwell, N.J.: Progress, 1958.

Hixson, William B., Jr. *Moorfield Storey and the Abolitionist Tradition*. New York: Oxford University Press, 1972.

Hobson, Barbara Meil. *Uneasy Virtue: The Politics of Prostitution and the American Reform Tradition*. Chicago: University of Chicago Press, 1990.

Hogsett, Vernetta Murchison. *The Golden Years: A History of the Idaho Federation of Women's Clubs, 1905–1955*. Caldwell, Idaho: Caxton, 1955.

Holden-Smith, Barbara. "Lynching, Federalism, and the Intersection of Race and Gender in the Progressive Era." *Yale Journal of Law and Feminism* 8 (1996): 31–78.

Holmes, William F. *The White Chief: James Kimble Vardaman*. Baton Rouge: Louisiana State University Press, 1970.

Homan, Gerlof D. "Mennonites and Military Justice in World War I." *Mennonite Quarterly Review* 66 (July 1992): 365–75.

Horne, John, and Alan Kramer. *German Atrocities, 1914: A History of Denial*. New Haven, Conn.: Yale University Press, 2001.

Horowitz, Helen Lefkowitz. *The Power and Passion of M. Carey Thomas*. New York: Knopf, 1994.

———. *Rereading Sex: Battles over Sexual Knowledge and Suppression in Nineteenth-Century America*. New York: Knopf, 2002.

Houde, Mary Jean. *The Clubwoman: A Story of the Illinois Federation of Women's Clubs*. Chicago: Illinois Federation of Women's Clubs, 1970.

———. *Reaching Out: A Story of the General Federation of Women's Clubs*. Chicago: Mobium, 1989.

Howlett, Charles F. "John Nevin Sayre and the American Fellowship of Reconciliation." *Pennsylvania Magazine of History and Biography* 114 (July 1990): 399–421.

Hunt, Rockwell D. *California and Californians*. Chicago: Lewis, 1926.

Hunter, Martha Lavinia. *A Quarter of a Century History of the Dallas Woman's Forum, 1906–1931*. Dallas: Clyde C. Cockrell, 1932.

Hunter, Tera W. *To 'Joy My Freedom: Southern Black Women's Lives and Labors after the Civil War*. Cambridge: Harvard University Press, 1997.

Ingalls, Robert P. *Urban Vigilantes in the New South: Tampa, 1882–1936*. Knoxville: University of Tennessee Press, 1988.

Jackson, Charles O. "William J. Simmons: A Career in Ku Kluxism." *Georgia Historical Quarterly* 50 (December 1966): 351–65.

Jacobs, Meg. " 'How About Some Meat?' The Office of Price Administration, Consumption Politics, and State Building from the Bottom Up, 1941–1946." *Journal of American History* 84 (December 1997): 910–41.

———. *Pocketbook Politics: Economic Citizenship in Twentieth-Century America*. Princeton, N.J.: Princeton University Press, 2005.

Jacobson, Matthew Frye. *Whiteness of a Different Color: European Immigrants and the Alchemy of Race*. Cambridge: Harvard University Press, 1998.

Jeffreys-Jones, Rhodri. *Violence and Reform in American History*. New York: New Viewpoints, 1978.

Jensen, Joan M. "Canning Comes to New Mexico: Women and the Agricultural Extension Service, 1914–1919." *New Mexico Historical Review* 57, no. 4 (1982): 361–86.

———. *The Price of Vigilance*. Chicago: Rand-McNally, 1968.

Jensen, Vernon H. *Heritage of Conflict: Labor Relations in the Nonferrous Metals Industry up to 1930*. Ithaca, N.Y.: Cornell University Press, 1950.

Jenson, Carol E. *Agrarian Pioneer in Civil Liberties: The Nonpartisan League in Minnesota during World War I*. New York: Garland, 1986.

John, Richard R. *Spreading the News: The American Postal System from Franklin to Morse*. Cambridge: Harvard University Press, 1995.

Johnson, Benjamin Heber. *Revolution in Texas: How a Forgotten Rebellion and Its Bloody Suppression Turned Mexicans into Americans*. New Haven, Conn.: Yale University Press, 2003.

Johnson, Charles Thomas. *Culture at Twilight: The National German-American Alliance*. New York: Peter Lang, 1999.

Johnson, David A. "Vigilance and the Law: The Moral Authority of Popular Justice in the Far West." *American Quarterly* 33 (Winter 1981): 558–86.

Johnson, Donald. *The Challenge to American Freedoms*. Lexington: University of Kentucky Press, 1963.

———. "Wilson, Burleson, and Censorship in the First World War." *Journal of Southern History* 28 (February 1962): 46–58.

Johnston, Paul I. "Freedom of Speech Means Freedom to Teach: The Constitutional Battle in Nebraska, 1919–1923." *Concordia Historical Institute Quarterly* 52 (Fall 1979): 118–24.

Jones, Beverly Washington. *Quest for Equality: The Life and Writings of Mary Eliza Church Terrell, 1863–1954*. Brooklyn, N.Y.: Carlson, 1990.

Jones, Lester M. *Quakers in Action: Recent Humanitarian and Reform Activities of the American Quakers*. New York: Macmillan, 1929.

Jones, Richard Seelye. *A History of the American Legion*. Indianapolis, Ind.: Bobbs-Merrill, 1946.

Jones, Rufus M. *A Service of Love in War Time: American Friends Relief Work in Europe, 1917–1919*. New York: Macmillan, 1920.

Jordan, William. " 'The Damnable Dilemma': African-American Accommodation and Protest in World War I." *Journal of American History* 81 (March 1995): 1562–83.

Judson, Sarah Mercer. " 'Leisure Is a Foe to Any Man': The Pleasures and Dangers of Leisure in Atlanta during World War I." *Journal of Women's History* 15 (Spring 2003): 92–115.

Juhnke, James C. "The Agony of Civic Isolation: Mennonites in World War I." *Mennonite Life* 25 (January 1970): 27–33.

——. "John Schrag Espionage Case." *Mennonite Life* 22 (July 1967): 121–22.

——. "Mob Violence and Kansas Mennonites in 1918." *Kansas Historical Quarterly* 43 (Autumn 1977): 334–50.

Käsler, Dirk. *Max Weber: An Introduction to His Life and Work*, trans. Philippa Hurd. Cambridge, U.K.: Polity, 1988.

Katznelson, Ira. "Rewriting the Epic of America." In *Shaped by War and Trade: International Influences on American Political Development*, ed. Ira Katznelson and Martin Shefter. Princeton, N.J.: Princeton University Press, 2002.

Kauffman, Christopher J. *Faith and Fraternalism: The History of the Knights of Columbus, 1882–1982*. New York: Harper and Row, 1982.

Kaufman, Jason. *For the Common Good? American Civic Life and the Golden Age of Fraternity*. New York: Oxford University Press, 2002.

Kaufman, Martin. "The American Anti-Vaccinationists and Their Arguments." *Bulletin of the History of Medicine* 41 (September–October 1967): 463–78.

Kazal, Russell A. *Becoming Old Stock: The Paradox of German-American Identity*. Princeton, N.J.: Princeton University Press, 2004.

Keeley, Mary Paxton. "A.E.F. English: Some Delimitations." *American Speech* 5 (June 1930): 372–86.

Keene, Jennifer D. *Doughboys, the Great War, and the Remaking of America*. Baltimore: Johns Hopkins University Press, 2001.

Keim, Albert N., and Grant M. Stolzfus, eds. *The Politics of Conscience: The Historic Peace Churches and America at War, 1917–1955*. Scottdale, Pa.: Herald, 1988.

Keith, Jeannette. *Rich Man's War, Poor Man's Fight: Race, Class, and Power in the Rural South during the First World War*. Chapel Hill: University of North Carolina Press, 2004.

Keller, Morton. *Affairs of State: Public Life in Late Nineteenth Century America*. Cambridge: Harvard University Press, 1977.

Keller, Phyllis. *States of Belonging: German-American Intellectuals and the First World War*. Cambridge: Harvard University Press, 1979.

Kellogg, Charles Flint. *NAACP: A History of the National Association for the Advancement of Colored People*. Baltimore: Johns Hopkins University Press, 1967.

Kenneally, James J. *The History of American Catholic Women*. New York: Crossroad, 1990.

Kennedy, David M. *Over Here: The First World War and American Society*. New York: Oxford University Press, 1980.

Kennedy, Kathleen. *Disloyal Mothers and Scurrilous Citizens: Women and Subversion during World War I*. Bloomington: Indiana University Press, 1999.

Kerber, Linda K. *No Constitutional Right to Be Ladies: Women and the Obligations of Citizenship*. New York: Hill and Wang, 1998.

——. "The Stateless as the Citizen's Other: A View from the United States." *American Historical Review* 112 (February 2007): 1–34.

———. "Toward a History of Statelessness in America." *American Quarterly* 57 (September 2005): 727–49.

Kerr, K. Austin. *Organized for Prohibition: A New History of the Anti-Saloon League.* New Haven, Conn.: Yale University Press, 1985.

Kevles, Daniel J. "Testing the Army's Intelligence: Psychologists and the Military in World War I." *Journal of American History* 55 (December 1968): 565–81.

Kight, Lawrence Edward. "'The State Is on Trial': Governor Edmund F. Noel and Defense of Mississippi's Legal Institutions against Mob Violence." *Journal of Mississippi History* 60 (Fall 1998): 191–222.

Kimball, David. *Venerable Relic: The Story of the Liberty Bell.* Philadelphia: Eastern National Park and Monument Association, 1989.

Klejment, Anne. "The Radical Origins of Catholic Pacifism: Dorothy Day and the Lyrical Left during World War I." In *American Catholic Pacifism: The Influence of Dorothy Day and the Catholic Worker Movement,* ed. Anne Klejment and Nancy L. Roberts. Westport, Conn.: Praeger, 1996.

Klosko, George. *Political Obligations.* New York: Oxford University Press, 2005.

Kohn, Stephen M. *American Political Prisoners: Prosecutions under the Espionage and Sedition Acts.* Westport, Conn.: Praeger, 1994.

———. *Jailed for Peace: The History of American Draft Law Violators, 1658–1985.* Westport, Conn.: Greenwood, 1986.

Kohrman, Allan. "Respectable Pacifists: Quaker Response to World War I." *Quaker History* 75 (Spring 1986): 35–53.

Korman, Gerd. *Industrialization, Immigrants, and Americanizers: The View from Milwaukee, 1866–1921.* Madison: State Historical Society of Wisconsin, 1967.

Kornweibel, Theodore, Jr. "Apathy and Dissent: Black America's Negative Responses to World War I." *South Atlantic Quarterly* 80 (Summer 1981): 322–38.

———. *"Investigate Everything": Federal Efforts to Compel Black Loyalty during World War I.* Bloomington: Indiana University Press, 2002.

———. "Race and Conscientious Objection in World War I: The Story of the Church of God in Christ." In *Proclaim Peace: Christian Pacifism from Unexpected Quarters,* ed. Theron F. Schlabach and Richard T. Hughes. Urbana: University of Illinois Press, 1997.

Kuklick, Bruce. *Josiah Royce: An Intellectual Biography.* Indianapolis, Ind.: Bobbs-Merrill, 1972.

Lamson, Peggy. *Roger Baldwin: Founder of the American Civil Liberties Union.* Boston: Houghton Mifflin, 1976.

Langum, David J. *Crossing over the Line: Legislating Morality and the Mann Act.* Chicago: University of Chicago Press, 1994.

Lawrence, Jon. *Speaking for the People: Party, Language, and Popular Politics in England, 1867–1914.* New York: Cambridge University Press, 1998.

Leach, Eugene E. "Chaining the Tiger: The Mob Stigma and the Working Class, 1863–1894." *Labor History* 35 (Spring 1994): 187–215.

———. "The Literature of Riot Duty: Managing Class Conflict in the Streets, 1877–1927." *Radical History Review* no. 56 (Spring 1993): 23–50.

Lee, David D., ed. *Sergeant York: An American Hero.* Lexington: University Press of Kentucky, 1985.

Lee, Erika S. *At America's Gates: Chinese Immigration during the Exclusion Era*. Chapel Hill: University of North Carolina Press, 2003.

Leff, Mark H. "The Politics of Sacrifice on the American Home Front in World War II." *Journal of American History* 77 (March 1991): 1296–1318.

Lendler, Marc. " 'Equally Proper at All Times and Equally Necessary': Civility, Bad Tendency, and the Sedition Act." *Journal of the Early Republic* 24 (Fall 2004): 419–44.

Levi, Margaret C. *Consent, Dissent, and Patriotism*. New York: Cambridge University Press, 1997.

Levi, Steven C. *Committee of Vigilance: The San Francisco Chamber of Commerce Law and Order Committee, 1916–1919: A Case Study in Official Hysteria*. Jefferson, N.C.: McFarland, 1983.

Levy, Leonard Williams. *Legacy of Suppression: Freedom of Speech and Press in Early American History*. Cambridge: Harvard University Press, 1960.

Lewis, David Levering. *W. E. B. Du Bois: Biography of a Race, 1868–1919*. New York: Henry Holt, 1993.

Lich, Glen E. *The German Texans*. San Antonio: University of Texas Institute of Texan Cultures, 1981.

Lindley, John M. *"A Soldier Is Also a Citizen": The Controversy over Military Justice, 1917–1920*. New York: Garland, 1990.

Lindquist, John H., and James Fraser. "A Sociological Interpretation of the Bisbee Deportations." *Pacific Historical Review* 37 (November 1968): 401–22.

Linn, James Weber. *Jane Addams: A Biography*. New York: Greenwood, 1968 [1935].

Litwack, Leon F. *Trouble in Mind: Black Southerners in the Age of Jim Crow*. New York: Knopf, 1998.

Lockmiller, David A. *Enoch H. Crowder: Soldier, Lawyer, and Statesman*. Columbia: University of Missouri Studies, 1955.

Loss, Christopher P. "Reading between Enemy Lines: Armed Services Editions and World War II." *Journal of Military History* 67 (July 2003): 811–34.

Lovett, Robert Morss. *Jane Addams and the Women's International League for Peace and Freedom*. Chicago: WILPF, 1946.

Lovin, Hugh T. "World War I Vigilantes in Idaho, 1917–1918." *Idaho Yesterdays* 18 (Summer 1974): 2–11.

Lowenthal, Max. *The Federal Bureau of Investigation*. New York: William Sloane Associates, 1950.

Luebke, Frederick C. *Bonds of Loyalty: German-Americans and World War I*. DeKalb: Northern Illinois University Press, 1974.

———. "Legal Restrictions on Foreign Languages in the Great Plains States, 1917–1923." In *Languages in Conflict: Linguistic Acculturation on the Great Plains*, ed. Paul Schach. Lincoln: University of Nebraska Press, 1980.

Lunardini, Christine A. *From Equal Suffrage to Equal Rights: Alice Paul and the National Woman's Party, 1910–1928*. New York: New York University Press, 1986.

———, and Thomas J. Knock. "Woodrow Wilson and Woman Suffrage: A New Look." *Political Science Quarterly* 95 (Winter 1980–81): 655–71.

Lynch, Michael J., III. "The Role of J. T. Canales in the Development of Tejano Identity and Mexican American Integration in Twentieth Century South Texas." *Journal of South Texas* 13 (Fall 2000): 220–39.

MacDonald, Anne S. *No Idle Hands: The Social History of American Knitting*. New York: Ballantine, 1988.

MacLean, Nancy. *Behind the Mask of Chivalry: The Making of the Second Ku Klux Klan*. New York: Oxford University Press, 1994.

Maier, Pauline. "Popular Uprisings and Civil Authority in Eighteenth-Century America." *William and Mary Quarterly*, 3rd ser. 27 (January 1970): 3–35.

Maines, Rachel. "Wartime Allocation of Textiles and Apparel Resources: Emergency Policy in the Twentieth Century." *Public Historian* 7 (Winter 1985): 29–51.

Marchand, C. Roland. *The American Peace Movement and Social Reform, 1898–1918*. Princeton, N.J.: Princeton University Press, 1972.

Mason, Alpheus Thomas. "Harlan Fiske Stone: In Defense of Individual Freedom, 1918–1920." *Columbia Law Review* 51 (February 1951): 147–69.

———. *Harlan Fiske Stone: Pillar of the Law*. New York: Viking, 1956.

Mattson, Kevin. *Creating a Democratic Public: The Struggle for Urban Participatory Democracy during the Progressive Era*. University Park: Pennsylvania State University Press, 1998.

———. "The Librarian as Secular Minister to Democracy: The Life and Ideas of John Cotton Dana." *Libraries and Culture* 35 (Fall 2000): 514–34.

Mayhall, Pamela. "Bisbee's Response to Civil Disorder." *The American West* 9 (May 1972): 22–31.

Mazower, Mark. "Violence and the State in the Twentieth Century." *American Historical Review* 107 (October 2002): 1158–78.

McAvoy, Thomas T. "The Catholic Church in the United States between Two Wars." *Review of Politics* 4 (October 1942): 409–31.

McCallum, Jack. *Leonard Wood: Rough Rider, Surgeon, Architect of American Imperialism*. New York: New York University Press, 2006.

McCartin, Joseph A. *Labor's Great War: The Struggle for Industrial Democracy and the Origins of Modern American Labor Relations, 1912–1921*. Chapel Hill: University of North Carolina Press, 1997.

McConnell, Stuart. *Glorious Contentment: The Grand Army of the Republic, 1865–1900*. Chapel Hill: University of North Carolina Press, 1992.

McKeown, Elizabeth. *War and Welfare: American Catholics and World War I*. New York: Garland, 1988.

McNally, Michael J. *Catholic Parish Life on Florida's West Coast, 1860–1968*. N.p.: Catholic Media Ministries, 1996.

McNeal, Patricia. "Catholic Pacifism in America." In *Catholics in America, 1776–1976*, ed. Robert Trisco. Washington, D.C.: National Conference of Catholic Bishops, 1976.

McPherson, James M. *For Cause and Comrades: Why Men Fought in the Civil War*. New York: Oxford University Press, 1997.

McQuillan, D. Aidan. *Prevailing over Time: Ethnic Adjustment on the Kansas Prairies, 1875–1925*. Lincoln: University of Nebraska Press, 1990.

Medley, Mary L. *History of Anson County North Carolina, 1750–1976*. Wadesboro, N.C.: Anson County Historical Society, 1976.

Melendy, H. Brett. *Walter Francis Dillingham, 1875–1963: Hawaiian Entrepreneur and Statesman*. Lewiston, N.Y.: Edwin Mellen, 1996.

Mellinger, Philip J. *Race and Labor in Western Copper: The Fight for Equality, 1896–1918*. Tucson: University of Arizona Press, 1995.

Members of the Past Presidents Association of The Dallas Federation of Women's Clubs, eds. *History of The Dallas Federation of Women's Clubs, 1898–1936*. Dallas: Clyde C. Cockrell and Son, 1936.

Meyer, Susan E. *James Montgomery Flagg*. New York: Watson-Guptill, 1974.

Michels, Eileen Manning. "Alice O'Brien: Volunteer and Philanthropist." In *Women of Minnesota: Selected Biographical Essays*, rev. ed., ed. Barbara Stuhler and Gretchen Kreuter. St. Paul: Minnesota Historical Society Press, 1998.

Mitchell, W. J. T. *What Do Pictures Want? The Lives and Loves of Images*. Chicago: University of Chicago Press, 2005.

Mjagkij, Nina. *Light in the Darkness: African Americans and the YMCA, 1852–1946*. Lexington: University Press of Kentucky, 1994.

Moller, George Long. *The Hoboken of Yesterday*. Hoboken, N.J.: G. L. Moller, 1964.

Monkkonen, Eric H. *The Police in Urban America, 1860–1920*. New York: Cambridge University Press, 1981.

Moore, Leonard J. *Citizen Klansmen: The Ku Klux Klan in Indiana, 1921–1928*. Chapel Hill: University of North Carolina Press, 1991.

———. "Historical Interpretations of the 1920s Klan: The Traditional View and Recent Revisions." In *The Invisible Empire in the West: Toward a New Historical Appraisal of the Ku Klux Klan of the 1920s*, ed. Shawn Lay. Urbana: University of Illinois Press, 1992.

Moore, William Haas. "Prisoners in the Promised Land: The Molokans in World War I." *Journal of Arizona History* 14 (Fall 1973): 281–302.

Morgan, Francesca. *Women and Patriotism in Jim Crow America*. Chapel Hill: University of North Carolina Press, 2005.

Morgan, H. Wayne, and Anne Hodges Morgan. *Oklahoma: A Bicentennial History*. New York: Norton, 1977.

Morgan, William M. *Questionable Charity: Gender, Humanitarianism, and Complicity in U.S. Literary Realism*. Hanover, N.H.: University Press of New England, 2004.

Morlan, Robert L. *Political Prairie Fire: The Nonpartisan League, 1915–1922*. Minneapolis: University of Minnesota Press, 1955.

Morn, Frank. *"The Eye That Never Sleeps": A History of the Pinkerton National Detective Agency*. Bloomington: Indiana University Press, 1982.

Mullendore, William Clinton. *History of the United States Food Administration, 1917–1919*. Stanford, Calif.: Stanford University Press, 1941.

Muncy, Robyn. *Creating a Female Dominion in American Reform, 1890–1935*. New York: Oxford University Press, 1991.

Murphy, Paul L. *World War I and the Origin of Civil Liberties in the United States*. New York: Norton, 1979.

Murray, Paul T. "Blacks and the Draft: A History of Institutional Racism." *Journal of Black Studies* 2 (September 1971): 57–76.

Murray, Robert K. *Red Scare: A Study in National Hysteria, 1919–1920*. Minneapolis: University of Minnesota Press, 1955.

Myers, Gloria E. *A Municipal Mother: Portland's Lola Greene Baldwin, America's First Policewoman*. Corvallis: Oregon State University Press, 1995.

Nagler, Jörg. *Nationale Minoritäten im Krieg: Feindliche Ausländer und die Amerikanische Heimatfront während des Ersten Weltkriegs*. Hamburg: Hamburger Edition, 2000.

———. "Victims of the Home Front: Enemy Aliens in the United States during the First World War." In *Minorities in Wartime: National and Racial Groupings in Europe, North America, and Australia during the Two World Wars*, ed. Panikos Panayi. Providence, R.I.: Berg, 1993.

Nash, Jay Robert. *Citizen Hoover: A Critical Study of the Life and Times of J. Edgar Hoover and His FBI*. Chicago: Nelson-Hall, 1972.

Nathans, Eli. *The Politics of Citizenship in Germany: Ethnicity, Utility and Nationalism*. New York: Berg, 2004.

Nelson, Clifford L. *German-American Political Behavior in Nebraska and Wisconsin, 1916–1920*. Lincoln: University of Nebraska–Lincoln Publication, 1972.

Nelson, E. Clifford. *Lutheranism in North America, 1914–1970*. Minneapolis: Augsburg, 1972.

Neth, Mary. *Preserving the Family Farm: Women, Community, and the Foundations of Agribusiness in the Midwest, 1900–1940*. Baltimore: Johns Hopkins University Press, 1995.

Newman, Louise Michele. *White Women's Rights: The Racial Origins of Feminism in the United States*. New York: Oxford University Press, 1999.

Ngai, Mae M. *Impossible Subjects: Illegal Aliens and the Making of Modern America*. Princeton, N.J.: Princeton University Press, 2004.

Nichols, May Ellis. *A History of the Meridian*. Brooklyn, N.Y.: n.p., 1934.

Nielsen, Kim E. *Un-American Womanhood: Antiradicalism, Antifeminism, and the First Red Scare*. Columbus: Ohio State University Press, 2001.

Norwood, Stephen H. "Bogalusa Burning: The War against Biracial Unionism in the Deep South, 1919." *Journal of Southern History* 63 (August 1997): 591–628.

Novak, William J. "The American Law of Association: The Legal-Political Construction of Civil Society." *Studies in American Political Development* 15 (Fall 2001): 163–88.

———. "The Legal Transformation of Citizenship in Nineteenth-Century America." In *The Democratic Experiment: New Directions in American Political History*, ed. Meg Jacobs et al. Princeton, N.J.: Princeton University Press, 2003.

———. *The People's Welfare: Law and Regulation in Nineteenth-Century America*. Chapel Hill: University of North Carolina Press, 1996.

Novick, Peter. *That Noble Dream: The "Objectivity Question" and the American Historical Profession*. New York: Cambridge University Press, 1988.

Novick, Sheldon M. "The Unrevised Holmes and Free Expression." *Supreme Court Review* (1991): 303–90.

O'Leary, Cecilia Elizabeth. *To Die For: The Paradox of American Patriotism*. Princeton, N.J.: Princeton University Press, 1999.

Olson, James C., and Ronald C. Naugle. *History of Nebraska*, 3rd ed. Lincoln: University of Nebraska Press, 1997.

O'Neal, Bill. "Captain Harry Wheeler, Arizona Lawman." *Journal of Arizona History* 27 (Autumn 1986): 297–314.

O'Neill, Colleen. "Domesticity Deployed: Gender, Race, and the Construction of Class Struggle in the Bisbee Deportation." *Labor History* 34 (Spring–Summer 1993): 256–73.

Osborn, Norris Galpin, ed. *History of Connecticut in Monographic Form*. New York: States History, 1925.

Osterweis, Rollin G. *Three Centuries of New Haven, 1638–1938*. New Haven, Conn.: Yale University Press, 1953.

Palmer, Maude G., comp. *The History of the Illinois Federation of Women's Clubs, 1894–1928*. N.p.: Illinois Federation of Women's Clubs, 1928.

Parish, Arlyn John. *Kansas Mennonites during World War I*. Fort Hays, Kan.: Fort Hays Studies, 1968.

Pateman, Carole. *The Problem of Political Obligation: A Critique of Liberal Theory*. Berkeley: University of California Press, 1985.

Pearlman, Michael. *To Make Democracy Safe for America: Patricians and Preparedness in the Progressive Era*. Urbana: University of Illinois Press, 1984.

Pegram, Thomas R. *Battling Demon Rum: The Struggle for a Dry America, 1800–1933*. Chicago: Ivan R. Dee, 1998.

Pencak, William. *For God and Country: The American Legion, 1919–1941*. Boston: Northeastern University Press, 1989.

Perkins, Mrs. Lawrence B. *One Hundred Years of Christian Service*. Evanston, Ill.: First Congregational Church of Evanston, 1970.

Perry, Bliss. *Life and Letters of Henry Lee Higginson*. Freeport, N.Y.: Books for Libraries Press, 1972 [1921].

Peters, Shawn Francis. *Judging Jehovah's Witnesses: Religious Persecution and the Dawn of the Rights Revolution*. Lawrence: University Press of Kansas, 2000.

Peterson, H. C., and Gilbert C. Fite. *Opponents of War, 1917–1918*. Seattle: University of Washington Press, 1968 [1957].

Pfeffer, Paula F. *A. Philip Randolph: Pioneer of the Civil Rights Movement*. Baton Rouge: Louisiana State University Press, 1990.

Pfeifer, Michael J. *Rough Justice: Lynching and American Society, 1874–1947*. Urbana: University of Illinois Press, 2004.

Piper, John F., Jr. *The American Churches in World War I*. Athens: Ohio University Press, 1985.

Pivar, Donald J. "Cleansing the Nation: The War on Prostitution, 1917–1921." *Prologue* 12 (Spring 1980): 29–40.

Polenberg, Richard. *Fighting Faiths: The Abrams Case, the Supreme Court, and Free Speech*. New York: Viking, 1987.

Powell, Allan Kent. *Splinters of a Nation: German Prisoners of War in Utah*. Salt Lake City: University of Utah Press, 1989.

Powers, Richard Gid. *Secrecy and Power: The Life of J. Edgar Hoover*. New York: Free Press, 1987.

Preston, William, Jr. *Aliens and Dissenters: Federal Suppression of Radicals, 1903–1933*, 2nd ed. Urbana: University of Illinois Press, 1994.

Price, Alan. *The End of the Age of Innocence: Edith Wharton and the First World War*. New York: St. Martin's, 1996.

Przybyszewski, Linda. "Judicial Conservatism and Protestant Faith: The Case of Justice David J. Brewer." *Journal of American History* 91 (September 2004): 471–96.

Purdy, Jedediah. *For Common Things: Irony, Trust, and Commitment in America Today*. New York: Knopf, 1999.

Putnam, Robert D. "Bowling Alone: America's Declining Social Capital." *Journal of Democracy* 6 (January 1995): 65–78.

———. *Bowling Alone: The Collapse and Revival of American Community*. New York: Simon & Schuster, 2000.

Rabban, David M. *Free Speech in Its Forgotten Years*. New York: Cambridge University Press, 1997.

Radice, Lisanne. *Beatrice and Sidney Webb: Fabian Socialists*. New York: St. Martin's, 1984.

Ragan, Fred D. "Justice Oliver Wendell Holmes, Jr., Zechariah Chafee, Jr., and the Clear and Present Danger Test for Free Speech: The First Year, 1919." *Journal of American History* 58 (June 1971): 24–45.

———. "An Unlikely Alliance: Tom Watson, Harry Weinberger, and the World War I Draft." *Atlanta Historical Journal* 25 (Fall 1981): 19–36.

Randel, Mrs. Ralph E., ed. *A Time to Purpose: A Chronicle of Carson County*. 4 vols. Hereford, Tex.: Pioneer, 1966–72.

Rawls, John. "Legal Obligation and the Duty of Fair Play." In *Law and Philosophy: A Symposium*, ed. Sidney Hook. New York: New York University Press, 1964.

———. *A Theory of Justice*. Cambridge: Harvard University Press, 1971.

Rawls, Walton. *Wake Up, America! World War I and the American Poster*. New York: Abbeville, 1988.

Reich, Steven A. "Soldiers of Democracy: Black Texans and the Fight for Democracy, 1917–1921." *Journal of American History* 82 (March 1996): 1478–1504.

Reis, Elizabeth. "The AFL, the IWW, and Bay Area Cannery Workers." *California History* 64 (Summer 1985): 174–91.

Rich, Melanie. " 'She Would Raise Hens to Aid War': The Contributions of Oklahoma Women during World War I." *Chronicles of Oklahoma* 91 (Fall 2003): 334–55.

Richards, Leonard L. *Gentlemen of Property and Standing: Anti-Abolitionist Mobs in Jacksonian America*. New York: Oxford University Press, 1970.

Rieff, Lynne A. " 'Go Ahead and Do All You Can': Southern Progressives and Alabama Home Demonstration Clubs, 1914–1940." In *Hidden Histories of Women in the New South*, ed. Virginia Bernhard et al. Columbia: University of Missouri Press, 1994.

Rippley, LaVern J. "Ameliorated Americanization: The Effect of World War I on German-Americans in the 1920s." In *America and the Germans: An Assessment of a Three-Hundred-Year History*, ed. Frank Trommler and Joseph McVeigh. Philadelphia: University of Pennsylvania Press, 1985.

———. "Gift Cows for Germany." *North Dakota History* 40 (Summer 1973): 4–15.

Rippley, LaVern J., with Robert J. Paulson. *German-Bohemians: The Quiet Immigrants*. Northfield, Minn.: St. Olaf College Press, 1995.

Robinson, Charles M., III. *The Men Who Wear the Star: The Story of the Texas Rangers*. New York: Random House, 2000.

Rodgers, Daniel T. *Atlantic Crossings: Social Politics in a Progressive Age*. Cambridge: Harvard University Press, 1998.

———. *Contested Truths: Keywords in American Politics since Independence*. New York: Basic Books, 1987.

Rodgers, Jack W. "The Foreign Language Issue in Nebraska, 1918–1923." *Nebraska History* 39 (March 1958): 1–22.

Rogow, Faith. *Gone to Another Meeting: The National Council of Jewish Women, 1893–1993*. Tuscaloosa: University of Alabama Press, 1993.

Rohrs, Richard C. *The Germans in Oklahoma*. Norman: University of Oklahoma Press, 1980.

Rosen, Ruth. *The Lost Sisterhood: Prostitution in America, 1900–1918.* Baltimore: Johns Hopkins University Press, 1982.

Rosenbaum, H. Jon, and Peter C. Sederberg, eds. *Vigilante Politics.* Philadelphia: University of Pennsylvania Press, 1976.

Rosenberg, Norman L. *Protecting the Best Men: An Interpretive History of the Law of Libel.* Chapel Hill: University of North Carolina Press, 1986.

Rosewater, Victor. *The Liberty Bell: Its History and Significance.* New York: D. Appleton, 1926.

Ross, William G. *Forging New Freedoms: Nativism, Education, and the Constitution, 1917–1927.* Lincoln: University of Nebraska Press, 1994.

Rouse, Jacqueline Anne. *Lugenia Burns Hope: Black Southern Reformer.* Athens: University of Georgia Press, 1989.

Ruckman, Jo Ann. " 'Knit, Knit, and Then Knit': The Women of Pocatello and the War Effort of 1917–1918." *Idaho Yesterdays* 26 (Spring 1982): 26–36.

Rumer, Thomas A. *The American Legion: An Official History, 1919–1989.* New York: M. Evans, 1990.

Salvatore, Nick. *Eugene V. Debs: Citizen and Socialist.* Urbana: University of Illinois Press, 1982.

Salyer, Lucy E. "Baptism by Fire: Race, Military Service, and U.S. Citizenship Policy, 1918–1935." *Journal of American History* 91 (December 2004): 847–76.

Samet, Elizabeth D. *Willing Obedience: Citizens, Soldiers, and the Progress of Consent in America, 1776–1898.* Stanford, Calif.: Stanford University Press, 2004.

Sandel, Michael J. *Democracy's Discontent: America in Search of a Public Philosophy.* Cambridge: Harvard University Press, 1996.

Schaffer, Ronald. *America in the Great War: The Rise of the War Welfare State.* New York: Oxford University Press, 1991.

Scharff, Virginia. *Taking the Wheel: Women and the Coming of the Motor Age.* New York: Free Press, 1991.

Scheiber, Harry N. *The Wilson Administration and Civil Liberties, 1917–1921.* Ithaca, N.Y.: Cornell University Press, 1960.

Schlossman, Steven L. "Is There an American Tradition of Bilingual Education? German in the Public Elementary Schools, 1840–1919." *American Journal of Education* 92 (February 1983): 139–86.

Schmidt, Henry J. "The Rhetoric of Survival: The Germanist in America from 1900 to 1925." In *America and the Germans: An Assessment of a Three-Hundred-Year History,* ed. Frank Trommler and Joseph McVeigh. Philadelphia: University of Pennsylvania Press, 1985.

Schmidt, Paul C. "The Press in North Dakota." *North Dakota History* 31 (October 1964): 217–22.

Schmidt, Regin. *Red Scare: FBI and the Origins of Anticommunism in the United States, 1919–1943.* Copenhagen: Museum Tusculanum Press, 2000.

Schott, Linda K. *Reconstructing Women's Thoughts: The Women's International League for Peace and Freedom before World War II.* Stanford, Calif.: Stanford University Press, 1997.

Schottenhamel, George. "How Big Bill Thompson Won Control of Chicago." *Journal of the Illinois State Historical Society* 45 (Spring 1952): 30–49.

Schwantes, Carlos A., ed. *Bisbee: Urban Outpost on the Frontier.* Tucson: University of Arizona Press, 1992.

Schwartz, E. A. "The Lynching of Robert Prager, the United Mine Workers, and the Problems of Patriotism in 1918." *Journal of the Illinois State Historical Society* 96 (Winter 2003): 414–37.

Scott, Anne Firor. "Most Invisible of All: Black Women's Voluntary Associations." *Journal of Southern History* 56 (February 1990): 5–22.

———. *Natural Allies: Women's Associations in American History.* Urbana: University of Illinois Press, 1991.

Sellars, Nigel Anthony. *Oil, Wheat, and Wobblies: The Industrial Workers of the World in Oklahoma, 1905–1930.* Norman: University of Oklahoma Press, 1998.

Sessions, Gene. "Espionage in Windsor: Clarence H. Waldron and Patriotism in World War I." *Vermont History* 61 (Summer 1993): 133–55.

Shaw, Stephanie J. "Black Club Women and the Creation of the National Association of Colored Women." *Journal of Women's History* 3 (Fall 1991): 10–25.

Shenk, Gerald E. *"Work or Fight!": Race, Gender, and the Draft in World War One.* New York: Palgrave Macmillan, 2005.

Shields, Sarah D. "The Treatment of Conscientious Objectors during World War I: Mennonites at Camp Funston." *Kansas History* 4 (Winter 1987): 255–69.

Shklar, Judith N. *American Citizenship: The Quest for Inclusion.* Cambridge: Harvard University Press, 1991.

Shore, Elliott, et al., eds. *The German-American Radical Press: The Shaping of a Left Political Culture, 1850–1940.* Urbana: University of Illinois Press, 1992.

Sibley, Milford Q., and Philip E. Jacob. *Conscription of Conscience: The American State and the Conscientious Objector, 1940–1947.* Ithaca, N.Y.: Cornell University Press, 1952.

Skocpol, Theda. *Protecting Soldiers and Mothers: The Political Origins of Social Policy in the United States.* Cambridge: Harvard University Press, 1992.

———, et al. "A Nation of Organizers: The Institutional Origins of Civic Voluntarism in the United States." *American Political Science Review* 94 (September 2000): 527–46.

———, et al. "Patriotic Partnerships: Why Great Wars Nourished American Civic Voluntarism." In *Shaped by War and Trade: International Influences on American Political Development,* ed. Ira Katznelson and Martin Shefter. Princeton, N.J.: Princeton University Press, 2002.

———, and Morris P. Fiorina, eds. *Civic Engagement in American Democracy.* Washington, D.C.: Brookings Institution Press, 1999.

Skowronek, Stephen. *Building a New American State: The Expansion of National Administrative Capacities, 1877–1920.* New York: Cambridge University Press, 1982.

Slotkin, Richard. *Gunfighter Nation: The Myth of the Frontier in Twentieth-Century America.* New York: Atheneum, 1992.

———. *Lost Battalions: The Great War and the Crisis of American Nationality.* New York: Henry Holt, 2005.

Smith, Jason Scott. "New Deal Policy Works at War: The WPA and Japanese American Internment." *Pacific Historical Review* 72 (February 2003): 63–92.

Smith, Rogers M. "Beyond Tocqueville, Myrdal, and Hartz: The Multiple Traditions in America." *American Political Science Review* 87 (September 1993): 549–66.

——. *Civic Ideals: Conflicting Visions of Citizenship in U.S. History.* New Haven, Conn.: Yale University Press, 1997.

Snyder, Thomas D., ed. *120 Years of American Education: A Statistical Portrait.* Washington, D.C.: National Center for Education Statistics, 1993.

Spratt, John S., Sr. *Thurber, Texas: The Life and Death of a Company Coal Town,* ed. Harwood P. Hinton. Austin: University of Texas Press, 1986.

Stanfield, John H., II. "The Dilemma of Conscientious Objection for Afro-Americans." In *The New Conscientious Objection: From Sacred to Secular Resistance,* ed. Charles C. Moskos and John Whiteclay Chambers II. New York: Oxford University Press, 1993.

Stansell, Christine. *American Moderns: Bohemian New York and the Creation of a New Century.* New York: Metropolitan, 2000.

Steel, Ronald. *Walter Lippmann and the American Century.* Boston: Little, Brown, 1980.

Steinson, Barbara J. *American Women's Activism in World War I.* New York: Garland, 1982.

Stentiford, Barry M. *The American Home Guard: The State Militia in the Twentieth Century.* College Station: Texas A&M University Press, 2002.

Sterba, Christopher M. *Good Americans: Italian and Jewish Immigrants during the First World War.* New York: Oxford University Press, 2003.

Stockley, Grif. *Blood in Their Eyes: The Elaine Race Massacres of 1919.* Fayetteville: University of Arkansas Press, 2001.

Stone, Geoffrey R. *Perilous Times: Free Speech in Wartime from the Sedition Act of 1798 to the War on Terrorism.* New York: Norton, 2004.

Stroup, Herbert Hewitt. *The Jehovah's Witnesses.* New York: Columbia University Press, 1945.

Stucky, Gregory J. "Fighting against War: The Mennonite *Vorwaerts* from 1914 to 1919." *Kansas Historical Quarterly* 38 (Summer 1972): 169–86.

Sullivan, Mark. *Our Times: The United States, 1900–1925.* New York: Scribner's, 1933.

Sun, Yumei. "San Francisco's *Chung Sai Yat Po* and the Transformation of Chinese Consciousness, 1900–1920." In *Print Culture in a Diverse America,* ed. James P. Danky and Wayne A. Wiegand. Urbana: University of Illinois Press, 1998.

Swanberg, W. A. *Norman Thomas: The Last Idealist.* New York: Scribner's, 1976.

Tabrah, Ruth. *Hawaii: A Bicentennial History.* New York: Norton, 1980.

Taylor, Kieran. " 'We Have Just Begun': Black Organizing and White Response in the Arkansas Delta, 1919." *Arkansas Historical Quarterly* 58 (Autumn 1999): 265–84.

Taylor, Robert M., Jr., and Connie A. McBirney, eds. *Peopling Indiana: The Ethnic Experience.* Indianapolis: Indiana Historical Society, 1996.

Terborg-Penn, Rosalyn. *African American Women in the Struggle for the Vote, 1850–1920.* Bloomington: Indiana University Press, 1998.

——. "African-American Women's Networks in the Anti-Lynching Crusade." In *Gender, Class, Race, and Reform in the Progressive Era,* ed. Noralee Frankel and Nancy S. Dye. Lexington: University Press of Kentucky, 1991.

——. "Discontented Black Feminists: Prelude and Postscript to the Passage of the Nineteenth Amendment." In *Decades of Discontent: The Women's Movement, 1920–1940,* ed. Lois Scharf and Joan M. Jensen. Westport, Conn.: Greenwood, 1983.

Theoharis, Athan G. *The FBI and American Democracy: A Brief Critical History.* Lawrence: University Press of Kansas, 2004.

———, and John Stuart Cox. *The Boss: J. Edgar Hoover and the Great American Inquisition.* Philadelphia: Temple University Press, 1988.

Thomas, Helen Shirley. *Felix Frankfurter: Scholar on the Bench.* Baltimore: Johns Hopkins Press, 1960.

Thorsen, Niels. *The Political Thought of Woodrow Wilson, 1875–1910.* Princeton, N.J.: Princeton University Press, 1988.

Thurner, Manuela. "'Better Citizens without the Ballot': American Antisuffrage Women and Their Rationale during the Progressive Era." *Journal of Women's History* 5 (Spring 1993): 33–60.

Tilly, Charles. "War Making and State Making as Organized Crime." In *Bringing the State Back In*, ed. Peter Evans et al. New York: Cambridge University Press, 1985.

Tindall, George Brown. *The Emergence of the New South, 1913–1945.* Baton Rouge: Louisiana State University Press, 1967.

Tischler, Barbara L. "One Hundred Percent Americanism and Music in Boston during World War I." *American Music* 4 (Summer 1986): 164–76.

Tonn, Joan C. *Mary P. Follett: Creating Democracy, Transforming Management.* New Haven, Conn.: Yale University Press, 2003.

Torpey, John. "The Great War and the Birth of the Modern Passport System." In *Documenting Individual Identity: The Development of State Practices in the Modern World*, ed. Jane Caplan and John Torpey. Princeton, N.J.: Princeton University Press, 2001.

Tuttle, William M. *Race Riot: Chicago in the Red Summer of 1919.* New York: Atheneum, 1970.

Tyler, Helen E. *Where Prayer and Purpose Meet: The WCTU Story, 1874–1949.* Evanston, Ill.: Signal, 1949.

Unruh, John D. "The Hutterites during World War I." *Mennonite Life* 24 (July 1969): 130–37.

Urofsky, Melvin I. *Louis D. Brandeis and the Progressive Tradition.* Boston: Little, Brown, 1981.

Vacha, J. E. "When Wagner Was Verboten: The Campaign against German Music in World War I." *New York History* 64 (April 1983): 171–88.

VanBurkleo, Sandra F. "Words as Hard as Cannon-Balls: Women's Rights Agitation and Liberty of Speech in Nineteenth-Century America." In *Constitutionalism and American Culture: Writing the New Constitutional History*, ed. Sandra F. VanBurkleo et al. Lawrence: University Press of Kansas, 2002.

Van Voris, Jacqueline. *Carrie Chapman Catt: A Public Life.* New York: Feminist Press, 1987.

Vaughn, Stephen. *Holding Fast the Inner Line: Democracy, Nationalism, and the Committee on Public Information.* Chapel Hill: University of North Carolina Press, 1980.

Wagenknecht, Edward. *Daughters of the Covenant: Portraits of Six Jewish Women.* Amherst: University of Massachusetts Press, 1983.

Waldrep, Christopher. *The Many Faces of Judge Lynch: Extralegal Violence and Punishment in America.* New York: Palgrave Macmillan, 2004.

———. "War of Words: The Controversy over the Definition of Lynching, 1899–1940." *Journal of Southern History* 66 (February 2000): 75–100.

Walker, Mack. "The Old Homeland and the New." In *German Culture in Texas: A Free Earth,* ed. Glen E. Lich and Dona B. Reeves. Boston: Twayne, 1980.

Walker, Samuel. *In Defense of American Liberties: A History of the ACLU*, 2nd ed. Carbondale: Southern Illinois University Press, 1999.

Walzer, Michael. *Obligations: Essays on Disobedience, War, and Citizenship*. Cambridge: Harvard University Press, 1970.

Wechsler, Herbert. "Harlan Fiske Stone." *New York History* 69 (April 1988): 154–62.

Wedin, Carolyn. *Inheritors of the Spirit: Mary White Ovington and the Founding of the NAACP*. New York: Wiley, 1998.

Weinberg, Carl R. *Labor, Loyalty, and Rebellion: Southwestern Illinois Coal Miners and World War I*. Carbondale: Southern Illinois University Press, 2005.

Weisenfeld, Judith. *African American Women and Christian Activism: New York's Black YWCA, 1905–1945*. Cambridge: Harvard University Press, 1997.

Westbrook, Robert B. "Fighting for the American Family: Private Interests and Political Obligation in World War II." In *The Power of Culture: Critical Essays in American History*, ed. Richard Wightman Fox and T. J. Jackson Lears. Chicago: University of Chicago Press, 1991.

———. "'I Want a Girl, Just Like the Girl That Married Harry James': American Women and the Problem of Political Obligation in World War II." *American Quarterly* 42 (December 1990): 587–614.

———. *John Dewey and American Democracy*. Ithaca, N.Y.: Cornell University Press, 1991.

———. *Why We Fought: Forging American Obligations in World War II*. Washington, D.C.: Smithsonian Institution Press, 2004.

"What We See and Can't See in the Past: A Round Table." *Journal of American History* 83 (March 1997): 1217–72.

Whayne, Jeannie M. "Low Villains and Wickedness in High Places: Race and Class in the Elaine Riots." *Arkansas Historical Quarterly* 58 (Autumn 1999): 285–313.

Whitaker, Walter E. *Centennial History of Alamance County, 1849–1949*. Burlington, N.C.: Burlington Chamber of Commerce, 1949.

Whitcomb, Carrie Niles. *Reminiscences of the Springfield Women's Club, 1884–1924*. N.p.: n.d. [1924].

White, Deborah Gray. *Too Heavy a Load: Black Women in Defense of Themselves, 1894–1994*. New York: Norton, 1999.

White, G. Edward. *Justice Oliver Wendell Holmes: Law and the Inner Self*. New York: Oxford University Press, 1993.

Whitehead, John S. "Western Progressives, Old South Planters, or Colonial Oppressors: The Enigma of Hawai'i's 'Big Five,' 1898–1940." *Western Historical Quarterly* 30 (Autumn 1999): 295–326.

Wiebe, Robert H. *The Search for Order, 1877–1920*. New York: Hill and Wang, 1967.

Wiegand, Wayne A. *An Active Instrument for Propaganda: The American Public Library during World War I*. Westport, Conn.: Greenwood, 1989.

Williams, David. "The Bureau of Investigation and Its Critics, 1919–1921: The Origins of Federal Political Surveillance." *Journal of American History* 68 (December 1981): 560–79.

Williams, Raymond. *Keywords: A Vocabulary of Culture and Society*. New York: Oxford University Press, 1976.

Willis, James F. "The Cleburne County Draft War." *Arkansas Historical Quarterly* 26 (Spring 1967): 24–39.

Willrich, Michael. *City of Courts: Socializing Justice in Progressive Era Chicago*. New York: Cambridge University Press, 2003.

———. "'The Least Vaccinated of Any Civilized Country': Personal Liberty and Public Health in the Progressive Era." *Journal of Policy History* 20 (January 2008).

Witcover, Jules. *Sabotage at Black Tom: Imperial Germany's Secret War in America, 1914–1917*. Chapel Hill, N.C.: Algonquin, 1989.

Witt, John Fabian. *The Accidental Republic: Crippled Workingmen, Destitute Widows, and the Remaking of American Law*. Cambridge: Harvard University Press, 2004.

———. "Crystal Eastman and the Internationalist Beginnings of American Civil Liberties." *Duke Law Journal* 54, no. 3 (2004): 705–64.

———. *Patriots and Cosmopolitans: Hidden Histories of American Law*. Cambridge: Harvard University Press, 2007.

Wittke, Carl. *German-Americans and the World War*. Columbus: Ohio State Archaeological and Historical Society, 1936.

Wood, Gordon S. *The Creation of the American Republic, 1776–1787*. New York: Norton, 1967.

Woodruff, Nan Elizabeth. "African-American Struggles for Citizenship in the Arkansas and Mississippi Deltas in the Age of Jim Crow." *Radical History Review* no. 55 (Winter 1993): 33–51.

Woodward, C. Vann. *Tom Watson: Agrarian Rebel*. New York: Oxford University Press, 1963 [1936].

Wylder, Delbert E. *Emerson Hough*. Boston: Twayne, 1981.

Young, Arthur P. *Books for Sammies: The American Library Association and World War I*. Pittsburgh, Pa.: Beta Phi Mu, 1981.

Young, Nancy Beck. *Lou Henry Hoover: Activist First Lady*. Lawrence: University Press of Kansas, 2004.

Young, Pauline V. *The Pilgrims of Russian-Town*. Chicago: University of Chicago Press, 1932.

Zangrando, Robert. *The NAACP Crusade against Lynching, 1909–1950*. Philadelphia: Temple University Press, 1980.

Zeiger, Susan. "She Didn't Raise Her Boy to Be a Slacker: Motherhood, Conscription, and the Culture of the First World War." *Feminist Studies* 22 (Spring 1996): 6–39.

———. *In Uncle Sam's Service: Women Workers with the American Expeditionary Force, 1917–1919*. Ithaca, N.Y.: Cornell University Press, 1999.

Zimmerman, Jonathan. "Ethnics against Ethnicity: European Immigrants and Foreign-Language Instruction, 1890–1940." *Journal of American History* 88 (March 2002): 1383–1404.

Zissu, Erik. "Conscription, Sovereignty, and Land: American Indian Resistance during World War I." *Pacific Historical Review* 64 (November 1995): 537–66.

Zonderman, David. "Over Here: The Wisconsin Homefront during World War I." *Wisconsin Magazine of History* 77 (Summer 1994): 295–300.

Dissertations

Benton, Katherine A. "What about Women in the White Man's Camp? Gender, Nation, and the Redefinition of Race in Cochise County, Arizona, 1853–1941." Ph.D. dissertation, University of Wisconsin, 2002.

Brownell, Penelope Noble. "The Women's Committees of the First World War: Women in Government, 1917–1919." Ph.D. dissertation, Brown University, 2003.

Feimster, Crystal Nicole. "'Ladies and Lynching': The Gendered Discourse of Mob Violence in the New South, 1880–1930." Ph.D. dissertation, Princeton University, 2000.

Fraser, Bruce. "Yankees at War: Social Mobilization on the Connecticut Homefront, 1917–1918." Ph.D. dissertation, Columbia University, 1976.

Jenkins, Maude T. "The History of the Black Woman's Club Movement in America." Ph.D. dissertation, Teachers College, Columbia University, 1984.

Jensen, Kimberly S. "Minerva on the Field of Mars: American Women, Citizenship, and Military Service in the First World War." Ph.D. dissertation, University of Iowa, 1992.

Nehls, Christopher. "A Grand and Glorious Feeling: The American Legion and American Nationalism between the Two World Wars." Ph.D. dissertation, University of Virginia, 2007.

Provost, Tracie Lynn. "The Great Game: Imperial German Sabotage and Espionage against the United States, 1914–1917." Ph.D. dissertation, University of Toledo, 2003.

Ribb, Richard Henry. "José Tomas Canales and the Texas Rangers: Myth, Identity, and Power in South Texas, 1900–1920." Ph.D. dissertation, University of Texas, 2002.

Thomas, William Henry, Jr. "The United States Department of Justice and Dissent during the First World War." Ph.D. dissertation, University of Iowa, 2002.

Weinberg, Carl. "The Tug of War: Labor, Loyalty, and Rebellion in the Southwestern Illinois Coalfields, 1914–1920." Ph.D. dissertation, Yale University, 1995.

Williams, Chad Louis. "Torchbearers of Democracy: The First World War and the Figure of the African-American Soldier." Ph.D. dissertation, Princeton University, 2004.

Index

Page numbers in italics refer to illustrations.